1812

Early American Studies

SERIES EDITORS
*Daniel K. Richter, Kathleen M. Brown, Max Cavitch,
and David Waldstreicher*

Exploring neglected aspects of our colonial, revolutionary, and early national history and culture, Early American Studies reinterprets familiar themes and events in fresh ways. Interdisciplinary in character, and with a special emphasis on the period from about 1600 to 1850, the series is published in partnership with the McNeil Center for Early American Studies.

A complete list of books in the series is available from the publisher.

1812

War and the Passions of Patriotism

Nicole Eustace

PENN

UNIVERSITY OF PENNSYLVANIA PRESS

Philadelphia

Published by
University of Pennsylvania Press
Philadelphia, Pennsylvania 19104–4112
www.upenn.edu/pennpress

Printed in the United States of America on acid-free paper
10 9 8 7 6 5 4 3 2 1

Library of Congress Cataloging-in-Publication Data

Eustace, Nicole.
1812 : war and the passions of patriotism / Nicole Eustace. — 1st ed.
p. cm. — (Early American studies)
Includes bibliographical references and index.
ISBN 978-0-8122-4431-1 (hardcover : alk. paper)
1. United States—History—War of 1812. 2. Patriotism—United States—
History—19th century. 3. Emotions—Social aspects—United States—
History—19th century. I. Title. II. Title: Eighteen twelve. III. Series: Early
American studies.
E354.E97 2012
973.5'2—dc23
2012004750

For
James Louis Eustace Klancnik,
Alexander Thomas Eustace Klancnik
and
James Michael Klancnik, Jr.

❧

Contents

Preface

Emotion, Persuasion, and the Meaning of War

When John Blake White's younger brother James announced that he planned to enlist in the U.S. Army in the spring of 1814, the elder White reacted with dismay. To his journal, he confided his "grief and mortification" at the news of his brother's plan. It was not that John opposed the war in progress, the British-American dispute now known as the War of 1812. A successful South Carolina lawyer and small-time slaveholder, John was also a patriotic amateur playwright and painter with a flair for taking on artistic projects with nationalist themes. Back when war had first been declared in June 1812, John had exclaimed that the news of the declaration, "though Melancholy," had "nevertheless inspired the heart of every American with animation and delight." Yet, despite the emotional pleasure he claimed to take in the war, when it came to the possibility of seeing his younger brother take on a combat role, he "remonstrated with him" and did "all in [his] power to demonstrate the impropriety of doing so." The idea of war filled John with agreeable feelings of "delight." Current events moved him to many creative flights of fancy. But he remained appalled at the thought that his brother wanted to take an active part in the fighting.[1]

A member of his local militia, John Blake White boasted the rank of captain and turned up to parade with his fellow militia members a couple of times a year. But he never performed any service more demanding than that and the war did nothing to interfere with the pleasant rounds of plays and parties that leavened his workaday world. White preferred to make his national contributions with pen and paintbrush rather than with sword or musket. Throughout the war years, he produced theater pieces and history paintings. He recorded often in his diary his "endeavour[s] to amuse myself with my pencil," noting that his inspiration was "furnished by the barbarities of the enemy with whom we are at War." White likely would have been perfectly willing to see his brother follow his example and assume honorary status in the militia. What filled him with concern was the fact that his brother had decided to enter the regular army.[2]

In the official census of 1810, the United States of America claimed a population of 7.2 million people. Of this number, more than half a million served in the war in some capacity. But the half-million figure is deceptive in that most of those men were militia members who served very brief terms, often contributed services that were more ceremonial than actual, and frequently refused to cross state lines to render assistance any place where it was actually needed. Only about 57,000 men served as regular enlisted soldiers during the war, and of these only 2,260 were killed. By contrast, the best estimates for the Civil War put total enlistments North and South at 2.5 million men out of a population of approximately 31.5 million. And of these soldiers, approximately 617,000 met their deaths. Proportionately, less than half of one percent of all servicemen died during the War of 1812, while a staggering one-fourth of all soldiers died in the Civil War. Statistics like these seem to argue against the historical significance of the War of 1812.[3]

Yet the life of John Blake White suggests that the meaning of the War of 1812 can be found as much in books and broadsides as on battlefields. If we truly wish to assess the impact and importance of the War of 1812, we need to consider it as a cultural event as much as a military one. Like John Blake White, many more people in the United States read and wrote about the War of 1812 than fought in it.[4]

c∞ɔ

The War of 1812 enjoys the uneasy distinction of being the first war ever to be declared in a modern democracy. Unlike the American Revolution, which developed piecemeal out of the patriot protest movement, and unlike the many quasi wars and campaigns conducted in the first quarter century or so of the new nation's history, the War of 1812 was begun by formal constitutional process. James Madison made a detailed case against Great Britain in a June 1 message to members of Congress. They duly responded with a formal statement of hostilities, a bill that Madison quickly signed into law on June 18, 1812. Enormously controversial with members of the Federalist Party from the moment it began, the war received a sort of popular referendum in the next two presidential elections, of 1812 and 1816. Madison easily won reelection in November 1812 and his hand-picked successor and former secretary of war, James Monroe, enjoyed landslide success four years later, in 1816. Hundreds of thousands of men cast Democratic-Republican votes in these contests. The war, in other words, proved to be a popular success.[5]

In strict military and diplomatic terms, the War of 1812 accomplished almost nothing at all. The declared foe was Great Britain and the desired object was Canada. Among a host of complaints against the British, the United States charged that nation with violating its international shipping rights and with impressing its sailors into forced service in the Royal Navy. By the war's end in 1815, after the British had burned Washington, D.C., to the ground and the national debt had nearly tripled, from $45 million to $127 million, all that the United States had managed was to convince the British to return all territorial boundaries and diplomatic disputes to their prewar status. Yet somehow, the population at large regarded the war as a rousing triumph.[6]

In a democracy, public opinion matters more than anything else. Politicians gain and maintain power with the approval of the populace. The War of 1812 provided an ideal moment for Americans, from virtual unknowns such as John Blake White to leading national statesmen, to experiment with shaping popular public opinion. How could a war that might easily have been dismissed as a terrific waste of time and money, if not deplored as a disastrous display of hubris, instead have sparked what one newspaper famously described as an "era of good feelings"? Feeling, it turned out, was everything. And good feelings were not hard to generate when most people did not experience the war firsthand, but only through their imaginations, as sparked by words and images on the printed page.[7]

When President James Madison addressed the nation to announce that war had been declared, he said: "I . . . exhort all the good people of the United States, as they love their country, as they value the precious heritage derived from the virtue and valor of their fathers; as they feel wrongs . . . that they exert themselves." Immediately printed in pamphlet form in Washington and widely circulated in newspapers, Madison's call made clear the expectation that showing love of country required supporting the war. Emotion was required for morality; feeling would motivate the actions and exertions of "good people."[8]

Both those who welcomed the coming of war and those who opposed it believed that marshaling the support of the U.S. population required mounting emotional appeals that would stir the soul. In 1812, Daniel Webster, an anti-war Federalist whose vocal opposition to the war would soon land him a seat in Congress, was an up-and-coming young lawyer with a flair for oratory. Rousing an audience of war opponents in the Federalist preserve of Portsmouth, New Hampshire, on July 4, 1812, just weeks after the president's statement, Webster proclaimed that James Madison's war went against the traditions of George Washington. He knew this, he declared, because of the way the war made him feel.[9]

"There is," Daniel Webster asserted, "not only a transmission of ideas and of knowledge, from generation to generation; there is also a traditional communication of sentiments and feelings." For Webster, it seemed obvious that anyone who was truly sentient would recoil from the prospect of an unnecessary war. Casting an eye toward "the horrible pit of European suffering and calamity," created by the Franco-British conflict in Europe, he urged his audience to share his vision. Reason alone might not be enough to sway the undecided. But emotional persuasion offered another way out. "If they will not hearken to the *warning voice*," he urged, "they may perhaps be shocked into some feeling by the evidence of their own senses." Webster believed that if only people felt the horror of war vividly, they would also oppose it avidly.[10]

But the shock of feeling could easily cut the other way. War boosters well understood this and traded on emotion in their turn. Few people would witness the war with "their own senses," whereas many more would enjoy the pleasurable sensory experience of artistic and literary representations of war. Although war critics offered their audiences the discomfort of pain and fear, supporters presented far more enticing emotional options. When John Blake White created a "National Picture" featuring an Indian massacre and presented it for public viewing in his hometown of Charleston in August 1813, the local newspaper the *City Gazette* pronounced that, "the subject, though horrible beyond measure, is rich and glowing." White described in his journal the effect such paintings had on himself as artist and on his audience as viewers by explaining, "while it fully occupies the mind and exercises the imagination, of the artist, painting affords pleasure to the beholder, by elevating and enlarging the mind." In White's telling, even the worst moments of the war could produce an appealing sort of emotional frisson in the casual observers who visited the free exhibition of his art at the Charleston courthouse and commercial exchange.[11]

The task White and other war boosters set for themselves was nothing less than the transformation of Webster's "horrible pit of suffering and calamity" into "rich and glowing" pleasure. To recast suffering as elevation and calamity as mental enlargement required performing a kind of emotional alchemy. Yet through just such "exercises [of] the imagination," many U.S. residents in 1812 came to view the war as a positive good.

⌐∞⌐

Ostensibly a conflict with Britain over naval rights, the American War of 1812 quickly became a test of the strength and meaning of American patriotism in a nation torn by sectional and political factionalism. While Federalist war opponents based in New England often attempted to elicit feelings of disgust about the conflict, Democratic-Republican advocates concentrated in the South and West more often tried to evoke delight. Throughout the war years, Republicans worked to portray the war as a romantic adventure, one in which dashing young men went to war to win the hearts of patriotic maidens and in which the thrill of romantic love contributed directly to the surge of patriotism. From generic songs and poems to specific descriptions of particular military engagements, war supporters relied on a new language of romantic patriotism to tell the story of the war. From the desks of high military officers and prominent politicians, the presses of the nation's burgeoning newspaper and pamphlet printers, and the kitchen tables of ordinary scribblers came a flood of professional and amateur efforts.[12]

While Federalists relied largely on feelings of fear and revulsion in their efforts to dissuade people from supporting the war, Democratic-Republicans saved their attempts to provoke disgust for descriptions of the enemy, including the British and their Indian allies. The Federalists failed to make a persuasive case against the war and one clear consequence of this was the way they faded forever from national power with the close of the conflict. Republican writers had all too successfully discovered the effectiveness of making war support the measure of love of country, and of likening love of country to ordinary romantic affections.

In American popular culture, in the era of the War of 1812, war stories and love stories intertwined. Many claims of equivalence were open and unrepentant. One of the first novels to come out of the war was an 1816 production

by a New York writer named Samuel Woodworth with the unwieldy but suggestive title *The Champions of Freedom; or, The Mysterious Chief, a Romance of
the Nineteenth Century, Founded in the Events of the War Between the United
States and Great Britain, Which Terminated in March 1815.* The book interwove seduction plots worthy of a sentimental romance novel with detailed historical descriptions of all the major events of the war. As a chapter titled "Love
and Patriotism" made clear, the novel juxtaposed these seemingly unrelated
story lines the better to showcase the essential relationship between romantic
love and martial action. The chapter began with an epigram: "Love rais'd his
noble thoughts to brave achievements / For love's the steel that strikes upon
the flint . . . / And spreads the sparkles round to warm the world." Here love
and bravery both appeared as inflammatory states, libidinal heat the spur of
military honor. Americans of the early republic largely enjoyed the notion of
romantic love as national duty.[13]

Meanwhile, Woodworth's complex title elided the difference between the
stated opponent of the United States—Britain—and the war's ghostly proxy
losers, the "mysterious" Indians whose lands were overrun by the "champions of freedom." As war supporters well knew, the connections between war
and romance were literal as well as figurative. Every time war boosters joined
the prosecution of the war to the private love of courting couples, they made
the takeover of Indian lands into a romantic possibility and a patriotic duty.
Though the United States won no changes in British policy as a result of the
war, the country did gain undisputed control of substantial Western territories once claimed by Indians, lands that would soon be settled by whites and
cultivated in substantial part by enslaved men and women. In an age when
starting a family usually meant clearing a farm, the population's fertility and
the land's fecundity were closely linked. Yet in Woodworth's telling, as in the
accounts of many self-appointed polemicists of the day, a war fraught with
moral, political, and practical problems could be successfully portrayed both
as a righteous cause *and* as a pleasurable romantic romp.

⚬∞⚬

When it came to shaping public opinion, John Blake White, Samuel
Woodworth, and thousands of other Democratic-Republicans quickly discovered how strongly emotions influenced judgments. By attaching delightful
feelings to dire events, they could transform both how people felt about the
war *and* how they thought about it. Blood and anguish held little appeal, but

love and sex were hard to resist. Death and destruction stood little chance of support, but family formation and procreation spoke to universal aspirations. If the experience of the latter could be made to stand in for the former, then liberty and equality could emerge from slavery and territorial aggression.[14]

Today, neuropsychologists can use sophisticated imaging techniques to study the way specific regions of the brain process stimuli. They have found that areas such as the amygdala and the frontal insula make instant evaluations of delight or disgust that can add positive or negative moral coloration to otherwise neutral prompts. As one scholar explains it, the amygdala "tilts" the mental "pinball machine." When a new stimulus of undetermined value is introduced by a prior stimulus with strongly positive or negative appeal, a person's reaction can be artificially shifted toward approach or avoidance. Powerful snap judgments about the practical and moral worth of a given course of action can result from the emotional reaction a person has to otherwise unrelated ideas and events. In the case of war debates during the era of 1812, partisans on both sides did what they could to shape people's political judgments by first coloring their emotional responses.[15]

Of course, no one in the era of 1812 had access to an MRI machine. But they could find a guide for their efforts in the work of the English philosopher Edmund Burke. Burke had published his famous treatise on aesthetics in London all the way back in 1757. But not until 1806, as tensions with Britain began to heighten daily, would *A Philosophical Inquiry into the Origin of Our Ideas of the Sublime and Beautiful* first be printed in America. The final and climactic section of that work, "How Words Influence the Passions," spoke directly to the efforts of would-be opinion makers during the War of 1812.[16]

Edmund Burke recognized that nothing shaped emotion as much as language did, saying, "there are no tokens which can express all the circumstances of most passions so fully as words." Yet he also posited that language could provide only the most imperfect and indirect approximation of actual experience. He argued, "the influence of most things on our passions is not so much from the things themselves, as from our opinions concerning them; and these again depend very much on the opinions of other men, conveyable, for the most part by words only." If politically active writers and speakers wished to exert decisive public influence, their best means of shaping opinion was by evoking emotion.[17]

Burke alerted people that words and things were not one and the same. Yet the shadow could matter more than the substance, especially when the emotions evoked concerned events of death and war. Burke reasoned: "there are many things of a very affecting nature, which seldom can occur in the reality, but the words which represent them do; and thus they have an opportunity of making a deep impression and taking root in the mind, whilst the idea of the reality was transient; and to some, perhaps, never really occurred in any shape, to whom it is, notwithstanding, very affecting, as war, death, famine, etc." As America entered into a state of war, very few ordinary people would experience any direct impact of the conflict. For them military confrontation "never really occurred in any shape." In the War of 1812, the numbers of men mustered for the fight were few and their terms of service brief. Most major war actions occurred in theaters far from U.S. population centers, on the fringes of the frontiers or on the waters of the Atlantic Ocean and the Great Lakes. Yet the words representing the war did have the "opportunity of making a deep impression and taking root in the mind." People's feelings about the war, and the moral judgments they made based on those feelings, would come not from direct experience but from the stories told and opinions expressed all around them, particularly in the public prints.[18]

❧

Historian Alan Taylor has recently proposed that we consider the War of 1812 as a civil war, as one of the first conflicts to test the bonds of people in the United States. If this is so, it must be significant that, at the time it occurred, the War of 1812 was successfully portrayed as such good fun. If war was a frolic and patriotism the natural result of indulging romantic passions, who could ever have predicted the devastation of the Civil War? Likening war to an exercise in love hardly prepared anyone to undertake the studied assessment of the moral implications of conflict. The first major battle of the Civil War, the Battle of Bull Run, caught contemporaries by surprise. Spectators with picnic hampers who had turned out to cheer the action were shocked to the core by the carnage: five thousand dead in a single day, more than in all the years of the War of 1812. Small wonder that a population reared on popular stories of war as pleasure had given so little weight to the true costs of armed struggle.[19]

Throughout the War of 1812, popular conclusions about the meaning of events were liable to be based more on the emotional language used to describe them than on rational appraisal of what had occurred. No matter how dire the events of the day, prowar commentators could always be counted on to put a romantic gloss on public accounts. Edmund Burke had warned that emotional words could distort reality even as they shaped understanding. He had noted, "we do not sufficiently distinguish, in our observations upon language, between a clear expression and a strong expression." People ought to be more careful in discriminating between the two modes of expression because "the former regards the understanding; the latter belongs to the passions: the one describes a thing as it is; the other describes it as it is felt." Though Burke had wished only to expose this tendency, many American polemicists in the era of 1812 proved highly eager to exploit it.[20]

American prowar commentators—from elite politicians to parlor poets and tavern hacks—displayed no qualms about inverting Burke; his dire warnings nearly amounted to a road map for American tacticians. Writers could glory in Burke's observation that "by the contagion of our passions, we catch a fire, already kindled in another, [a match] which probably might never have been struck . . . by the object described." From prewar attempts to build public support for taking up arms to postwar efforts to cement the significance of the conflict's climactic battle, emotion played a key part in shaping public ideas. As American opinion makers would quickly discover, romance could provide the flint with which to fire a war.[21]

Chapter 1

❦

Celebrating Love, Liberty, and Progeny
UNITED STATES, CIRCA 1811

Hezekiah Niles nurtured a visceral antagonism toward the British. The founder and editor of the *Niles Weekly Register*, who began publishing out of Baltimore in 1811, claimed that, back during the American Revolution, British soldiers had menaced his pregnant mother and almost killed him in utero. As he told the story in the pages of his paper, he "nearly perished with his mother a short time before he was born. A British grenadier *gallantly* attacked her with his bayonet, but she was saved as though by the interposition of Providence." In relating this episode, Niles no doubt hoped, as he did with every article he wrote, that he had "done a good deal to . . . rouse . . . a *national feeling* and [to] buil[d] up [a] pride of character hitherto too much neglected." Born in 1777 to Pennsylvania Quakers, by 1811 Niles was himself a family man in his prime, a Republican newspaper publisher with firm nationalist views, and—his religious roots notwithstanding—a steady promoter of renewed war with Britain.[1]

Niles's tale of his near miss with feticide carried significant political charge. Like many of his fellow Republicans, Niles had come to believe that population strength provided the key to American national power. Beyond inflicting personal tragedy, disrupting reproduction imperiled the nation. Niles's concern with population questions ran deep. He recounted his own story in March 1812, just three months before the United States declared war on Britain, and in the same weekly issue in which he also featured an installment of an article he titled "An Analytical Review of the 'Essay on the Principle of Population, by T. R. Malthus, A.M.' with Some Remarks

More Particularly Applicable to the Present and Probable Future State of the United States."[2]

Niles presented Malthus to the public only to contradict him. His "analytical review" of the *Essay on Population* aimed to explain why the British theorist's arguments in favor of population restriction were not "particularly applicable" to the United States. Perhaps Niles's remembrance of his family anecdote was spurred by his close engagement with contemporary political economy. Or perhaps his interest in the role of reproduction in national progress stemmed from the knowledge of his own prenatal danger. Either way, Niles took it upon himself to increase public awareness of the interconnections between individual reproduction and national population, the better to inspire his fellow Americans with patriotic fervor at a moment of national crisis.

⁊⦵⦵⦶

All wars put population strength at a premium and create strong public interest in personal attachment to the nation. Resident populations must be mobilized, neutralized, and/or defended. Wars always ask people to give themselves to their country. But in America, in 1812, the very idea of entering into open battle remained highly controversial. Since the constitutional founding of the United States in 1789, the nation had never yet made a formal declaration of war. The decision to do so generated intense debate. Members of President James Madison's Democratic-Republican Party, predominant in the South and West, broadly supported military action against Britain, from challenging the Royal Navy at sea to mounting a conquest of Canada. Members of the opposition Federalist Party railed against war from their New England base. Wide swaths of the population remained more or less open to persuasion. Interlinked arguments about family generation and national expansion were at the center of these vigorous discussions. The population practices and patriotic emotions that emerged during the United States' inaugural war would shape the nation for many ages to come.[3]

Growth-oriented Republicans embraced a polarizing vision of national progress in which people would become endeared to the nation through unfettered freedom to reproduce. Procreation functioned simultaneously as a fundamental right and an essential obligation. A nation that protected the natural human drive to beget children deserved the love and loyalty of its inhabitants. In return, those who enjoyed these liberties owed their offspring to the nation, the very embodiment of patriotic love.[4]

Even before the American Revolution, local commentators and international observers had remarked on the fantastic fecundity of North America. Its lands were fertile and so were its people. Ironically, the English had first established colonies in part out of concern over perceived population excesses in their small island nation. But on the vast continent of North America, population came to be appreciated as the basis of national potency. In what many Euro-Americans saw as a virtuous cycle, but many Native Americans and their British and Canadian allies viewed as a vicious circle, the continent's wide-open grounds supported demographic expansion even as the increasing U.S. population enabled the seizure and settlement of new land. The resultant divergence in British and American attitudes toward the merits of population significantly increased tensions between the two nations.[5]

Throughout the first quarter century of U.S. independence, Britons and Americans had chafed each other about questions of population: its regulation, limitation, or optimization. Even as white Americans claimed to need enslaved Africans and African Americans to people their labor force, they coveted Indian lands to support the ever-growing number of the nation's people. The British interfered with U.S. plans on both counts. On the continent, the British continued to cultivate diplomatic and economic partnerships with Indians, supporting the rival population from whom the United States perceived the greatest immediate threat. On the ocean, Britain controlled Atlantic shipping, forbidding the African slave trade after 1807 and harassing U.S. merchant vessels. Meanwhile, at sea, Britain's traditional goal of population limitation was reversed. The Royal Navy needed every hand it could find on deck. The consequent British practice of boarding American ships to round up vagabond British seamen provoked enormous controversy, the more so since these efforts could sometimes sweep Americans into British nets.[6]

In the midst of such moral and political confusion, both Americans and Britons made scattershot efforts to maintain the better claim to virtue. Though the United States boasted of being the land of the free, it drew sharp distinctions between the citizenship rights of native-born, property-holding, white men and the options available to all those national denizens not recognized as formal citizens. The British lambasted Americans for the way their practices constricted liberty—even though their own impressment tactics flouted the rights of American citizenry and their dominion of the seas supported their own imperial efforts in India and beyond. The rising crisis with Britain compounded every element of the promise and problems of population in the United States. As they argued the ethics of population increases and the merits of territorial expansion, Americans debated the implications of allowing family formation to play a key philosophical and practical role in the building of the nation.[7]

Polemicists such as Hezekiah Niles brought the abstractions of political economy to the entertainments of popular culture. Print was a key arena where public and private intersected, where personal behavior could be glossed with political meaning. In this context, even those with no formal voice in government could be asked to lend their weight. Maximizing the number of people who could be mustered for the country meant relaxing barriers to public participation, finding new ways to inspire loyalty to the nation, and encouraging reproduction. With the stress of war making every person's contribution count, personal feelings and patriotic feats became connected in new ways.[8]

⌒∞⌒

Thomas Robert Malthus, who would grow up to become an Anglican clergyman and celebrated British theorist of political economy, was ten years old in 1776 when civil war first broke out between Great Britain and its North American colonies. Throughout the formative years of his adolescence, his ears must have echoed with American cries for liberty. For many Britons, the idealistic rhetoric of the Declaration of Independence could not have been more jarring. American hypocrites trumpeted a new universal philosophy of natural rights, scorning the traditional rights of Englishman rooted in the Magna Carta, even as they continued to practice racial slavery. British commentators, such as Samuel Johnson, demanded to know, "how is it we hear the loudest yelps for liberty from the drivers of Negroes?" Coming of age just as the British signed a peace treaty in 1783 and ratified American Independence, Malthus would eventually take British skepticism of American liberty to new heights.[9]

Malthus first set forth his ideas in 1798 in a book-length treatise, *Essay on the Principle of Population*, that is now widely regarded as a direct precursor of Darwin's work on evolution. His central hypothesis was that populations increase geometrically, while the means of subsistence increase arithmetically. Expanding populations inevitably outstrip food supplies. Yet despite his modern reputation, Malthus was a political economist before he was a biologist. His main interest in studying population was not to understand ecological patterns, but rather imperial ones. And by the time Malthus published in

1798, the Napoleonic Wars of France were already in full swing. From his English island redoubt, Malthus cast one critical eye across the Atlantic at America, another baleful glance over to France on the continent.[10]

Malthus offered his model of population not as a scientific abstraction but rather as a concrete analysis of geopolitics. The often-omitted full title to his famous work signals his intentions. He began in 1798 by calling it *An Essay on the Principle of Population as it Affects the Future Improvement of Society*. Yet just five years later, in 1803, he was subtitling the second edition of his study of population *An Inquiry into Our Prospects Respecting the Future Removal or Mitigation of the Evils which It Occasions*. Viewing overpopulation as the main cause of famine and suffering, Malthus censured unrestrained reproduction as one of the main moral "evils." Efforts to stave off starvation by staking out new territory would only create new misery. The occupying population could only prosper at the expense of the natives. Meanwhile, once the invaders' numbers multiplied to the point that they again overran available resources, as they inevitably would, the final number of suffering people would have increased exponentially.[11]

By the time Malthus issued a third edition of his essay in 1807, Britain had formally declared war on France, while the United States had purchased from France the right to claim the vast tract of the North American interior known as the Louisiana Territory. Meanwhile, the United States, according to its own calculations, had sustained dramatic increases in population begun in the eighteenth century. From the first national census taken in 1790 to the second taken in 1800, the nation's numbers expanded from approximately 3.9 million to approximately 5.3 million. They continued to rise sharply, reaching 7.2 million by the third official census of 1810. In total, the nation's numbers increased nearly twofold in just two decades. With no rival European claims to contend with, nothing stood in the way of a doubling of U.S. lands, and a redoubling of the U.S. population, save the thousands of Indians who continued to live on their native ground. The United States thus provided the perfect object lesson for Malthus's claims that excess population fueled territorial aggression.[12]

Taking a hard look at U.S. ambitions to exert ever greater control over the continent, Malthus concluded, "if America continue increasing, which she certainly will do . . . the Indians will be driven further and further back into the country, till the whole race is ultimately exterminated." How could the United States claim to be the globe's strongest defender of freedom when it denied the basic right of survival to Native Americans? Malthus declared:

"the right of exterminating, or driving to a corner where they must starve, even the inhabitants of thinly peopled regions, will be questioned in a moral view." Though the British army had not beaten American revolutionaries on the battlefield, British commentators could reverse the triumph of American liberty through moral critique.[13]

⸎

Many Americans of the era rejected Malthusian analysis and instead tracked the nation's population gains with pride. The official national census ensured widespread awareness of America's remarkable demographic success in its first decades of existence. Americans did not view census reports as dry documents, of concern to only a few government policymakers. On the contrary, they took avid interest in the nation's numbers. Census totals were reported in countless regional and local newspapers as soon as returns came in. Complete census reports were printed, with county-by-county compilations, and made available for public purchase. Census numbers featured in most standard almanacs, part of the basic information that even ordinary farm folk wanted to have at their fingertips. Some people went so far as to purchase decorative certificates in which census data was presented in ornamental graphic form suitable for framing and viewing (Figure 1). For many people in the United States, then, Thomas Malthus's work represented a stunning rebuke of a signal American success. As U.S.-British frictions began to rub raw at the turn of the century, he was advancing an analysis of American demography that amounted to a stinging critique of American society.[14]

American reproductive boasts reached back to the previous century. Benjamin Franklin, printer, politician, and thinker, started things off by including among his wide-ranging contributions to science and civics a significant early study of demography: the 1755 pamphlet *Observations Concerning the Increase of Mankind and the Peopling of Countries*. Franklin, still a proud member of the British Empire when he wrote his *Observations*, made no apologies for American fecundity. He had boasted that, though only eighty thousand Englishmen had migrated to North America since the beginning of colonization, there were "upwards of one million English souls in North America" by 1755. He had celebrated the prospect that "in another century ... the greatest number of Englishmen will be on this side of the water. What an accession of power to the British empire by sea as well as land!" In Franklin's writing, population equaled power, pure and simple.[15]

Thomas Malthus freely acknowledged an intellectual debt to Benjamin Franklin. In the opening pages of his *Essay on Population* he leaned on

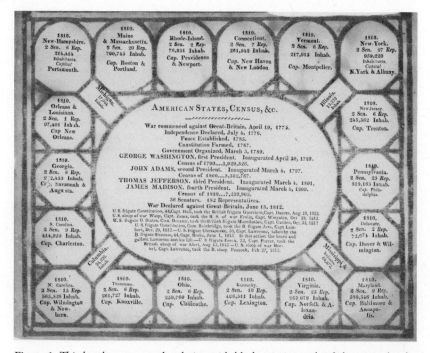

Figure 1. This handsome two-color design with black printing and red decorative border was meant for display. Note the graphic representation of the states as octagons, with the territories included as rectangular ornamental details. The "inhabitants" of each state and territory are enumerated. While the inclusion of information on congressional representation suggests that population figures were of interest for their domestic political implications, the juxtaposition of census figures with the political and military timeline featured in the central oval of the certificate hints that the role of population in geopolitics was also a prominent contemporary concern. "American States, Census, &c.," c. 1813, Collections of the American Antiquarian Society.

Franklin's ideas directly. He noted: "It is observed by Dr. Franklin, that there is no bound to the prolific nature of plants or animals, but what is made by their crowding and interfering with each others means of subsistence. Were the face of the earth, he says . . . empty of other inhabitants, it might in a few ages hence be replenished from one nation only, as for instance with English-men. This is incontrovertibly true." The two men easily agreed that people, like all living things, occupied as much habitat as biological competition would allow.[16]

Both men argued that marriage was key to the population process, a crucial theoretical point with considerable political importance. In human societies, where culture shaped reproduction as much as nature, marriage traditions had the greatest influence on the rise of population. Franklin argued, "people increase in proportion to the number of marriages . . . when families can be easily supported, more persons marry, and earlier in life." Malthus echoed this, saying, "the dictate of nature and virtue seems to be an early attachment to one woman; and where there were no impediments of any kind in the way of a union [that is no laws to limit marriage] . . . the increase of the human species would be evidently much greater than any increase which has been hitherto known." In countries where youthful, "early" marriages were common, couples had added time to produce extra children and maximize their contributions to the total population.[17]

Significantly, each regarded the increase of European populations in America as the surest proof of these assertions. Franklin reported that "marriages in America are more general, and more generally early, than in Europe . . . reckoning one with another . . . our people must at least be doubled every twenty years." Malthus confirmed that in "America, where . . . the . . . checks to early marriages [have been] fewer than in any of the states of Europe, the population has been found to double itself, for above a century and a half successively, in less than . . . twenty-five years." Only if the average age of marriage were significantly raised would the number of children born to each couple decline and the progress of population be diminished.[18]

Where Franklin saw American reproductive success as cause for celebration, in Malthus it induced only moral indignation. Malthus would go on to argue, as we have seen, that Euro-Americans' continual increase had to be "questioned in a moral view" in light of the potential of expanding white populations to exterminate Indians. Franklin, by contrast, rested his case on the notion that Indians, "having large tracts, were easily prevailed upon to part with portions of territory to the new-comers, who did not much interfere with the natives." In Franklin's sanguine assessment, "so vast" was "the territory of North America that it w[ould] require many ages to settle fully." Despite their similar staring points, Franklin and Malthus arrived at markedly different analytic destinations. Not surprisingly, proexpansionist Americans of the early republic preferred to travel with Franklin.[19]

⌒∞⌒

Franklin's eighteenth-century ideas on population remained well known down through the years to 1812. Many affirmed his view of the connections between population increases and national power and joined his celebration of the American habit of "early marriage." Some learned of Benjamin Franklin's ideas by reading his *Observations Concerning the Increase of Mankind* directly. Reprints of the full tract remained available throughout the early nineteenth century in multivolume editions of Franklin's collected works.[20]

Yet most Americans who joined Franklin in regarding population as a source of pride had no need of straining to follow the formal theoretical propositions of the learned treatise that so engaged and antagonized Malthus. Instead, readers could become familiar with Franklin's views through an entertaining two-page essay that was republished in numerous newspapers and inexpensive anthologies throughout the late eighteenth century and early nineteenth century. Originally written as a congratulatory letter upon a friend's marriage, these scribbles soon became a significant piece of published humor that did much to transform Franklin's controversial views on political economy into accepted folk wisdom.[21]

"Dear Jack," began Franklin's studiously casual note to the new groom John Alleyne, "you desire, you say, my impartial thoughts on the subject of early marriage." Sly Franklin may not have been "impartial," but he was emphatic. "With us in America," he said, "marriages are generally in the morning of life." Basking in the American dawn, Franklin explained, "by these early marriages, we are blessed with more children. . . . Hence the swift progress of population amongst us, unparalleled in Europe!" Franklin taught that each man could contribute to his country by establishing a family. Jack, he said, was "now in the way of becoming a useful citizen" who had "escaped the unnatural state of *celibacy for life*," which, as everyone knew, was "a situation that greatly lessens a man's value." Franklin also offered praise for fecund American mothers. The country's reproductive feats could be credited in no small measure to "the mode amongst us, founded in nature, of every mother suckling and nursing her own child," which meant that of the many babies born, "more of them [we]re raised" to adulthood.[22]

If youthful marriages and maximized reproduction made American men and women "useful" members of the public, Franklin promised that these choices would also make people personally fulfilled. In fact, of all the marriages he'd seen, Franklin was "inclined to think that early ones stand the best chance of happiness." In short, men and women were meant for marriage: "what think you," Franklin demanded, "of the odd half of a pair of scissors—it can't well cut anything—it may possibly serve to scrape a trencher." Franklin was winking at his reader, injecting comedy into a commentary on morality that also offered polemical instruction in political economy.[23]

As amusing "miscellany" sections became more common in newspapers across the country and pamphlet literature that aimed equally to entertain and instruct became widespread, casual references to Franklin's theory multiplied. For many commentators, the intersection of the personal and the political in the formation of families was exactly what made opining on marriage such serious fun. Mason Locke Weems, now more often celebrated as the author of the *Life of George Washington*, gave as much attention to pedantry as to biography. In 1800, the same year that he published on Washington, he offered a lighthearted take on political economy in the form of a humorous pamphlet he called *Hymen's Recruiting-Serjeant; or, The New Matrimonial Tat-too, For the Old Bachelors*. Weems specialized in writing patriotic literature marketed at inexpensive prices to southern audiences; in the topic of population he found a useful new trope.[24]

Weems opened his endorsement of matrimony by making an explicit case that reproduction lent power to nations and that strong marriages could provide a country's best defense. He made clear that population expansion offered the United States' best assurance of success over both British and French rivals. Without slighting the importance of American fighting forces, he insisted that family formation mattered more. He said: "I am very clear that our *Buckskin heroes* are made of, at least, as *good* stuff as any the *best* of the *beef* or *frog-eating* gentry on t'other side of the water." But, he insisted, nothing could save the United States "while they can out-number us *ten to one!* No, my friends, 'tis population, 'tis *population alone*, that can save our Bacon." If this wasn't explicit or witty enough as a motto, Weems then laid it on even thicker, telling bachelors and "Maidens fair," "if truly you love your country dear . . . *marry and raise up soldiers might and main* / Then laugh you may, at England, France, and Spain." Crediting Franklin directly as a source of inspiration, Weems added, late in the pamphlet, "Franklin, we dare mention . . . says . . . *Early Marriages* are best." Tracts like this one went far to disseminate Franklin's ideas and to concentrate the public's attention on their military implications. Weems's rallying cry went through five editions by 1806 and then came back into print after the conclusion of the war, appearing in at least two more editions in 1816 and 1817.[25]

Another light essay, this one by an anonymous minister that originated in a newspaper called the *Port Folio* and circulated widely in New England throughout the early 1800s announced, "'Two are better than one.' Dr. Franklin thought so, when he recommended early marriages." Taking the view that marriage protected personal morality by discouraging promiscuity, the good clergyman concluded, "it is better to marry than burn." Was the Franklin of this reference the author of the formal treatise or of the witty variety column? Was the message of the miscellany purely personal or implicitly political? No matter, the value of early marriage was being engraved in the culture.[26]

By the time references to Franklin's views on marriage began circulating under the *Port Folio* dateline in 1803, Thomas Jefferson had won the presidency, the nation was swinging from Federalism to Republicanism, the contract was closed on the Louisiana Purchase, and Franklin's claim that vast tracts of North America would lay open to generations of Euro-Americans seemed more prescient than ever before.[27]

President Jefferson seems to have had the Franklin-Malthus debate directly in mind when he orchestrated transfer of the Louisiana territory from France to the United States. The United States took formal possession of the region on December 30, 1803. Exactly one month later, on February 1, 1804, Jefferson wrote a letter in which he confessed to "giving the leisure moments I rarely find, to the perusal of Malthus's work on population." Though careful to acknowledge that Malthus's work was indeed one of "sound logic," he insisted that the Englishman's theories could not be applied to the United States because "the differences of circumstance between this and the old countries of Europe, furnish differences of fact whereon to reason, in questions of political economy, and will consequently produce sometimes a difference of result." He concurred with Malthus that in Europe, "the quantity of food is fixed, or increasing in a slow and only arithmetical ratio" with the regrettable result that "supernumerary births consequently add only to . . . mortality." But in accepting European weakness, he did nothing to concede American strength.[28]

With logic that could only be called Franklinian, Jefferson concluded that, in America, "the immense extent of uncultivated and fertile lands enables every one who will labor to marry young, and to raise a family of any size." If Malthus claimed that America's burgeoning population forced territorial expansion, Jefferson inverted this logic. He asserted that the virtually limitless availability of American lands assured that for practical purposes there could be no such thing as excessive population. "Our births," Jefferson assured his correspondent, "however multiplied, become effective." In Jefferson's survey of the situation, Indians were conveniently overlooked altogether.[29]

For Jefferson, as for Franklin, the personal and the political created powerful synergy. Jefferson believed that increasing American births would be "effective" for the U.S. nation. Yet he also understood that for many ordinary men, the right to "marry young and to raise a family of any size" was a deeply appealing part of republican manhood. And while Jefferson referred confidently to "political economy," displaying easy mastery of the leading academic theories of his day, he also knew that his intellectual opposition to Malthus would hold real-world appeal for many American constituents. Jefferson's political fortunes and governing philosophy depended on interconnections between family and state, between individual desires for marriage and parenthood and the collective will to acquire a continental empire.[30]

When Jefferson contradicted Malthus, he also took a stand in an international debate with significant consequences for transatlantic policy and diplomacy. He made his dismissive comments in a letter to Jean Baptiste Say, a French theorist of the physiocrat school and an open competitor with Malthus. Say and his fellow French philosophers believed that there was a necessary relationship between "population, the power of states, and the happiness or misery of peoples." Unlike Malthus, they did not think the state should encourage people to delay marriage and restrict reproduction in order to prevent the "evils occasioned" by excess population. On the contrary, they took the liberal position that maximal freedom of circulation, of people as well as of capital, was required to optimize social welfare. Where Malthus favored tariffs, Jefferson and his French allies favored free trade. Where Malthus promoted population restriction, Jefferson advocated land acquisition. As Britain and France squared off in the Napoleonic Wars, and Jefferson sought to engage in a diplomatic balancing act between the two European powers, his philosophical sympathy with the French meant that his foreign relations would often seem to favor them as well.[31]

⸲∞⸲

In writing to Say, Jefferson engaged in a privileged private conversation that few common people in America could have followed closely. Exposure to Franklin's humorous marital advice did not equip the average person to engage in elevated debates about political economy. Yet at that very moment, American writers and editors were working to expand the narrow boundaries of polite culture and political debate. If ordinary decisions about when and whether to wed and have children could be considered political acts, the fate of the nation hung on just this sort of cultural instruction.[32]

In 1804, the Richmond lawyer (and later U.S. attorney general) William Wirt collaborated on an anonymous essay series for the *Richmond Enquirer* called "The Rainbow" that became a stepping-stone toward bringing Malthus to the masses. Wirt was a self-taught lawyer and frequent newspaper contributor from Maryland who later became U.S. attorney general. In his first essay for the *Enquirer*, published in August 1804, he conceded that "the mass of people cannot be profound." But he recoiled from the idea that "they should be excluded from every degree of intellectual improvement." On the contrary, he declared that in America, where ideals of equality held sway, "all that seems wanting to ripen the harvest of national happiness . . . is a more extensive diffusion of useful knowledge." Putting himself forward for the task he asked, "may not the regular insertion of miscellaneous essays on useful subjects, be employed with the happiest effects, for this important purpose?" In Wirt's eyes, the burgeoning American print trade in newspapers and pamphlets provided the ideal forum for public instruction and essays like his the perfect medium.[33]

William Wirt was equally firm in his opinion regarding the ideas Americans most needed to know about: those of Thomas Malthus. It is difficult to imagine a more energetic endorsement of Malthus's *Essay on Population* than Wirt's. He declared that "from the perusal of this great work," he had "derived more original and valuable information than from any other book, or from all the other books he ha[d] ever read." Wirt's enthusiasm for Malthus made him an idiosyncratic Republican and it is hardly surprising that he ultimately left the Republican Party altogether. However, in his belief that periodical literature had a key role to play in the education of Americans and in his conviction that population was *the* key issue of his day, he was very much in the mainstream.[34]

Wirt approached the famous *Essay on Population* focused on exactly the same issues of marriage and family that mattered so much to his contemporaries. In a later essay for the "Rainbow" series, a piece titled "On Celibacy" published in November 1804, Wirt made a point of reminding readers that "the marriage state has its miseries, its peculiar excruciating torments, from which celebracy [sic] is totally exempt." He warned against "the politician" who "will tell you that however hard this may bear upon individuals . . . yet the strength of nations consists in numbers and population ought to be encouraged and marriage considered patriotic and honorable." Wirt saw clearly that individual life-cycle choices were being weighted with national political consequences. Though he opposed the trend himself, he thought people had a right to know the full range of philosophical opinion on the actual personal impact and public implications of private decisions. Ironically for Wirt, his efforts to increase awareness of Malthus were much more successful than his attempts to persuade people to adopt the Englishman's point of view.[35]

In the years after the "Rainbow" essays appeared, discussions of the *Essay on Population* increased, but so did the range and variety of criticisms of it. Indeed, while Wirt's urgent call for his contemporaries to familiarize themselves with Malthus gained wide currency, his concern about the political pressures in favor of marriage and procreation did not. His first newspaper essay was republished in an anthology released late in 1804. His second, "On Celibacy," never again saw the light of day.[36]

Instead, another politically active publisher named Roger Chew Weightman co-opted Wirt's hearty praise of Malthus for his own purposes. A young man on the make, Weightman had moved to Washington, D.C., as a teenager. By 1807, at the age of twenty, he had learned enough of the print trade to buy his own publishing office. He soon took on the role of congressional printer and, from that year forward, would print hundreds of documents for the legislature. Before long, Weightman's Republican leanings would lead him to join Madison's Washington establishment in supporting war against Britain. He would join the D.C. militia and be elected to the D.C. council by the age of twenty-six. In the meantime, with keen political as well as entrepreneurial instincts, he also embarked on a significant new publication project: the production of the first-ever American imprint of Malthus's *Essay on Population* (Figure 2).[37]

Counterintuitive as it first appears, Madison administration allies were eager to see Malthus in circulation among lawmakers and opinion shapers. With the help of several other booksellers, Weightman began advertising for advance subscriptions to underwrite publication. The first such advertisement, which appeared in the newspaper the *United States Gazette* in 1807, quoted Wirt's "Rainbow" article verbatim, notifying "such of his readers as may not have been fortunate enough to peruse the 'Essay on Population' by Malthus, that from the perusal of this great work, he ha[d] derived more original and valuable information . . . than . . . from all the other books he ha[d] ever read."

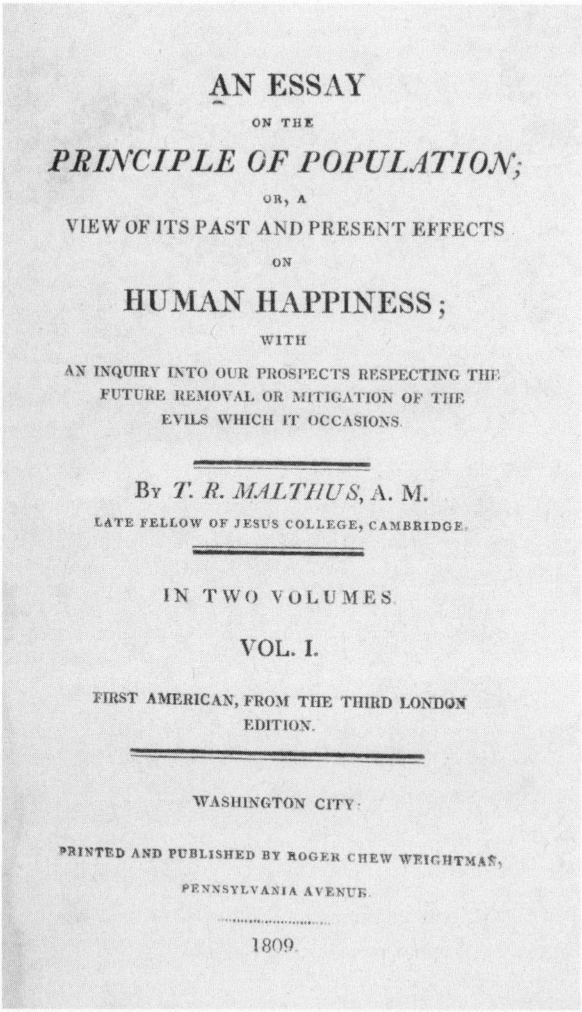

AN ESSAY

ON THE

PRINCIPLE OF POPULATION;

OR, A

VIEW OF ITS PAST AND PRESENT EFFECTS

ON

HUMAN HAPPINESS ;

WITH

AN INQUIRY INTO OUR PROSPECTS RESPECTING THE
FUTURE REMOVAL OR MITIGATION OF THE
EVILS WHICH IT OCCASIONS.

By *T. R. MALTHUS*, A. M.

LATE FELLOW OF JESUS COLLEGE, CAMBRIDGE.

IN TWO VOLUMES.

VOL. I.

FIRST AMERICAN, FROM THE THIRD LONDON
EDITION.

WASHINGTON CITY:

PRINTED AND PUBLISHED BY ROGER CHEW WEIGHTMAN,

PENNSYLVANIA AVENUE.

1809.

Figure 2. Title page of the first American edition of the *Essay on the Principle of Population*. Collections of the American Antiquarian Society.

Making mock apology for the boldness of offering an American reprint, the advertisement concluded: "for surely a work of such inestimable value and celebrity must already be in the hands of every man who aspires to discharge the functions of an editor, legislator, or instructor." The appeal to legislators and editors to read Malthus would be featured in Weightman advertisements repeatedly in Republican-leaning newspapers in New York, Pennsylvania, and Virginia in 1807.[38]

Those who wished to take a hard line against Britain reveled in Malthus's scientific documentation of American fertility without feeling the least obligation to honor the conclusions he drew from his evidence. Praising Weightman's efforts directly, the New York paper *American Citizen*, in May 1809, paid the usual formulaic respects to Malthus in saying "the American Press could not ... have conferred a higher benefit on the public than has been done by the recent publication of *Malthus's Treatise on the Principle of Population*." Yet the article simultaneously labored to undermine the Englishman's reasoning. Noting that Malthus, "recommends ... forebearance to marry until the parties possess the probable means of maintaining their children," the essay explained that "he contends that nothing has been so fertile in the creation of misery as early marriages ... and infers that it is our duty so to regulate our conduct and passions as to avoid a step which cannot fail ... of ... entailing wretchedness on our children." Nevertheless, the article concluded, "these inferences ... however they may hereafter apply to this country are happily at present in great measure inapplicable." Sounding a note of American exceptionalism, the author declared, "the means of subsistence are so prodigiously produced among us, as invariably even to exceed the unprecedented growth of our numbers."[39]

Belief in the boundlessness of American land, no doubt strongly bolstered by the just-completed Louisiana Purchase, allowed those of an expansionist bent to celebrate Malthus's data even as they sought to refute his analysis. Americans remained free to follow their "passions" and to "conduct" themselves however they wished.

☙❧

By the time that Weightman's imprint became available in 1809, U.S.-British relations had grown more strained than ever. Treaty negotiations over the issue of impressment were already near a standstill in 1807 when the British incited new hostility by trying to board the USS *Chesapeake* to search for deserters from the Royal Navy, then firing on the frigate when the Americans refused to allow them to do so. Three Americans were killed in the incident and four sailors were taken into British custody, while American dignity was severely wounded. Resisting calls for war, then-president Jefferson instead favored responding with an embargo of British goods. But by March 1809, when James Madison entered office, the embargo too was considered a failure, especially by New England Federalists hurt by the reduction of trade. Congress repealed it in favor of a non-intercourse act, which allowed neither imports from, nor exports to, England or France. In this politically charged atmosphere, as Republicans and Federalists squared off against each other and the United States careened between confrontations with Britain and France, debates about population took on added urgency. Countering Malthus could both help to overcome Federalist objections to the idea of war and help to undercut British claims to be the best guarantors of liberty.[40]

The political importance of Malthusian debates was open knowledge among the reading public on both sides of the Atlantic. When a British writer groused that "many politicians in the United States affect to deride all the great and important principles laid down by Mr. Malthus as absurd and visionary," the complaint perversely pleased Americans so much they reprinted it in the States. Often, when Americans did offer any approval of Malthus, it was only to applaud his exact and methodical accounting of American population strength, not to agree with his argument that future increases should be curtailed. A letter to the editor that appeared in the New York *Public Advertiser* in the summer of 1809 shows how commentators tried to turn Malthus's critique against itself: "Mr. Malthus, in his essay on population . . . speaking of the importance of America . . . to the very existence of great Britain . . . uses . . . remarkably strong and truly just expressions." If only the British would focus on America's "importance" and respect American strength instead of opposing it, the two rivals might yet act as partners. Driving home the significance of the remarks for both domestic and international politics, the author added, "Republican editors in this state, friendly to the administration, are requested to publish these papers." This wish, at least, was granted. The letter was reprinted in different papers at least twice in the next two months.[41]

While newspaper writers swiped at Malthus, American political economists began sharpening their quills to launch a sustained defense of American population practices. When the Massachusetts philosopher and civic innovator Loammi Baldwin, who would soon be busy directing the fortification of Boston's harbor during the war, set forth his *Thoughts on the Study of Political Economy* in 1809, he tipped his hat to Malthus. He quoted the *Essay on Population* approvingly as "endeavouring to impress as strongly as possible on the public mind, that it is not the duty of man simply to propagate his species, but to propagate virtue and happiness." Still, despite paying token respects to Malthus, Baldwin felt no hesitation in asserting that "in every nation . . . the number of inhabitants is the best index of its power and as the ratio of increase or decrease varies, national strength and happiness will fluctuate." Malthus thought excess propagation a threat to happiness; Baldwin insisted that the level of population was the very measure of happiness itself.[42]

For Baldwin, adherence to Malthus's strictures promoting virtue in no way precluded belief in a positive correlation between the strength of nations and the size of populations. He boasted that "the increase in the Union exceeds in a very considerable degree, any ratio that the states of Europe have exhibited for ages." Far from provoking self-critique about the moral implications of American expansionism, Malthus's warnings often seemed only to add support to beliefs in the unlimited potential of American expansionism.[43]

Like Franklin and Jefferson before him, Baldwin tied American fertility and American freedom directly to the ability to marry. He applauded the fact that "we have no impolitic or pernicious institutions concerning marriage; and without any . . . we have only to study how to improve our natural advantages . . . to accelerate the progress of national strength and national happiness." Malthus himself made no policy recommendations favoring new government regulations on marriage, no arguments supporting what Baldwin derided as "impolitic or pernicious institutions concerning marriage." But American opponents often pretended he did. They wrote as if he called for undermining natural human rights. Making marriage and reproduction central to the pursuit of personal and national "happiness" relocated the site of Americans' most basic inalienable rights from the public to the private realm.[44]

∽∞∾

By the time Hezekiah Niles decided in 1811 to describe to readers of his newly founded newspaper, the *Weekly Register*, just why the "Evils" apprehended by Thomas Malthus were *not* "Particularly Applicable to the Present and Probable Future State of the United States," he could count on a wide domestic audience eager to agree with him. Niles had a new kind of project in mind. He proposed to offer his customers a detailed yet compact synopsis of Malthus's *Essay*, giving his audience a chance to form independent opinions, before adding any commentary of his own. He promised that by providing a window into Malthus, he would open to every reader's "view the causes of emigration, revolutions, wars, colonization &c." Nile's extensive summary went further even than Weightman's American reprint of the *Essay* to bring the complex ideas of political economists within the reach of common readers.[45]

However, in Niles's hands, editing Malthus meant expurgating him. Despite his promise to explain the causes of wars and colonization, the *Register* made no mention of Malthus's critique of American takeovers of Indian lands, no comment on the fact that population expansion and territorial aggression were linked in the analysis of the British political economist. Niles's summaries of Malthus were fairly accurate as far as they went. Though he did not often quote Malthus directly, it is possible to sit down with the *Weekly Register* in one hand, the *Essay* in the other, and see clearly where he gathered his material. However, it is also clearly evident that Niles strategically culled from the full work.

Niles champed at the bit to confront Britain. Before beginning to publish the *Weekly Register* in 1811, he editorialized for years in the *Evening Post* about the inevitability of conflict with Britain and the need for American military preparedness. He introduced his readers to Malthus only to bring them the triumphal information that, because of a combination of natural and cultural factors, American reproduction was far superior to that ever achieved by any other people anywhere in the world.[46]

The Niles report on Malthus stretched over many issues of the *Register* published in the fall of 1811 through the spring of 1812. In abstracting Malthus, Niles offered his own primer on how reproductive potency could assure national power. Malthus urged all people to exercise moral restraint, to delay sexual activity as long as possible in order to limit their total number of offspring. Niles duly reported this, but perversely tailored his presentation of Malthus to emphasize information on how the sexual and romantic mores of Euro-Americans could confer a fertility advantage over Native Americans as well as Europeans and Africans (Figure 3).

In the first segment, published in September 1811, Niles stressed Malthus's finding that among "American Indians . . . the women are by no means prolific, having seldom more than two or three children." As Malthus argued and Niles reported, there were a number of possible factors that could have shaped Indian demography. They rejected the idea that Indian women might have borne few children simply because their men were "naturally void of amorous or lustful affections." Though the figure of the passionless and inhuman

A PERSPECTIVE VIEW OF NIAGARA FALLS, copied from a drawing made on the spot, and here presented, not only as an appropriate Emblem of the Subject below, but as a testimony of one valuable property in the new LETTER-PRESS, invented by the Author of this Proposal, enriching the Printer's Art with the means of displaying any Number of Colours.

IMPROVE NATURE's BOUNTY.

A PROPOSAL,
FOR REMOVING THE INCONVENIENCIES INCIDENT TO LOCKS AND INCLINED PLANES, IN
TRANSFERRING CANAL-BOATS FROM ONE LEVEL TO ANOTHER.

THE numerous expedients which have been tried in Europe, as remedies for the disadvantages attendant on Locks in canal-navigation, have not yet so far succeeded, as to preclude the hope for something superior to any substitute hitherto devised. lower, by every boat of any considerable magnitude, which descends with a full cargo, and rises empty. In a trade therefore which is altogether descending, the upper level will thereby constantly gain water from the lower; and the contrary if the trade

Figure 3. This decorative image stresses both the natural abundance of North America and the need to "improve nature's bounty." Note the pair of figures in the right foreground, a seated man in jacket and breeches on the left, a standing woman in full-skirted dress on the right, a male-female couple who together will develop the land. The image documents the self-conscious role assumed by practitioners of the "printer's art" in promoting national growth, applying the latest technology in color printing to entice expansionist desires. "A Perspective View of Niagara Falls," c. 1813, Collections of the American Antiquarian Society.

Indian was one popular image on both sides of the Atlantic, neither Malthus nor Niles hesitated to confirm the prevalence of "dissolute and libertine manners" among some tribes as well as "the early prostitution of the females." With Malthus insisting that excess procreation, even within marriage, should be regarded as a social and moral evil, Americans like Niles readily emphasized extreme Indian sexuality, the better to rehabilitate Euro-American claims to comparative virtue.[47]

Yet Niles did slant Malthus's analysis in key ways. In one deliberate addition to the discussion of Indian sexual practices, Niles threw in a belated acknowledgment that Indians "were being driven from their former lands by the more powerful whites, to a narrow extent of territory." But he did so only to reject lack of land as an explanation for low Indian fertility. In Niles's silent revision of Malthus, Indians should have been grateful for the loss of hunting lands because, in consequence, they were "obliged to learn from their conquerors something of agriculture." Niles went on to argue that "this progress towards civilization would naturally give a spur to procreation . . . but a counterbalance may be found in the introduction of intoxicating liquors among them." Malthus himself did mention the problem of alcohol—in another section of the *Essay* entirely. But in his account, this health risk was only a minor population factor in comparison with the contraceptive effects of delayed weaning among breastfeeding Indian women. And Malthus certainly offered no credit to the "conquerors" for instructing Indians in the civilized ways that could lead to maximized reproduction.[48]

Niles made no secret of his own belief that American lands belonged in Euro-American hands. His critiques of Indian sexual mores advanced a concerted effort to justify U.S. territorial expansion on moral grounds. Just months after war finally broke out, Niles would feature an article in the *Register* proclaiming, "Imagination looks forward to the moment when all the southern Indians shall be pushed across the Mississippi: when the delightful countries now occupied by them shall be covered with a numerous and industrious population." The contrast with Malthus could not be more complete. Where Malthus bemoaned the fact that Indians were being "driven further and further back into the country," Niles boasted that all Indians would soon be "pushed across the Mississippi." And while worries that Indians would be "exterminated" by invading hordes from the United States plagued Malthus, the potential rise of "a numerous and industrious population" furnished the subject for Niles's fondest imaginings.[49]

Meanwhile, in his second installment in the *Essay on Population* series, published in October, Niles enticed his readers with a subtle but highly significant shift in analysis that undermined Malthus's true intentions while advancing his own. After skipping over most of Malthus's review of European population history because he "deem[ed] it unnecessary to pursue him through the long detail of historical facts," Niles paused to linger at length over a discussion of "laws and customs of the ancient German nations" that Malthus in turn had based on the findings of the Roman historian Tacitus. Niles took special interest in this section of Malthus's *Essay* because, as the American editor put it, the ways of the Germans were "eminently calculated to promote the spirit of procreation." Although Malthus studied the Germans as a cautionary tale of how barbarian hordes had managed to conquer civilized Rome, Niles found in their story a ready source of inspiration.[50]

Niles recounted Mathus's initial observations faithfully enough. He related that German women were "treated with the most marked attention and regard," a commonplace point of contrast with Indian women made by European observers from the earliest days of colonization. He joined Malthus in approving the fact that "marriages were everywhere strongly inculcated and matrimonial infidelity was scarcely known." And he applauded along with the Englishman the information that prostitutes were treated as outcasts, while any "man who debauched a woman was obliged either to marry her, to give her a portion, or to suffer death." Though the Anglican clergyman advocated delayed marriages as the most effective voluntary means of checking population, he did so only in the context of calling for chastity before marriage and fidelity after.[51]

Yet Niles brought *his* survey of the Germans to a markedly different conclusion from that of the author he was supposedly summarizing. Malthus wrapped up his observations on the ancient Germans by deploring "the disgusting details of those unceasing wars" and lamenting the "prodigal waste of human life, which marked these barbarous periods." Niles, in contrast, used sarcasm to ridicule Malthus for his critique: "These people were called *barbarians*; how unlike the *civilized* people of the present *enlightened* age! Who can smile at seduction, as a fashionable pastime, and encourage the harlot to look down on the virtuous woman." No matter that Malthus in no way countenanced sexual debauchery. Niles implied that the decadent modern English were more tolerant of lewd behavior than the simple and moral members of the United States, who confined their sexuality to procreative purposes within marriage. Though the Englishman challenged Americans to a contest of virtue, Niles was confident he could gain the upper hand.[52]

Finally, on the subject of African fertility, Niles reached new heights of righteous bigotry and intellectual incoherence. On the one hand, in an apparent effort to assert that the slave trade had done no harm to the continent's people, Niles claimed, "in different parts of Africa, we have reason to be astonished at the *principle* of increase which is found to be sufficient to keep up the population under so many impediments." On the other hand, he quickly reported that Malthus observed shorter life spans in Africa than in Europe or America, "a circumstance which our author is inclined to attribute chiefly to the heat of the climate." Not for Niles such a value-neutral explanation of mortality. "But we do not find this to be the case in other hot climates," he complained. He much preferred the virulent condemnation of the Comte de Buffon, who, "with greater propriety, attributes the shortness of life in Africa to the early intercourse of the sexes. The children are so debauched . . . that from the age of ten or eleven they give themselves up to every species of lustful practices." Such statements were anathema to Malthus, who vigorously and openly opposed the slave trade and defied anyone to use his theories to support it. But they fit neatly with Niles's efforts to burnish Euro-American fertility with the sheen of special morality.[53]

⟨∞⟩

At the time that Niles first offered his gloss on Malthus, in September and October 1811, the United States was formally at peace, though already many observers could predict the conflict with Britain that would break out in the spring. Meanwhile, before Niles could even bring the third installment of his Malthus series to press, the United States did engage in open battle—with the Indian confederacy led by the Shawnee leader Tecumseh. Indiana territorial governor William Henry Harrison led the troops that defeated Tecumseh's fighters on November 7, 1811, in the confrontation that became known as the Battle of Tippecanoe. Despite the success of the maneuver, the United States left the field more concerned about evidence that the British were supporting Indians in the western portion of U.S.-claimed territories than content with their show of prowess. In this fraught atmosphere, Niles did everything he could to transform Malthusian critiques of American imperialism into a manual of martial inspiration.[54]

As war with Britain shifted from future prospect to present danger, Niles began to denounce Malthus directly. By the spring of 1812, when President Madison was daily deliberating on asking Congress for a declaration of war, Niles was arguing that England's relatively small population owed more to the indulgence of extramarital sexuality, with related increases in venereal disease and consequent infertility, than to any exercise in moral restraint. "Upon the whole," he sneered, "we conceive our author would have been more consistent to have attributed the small proportion of births in England . . . to the very great licentiousness of manners which prevails to so great a degree . . . owing to the facility of sexual intercourse." Niles depicted the British as too debauched to serve as moral arbiters of the United States.[55]

By the summer, when war had finally been formally declared, Niles was warning readers against "the impropriety of trusting to impressions made upon us by the ingenuity of foreign writers, most of whom in respect to the United States, are governed either by erroneous views or sinister motives." Dismissing Malthus after providing him months of hospitality in the pages of his newspaper, Niles promised readers that they need pay no heed to any of Malthus's warnings because the huge territory available to the United States gave them "the means . . . of escaping the evils which follow an excess of increase" in human population.[56]

Instead, he told readers they should take pride in the effects of unfettered fertility on American society. In attacking U.S. imperialism, he argued, Malthus was actually undermining American egalitarianism. He announced, "we shall . . . here close our analysis of Mr. Malthus and take a slight review of the United States in the course of which we shall endeavor to prove, that we are far removed from the operation of those evils which, it has been contended, so powerfully threaten the system of equality." According to Niles, the ready availability of land and the consequent limitless potential for reproduction was the very basis on which American equality was built.[57]

If equality was one happy result of the United States' acceptance of unlimited progeny, liberty was the other. Niles argued that by providing lands not only for its own peoples but also for many fleeing war-torn Europe, the United States was in fact upholding the very liberty that Britain could not claim to provide. He ended his analysis by boldly proclaiming that the United States was "the only asylum, which the tyranny and rapacity of the despots of the old world have left, to the oppressed and afflicted members of the human family." Instead of continuing to provide a platform, tilted as it was, for Malthusian ideas, Niles now declared his open opposition to applying the Englishman's arguments in America. The United States was unique in its fertility and, as a direct consequence, in its protection of liberty.[58]

Nile's final repudiation of Malthus came in the same issue of the *Register* as the story of how his own birth had been brutally menaced by the British. At this moment—as he sought to rev up American memories of the revolutionary movement for Independence, the better to motivate a new movement for war—Niles launched into the story of his family's ordeal. The image of the bayonet brandished against his mother's swollen belly dramatized the stakes of population concerns in a way that could not have been more concrete.[59]

⤜∞⤏

Transforming the sense of personal crisis into political commitment was a crucial element of raising support for a war that many regarded as ill advised, unnecessary, and even immoral. If Republicans who supported the war could cite a long train of British provocations, from impressment on the seas and interference with U.S. shipping to material support for Indian opponents and even occasional attacks on U.S. navy vessels, Federalists who opposed it questioned the motives of the bellicose. They claimed that France had paid no more heed to American attempts at neutrality than had the British and were as deserving of U.S. opposition. They argued that war with Britain, far from protecting U.S. commerce, would halt it altogether. They pointed out that even if war were desirable, the United States was gravely unprepared to fight, with a tiny navy and an ineffectual volunteer army. They worried that war supporters were turning the nation in the direction of Napoleonic despotism. And they charged that southern and western slaveholders, not content with expanding the geographic reach of slavery through the acquisition of the Louisiana territory, sought to further their grasp on the nation through the invasion and annexation of Canada.[60]

In the run-up to war, Republicans and Federalists increasingly squared off against each other on the basis of pro- or anti-Malthusian attitudes. Republican-leaning newspapers like the Philadelphia *Weekly Aurora* complained that "not a few of our *piddling* politicians have been led astray . . . by . . . the able but artful and insidious misanthropy of Malthus." In Federalist regional strongholds like New Hampshire, newspaper commentators did not even try to argue against the importance of policies favoring increasing population for the advancement of the United States. Instead, they were reduced to trying to convince people, in the words of one repeatedly reprinted article, from the spring of 1812, that "early marriages are a public blessing: but unhappy matches a private curse." While some people may have been persuaded by warnings against the dangers of hasty youthful marriages, opinion did not shift enough to earn the other elements of Malthus's critique a full American hearing. As it was, from the Republican press, as from the pages of political tracts, came the continuous assertion that a key component of American happiness, public and personal alike, was the right to maximize reproduction.[61]

It took another English minister and sometime newspaper editor, this one a Republican-leaning Presbyterian who fled Britain for the United States, to articulate exactly how Malthus's analysis could be inverted in America. The Reverend George Bourne, by then a resident in Virginia, made Malthus the chief target of his wartime work, *Marriage Indissoluble and Divorce Unscriptural*. He complained, "Mr. Malthus's information may enable us to contrast the wretchedness and misery of European climes with Columbia's enjoyments: but the design of his essay on Population cannot be sufficiently condemned." According to Bourne, "the grand conclusion which is drawn from his survey 'that persons should not marry until they are advanced in years,' is one of the most iniquitous and destructive positions, that ever was promulgated under the name of moral and political philosophy." From there, Bourne went on to accuse Malthus of encouraging prostitution and assorted other personal and social ills.[62]

Furthermore, Bourne, like Niles before him, easily linked his defense of marriage directly to issues of geopolitics. And, just like Niles, Bourne found a champion in the Roman writer Tacitus. Bourne asserted, quoting that ancient historian, that "early marriages are the soul and chief prop of empire." If the United States wanted an empire to rival Britain's, it could do no better than to promote youthful marriage and maximized population. Malthus might try to discredit both undisciplined sexual reproduction and unrestricted territorial expansion as profoundly immoral. But opponents like Bourne stood ready to claim that Malthus and his fellow Britons were the ones with the deficit of virtue. Expansionist Americans of the 1812 era openly sought to advance the building of a U.S. empire. Self-styled American "republicans" could cast themselves as more martial than Romans when they entered marriages and produced children.[63]

In the United States, polemicists did not hesitate to tie the right to marry directly to the contest to carry liberty's standard that the British and Americans continued to fight on many fronts. In this analysis, true political liberty required unlimited emotional freedom. And the most exalted emotion was romantic love. As Virginia plantation owner and political theorist John Taylor explained it, Malthus was in favor of "resorting to law for suppressing love." He exclaimed, "Malthus teaches us, that the English system . . . will devote one part of the community to death by famine, or to the necessity of living above half their lives without affections." According to Taylor, England offered its people only the stark choice between mass starvation or marital delay, population limitation, and emotional privation.[64]

Some southerners even went so far as to use opposition to Malthus as a means of justifying slavery. They taxed Malthus with imposing a kind of moral slavery on his followers that was worse than legal slavery. If Malthus "proposes to introduce a papistical system of celibacy," John Taylor asked, who could fail to notice "the difference in point of benevolence, between indirect slavery to a separate interest, and direct slavery to an absolute master?" In Taylor's America, even those subjected to "direct slavery to an absolute master" retained the right to reproduce. No matter all the other freedoms denied the enslaved, including the right to legal marriage and, indeed, the right even to "own" their own children. U.S. slaveholders could boast that African Americans in bondage enjoyed greater basic privileges of procreation than did supposedly "freeborn" Englishmen. Meanwhile, American whites enjoyed natural rights to love and marriage under attack in Malthus's Britain. The insidious logic that linked liberty, equality, and fecundity could be used not only to justify the seizure of Indian lands but also to address the most fundamental ethical dispute with Britain: slavery itself.[65]

⸎

Anti-Malthus Republicans mixed a complex brew in their effort to distill American moral legitimacy from British assertions of supremacy. If population was the basic malt of the American argument, romantic love supplied the heat of fermentation. Sexual attraction could motivate national action. Niles used his "analysis" of Malthus to introduce this idea with a key sleight of hand. Though Niles suffered no qualms about offering a highly selective presentation of Malthus, he objected that Malthus himself recognized no obligation to report every idea of Tacitus. Some of the latter's observations seemed to Niles to positively require consideration. And so in his summary of the *Essay on Population*, he simply interwove his own chosen lines of loose translation from Tacitus within and among sentences that corresponded closely to those actually composed by Malthus. Uninformed readers were left to assume that Malthus himself had included material from Tacitus that had actually been inserted directly by Niles. Of special interest to Niles were hints that Tacitus provided about the role of romance in the winning of war.[66]

Niles wished readers to consider that martial ardor owed its origin to marital desire. Immediately after accurately summing up Malthus's rendition of Tacitus's comments on the "attention and regard" paid to German women, and directly before mentioning those on the "infrequency of marital infidelity" among the Germans, Niles injected a claim from Tacitus entirely absent from the *Essay on Population*. He said that German men "sometimes carried their women with them into the field of battle, where their presence served to animate them with martial ardor." Niles here conjured quite a spectacle: women on the battleground, men inspired by sexual ardor to martial feats and military victory.[67]

Niles followed up these claims on the origins of German "martial ardor" with further information highly relevant to population concerns. Fighting before the eyes of women, Niles noted with Tacitus, served "often to turn the fate of a battle, when they would have ingloriously retreated or suffered themselves to be taken captives." If population strength was the measure of nations, then being captured by the enemy, and forced to join their ranks, was literally a fate worse than death.[68]

In 1812, Hezekiah Niles was still an upstart young printer trying to make his name and fortune with the newspaper he called the *Weekly Register*. Whoever his readers were, they probably did not include many at the highest levels of U.S. policy circles. Yet by 1817, Niles would be bold enough to address a private letter to James Madison asking the former president to endorse his newspaper. It was to Madison that Niles made the declaration that he had "been flattered with the belief that the *Weekly Register* . . . ha[d] done a good deal to the rouse of a *national feeling* and built up pride of character hitherto too much neglected." Niles's own understanding of his work involved much more than the simple reportage of news and facts. It extended to the intentional manipulation of emotion, the creation of "national feeling."[69]

∽∞∽

How was "national feeling" supposed to feel in the era of 1812? The United States of the early nineteenth century could not rely on any traditional form of patriotism. American inhabitants could not claim the ties of birth, of lineal descent from a shared progenitor, that bound together the historic peoples of established countries. Lacking true natal ties, nationalists in the era of the early republic had to develop deliberately the feelings they could not inherit naturally. Writers like Hezekiah Niles understood that calls to "patria," to literal love of "fatherland," could have only limited effectiveness in the United States. Instead, Niles and those of his ilk made a strategically significant shift of emphasis from fathers to lovers. Promoting patriotism in a new democracy, they decided to foreground the future over the past, the chosen love of heterosexual romance over the obligatory obeisance of filial duty. They insisted that, in symbolic terms, men and women ought to enter the field of battle together.[70]

When President James Madison addressed the nation in response to Congress's declaration of war in June of 1812 he "exort[ed] all the good people of the United States, as they love their country . . . that they exert themselves," an apparently conventional call to arms. But in the America of 1812, there were few established standards to rely on. Every element of Madison's exhortation posed potential problems. Just who were "the good people of the United States" and how should they be called to account? How exactly could people be roused to "exert themselves" and what specifically would their exertions entail? What precisely were the emotional contours of "love" of country?

Appealing to national loyalty was a complex proposition in a country as divided as the new United States. The country's Constitution, the founding document that defined the United States, declared that "we the people" had come together "in order to form a more perfect union." But just who were the "people" who gave voice to the constitution and how close a union did they propose to form? Were they the same as Madison's "good people of the United States"?

While only propertied white men could boast full citizenship under the terms of state and federal constitutions, the wartime emergency seemed to require a wider appeal to—and a fuller reliance on—the population of the United States as a whole. At the most basic level, counting the nation's people required making a straightforward numerical tally. But choosing the criteria by which to enumerate the country's inhabitants involved social and cultural calculations as much as mathematical ones. If Americans of the early republic were no longer royal subjects forced to submit to the British Crown, neither were many of the nation's inhabitants—from enslaved blacks to most Indians to all women—full democratic citizens. Instead, as a collective, they constituted a new broad category: the population.[71]

The Constitution's strange triangulations and circumlocutions on this point—from measuring the enslaved as "three-fifths" of a person to referring awkwardly to "Indians not taxed"—are well known. Such practical compromises over the nomenclature of citizenship are now sometimes judged to be a simple matter of flawed logic, unfulfilled promise, or political expediency. Or these choices can be viewed more critically as having compromised the justice of the Constitution at the core, vivifying the rights of white male citizens only by vitiating those of everyone else. Yet what any analysis of the Constitution's exclusions overlooks is that in some real sense the nation did rely on vital contributions from *all* "the people" referred to therein. Wartime demands for the productive and reproductive labor of *all* the nation's inhabitants required a new vocabulary of provisional inclusion. "Population" filled the bill.[72]

With military pressures making population a more important asset than ever, early American nationalists had marked incentives to make population as broad a category as possible. By contributing patriotic service, on battlefield or in childbed, anyone—including women, enslaved Africans, and new immigrants—could show love of country and be counted a useful part of the population. And in the process, each could claim liberty in its most elemental form: the right to produce progeny.

Neither requiring consent nor guaranteeing rights, the category of "population" nevertheless promised a degree of national protection and affiliation. The associated activities of warfare and childbirth allowed men and women alike access to a new form of national belonging. Of course, integration in the population in this sense conveyed far fewer rights than did formal recognition as a citizen. To be incorporated into the country as a simple member of the population imposed demands for personal service without conferring corresponding political privileges. Yet this was the de facto basis on which the majority of American inhabitants lived within the nation. Meanwhile, as for the Indians who refused to offer up their bodies to the body politic, many Americans preferred to cast them as corpses.

When Americans of the 1812 era discussed "population," they were invoking both a key social and political category and an important kind of activity. In theory, populating the country required only that it be filled with inhabitants, a process that could rely on foreign migration as much as on procreation. Yet in practice, when Americans of the 1812 era discussed "population" as an action, they often had reproduction explicitly in mind. Loammi Baldwin's published *Thoughts on Political Economy* publicly articulated such views in saying "the union of the sexes is the most important, and in a political view, the only desirable source of population to a state." Ultimately the *activity* of populating the nation was the surest way of being included in population as a *category* of national belonging.[73]

Moving the population to action on behalf of the nation presented a critical emotional challenge. While nationalism is often said to require a unified sense of identity, it may also proceed from a more easily achieved—and more readily restricted—commitment to joint action. In searching for the emotions of early American nationalism, then, we might do well to focus less on those supposed to advance the formation of "identity" and more on those who might enhance instrumentality. In the United States in 1812, the nation needed to draw strength from the actions of its entire population, but its leaders neither needed nor desired to grant every member of the populace the same kind of status. All Americans were not citizens; in this way, their unity was sharply limited. Yet by acting cooperatively to support the country in an hour of crisis, they could coordinate their interests. Patriotism may as often arise from shared pursuits as from shared personhood.[74]

By 1812, American expansionists sought above all to foment military action: to force Indians to relinquish lingering territorial rights to the lands of the Great Lakes and the Mississippi basin and to compel the British to abandon all diplomatic and trading ties to American Indians. They needed, ultimately, to fuel lust for geographic gains. Quite conversant with the notion that there is an inherent connection between passion and action, Americans at the turn of the nineteenth century knew that they had to stoke longing before they could stake claim to new lands. It was no accident, then, that the love that underlay early American nationalism was an explicitly yearning kind, one that grew out of ordinary desires to expand families and acquire farms.[75]

⌘

When the War of 1812 at last drew to a close in 1815, President James Madison could celebrate no change in the formal terms of British-American relations. Considered as a military confrontation with Great Britain, the War of 1812 accomplished little. By most measures, indeed, it was a grave American embarrassment. Multiple attempts to invade Canada failed, while the British succeeded in burning the public buildings of the nation's capital to the ground.

The United States' single major land victory, achieved at New Orleans at the last minute, was immediately rendered moot by a prior peace treaty, an accord that itself did little to redress the stated provocations of the conflict. Still, Madison triumphed that "the United States are in the tranquil enjoyment of a[n] . . . honorable peace. . . . The strongest features of its flourishing condition are seen, in a population rapidly increasing, on a territory as productive as it is extensive." Taken out of context, Madison's remarks could seem to be a simple observation that the vast terrain of the American continent allowed the continuing growth of the U.S population. Considered in light of the Republicans' preferred anti-Malthusian ideas of political economy, however, his comments take on another color.[76]

Sexual reproduction took pride of place in the early republic's geopolitical imagination. As much as technical military might, the "natural" force of demography could fundamentally alter the shape of national geography. In the depths of the war, when the military outlook seemed bleak to many, former president Thomas Jefferson privately reassured a friend, "We shall indeed survive the conflict." He argued, "breeders enough will remain to carry on population. We shall retain our country, beat our enemy, & probably drive him from the continent. We have men enough." Many contemporaries viewed the production of progeny as a foundational element of military planning.[77]

Like his predecessor in office, President James Madison preferred the ideas of French physiocrats to those of English political economists like Malthus. The two presidents shared the perspective of their mutual wartime correspondent Pierre Samuel du Pont de Nemours, who stressed that freedom of circulation required not only untrammeled trade but also unrestrained reproduction. As Jefferson wrote to de Nemours at the war's end in 1815, his fondest "hope" for his country was that, with the British vanquished, Americans would at last be "permitted to proceed peaceably in making children, and maturing and moulding our strength and resources." Despite the fiction that lay at the base of this hope, that "making children" could be a wholly peaceable process, the official Republican view that population was essential to American national strength became one of the most enduring legacies of the war.[78]

The plentiful lands of North America could support population increases undreamed of in Britain. But the converse proposition also applied. The rapid rise of the U.S. population gave it the manpower needed to seize and settle new ground. Ordinary people consciously participated in the project of enlarging the nation's territory by expanding its population. In 1816, in the immediate wake of the war, a petition to Congress announced that the "inhabitants and native Citizens of the Northern and Eastern section of the United States" were seeking to settle lands in the Northwest Territory not only from an "ambition to advance their own [interests]" but also from a desire "to extend the population and the power of the United States." The phrase "inhabitants and native Citizens" seems significant here. The action of populating the nation could in itself ensure inclusion in the nation's population, even for those inhabitants who were not full legal citizens.[79]

As Governor Ninian Edwards of the Illinois Territory observed to Secretary of War William Crawford at the close of the war, although Indian "hostility" had the potential to "put an end to the surveying, or occupying of the military lands," in the short term, within just a few years, "the growth of our population . . . will prevent all future danger." High fertility in the territories was not just an unremarkable effect of the normal conditions of a "frontier" political economy, much less the unintended result of the "natural" demographic decline of doomed Indians. On the contrary, the linked effects of population augmentation and territorial aggression may well have been the fruit of studied strategy. As the Reverend George Bourne had observed, quoting Tacitus: "early marriages are the soul and chief prop of empire." An expanding state had a direct interest in encouraging the optimized levels of reproduction made possible by youthful marriages.[80]

George Bourne's approving quotation from Tacitus gained popularity from southern parlors like his own to the hardscrabble settlements of frontier areas in western Pennsylvania. In November 1815, in the wake of the war, the *Carlisle Gazette* published yet another round of praise for the role of reproduction in the seizure of land. The paper declared, "Tacitus says, early marriage makes us immortal. It is the soul and chief prop of empire." Here the merging of high political economy and popular culture seems near complete. The article concluded by warning that "the man who resolves to live without woman, and the woman who resolves to live without man, are enemies to the community in which they dwell." Again and again word came down that any community dweller, whether man or woman, whether full citizen or simple inhabitant, could contribute vital force to the country.[81]

So long as population was *the* fundamental source of strength for the country then anyone's sexuality could not only foster personal happiness but

WREATHS FOR THE

CHIEFTAIN;

TOGETHER WITH

I'D RATHER BE EXCUS'D.

WREATHS for the Chieftain we honor! who planted
  The Olive of peace in the soil that he gain'd,
Freemen his praise, 'neath its shelter have chaunted,
  Secure in its branches the Ringdove remain'd.
    War blasts have scatter'd it !
    Rude hand have shatter'd it !
Flown the nettler, that tenanted there?
  Long from the pelting storm
  None sought its blighted form,
Save the lone Raven, that scream'd in despair.

Hossannas the high vaults of heaven ascending,
  Hallow the day when our Chieftain was born !
The Olive he planted revives, and is blending,
  Its leaves with the laurel that blooms o'er its urn.
    Ne'er may the sacred tree,
    Shorn of its verdure be ;
Ne'er may the blast, that hath scatter'd it, blow,
  " Heaven send it happy dew,
  Earth send it sap anew,
Gaily to blossom and broadly to grow."

Sunk be the blaze of the balefire forever !
  Hush'd be the trump in the slumbers of years !
Seraphs sound Pæans of praise to the giver,
  Peace hath illumin'd a nation in tears !
    May she in triumph reign
    Over our land again ;
Ne'er may her fair floating banners be furl'd,
  Still be the orphans moan,
  Silent the widow's groan,
Lost, for a time, in the joy of the world.

I'd rather be Excus'd.

RETURNING from a fair, one eve,
  Across yon verdant plain ;
Young Harry said he'd see me home
  A tight and comely swain,
He begg'd I would a fairing take,
  And would not be refusing take,
Then ask'd a kiss refus'd ;
  I'd rather I blush'd and cry'd,
    be excus'd.

You're coy said he, my pretty maid ;
  I mean no harm I swear.
Long time I have in secret sigh'd,
  For you my charming fair ;
But if my tenderness offends,
  And if my love's refus'd,
I'll leave you, what along, said I,
  I'd rather be excus'd.

He press'd my hand, and on we walk'd,
  He warmly urg'd his suit ;
But still, to all he said, I was
  Most obstinately mute.
At length got home, he angry cry'd,
  My passion is abus'd ;
Then die a maid, indeed, said I,
  I'd rather be excus'd.

Printed by Nathaniel Coverly, Jun. Boston.

Figure 4. This broadside produced at the war's end by the prolific printer and unabashed nationalist Nathaniel Coverly juxtaposes two poems and accompanying images that graphically document the convergence of militaristic, imperialistic, romantic, and reproductive themes in popular culture. The image on the left commemorates the return of the nation to peace and with it the homecoming of a venerable old soldier. The first lines of the corresponding poem declare, "WREATHS for the Chieftain we honor! who planted / The Olive of peace in the soil that he gain'd." The apparently unrelated image on the right shows a suitor extending his hand to a maiden who throws up her hands in surrender, consenting to wed. Note that on his outstretched hand rests a miniature person, a symbolic reference to the reproductive promises implied in a marriage pact. In the first lines of the corresponding poem, the "comely swain … ask'd a kiss" and the female narrator recounts, "I blushed and cry'd, / I'd rather be excused." By the last lines of the poem, however, the narrator relents. Rather than face life as a spinster she declares, "Then die a maid, indeed, said I / I'd rather be excus'd." Together these coordinating poems and images suggest how intertwined love and war would become in the popular imagination as well as in formal political economy. "'Wreaths for the Chieftain;' together with 'I'd Rather Be Excus'd,'" Nathaniel Coverly, Jr., Boston, c. 1815, Collections of the American Antiquarian Society.

also contribute to the very foundation of the nation. Love of country had literal genesis in romantic feeling (Figure 4). And with neat circular logic, as falling in love and beginning wedded life became patriotic duties, the rights to copulate and procreate in turn defined the essence of liberty.[82]

Many American nationalists of the 1812 era centered their emotional efforts on romantic love as the wellspring of patriotism. When Niles suggested with Tacitus that ardent love for women could inspire military ardor, he made a formal theoretical proposition out of something that was fast becoming an unremarkable element of popular culture. As would become abundantly clear over the months and years to come, proponents of the war often appealed directly to national "ardor" in the effort to rouse the populace.

Chapter 2

❧❦❧

Failures of Feeling as National Disasters
DETROIT, AUGUST 1812

When the men first saw a blue-and-red-striped marquee tent rising in the American camp on the Detroit River, "a singular structure never before seen in this army," many may have shrugged it off as just one more example of indulgence by "so many fops" given to "so much parade and no action among them." But when the officers and soldiers of the Northwestern Army of the United States later watched a white flag being raised over that tent, they were "struck with astonishment." The first American effort at invading Canada, intended as the grand opening of the War of 1812, had just ended in utter defeat.[1]

The author of those observations, Captain Robert Lucas, swore in a journal entry dated that day, August 16, that "in entering into this capitulation" to the British forces amassed under General Isaac Brock, General William Hull "only consulted his own feelings. Not an officer was consulted, not one anticipated a Surrender till they saw the white flag displayed." Worse was still to come. Lucas exclaimed, "when our troops was marched out our Coulours Struck and the British Coulours hoisted in their Stead, my feelings was Affected beyond expression." He claimed that all but one person shared his emotions: "even the women were indignant at so shameful a degradation of the American character and all felt as they should have felt save he who held in his hands the reigns of authority." Lucas's words were destined to be widely repeated.[2]

Colonel Lewis Cass, who had not himself witnessed the moment of surrender, liked Lucas's account of it so much that he incorporated it into an official report on the capitulation that he prepared for the secretary of war the next month, quoting Lucas's words verbatim and without attribution. Hull's officers rushed together to blame the national military failure on Hull's individual emotional flaws. "All felt as they should have felt," save General Hull whose "own feelings" had led the country to disaster.[3]

Hauled before a court-martial in Albany, New York, in January 1814, Hull would find that emotional transgressions loomed large in the capital charges he faced, from "TREASON against the United States" to "COWARDICE at and in the neighborhood of Detroit" to "NEGLECT OF DUTY and UNOFFICER-LIKE CONDUCT." The court, in detailing what was meant by the charge of "un-officer like conduct" declared that "the officers and soldiers" had "been dissatisfied and disgusted by a scene of inactivity, irresolution and procrastination" by which "the general ardor of the army insensibly abated." According to the court, maintaining the emotional ardor of his fighting force was one of the general's most important duties.[4]

The crimes Hull stood accused of lay as much in damaging the friable feelings of his men as in failing to exhibit courage himself. Summing up the scene at Detroit, the court held that "the northwestern army of the United States then and there being in fine spirits, and eager to meet the approaching enemy in battle" had been thwarted by a general willing to "enter into a shameful capitulation." In sum, the court charged, "a brave army [was] wantonly sacrificed by the personal fears of its commander." Soldiers who had once been in "fine spirits" had had their ardor "insensibly abated."[5]

Colonel Lewis Cass's critique of Hull's negative impact on the ardent feelings of the troops helped round out the formal counts against the general. In the official memorandum he prepared for the government in September 1812, Cass provided extensive commentary on the changing emotions of the American fighting corps and the strategic significance of these shifts in sentiment. According to Cass, "when the forces landed in Canada, they landed with an ardent zeal," and then maintained their emotional arousal in readiness for action. When General Brock first demanded surrender on August 15, "stating he could no longer restrain the fury of the savages" allied with him against the United States, an "immediate and spirited refusal was returned" by men whose emotions were primed for victory. Cass avowed "that we were far superior to the enemy; that upon any ordinary principles of calculation we would have defeated them, the wounded and indignant feelings of every man there will attest." Strikingly, Cass offered emotion not simply as proof of intention, but as the veritable proxy of achievement. The "feelings of every man there" were enough to "attest" to the inevitability of an American victory, had they only been given the opportunity to enter the field. Having drilled themselves in correct feeling, the troops were sure to win any fight.[6]

Hull, however, had dashed the men's spirits with his cowardly refusal to face the enemy. "Confident I am," Cass asserted, "that had the courage and conduct of the General been equal to the spirit and zeal of the troops, the event would have been as brilliant and successful as it now is disastrous and dishonorable." Meanwhile, the full implications of Hull's actions could only be understood through reference to their impact on the army's emotions. Cass did not skip a detail: "to see the whole of our men flushed with the hope of victory, eagerly awaiting the approaching contest, to see them afterwards dispirited, hopeless and desponding, at least 500 shedding tears because they were not allowed to meet their country's foe and fight their country's battles, excited sensations, which no American has ever before had cause to feel." In Cass's view, the "ardent zeal" of "spirited" men could quickly give way to the hopeless despondence of the "dispirited." He claimed that emotional control was the core of military discipline.[7]

General William Hull approached his capital trial determined to keep the focus on the factual rather than the emotional. In defending his decision to surrender, he would lay out for the tribunal a clear account of the organizational challenges he faced, from limited supplies of food and medicine to inadequate arms to insufficient, insubordinate, and inexperienced soldiers. Of course, he categorically denied the charge that he himself had shown cowardice in taking pragmatic action to save the lives of his otherwise doomed troops. But more importantly still, he emphatically disputed Cass's claims that emotional priming had any useful effect on military preparedness. Hull argued that the men, "though, they were very ardent and patriotic in their expressions, had had no service and neither men nor officers had ever been tried. It is not extraordinary that I should have felt some want of confidence in these raw troops." Hull insisted that patriotic ardor was no substitute for armed effectiveness. No matter how emotionally moving Cass's stories of spirited men reduced to tears were, Hull tried to steer the trial back to a clear-sighted accounting of the true challenges facing a nation that had gone to war with only the most minimal military infrastructure.[8]

Hull and Cass came from two different generations and represented opposite extremes in their attitudes toward emotion. The competition between them highlights fundamental social and political shifts under way in the early republic. Hull's claims to bravery as an innate character trait relied implicitly on theories that human nature could be categorized according to fixed moral divisions with clear social correlates. For himself, he claimed a constant "character for courage." In contrast, Cass and the men who dominated the court ascribed to a newer notion of human nature as infinitely malleable. Transient emotions could make and unmake men at every moment. Cass-style emphasis on emotional fluidity underpinned ideals of social mobility at a time when the Democratic-Republican Party was turning away from the idea of republicanism (with all that implied about leadership by the virtuous) and toward democracy (with its emphasis on equal participation for all).[9]

Whereas Hull, the experienced and tested veteran of the Revolutionary War, deplored the shortages of men and materiel that would humble the U.S. war effort from start to finish, Cass, a member of the rising generation, was convinced that the right emotional outlook mattered more than anything else. In practical terms, Hull's position was hard to dispute, but in symbolic terms, Cass's claims would carry the day. Throughout Hull's trial and many subsequent military disasters and defeats, popular enthusiasm for the war never flagged—so long as public representations of events played in an emotionally upbeat key.

War supporters warmed quickly to the notion that emotional ardor represented a key contribution to national projects even in the absence of any other achievements. Federalist war critics who disbelieved the war's stated objectives readily perceived war boosters' emotional strategies. From pulpit sermons to broadside posters, they deplored the way sinful passions were being used to promote bad public policies. But one man's sinful passion was another's soaring patriotism. War boosters found it highly profitable to promote the war by making use of emotional appeals that linked ardent love of country to pleasurable feelings; and they hit on an especially effective tactic when they linked war ardor to romantic and sexual ardor.

⁙

If Hull's problems came to fruition with his surrender on the Detroit River, they had taken root long before in the woods of the Old Northwest. From the moment Hull took command of his troops, problems arose. Commissioned in Washington in April 1812, Hull regarded the assignment to lead the Northwest Army as a natural extension of his duties as governor of the

Michigan Territory and a fitting cap for his long military career. He agreed to take command of a mix of troops including the Fourth U.S. Army Regiment (a unit of three hundred soldiers) and twelve hundred Ohio militia members. The combined forces were to reconnoiter in Urbana, Ohio, then cut a swath north through two hundred miles of untracked forest to the Canadian border at Detroit.[10]

Yet no sooner had General Hull taken over command of the militia forces from Governor Return Meigs of Ohio than a contingent of the Ohio militia refused to set off on the march. Hull ordered their officers to command them to depart, but still they refused. Finally, he sent the soldiers of the Fourth Regiment to force them to fall into line. Ever after, Hull cited the incident as evidence that from the moment he "first took the command of these troops" he had been concerned with "the want of discipline and the mutinous spirit which prevailed." As Hull told it, "the authority of their officers was not sufficient to command their obedience. . . . Nothing but the bayonets of the 4th regiment could have that effect." Far from leading to victory, the emotions of men devoted to democracy breathed only a "spirit" of mutiny. Left to lead a green militia that lacked any respect for crucial military procedures and routines, Hull could almost have foretold the disaster at Detroit.[11]

Hull saw the short-lived mutiny in Ohio as symptomatic of pervasive disorder among a new generation, a cohort unwilling or unable to live up to the standards of authority and deference on which army life depended. As he recounted at his trial, "the organization of the militia corps . . . was particularly calculated to create a distrust with respect to them." The difficulty lay in the fact that "all the officers held their commission in virtue of an election, mediate or immediate, of the men of whom they were the nominal commanders. . . . Elected officers can never be calculated upon as great disciplinarians." No more did men in a democratically organized military unit understand the duty of due subordination: "the man who votes his officer his commission, instead of being implicitly obedient, as every soldier ought to be, will be disposed to question and consider the propriety of the officer's conduct before he acts." Question and consider the propriety of Hull's actions the men most certainly did.[12]

These opposing viewpoints came to the fore in Hull's clash with Cass. In his letter to the secretary of war, Cass minced no words in describing the emotional effects that Hull's surrender inflicted on the troops, dwelling at length on the despondence of men who shed tears when they could not show arms. In response, at his trial, Hull took Cass to task from every angle. First of all, he pointed out that "the ungenerous letter which Colonel Cass wrote to the government" should rightfully be regarded as simple fiction. The colonel had not been in camp at the time of the capitulation (having led a detachment of men away on a side mission) and therefore could claim no authority as a witness. Picking apart Cass's account, Hull demanded to know "who were these weeping troops? It is not to be presumed that it was intended we should believe they were the regulars—they are not commonly given to such weeping." Hull categorically denied that true soldiers ever cried.[13]

Rejecting Cass's claims for the military efficacy of emotion, Hull insisted that only untried militiamen would ever resort to such feeble measures. He sneered, "the men then who shewed this very extraordinary sensibility must have been Colonel Cass's patriotic volunteers—the same *volunteers* who mutinied in the camp at Urbana and would not march 'till they were compelled to do so by regular troops." Rhetorically, Hull and Cass had reached a stalemate, the former deriding the notion of "sensibility," the latter dismissing "philanthropic" considerations in the conduct of war. Yet Cass's claims would prove to carry far more weight.[14]

Throughout the summer preceding the surrender, newspapers across the nation had been reporting the emotional status of the army, as though this was the most reliable possible barometer of the war's progress and prospects. News of Hull's fall was bound to come as a shock since so many papers had spent months affirming the abilities of "our brave troops." Various articles reported, for example, that the troops were "in fine spirits, and anxious to be led across to the enemy," that they were "all in high spirits and we feel confident of success," and that the "men moved on with great spirit and alacrity." The nation, like its soldiers, had emotionally prepared only for victory. And though New York's *Western Star* proclaimed "hopes and fears alternate rising," many people took optimism itself to be a kind of national duty.[15]

Culling newspaper comments over the preceding months, a critical reader could have isolated more alarming indicators than those provided by the supposedly sunny emotional outlook of the men. Troop strength fell far below Hull's strategic needs. Yet the Northwestern Army received little cooperation from the armies of other commanders. By mid-August, published news that General Henry Dearborn (in command of the U.S. Army forces on the Niagara) had agreed to a "suspension of arms" with the British but had not included Hull and his troops in the armistice should have raised alarms.

Failure to coordinate the Hull and Dearborn forces would prove fatal to U.S. efforts. Still, the news caused only a ripple of concern. Meanwhile, Hull's ragged forces were also short on supplies, including arms and ammunition. As the *Philadelphia Freeman's Journal* noted on August 17, "numerous difficulties had presented themselves" to Hull and his men; most dangerously, "our brave troops were without artillery." And all of the above concerns were duly relayed to the War Department in Washington in Hull's official correspondence. Nevertheless, the chorus of voices emphasizing emotional readiness and predicting easy victory drowned out those urging caution.[16]

Colonel Lewis Cass had worked busily behind the scenes to sow the notion that the army's ardor all but guaranteed quick success in Canada. In fact, the claim that "the men moved on with great spirit and alacrity" came directly from his pen, having been included in an official letter sent to Hull on July 17. Leaked to the press, the letter was widely reprinted in the week *after* Hull's surrender, yet a week *before* the capitulation became common knowledge. Carried verbatim in papers in Boston and Maryland on August 18, in New York and South Carolina on August 19, and in Maine on August 20, Cass's elaborate claims that the army and its officers "conducted" themselves "in the most spirited and able manner" plowed the way for the public to take defeat as a wholly unanticipated catastrophe that could be explained only by the unpredictable behavior of an unsteady commander, a man whose own emotions fell far short of those of his forces.[17]

To understand how a man's personal emotional lapse (if indeed it occurred at all) could be successfully prosecuted as a public crime, it helps to appreciate the extent to which everyone from academic philosophers to military tacticians to the public at large credited sexual and emotional arousal as the source of courage even as they debated American capacities for the same. European observers had begun discussing whether the North American environment was more likely to advance or retard human progress almost from the moment that colonization projects began. As moral philosophy became a dominant intellectual fashion in the eighteenth century, writers like Georges-Louis Leclerc, Comte de Buffon, and Henry Home, Lord Kames, began to focus their analysis on emotion and to assert that virtuous feelings faltered in the American habitat. By the early nineteenth century, figures like transatlantic intellectual Alexander von Humboldt (a German member of the American Philosophical Society) attempted to create elaborate classification systems distinguishing the emotions of savage versus civilized people in various climates. In such schemas, classical Greece and Rome inevitably featured as exemplars of virtue, beside which all non-European societies appeared debased.[18]

The question for U.S. citizens was whether the courageous ardor they derived from Europe had been strengthened or enervated by the North American climate and landscape. Much depended on whether Indians, the native inhabitants of the land, were themselves judged to be superior or inferior in point of character, since all commentators seemed in basic agreement that, once in America, Europeans inevitably began to take on local traits. In the era of 1812, the United States was simultaneously a postcolonial nation and a neocolonial power, struggling under the continued social and cultural sway of the British and subject to British decrees on the high seas even as it sought to further Native American subordination on the continent. As U.S. nationalists mounted the case for a war whose centerpiece was to be the invasion of western Indian lands along with British Canada, they sought to attain a perfect balance of Old and New World traits, to achieve what the New York physician Hugh Williamson described in his 1811 book *Observations on the Climate in Different Parts of America* as the most "favorable combination of courage and strength . . . and . . . political freedom."[19]

In the midst of the War of 1812, Alexander von Humboldt offered a new review of indigenous American societies that argued that courage failed to flourish on the American continent. According to Humboldt, the American habitat enabled lives of such ease and indolence that courage was never cultivated; when scholars studied Indians they could "discern . . . more submissive resignations to the decrees of the sovereign, than patriotic love for the country; passive obedience without courage for bold enterprise." Claiming that "no elevation of thought ennobled the character" of Indians, and no advancement in fine arts or literature could be found among them, he concluded that their culture could be recognized instead by "that dark and melancholy aspect, which forms a striking contrast with the elegant arts and soothing fictions of the people of Greece." Humboldt's analysis made clear that "love for . . . country" and "courage for bold enterprise" constituted the essence of classical virtue, the basis for artistic elevation, the foundation of republicanism, and the antithesis of savagery.[20]

For self-styled republicans of the new United States, eager to claim a classical legacy, all theories that American soil stunted the growth of virtuous emotions required vigorous opposition. With the stakes of cowardice versus courage set so high, U.S. theorists sought to discover just what emotions could be counted on to banish the former and bolster the latter. "Ardor" provided the answer, a fact that says a great deal about the reasons for Hull's troubles as well as about the rhetorical and political successes of the prowar faction in 1812.

Courageous actions were the outward manifestation of strong inward passions. Part and parcel of climate-based debates about American courage were speculations about the connections between environmental and emotional temperature and the effect of each on love and war. When a theorist like Alexander von Humboldt speculated that Indians lacked both love and courage, he drew on centuries-old claims that the two emotions were closely connected and that each suffered when subjected to chill. Indeed, the "melancholy aspect" that Humboldt claimed characterized Indian culture echoed classical humoral theories about the correspondence between cold temperatures and cold temperaments.[21]

Americans set out to counter such ideas. Samuel Stanhope Smith, American Philosophical Society member, Princeton University president, and author of the 1810 work *The Causes of the Variety of the Complexion and Figure in the Human Species*, inveighed against assumptions that the American atmosphere inhibited amorous desires and courageous outlooks. He declared: "American savages have often been represented by European writers as frigid towards the sex because they seldom avail themselves of . . . opportunities to violate the chastity of their females. . . . Infinitely fewer violations of female honor and safety take place than are found under the restraints and excitements of our civilized manners. On a like foundation cowardice has been imputed to the aboriginal natives of America." Smith insisted that Indians *were* brave and that any apparent lack of libido among them was a matter of false appearances. He argued that Indians experienced no temptations to rape women not because they lacked desire, but simply because their natural lifestyle allowed free flow for their sexual impulses. Without "civilized" restraints to frustrate them to the point of taking immoral action, Indians refrained from violating women. Smith regarded it as important to contradict the notion that the American climate could cause Indian frigidity and thus reduce them to cowardice. Whether or not he approved of sexual desire as a source of courage, Smith certainly felt bound to dispute the idea that Americans inhabitants suffered from either fearfulness or frigidity.[22]

Men waged war best when stirred by ardent emotion, by love that was not only patriotic but also composed of romantic and even erotic components. Smith made no direct mention of conflict with Indians or Britons in his 1810 piece. But by 1812 he would go to press with an essay, "Of Laws Relative to a State of War and of Neutrality," that critiqued the British explicitly; the existence of this second work helps illuminate the geopolitical concerns underlying his nearly contemporaneous comments on American courage.[23]

In his *Observations on the Climate*, Hugh Williamson likewise took as his organizing question the task of "determ[ining] whether there be any essential frigidity in the American atmosphere." The significance of the issue lay in the fact that "philosophers . . . who mention the coldness of our climate . . . state this allegation in support of another conjecture, viz. that animal nature must degenerate here." Williamson complained that "philosophers allege that the American Indian . . . has no beard; that he is more frigid, more weak, and more cowardly than the inhabitants of the old continent." Cold weather and cold libido went together in such analysis: Williamson sought to establish that America and Americans enjoyed optimal warmth. When men got hot enough, libidinous passions could prod courageous actions.[24]

Descriptions of ardent soldiers may now seem so commonplace as not to need explanation. At face value, a remark like that of General Hull's soldier Robert Lucas that "never was there a more Patriotic army, never was there an army possessing greater love of Country or a more ardent desire to render it important Services" can seem almost pro forma, devoid of any real connections to sexuality or emotionality. Yet we need to take seriously the extent to which arguments for war came packaged as invitations to romantic pleasures. Quite simply, philosophical theory and popular understanding alike claimed that the cure for fear was love, that amorous feelings and patriotic ardor each enflamed the other.[25]

It was not inevitable that ardent emotion would become the measure of patriotic contribution. The public at large did not necessarily have to embrace the argument that the American failure at Detroit was the direct result of the damage Hull did to the ardor of his men. The very earliest reports of the American setback at Detroit avoided mention of emotion or condemnation of Hull and stuck to tactical and procedural explanations. A letter of August 23 from Pittsburgh reprinted in Pennsylvania on August 28 reported that at the time General Hull was "taken," the "United States forces at Detroit

[we]re 1500" while the "English . . . had been reinforced by 4,000 Indians." A New York paper, citing Pittsburgh informants as the source of its news, said on August 31 that "the cause of the surrender was, *that the American forces were in a starving condition.*" Yet by early September, observers began to warn that Hull himself would be charged with sole culpability for the setback. Even as Hull's supporters justified his decision not to invade Canada on the purely practical grounds that his small army "without provisions or ammunition" was inadequate to attack "a force so superior" as that of the British, they correctly predicted that administration allies would seek to "impute the blame solely to the cowardice or treachery of Gen. Hull." As the *Alexandria Gazette* presciently noted on September 12, because "the indignant voice of the people is lifted up against the cabinet at Washington, the troops of the palace fondly hope, that they shall be able to render Hull a scape goat."[26]

Politically, a great deal was at stake in the assignment of blame. Hull's capitulation, coming just two months after war was declared, invited immediate public scrutiny of a military adventure that many criticized on moral grounds and still more critiqued on practical ones. With presidential elections looming in November, Hull faced censure from all sides, from Federalists who denounced the entire enterprise as dubious to Madison loyalists within the Democratic-Republican Party who preferred to lay blame on Hull personally rather than admit to any policy failure on the part of the administration. Political exigencies meant Hull would be tried in the press long before he ever had an opportunity to appear in court.

Slamming "Mr. Madison's War" on September 12, the *Cooperstown Federalist* deplored that "a whole Territory of the United States has been given up . . . and a brave band of the defenders of our country made over to the enemy." Of "the conduct of General Hull," the paper asserted, "treachery, duplicity, and cowardice . . . stalk hand in hand with all his proceedings." To Hull they offered the malediction, "blast the coward who thus has given up the land he governed!" With war boosters and war opponents equally sure of the importance of courage and the fact of Hull's cowardice, few were left to defend him.[27]

Colonel Lewis Cass stepped up to perform what little labor was needed to complete Hull's condemnation. No sooner did he arrive in Washington from Detroit than Cass composed his letter to Secretary Eustis. Playing exactly to the needs of the administration, Cass's report, datelined "Washington, September 10th," declared that he and his fellow officers "know and feel, that no circumstances . . . can excuse a capitulation so dishonorable and unjustifiable. This too is the universal sentiment among the troops." Relying on emotion to make his case, Cass asserted that the men's feelings alone were all the evidence needed to prove that Hull's decision not to fight was a lamentable example of failure and not a laudable instance of prudence. Cass succeeded in shoving Hull directly into the crosshairs.[28]

Even as newspapers like the *Alexandria Gazette* warned that the federal administration was urgently seeking a scapegoat, Cass's letter was being rushed to press. First reprinted in a Washington paper called the *Courier* on September 16, Cass's critique featured in numerous papers from South Carolina to Connecticut in the remaining two weeks of September alone. A few papers, such as the Philadelphia-based *Poulson's Daily Advertiser,* cautioned that "the public" should "weigh the statement of Colonel Cass to Doctor Eustis with all proper allowance" because it was "evidently written with an eye to the favor of the administration." *Poulson's* even went so far as to point out that "by the letter itself it appears that *Col. Cass was not with Gen. Hull at the surrender of Detroit.*" But many more publications did not bother with context or caution, simply reproducing Cass's text verbatim under a neutral heading, such as that provided by the *Farmer's Repository* of Charleston, in what is now West Virginia, which on September 25 ran the headline "Letter of Col. Cass of the army late under the command of Brig. General Wm. Hull to the Secretary of War, Washington, September 10th, 1812." Cass coached the country to turn its attention away from scrutinizing the strategic problems of the army (much less from debating the basic merits of the war) and to focus instead on analyzing the flawed emotions of the fallen general.[29]

⤜⊗⤛

Like his nemesis Lewis Cass, William Hull had spent the early summer of 1812 trying to wage war by winning over public opinion, though with markedly less success. Hull had begun by grandstanding in the opening days of the Canadian campaign. Upon arrival at the border on July 12 at the farming town of Sandwich, he had staged an elaborate ceremony of conquest. Moving his men upriver to Canada at first light, he had staked the U.S. flag on Canadian soil and issued a sweeping proclamation, "To the Inhabitants of Canada." Hull's address appeared to guarantee a speedy victory for the American side. Inviting Canadians to flock to the American standard, and himself making courage the issue of the moment, Hull had told them, "I doubt not your courage and firmness. . . . I will not doubt your attachment to liberty. The United States offer you peace, liberty, and security. Your choice lies between these, war, slavery, and destruction." Such rhetoric linked bravery closely to liberty, implicitly affirming connections between emotional outlook and political orientation.[30]

Perhaps the most confounding lines of all in Hull's pronouncement concerned his assessment of his army's strength. Hull claimed to the Canadians, "had I any doubt of eventual success, I might ask your assistance, but I do not. I come prepared for every contingency. I have a force which will break down all opposition, and that force is but the vanguard of a much greater." Did these words imply that Hull himself was wholly confident of the capabilities of his forces? If so, his comments could add weight to later charges that he alone was responsible for the failure of an otherwise irreproachable army. Or should Hull's remarks be scanned more closely, for the implication that his claims were based not on belief in the abilities of the troops at hand but rather on the expectation that further reinforcements would arrive to make good the threat of his "vanguard"? Hull afterward insisted on the latter. And he argued that War Department administrators, who had access to his full strategic reports and not only to his public relations efforts, could not reasonably have arrived at any other interpretation.[31]

In fact, Hull explained at the trial, he had only allowed himself to be goaded into the July 12 crossing into Canada in the first place because he had been trying to appease an overeager officer corps insistent on hasty action. He "determined to take a post in the enemy's country," he said, merely to "satisfy the impatience of my officers, and preserve the confidence of my army." Stressing once more the theme of generational conflict as well as the lack of respect the soldiers betrayed, Hull complained that his men "thought all generalship consisted in inconsiderate and impetuous advances." Far from respecting his own wisdom and judgment, his officers second-guessed every decision he made.[32]

For his part, Hull had always harbored grave doubts about the capacities of his men. Despite the resounding rhetoric of his official speech, he had had good reason to question whether his forces could "break down all opposition." As he told the court, "the young and inexperienced officers I had under my command . . . thought and said that they were very brave but . . . with a few exceptions, [they] do not know it to this day from any trials of their courage." Hard evidence supported Hull's concerns, for a significant contingent of the men had failed a key test only one day before the general invasion.[33]

On July 11, an advance scouting party had been sent to cross the Detroit River into Canada. Yet the members of two companies had refused the order. As diarist Robert Lucas recorded it, "the Genl demanded a list of the names of those that refused to Cross the river" and, in response, "the adjutan[t] rashly abused the whole Company as Cowards Traitors &c. and made a return of them to the Gnl under the head of a list of Cowards under the name of Militia." Hull thus likely made the brash claims of his proclamation more to impress his officers and stiffen his wavering men than to offer an objective assessment of the army's true strength. As he afterward described, he had been forced by circumstances into "representing myself as having the utmost confidence in the force I commanded. . . . With these views, I published my proclamation."[34]

Hull credited his men with enthusiasm but had little confidence in their actual abilities. As he explained at the trial, "my experience in the revolutionary war had fixed in my mind a distrust of the services of undisciplined militia, however ardent and valorous they might appear by language and even by actions, when not before the enemy." Cass might claim that the men's emotional arousal proved their readiness to fight, but Hull insisted that ardor without experience counted for little.[35]

If Hull's calculations were purely military, his opponents' considerations were mainly political. Feeling may have mattered little for army preparedness, but it meant everything for popular opinion. Nothing boosted love of country like an appeal to ardent passions. In the fall of 1812, Madison and his allies needed to be sure the public would not turn against the administration. Maintaining enthusiasm for the war and support for the president quite simply required keeping up people's spirits. Fortunately for the president, many people stepped up to offer just this kind of emotional ballast.

Prowar writers consistently asserted the existence of an essential connection between love and patriotism. Typical was the broadside ballad that exhorted:

Columbian soldiers look and see,
The bleeding cause of liberty;
Let patriotic love inspire
Our frozen hearts with freedom's fire.

In itself, this war booster's decision to invoke "patriotic love" is neither surprising nor particularly revealing. On the surface, it smacks of convention. Why linger over the claims by war boosters of the 1812 era that love should "inspire our frozen hearts with freedom's fire"?[36]

Even in New England, where Federalist opposition to the war was strongest, many people eagerly enjoyed the culture of patriotic ardor. In 1812, a highly successful Massachusetts printer by the name of Isaiah Thomas founded the American Antiquarian Society with the avowedly nationalist goal of preserving what he called "the literature of liberty." One of his key early gifts to the society included an assortment of broadsides from Massachusetts printers that he compiled in 1814, a collection that Thomas preserved as a record of the kind of print "in taste among the vulgar." Choice titles included poems about bundling (the practice, popular among courting couples, of an unmarried man and woman going to bed together clothed) and humorous songs about faithless suitors or straying wives. Yet many of the Isaiah Thomas broadsides combined sex and romance with calls to patriotism and support for the war. Giving serious scrutiny to the political content of the popular amusements printed and preserved by Thomas and others presents an opportunity to more deeply understand the terms and stakes of the War of 1812, while also more fully revealing the cultural contours of the early republic.[37]

Intended by their very nature to stir the blood, songs meant to motivate action also encouraged people to ignore the facts of war's mortal consequences. A ditty called "On Hobbies" (featured in the bombastically titled *National Song-Book . . . a Collection of Patriotic, Martial, and Naval Songs and Odes, Principally of American Composition*, published in 1813), for example, used the trope of the hobbyhorse to make explicit equations between sex and soldiery, love and liberty. Its rhymes are worth quoting at length:

The hobby of soldiers in time of great wars,
Is breaches and battles, with blood, wounds, and scars;
But in peace you'll observe that quite different their trade is
The hobby of soldiers in peace is the ladies.
    All on hobbies (All on hobbies,
    All on hobbies, gee up, and gee O)

The ladies, sweet creatures! Yes they now and then,
Get astride of their hobbies, too, just like the men:

With smiles and with simpers beguile us with ease;
And we gallop, trot, and amble, e'en just as they please.
    All on hobbies &c.

The Americans' hobby has long since been known:
No tyrant or king shall from them have a throne:
Their states are united and let it be said,
Their hobby is liberty, peace, and free trade.
    All on hobbies, all on hobbies,
    All on hobbies, gee up, and gee O.

As these verses help enunciate, when Americans of the early republic cast the sexual together with the martial, the perils of war could be entirely eclipsed by the erotic. Such songs encouraged people to imagine national service as personal pleasure.[38]

Whether songs verged on the comical or the sentimental, marital ardor figured as a key source of martial ardor. A war song titled "How to Nail 'Em" praised American "hammers" and "nails" but implied that husbands, not bachelors, knew best how to use them:

The Bachelor's a hob nail.
He rusts for want of use sir,
The misers they've no nails at all,
They're all a pack of screws sir;
The ENGLISHMEN will get some clouts,
If here they chance to roam, sir,
For AMERICANS like hammers, will
Be sure to drive them home, sirs.

Here marital sexuality was supposed to help American men best Englishmen militarily.[39]

Often, the loyal women waiting to reward America's military men were supposed to be betrothed. A broadside poem called "The Soldier's Return" imagined the reunion of "Allen" and "Sally" and asked what would happen if Allen arrived almost unrecognizable after the rigors of battle. Would Sally's "heart to some other [have] stray'd?" No, Sally assured Allen,

Oh! My delight, though altered as thou art,

Reduced by honest courage to this state,
Thou art the golden treasure of my heart,
My long lost husband and my wish'd for mate.

Many writers who offered ardor as an inducement to arms avoided condoning illicit sex and instead stressed the importance of marriage as the avenue through which pleasure was to be pursued.[40]

But other writers played still more flagrantly with the possibilities of extramarital sexuality. A broadside poem from the Isaiah Thomas Collection called "The Soldier and His Fair Maid" claimed that young women could safely give themselves up to the sexual advances of soldiers because military men were too honorable not to marry them should a pregnancy result. The poem began:

The soldier as he walk'd thro' the field,
To see what flowers the earth would yield,
It was there he spy'd a lady gay,
Without any gown a raking hay.

The image of a nude woman frolicking in a field could hardly have been more explicit, but the poem went on to describe how:

He treated her with wine and cake,
And with gold rings, fine ribbons and gloves,
Until he gained this fair maid's love.

When the gay lady found herself big with child, "She cursed the hour and the day / She went with the soldier and left her hay." Yet, the poem promised, she need not be concerned:

For soldiers they love to sport and play,
With pretty girls a raking hay,
And if by chance they play too hard,
They'll marry them for their reward.

Addressing women, directly, the poem advised:

Come pretty maids both fair and gay,

If e'er you go to raking hay,
And if by chance a soldier you see,
You must not slight his company.

The whole message of such verses was that women could support the country by "sporting" with soldiers. They ran no risk in doing so, for men who met their obligations to country would never fail to respect those to their sexual partners.[41]

Women served the nation not only as paragons of virtue but also as objects of desire. When we imagine women of the early republic today, we often envision wives and mothers being asked to exemplify spotless chastity. Sex is not supposed to sully the image of the gentle ladies whose most important political task was to moderate the unbridled passions of men. Yet the figure of the passionless middle-class matron of midcentury, wedded to ideals of bourgeois domesticity and determined to limit her fertility, has obscured the role of sex and reproduction at a key early moment in the emergence of American nationalism. Women had to do much more than simply embody virtue. Just as enslaved women's reproductive work built the fortunes of their masters and the might of the nation, so white women's reproductive contributions also aided national growth. In the era of 1812, all women were encouraged to incite in men the sexual ardor that both spurred population and stirred acts of patriotism.[42]

A song called "The Love of Country" spelled out precisely how the transubstantiation of conjugal into national love was supposed to occur:

A soldier is a gentleman,
His honor is his life,
And he that won't stand to his post,
Will ne'er stand by his wife.
. . . .
Since love and honor are the same,
Or are so near allied,
That neither can exist alone,
But flourish side by side
. . . .
Then farewell sweet-hearts for a while,
Ye pretty girls adieu!
And when we've drove the British dogs,
We'll kiss it out with you.

Here men were warned to beware the error of shirking from combat lest they be suspected of connubial inconstancy as well. At the same time, with the promise that "love and honor are the same," men and women alike were told that soldiers made the best husbands and lovers. The relationship between martial and marital ardor was cyclical; the same men roused to go to war would return again to "kiss it out" with pretty girls and sweethearts.[43]

While some poems urged women's efforts to use their sexuality to stir men's ardor with the promise that soldiers made more reliable partners than ordinary men, others tempted young men with the thought that their prospects on the marriage market would improve if they first proved their worth through military service. A poem on the Battle of Plattsburgh, a redeeming moment for U.S. forces in September 1814, shortly after the fall of Washington, told the story of a soldier in that fight who had strengthened the devotion of his fiancée by his display of determination in battle. Narrated in the voice of the woman, the song celebrated:

> Our squadron triumphant, our army victorious,
> With laurels unfaded, our spartans returned
> My eyes never dewlt on a scene half so glorious
> My heart with such raptures before never burn'd
> For Sandy my darling, that moment appearing
> His presence to every countenance cheering,
> Was render'd to me more than doubly endearing
> By the feats he performed.

The narrator "burn[e]d" "with . . . rapture" for the returning soldier as she never had before. His military action spurred her romantic attraction. Women's sexual love offered inspiration for the soldier going off to war and validation for the man returning. Men who risked their own deaths for the nation enjoyed a better shot at procreation.[44]

Isaiah Thomas dismissed such popular ditties as the purview of the "vulgar" masses. He encouraged people to regard the content of broadside ballads as evidence of attitudes on the popular fringe, far removed from the core concerns of the nation, from the considerations of men like President James Madison who urged people to support the war "as they love their country." Nevertheless, evidence does exist to suggest that we should hesitate before coming to such a conclusion.

If elite Americans did not share the popular taste for melding the sexual and the martial, it would be hard to explain how a Yale graduate of 1814, a young man by the name of Leonard Withington, came to pen a play called *Rustic Love*, performed by him and his fellow students before the polite audience in attendance at Yale's commencement. The play, which was never published yet survives in multiple manuscript copies, many made contemporaneously, involves the attempted seduction and betrayal of a virtuous farm girl by a genteel imposter by the name of Mr. Scoff, "a fellow with a powdered head & a great ruffle big enough for the main sail of a frigate."[45]

Scoff's plan (which hinges on convincing the heroine's father to break his word to her true love, an American sailor named Jack, and to promise her in marriage to Scoff instead) requires persuading the simple farmer that Scoff, purportedly a gentleman schooled in the ways of the English elite though actually a prison escapee, knows what is best for the family. When Jack returns to claim his bride, the father justifies his betrayal by arguing, "you and I don't know the world—we are poor ignorant people— why Mr. Scoff says the people in England make nothing of breaking their word." After many soliloquies, an abduction attempt, and a daring rescue, the lovers are at last reunited to learn the lesson that "politeness wasn't made for . . . honest people . . . but for the proud and the rich who have nothing else to do—It should be enough for us to be virtuous & live in love—to serve our fellows & to honor our maker." A triumphant wedding ensues in which the American sailor gets his reward.[46]

Yet this resolution does not occur before Jack, along with the heroine's uncle and brother, engages in numerous jokes about pleasure culture and prostitution. To cite one example, in searching for a way to describe the sweetness of his fiancée's voice, Jack asks her brother, "didn't you never go by a rendez-vous house when they are enlisting sailors?" Her brother replies, "You mean where they stick a flag over the door & you always hear a fiddle squeaking?" "Yes," Jack assures him, "her voice was a thousand times sweeter than that—bless my soul! When she sang you would think that all the fiddles and bagpipes in the world had struck up."[47] The play as a whole— tempting to dismiss as frivolous entertainment yet patently also an allegorical commentary on the British-American war and on those genteel New England Federalists suspected of supporting the British—helps make clear that ardor's allures captivated prowar Americans up and down the social spectrum.

"Love of country" is not a timeless and unchanging concept. Americans of the early republic drew on love in support of war in culturally specific and politically revealing ways. Thinkers going back to Aristotle have posited that love of country provides the basis for patriotism, that brotherly bonds form the foundation of virtuous citizenship. More recently, Benedict Anderson has reminded us to consider the role of "affective imaginings" in drives to war. In defining the nation as an "imagined community," he observed that "the nation is always conceived as a deep, horizontal comradeship" and argued that "it is this fraternity that makes it possible . . . to die for such limited imaginings." In fact, Anderson's argument that "horizontal" feelings of "fraternity" provide the essential impetus for killing and dying deserves further scrutiny. Close examination of the war culture of 1812 reveals that the "ardor" of the era relied less on male friendship than on heterosexual romance. Songster books and broadside ballad posters published between 1812 and 1815 show clearly how much public attention focused on the role of romantic courtship and passionate love in prowar arguments.[48]

The popularity of ardent patriotism not only had fatal personal and professional implications for General Hull but also dire political implications for the Federalist Party. Sexy war songs helped undercut the tedious moral calculations of war opponents. Federalist war critics could easily be dismissed as prudish sexual scolds. As the war ground on, bringing one defeat after another, even many army supporters came to agree that while emotion might fire imaginations, it was useless for firing cannons. By the autumn of 1814, by the time the nation's capital had been burned black by the British, even war boosters would start issuing warnings that "the mass of our citizens who have so patriotically taken up arms, however brave, are destitute of experience, of discipline, and of skill." The author of this lament, prominent Philadelphia printer Matthew Carey, asserted, "courage without skill is wholly unavailing." General William Hull could hardly have put the thought better himself. Yet, unfortunately for Hull, this was still a distinctly Federalist and decidedly minority view in the early days of the war when he was first saddled with accusations of cowardice.[49]

∞

Manifold challenges were facing Hull's army. These problems are worth lingering over because they help to establish that the factual basis for Hull's court-martial was likely to be less convincing than the emotional one. By July

29, according to an official brief that Hull sent to Secretary of War William Eustis, short reserves of flour and other provisions paired with difficulties in opening and guarding supply lines made it difficult to guarantee the men's most basic needs. Hull questioned whether his small and unsteady band of men was equal to the task of invading Canada, and was reduced to telling the secretary, in a marked instance of wishful thinking, "I have the fullest confidence that a force will be immediately ordered to this country sufficient to make an entire conquest of all enemies." Until then, because the army lacked heavy artillery, any serious assault on fortified British defenses was likely to prove far more difficult that the simple ceremonial planting of a flag in a riverbank.[50]

Preferring, therefore, not to take further action after issuing his proclamation, Hull had bided his time at Detroit, working to prepare artillery and hoping to receive word of arriving reinforcements from Ohio and Kentucky. His officers scoffed at such inactivity and indecision and challenged Hull's right to enforce idleness. In the days leading up to the capitulation, relations between Hull and his men deteriorated further and further. Given the chance to recount events in court, Hull declared, "I must not omit, painful as it is to me to advert to it, the unhappy terms in which I was with my officers. . . . They had lost all confidence in me." Yet Hull, for his part, had little faith in his staff and bristled at their apparent belief that they had the right to help direct strategy.[51]

When Hull called a meeting of his officers to discuss the merits of making an attempt on the British fortress of Malden in the absence of heavy cannon, he was dismayed to find that they seemed "to have thought that when a council of war was called, it was to be governed by the laws of a town meeting; and that a General was absolutely bound by the voice of the majority." The tension between Hull and his officers came down to a debate about authority and subordination as much as to any concrete conflict about tactics.[52]

For Hull, the ultimate proof of his wisdom in delaying attack lay in his officers' refusal to vouch for the "firmness," that is, for the manly courage, of their troops. Though they demanded an offensive, Cass and the other militia officers would not offer any guarantees for the conduct of the troops. As Hull argued at the trial, ardor without experience counted for little. He insisted, "It is not extraordinary that I should have felt some want of confidence in these raw troops . . . when their own officers were not willing to be responsible for their firmness in an assault." Alone among the officers, Lieutenant Colonel

James Miller, of the regular army, was willing to "answer for the men [he] commanded." At Hull's trial, Miller confirmed the general's basic account, noting that "the other [commanders] said they would not be responsible for their men, but believed they would behave well." Once again, Hull asserted that only the Fourth Regiment could really be trusted in combat. Although Cass and other militia officers swore that the feelings of their men attested to the fact that, until Hull faltered, the troops were on the verge of victory, Hull never varied in his contention that empty emotionalism counted for naught.[53]

Critics of the war agreed completely with Hull's position that men who claimed to feel great ardor before they had experienced any military action were mistaking shadow for substance, feeling for form. Across New England, from the first days of the war to the last, Calvinist clergymen and Federalist war opponents railed against the role of ardent passion in creating public support for the war. The Reverend John Lathrop, himself a seventy-two-year-old veteran of the Revolutionary War, took to his pulpit that first summer to assert that "men of high sensibility, and young men who know little of the sufferings of the camp, or the dangers of bloody conflict, may perceive in themselves an elevation of spirits when the trumpet sounds and they are called to arms." But, Lathrop emphasized, "such elevation of spirit" was nothing but an illusion. Emotional sensibility was less a source of strength in battle than an intoxicating elixir that lured would-be soldiers down a path to suffering and early death.[54]

According to Federalist-allied members of the New England clergy, men who joined the fight out of feelings of ardor acted out of delusion, responding like sheep to the promptings of sin. In the first month after the declaration of war, church ministers held days of prayers and fasting in which they asked their flocks to reflect on the meaning of war. "I feel as an American, love the country of my nativity," insisted pastor Kiah Bayley of New Castle, Maine, in a sermon he preached on a fast day on July 23, 1812. But he insisted that Christian love should supersede all other forms. "Christ requires us *'to love our enemies,'*" he told his audience, and such love surely could not coexist with ardor for war. On the contrary, he argued, "War proceeds from the worst passions of the human heart, and tends greatly to inflame them." Quoting from James 4, he demanded of the assembled parishioners, *"From whence come wars and fightings among you? Come they not hence even of your lusts, that war in your members?"* Federalists did not dispute that there was a deep connection between the sexual and the martial. But they insisted such lusts deserved renunciation, not celebration.[55]

When New Englanders thought about "lust" as a term, they had "carnal desire" directly in mind. This is the sole definition of "lust" that Noah Webster offered his readers when he created the first American-authored dictionary of the English language in 1806. To be "lustful," according to Webster, was to have "irregular desires," while to behave "lustfully" was do to something in a "lustful or lecherous manner." Moreover, "lusting" involved "the act of inordinate desire." Yet despite all these imputations of sexual sin and deviancy, Webster also noted that to do something "lustily" was to do it "stoutly, boldly, with courage." Connections between passion and action, between sexual arousal and courageous resolve were woven into the very vocabulary of American English in the era of 1812.[56]

Ministers opposed to passions found eager supporters among many of their parishioners. Along with formal sermons, printers also circulated ideas advanced by ordinary writers. One casual author, a man from Newport, Rhode Island, named William Allen, had the pleasure of seeing an antiwar poem he wrote circulated as a broadside poster:

War, carnage and devastation,
Many falls and bleeds and dies.
In the sacred page we read,
All these from our lusts proceed

From formal sermons to singsong couplets, war opponents easily accepted the association between violent actions and vile passions. The biblical basis of claims that wars resulted from lust was accepted as common knowledge across New England.[57]

In a sort of vicious circle, lust moved men to war, while soldiers in camp found themselves further corrupted by the loose atmosphere that prevailed there, where women serving as cooks and laundresses might well also engage in casual prostitution. "As war always comes from the lusts and vicious principles and habits of ungodly men," warned the Massachusetts minister John Smith in August 1812, "so it tends directly to increase the same lusts, principles, and habits. The camp is the birthplace of vice; and being nourished up there, it will necessarily go forth and corrupt the community." Wars encouraged unruly passions and ungodly morals even among people who did not participate in them directly.[58]

Soldiers spread sin wherever they went. Smith's warning was mild compared to the alarm sounded another year later by fellow Massachusetts minister Jacob Catlin. By July 1813, Catlin was blaring that "camps are the nurseries" of every sort of sin, but especially "of intemperance, of lewdness, of profanity." He too predicted such sin would prove highly contagious. Soldiers, "having presently imbibed libertine principles, and peculiar vices of the camp, mingle again with their natural connections and diffuse the deadly poison." Innocent family and friends were liable to have their morals corrupted by simple social interactions with men infected with the lewd and libertine ways of the military camp.[59]

How had Democratic-Republicans supposedly become embroiled in such practices? Federalists charged that their opponents had been duped into declaring war against the British by France, a nation that relied directly on passion to practice its deceptions. Reverend John Smith accused the French of "combining . . . the wildest passions with the most deliberate perfidy." That nation had mastered the art of temptation. "France has ransacked the globe . . . to collect the arts of fraud and seduction," Smith cautioned, adding, "her secret emissaries are employed to diffuse licentiousness, to break up sober habits, to divide the people and destroy their morals." Like young people hanging around with the wrong crowd, Democratic-Republicans had been led astray by the French.[60]

Reverend David Osgood of Cambridge, Massachusetts, claimed in 1812 that leading members of the opposing party, "liable to corrupt prejudices and passions," had "acknowledged themselves caught and entangled in the toils of Bonaparte, that rival of Satan himself in guile and mischief." Exactly where Osgood had seen or heard such an acknowledgment, he did not bother to reveal. But he did not hesitate to charge that "the authors of this war [were] in character nearly akin to the deists and atheists of France." He denounced them as "men of hardened hearts, seared consciences, reprobate minds and desperate wickedness." Once people had gone down the road of political passion, they should not be surprised to find themselves mired in the hell of war.[61]

Antiwar preachers did not shy away from linking religion and politics, calling directly from the pulpit for their congregants to support Federalists and vote out the Democratic-Republicans. In a sermon on the "Evil Effects of War" in which he sounded the by-then familiar biblical question, *From whence come wars and fightings among you? Come they not hence even of your lusts which war in your members?*" Benjamin Bell demanded, "do not the Federalists endeavor to gain their points by addressing themselves to the *reason*; and *understandings* of people?" Frustratingly, however, the public at large seemed immune only to the rational. "Alas! We have poor success," he lamented, "our opponents, knowing that people in general are governed more by their passions than by sober reason, have had infinitely better success in obtaining their votes to the ruin of the country." If public spirit and patriotic ardor, enflamed by sinful lusts and passions, influenced every effort to weigh the causes and consequences of the war, Federalists believed they could not fairly compete.[62]

In Massachusetts, a traditional Federalist stronghold, politicians claimed that Democratic-Republicans deliberately pandered to the people's basest instincts. By 1814, the members of the General Court of Massachusetts, denouncing a war "deemed by the great portion of our fellow citizens to be both wicked and unjust, and by a still more numerous class wanton and inexpedient," asserted that such wantonness resulted directly from the negative effect that emotion exerted on people's ability to arrive at critical moral judgments. The court warned people against "yielding to the dominion of the passions, of which a weak or wicked administration may take advantage to involve them in the deepest national calamity." Federalists equated emotional allurement with political disempowerment. Like General William Hull, they insisted that the fantasy of war, no matter how emotionally compelling, could never prepare people for the reality.[63]

On the eve of the debacle at Detroit, Hull was asking for performance guarantees that his staff would not make; his officers were demanding action that Hull would not take. Matters had reached the breaking point. On August 14, Hull maneuvered to send off two of his most troublesome critics, Colonels Lewis Cass and Duncan McArthur, by ordering them to take a detachment of three hundred men to escort some provisions being transported from the outlying River Raisin area. Cass friend and ally Robert Lucas argued in his diary that "it appears as if Colo McArthur and Cass had been sent a way on purpose by Gnl Hull So that he might have a fair opportunity of Surrendering the fort to the British." Whether or not that was true, Lucas's perspective would be incorporated in the official record when Cass quoted the diary without attribution in his letter to the secretary of war.[64]

Cass and the others afterward insisted that Hull's negative assessments of troop strength and supply levels were grossly misstated. In answer to the objection that Hull had fully documented the army's true situation in months of letters to Washington, they asserted that Hull must have systematically falsified records as part of a carefully laid plot to commit treason. Lucas pursued the treason theory even to the point of claiming to have been "apprehensive" that the red-and-blue-striped tent Hull had raised at the fort shortly before the surrender could have been "intended as Som Signal,—as he never before had a markee in camp since the army ha[d] been at Detroit." Their view prevailed to the extent that treason was the first of three capital charges leveled at Hull by the court-martial. Yet not even the court could ultimately countenance the accusation of treason. It threw the charge out on a technicality, while also admitting that there was no evidence to support the claim.[65]

In actuality, it would have been as difficult to prove definitively that the army could have succeeded with a better commander as it would have been to disprove Hull's claims that the army was outnumbered, undersupplied, and unready to fight. The government went a ways toward solving the latter problem by burdening Hull with responsibility for any failures of preparedness. The third formal charge against him, "neglect of duty," specified that Hull was to blame for the very lack of supply-line communication and troop strength that he himself had sought to document. Still, this alone might not have been enough to convince anyone that the general's disappointing performance constituted a capital crime. The key to the court's case against Hull came with the charge of "unofficer-like conduct" (included in the third charge) together with the second, central charge, that Hull had been guilty of "cowardice at and in the neighborhood of Detroit."[66]

⚬⚬⚬

From first to last, Hull deplored the idea that he could possibly be put to trial for failures of feeling. He protested to the court that actions, not emotions, were the only proper objects of censure, saying, "there never has been, and in justice never can be, a conviction under this charge of cowardice, but when a want of courage is indicated by the *omission* or *commission* of some act in violation of the duty of the person against whom the charge is made." Yet "conduct unbecoming" provided a very murky standard, a deep pool into which almost any charge could be flung and which would necessarily reflect the cultural concerns of the moment.[67]

In 1812, a rising generation of Americans believed that to measure the meaning of a person's conduct required identifying the emotions that motivated the actions at issue. With all eyes trained on General Hull, the question of just what he had felt at Detroit came to be paramount.

The first witness to take the stand was one Josiah Snelling, twenty-nine years old and newly commissioned at the time he served as a captain in Hull's army. After taking his oath before the court, he wasted no time in asserting: "I have been taught to believe that there are certain human passions which are indicated by appearances, and the appearances of General Hull, according to my mind, indicated fear." Snelling was especially struck that Hull, "apparently unconsciously, filled his mouth with tobacco, so that his cheeks were extended by it." Painting a vivid picture of the unfortunate result, Snelling continued, "the saliva ran from his mouth on his neckcloth and clothes. He often rubbed his face with his hands and distributed the tobacco juice about his face." Snelling's views were corroborated by the testimony of a second captain, Samuel McCormick, who averred that on the day of the surrender Hull's "face was discoloured with tobacco juice. It was over the lower part of his face and a spot was over his eye. I thought he was under the influence of fear. I had no doubt of it."[68]

By any account, Hull exhibited extreme emotion on August 16, the day of the surrender of the fort at Detroit. Hull made no effort to deny the point but asserted that it carried no significance. As Hull phrased it, "expressions of the human countenance, and the manners of men, are but fallible indications of the workings of the human mind." Warning against founding judgments in "the temporary physical condition of the body," Hull insisted that "the difference in appearances, produced by the excitements of different passions, are too subtle to admit of observations from which any conclusions can be drawn." In other words, the body produced passions while the mind molded character. The passions were ephemeral, while character was enduring; only character could be used to take the true measure of a man.[69]

Hull went on to assure the court that "if my countenance showed traces of what I felt, it must have shewn traces of the painful anxiety, by which I had been oppressed, and marks of the deepest regret for the measures I had been obliged to pursue." Though at first glance the difference between anxiety and fear may seem insignificant, for Hull the distinction was crucial. "Personal fear," of which he stood formally accused, signified overriding concern for the self, while "anxiety," however "painful," was something he had endured out of selfless concern for the people he led. In selfishness versus selflessness lay concerns of character that Hull liked to think rose above the trivialities of passing passions.[70]

Yet by inviting the court to consider whether the evidence indicated that his "countenance showed traces" of anxiety versus fear, Hull committed a fatal blunder. He inadvertently lent support to the very tactics his opponents were determined to pursue. A long parade of witnesses sat before the court and opined about the passions that Hull had displayed at Detroit. They sought to establish from the start the validity of emotional evaluation as the basis of legal opinion.

Hull could scarcely believe that the habit of chewing tobacco could provide proof for a capital conviction. Attempting to expose the farcicality of the situation, he demanded of the court: what if the witnesses "saw about me more of the marks of tobacco than was consistent with neatness. Are these grounds which will warrant a conclusion that is to effect the life of a man?" Incredulous that tobacco use should even arise as a topic of discussion, he concluded, "as to what has been said on this disgusting subject of the tobacco, I will dismiss it as to all the witnesses, with a reference to . . . the *excitement* which some of the witnesses who use tobacco, felt while they were under examination. [They] deluged this floor with their expectorations." Hull's revulsion at the brown streams of tobacco juice flowing from the witness stand was exceeded only by his repugnance toward the current of absurdity swirling through the court.[71]

However much his opponents might salivate over such embarrassing details, Hull's real vulnerability lay in the men's descriptions of his emotions. In slipping from questioning whether the evidence of emotion could ever be a sound basis for a criminal conviction to quibbling about just which variety of emotion—anxiety or fear—he actually felt, Hull had exposed his flank. He then compounded the error by entering into an argument about whether the young witnesses arrayed against him had sufficient experience and expertise to accurately identify emotions. He sneered, "Snelling, though a very young gentlemen, it is to be presumed has great acquirements; and it would seem, from his testimony that the human passions have been the object of his study." In mounting this critique of Snelling, Hull no doubt hoped to make the man's pretensions to discernment appear ridiculous. On a roll, Hull chuckled that "he has not told us in what school he acquired his science in physiognomy; nor has he given us the rules by which, when the mind may be under various excitements, he can distinguish the appearances which will indicate the prevalence of one over the other." Yet here too, Hull stumbled, only succeeding in betraying his grave ignorance of emotional attitudes of Snelling's generation.[72]

According to the best-accepted standards of science in the early republic, Hull's skepticism on the subject of physiognomy was very well founded. At the American Philosophical Society in Philadelphia, a leading literary and intellectual center of the day, an interested reader would find little information on the pseudoscience of physiognomy. The celebrated Pennsylvania physician Benjamin Rush mentioned the subject in his 1812 tome *Medical Inquiries and Observations, upon the Diseases of the Mind*, only to declare that would-be practitioners of physiognomy must themselves suffer from "a disease of the mind" that created an "inability of the mind to perform operations of judgment or reason." Rush then regaled his readers with the tale of the madness of "the strange, wild, eccentric Lavater," the European who had originated the theory of physiognomy. If Rush's amused dismissal had truly been the last word on physiognomy, Hull might have had the last laugh in court.[73]

Unfortunately for the general, however, popular culture left much more room for interest in physiognomy. Noah Webster's "compendious" American dictionary defined "Physiognomy" matter-of-factly as "*n.* the art of judging by the face" on the same page that it offered definitions for "Philology" ("*n.* grammatical learning") and "Philosophy" ("*n.* knowledge moral or natural"). Though defined as an "art," physiognomy was accorded the same lexicographic standing as any other branch of science.[74]

Moreover, unlike the case with other forms of scientific knowledge, a person needed no formal schooling to become a "judge of men by their faces." Publications from self-declared experts on the topic abounded. According to an 1807 work by one Richard Brown, *An Essay on the Truth of Physiognomy*, "physiognomy, as applied to man, means a knowledge of his physical, moral, and intellectual qualities and endowments, derived from an observance of his countenance, person, and deportment." Brown offered arguments exactly at odds with Hull's assumptions. As Brown explained it, physiognomy could be defined as "the science which treats of the external signs of the passions and emotions. It is a knowledge of the state or rather movements of the mind, derived from an observance of the appearance of the body." While Hull denied that the body could reveal the mind, much less that surface passions could offer insight into underlying moral and intellectual qualities, devotees of physiognomy argued that precisely this was possible. Perhaps most damning of all for Hull, Brown affirmed that knowledge of physiognomy was no "great acquirement." On the contrary, "infants, and even dogs and other animals are practical physiognomists."[75]

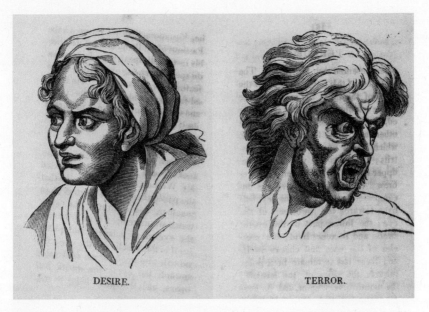

DESIRE.   TERROR.

Figure 5. These illustrations are from a popular instruction manual on physiognomy, "the art of judging by the face." While they do not quite portray "ardor" and "fear," the precise emotions that witnesses were asked to judge in Hull's capital trial, they come close. "Desire" and "Terror," instructional illustrations in George Brewer, *The Juvenile Lavater; or, A Familiar Explanation of the Passions* (New York: M'Dermut & Arden, 1815), Collections of the American Antiquarian Society.

Physiognomists took for granted that the science's chief attraction lay in the easy availability of the knowledge it provided. Books on the subject frequently emphasized how naturally children could glean information from simple interpretations of the face. *The Columbian Reader . . . Designed for the Use of Schools*, published in 1810, noted that those "who have learned physiognomy from their playfellows in their early years, understand the pleasurable or painful feelings of all with whom they converse, often even before their words are finished." Such views existed before the Hull trial and would persist after. In 1815, children's author George Brewer would offer *The Juvenile Lavater . . . Calculated for the Instruction and Entertainment of Young Persons* to the public without apology (Figure 5).[76]

In fact, physiognomy's popularity stemmed not from its associations with children, per se, but from its connection to rising trends of democracy. A pamphlet by Philadelphia author and social activist Thomas Branagan, published in 1813, the year before Hull's trial, provides a useful illustration of the importance of physiognomy as a tool of popular politics in the new republic. *The Charms of Benevolence and Patriotic Mentor; or, The Rights and Privileges of Republicanism, Contrasted with the Wrongs and Usurpations of Monarchy* explicitly linked emotional analysis with political decision making. A table of contents directed the reader to four chapters on the following topics: "I. Strictures on the Cogent Necessity of National Legislatures," "II. Remarks on the Importance of the Science of Physiognomy," "III. An Essay on the Excellency of Establishing Benevolent Institutions," and "IV. The Beauties of the 'Rights of Man.'" This book garnered such success that it appeared again in 1814 with the identical table of contents, now advertised as the fifth edition. According to Branagan and his many readers, the "rights and privileges of republicanism," the very "rights of man," rested on the knowledge to be gleaned from physiognomy. Physiognomy promised to allow ordinary readers to pierce the facades of social pretension, the better to discern which people's emotions were truly employed in the service of the nation.[77]

⌒∞⌒

When General Hull derided Captain Snelling as a man too immature to offer serious commentary on the state of a general's morals and motivations, he only displayed the extent of his own isolation. He predicted, "Snelling, I have no doubt, when he gains more age and experience, will find that the indications of appearances, in respect to the human mind, are fallacious." With physiognomy enjoying popularity because of, not in spite of, its accessibility to everyone down to infants, such objections could little aid Hull's cause.[78]

As witness after witness stepped forward in court to corroborate claims that Hull had showed cowardice at Detroit, the strong thread of his original argument against making emotion admissible as the basis of a criminal complaint began to fray. Hull could have simply maintained that his high moral character and long devotion to public service made it impossible to interpret his decisions at Detroit as anything other than a pragmatic response to a crisis that he himself had foreseen and that he had made every effort to prod the War Department to prevent.

Instead, he began to cavil about whether the witnesses against him had ever come near enough to him in the fort at Detroit to clearly see his face. Of one such witness, he snorted, "his power of judging of the human passions from appearances is superior even to Major Snelling's; because from his testimony, it seems, he can perceive the appearance when the object is at some distance." Underscoring just how far-fetched such claims were, he added, "they had, according to this testimony, perceived that I was frightened while I was on horseback in the face of the enemy's fire; and before they had approached me or spoke to me." In disputing such details, Hull reduced himself to shredding the ends of the prosecution's tightening noose.[79]

Hull found it almost inconceivable that the court could credit such evidence. He implored: "When the court considers my situation: how many causes there were to excite strong emotion; will they believe that the witnesses who have testified on this point were capable of such discrimination as would enable them to ascertain that the appearances which they have described procoeded [*sic*] from personal fear?" Why couldn't Hull simply let the issue of emotion rest? He, like his antagonists, believed that courage was the key requirement of military life. He squirmed under "imputations cast upon me by representations, intended to make me appear abjectly and disgustingly base."[80]

In Hull's worldview, those of elevated status should never be censured by, much less confused with, those who belonged among the debased. Hull's brief against physiognomy rested on its reputation as the sort of perception accessible to "dogs and other animals" incapable of reasoned judgment. Of Samuel McCormick, who had testified that he believed a face stained with tobacco juice showed clear evidence of fear, Hull complained, "he appeared to form his judgment on natural instinct." He pilloried McCormick along with his claim, saying it was "a claim which was out of the first stage of civilization: to which rank, notwithstanding his tawdry regimentals, it was evident he belonged." From first to last, Hull clung to the notion, popular with climate theorists, that human populations could be characterized by different gradations of civilization. Men could be sorted into discrete groups by moral distinctions with valid social coordinates.[81]

In opposing the right of his inferior officers to pass judgment upon him, Hull violated a rapidly hardening belief among a new generation of Democratic-Republicans: white leaders who claimed superior levels of cultivation bore a special burden to submit to regular emotional audits to determine how well their continuing accomplishments measured up to their potential. No longer could the supposedly settled cultural attainments of men like Hull be allowed to determine social status and moral worth. Hull sought to dismiss the witnesses against him as tawdry pretenders beneath his contempt only to find that his accusers subscribed to new democratic social standards with which he could not even begin to contend.

In throwing his own men into the same class with Indians and others conventionally ranked in the lowest "stage of civilization," Hull offered his corps the deepest possible insult. More fatally still, his negative comparison of U.S. soldiers to American Indians offended even Federalist war critics, the only ones left with an ounce of interest in his defense. If there was one point on which almost everyone could agree, it was that Indians were "savages" whose very existence threatened the survival and success of the United States. When the Massachusetts Federal Court offered its stinging indictment of the war in 1814, it asserted that "the real cause of the war must be traced . . . to a violent passion for conquest." Here was a clear accusation that the ultimate object of national lust was Indian land. Nevertheless, this denunciation implied less respect for Indians than distaste for the inhabitants of the South and West whose "cupidity" led them to covet "the wilderness reserved for the miserable aborigines." When the kindest description anyone could offer of Indians was that they were "miserable aborigines," Hull won himself no new allies in comparing a U.S. military officer to someone of the "first stage of civilization."

So widespread was anti-Indian sentiment that even many northerners who opposed the war used the figure of the menacing Indian in attempts to interrupt the patriotic fantasies of romantic pleasure that were basic to so many war songs and poems. The Reverend Benjamin Bell of New York, who joined the chorus of voices claiming that *"wars and fighting . . . come . . . hence even of your lusts which war in your members,"* nevertheless warned his flock that, "sometimes, while the husband is gone to the camp, the merciless savages break in *at dead of night,* upon the defenceless mother and helpless children, kill and scalp them, plunder and burn the house; and escape to the wilderness unrevenged." And indeed it was just such concerns that led many militiamen to refuse to travel far from their own hearths to pursue the British in Canada. Among war supporters and opponents alike, antagonists of the British or critics of the French, the idea that Indians were enemies prevailed.[82]

Another New York minister, the Reverend Samuel Whelpley, also reconciled his opposition to the passions of war with the conviction that Indians were undeserving barbarians condemned by God. In an 1813 sermon he called "The Fall of Wicked Nations," Whelpley said that among people and nations destined to be lost in a biblical "deluge . . . you will see little but what indicates the reign of the passions." Blaming evil lusts for the onset of the War of 1812, Whelpley said that "a war set on foot for conquest, is robbery and murder on the largest scale." Here was the classic Federalist critique that the War of 1812, far from being a justifiable war of self-defense, was in fact an imperial war of conquest. Whelpley advised his listeners to repent or face divine retribution.[83]

Yet Federalist complaints about the Republican lust for conquest should not be misunderstood as support for the territorial rights of Indians. Whelpley did not for a moment question that the United States was the favored nation of heaven, and Christians the chosen people of God. Painting a picture of a world at risk, he asserted: "God was pleased to open for our ancestors an asylum in this new world. To them the savages were caused to resign these fair regions." According to this common conceit, Europeans had not so much stolen the American continent by force as gratefully accepted the land as a mark of God's grace. Whelpley continued, "At the sound of the ax and the hammer the wild demon of barbarity and darkness fled away, and flourishing villages and cities rose . . . no nation ever made such progress in population, wealth, and power." Far from linking population increases to land seizures, Whelpley saw both land acquisition and population augmentation as independent blessings from God.[84]

For all but a few Federalists, opposition to the war stemmed from sectional, commercial, and domestic political considerations, not from any reservations about the morality of seizing the continent and settling it with Old World peoples and their descendants. Reverend Whelpley carried the argument to the point of claiming that Indians were practically minions of Satan, calling them nothing but "wild demons." For the most part, when Federalists like Whelpley scorned the idea of conquest, they meant only to speak in defense of British Canada, not to question the value and validity of seizing Indian territory for the United States.

Ultimately, the fact that British forces at Detroit had Indian allies at their sides proved to be a public-relations boon for the Madison administration. In an address to the nation in which he sought to put the best possible spin on the surrender at Detroit, President Madison declared, "A distinguishing feature in the operations of this adverse event, is the use made by the enemy of merciless savages under their influence." For Madison, this was the ultimate proof of British depravity. "The enemy has not scrupled to call to his aid their ruthless ferocity," he complained, before reassuring the country that "the national spirit rises according to the pressure on it. The loss of an important post and the brave men surrendered with it inspired everywhere new ardor and determination." When even the president relied first and foremost on the rise of ardor for the preservation of the nation, Hull stood little chance of winning his case on the basis of reasoned analysis alone.[85]

In the end, none of Hull's protestations, factual or characterological, could ultimately override the court's and the nation's embrace of the emotional. In a satiric history of the Detroit campaign, Jacob Bigelow, a young Massachusetts man with a quick pen, sought to cast Hull's plight into sharp relief. Comparing the prowar faction to a noisy flock of seagulls and dubbing General Hull the "Captain of the Gulls," he deftly summed up the essential points of the story line presented at the trial: "The unhappy and disconsolate commander of the Gulls, unwilling to shed the blood of his followers, by confronting their empty guns and hungry bellies with the brawny and beef-fed warriors of the north; with a heavy heart and rueful physiognomy, put his reluctant signature to the articles of surrender! . . . On the occurrence of this unexpected event, the whole army from the most iron hearted colonel, to the most delicate Naiad of a washer woman that followed in its train, was overwhelmed with a flood of shame, and shed tears of vexation and grief." Bigelow, a trained physician, was as skeptical as Hull about the use of physiognomy, as incredulous as the general at the idea of the entire army, including its most disreputable female followers, crying over Hull's performance. Many Federalists found it humorous to the point of absurdity that ardent emotions had emerged as the index of morality, serving as the first and last word on the proceedings of General Hull. Nevertheless, the portrait Bigelow offered of Hull as a sorry seagull, "plucked and roasted . . . for a blockhead, a coward, and a traitor," did little to help restore the general's stature. Federalists who believed Hull should have refused on principle to help prosecute the war were not going to go far to advance his defense.[86]

Hull fared little better in postwar satires. In *The Adventures of Uncle Sam in Search After His Lost Honor*, published in 1816, Hull made out rather well overall; the author summed up Hull's ordeal by asserting that he had been "tried with great form and solemnity . . . [and] was made the scape-goat, to carry the freight of the charge of mismanagement from the sensitive consciences of fortunate office holders." Still, even Frederick Augustus Fidfaddy, the pseudonymous author of this humorous work, had little respect for those who showed cowardice. Inverting Hull's claim that his decision to surrender was a selfless act made heedless of the personal cost to his reputation, Fidfaddy offered the following sarcastic conclusion about American soldiers at large:

> The coward only, ever fears
> The loss of reputation;
> This loss the real Hero bears,
> With hardened resignation.
>
> . . . .
>
> Far wiser he, that shuns the strife,
> And prudent bends to reason;
> Weighs well the value of his life,
> And learns to run in season.

Even among war critics, courage remained a signal American attribute, one that must be maintained at all costs. Hull's attempts to cast submission as compatible with courage were met mostly with incredulous laughter.[87]

Such was the power of the emotional argument that claims of Hull's fearfulness eclipsed every other consideration of the meaning of the capitulation. Appearing before the court bowed but unbroken, Hull tried to point out that political expediency—not military necessity or judicial integrity—had dominated his trial. Of the regiment arrayed against him, he pronounced, "they foresaw that a great reputation was to be purchased at so cheap a rate as appearing highly averse to the surrender; and afterwards publishing to the world all they said and did as evidence of my criminality and their own heroism." In fact, a great deal of truth supported Hull's claim.[88]

By the time of the trial, as Hull himself observed, Snelling had been promoted from captain to colonel, as had McCormick. Yet neither man had been on active duty since the time of the surrender. Robert Lucas, whose journal shadowed the trial and supported the assertions of Lewis Cass, later became governor of the state of Ohio and the territory of Iowa. Cass himself had immediately replaced Hull as governor of the Michigan Territory in 1813 and was further rewarded for his contributions to Hull's troubles by promotion to general. Ultimately, he became secretary of war in the Jackson administration. Meanwhile, Hull was left to receive a sentence of death from the trial judge—who was none other than General Henry Dearborn, the very man whose partial armistice with the British had done so much to leave Hull and his troops vulnerable at Detroit.[89]

⤬

Exactly as Lewis Cass had prescribed, emotional agility—the ability to alternately burst with ardor or burst into tears—brought the reward of upward mobility to an ambitious young generation determined to make a reputation for themselves and their nation. Cass had long argued that only through renewed war and reinvigorated emotional spirit could Americans reaffirm their worth; as early as 1809 he had sent a formal declaration to President Madison in which he asserted, "the same spirit which enabled our Fathers to achieve the Independence of these United States will enable their sons to defend it." Meanwhile, Hull's hidebound adherence to older notions of honor and status left him no quarter.[90]

Hull, of course, believed that he himself *was* one of the "fathers" of Independence. He clung to the notion that if he could only prove he was not, by nature, a "coward," he could then establish that his actions at Detroit had been motivated neither by personal fear nor by any concern for self. He swore in court that he well understood the consequences of surrender for himself and his country. He said, "I knew that the disappointment of the high expectations that had been raised would be charged to me, and that all the faults of others, to which in fact the failure of the expedition was owing, would be laid at my door." He insisted, "these considerations enlisted every private feeling against the surrender; my mind was agitated by the opposite demands of duty." Even knowing the peril in which capitulation would place him, he refused to send his troops to near-certain slaughter. Yet none of his comments in court could forestall the fate set in motion at Detroit. Hull closed his defense by demanding: "Will you believe that the years in which I have grown grey in my country's service, should have so far changed my nature, as that I could have been the base and abject thing my enemies have represented? No, gentlemen, that blood which animated my youth, age has not chilled. I at this moment feel its influence, and it makes me dare to say that no man ever did or can think me a coward." On the contrary, they could and they did. Even Hull's echo of George Washington's famous claim, "I have grown grey in the service of my country," had little effect. Nothing could lower the flag of failure that fluttered about him as plainly as that banner of surrender had flown at Detroit.[91]

William Hull's death sentence for cowardice so riveted contemporaries that when entrepreneurial author Thomas Clark published a fifty-two-page time line of American history in 1814, *American Chronology from the Discovery of the Western World*, his one-line summaries of all major events (beginning with, "1492: Columbus discovers America") climaxed with the entry: "1814: May 2nd: The sentence against General Hull this day promulgated. THE END." If it now seems ludicrous to imagine Hull's trial as the culmination of the history of the "Western World," it appeared plausible to people of his day. A key political and moral question framed the charges against Hull: did the American failure to invade Canada, much less to defend Detroit, result from the personal emotional failings of William Hull or from systemic national problems, from failures of military preparedness to the war's lack of accepted legitimacy? Hull's condemnation was to be the ground of the nation's exoneration.[92]

Despite his protestations against admitting emotional evaluations as judicial evidence, Hull himself shared the basic conviction that courage counted. Indeed, he went so far as to declare at the trial "that he had "no desire to preserve a life that shall be stigmatized by a conviction of this court on the charges of cowardice." Hull claimed he hardly cared if he lived or died if he were going to go down in history as a coward.[93]

It could have brought Hull no more than cold comfort then that his life was ultimately spared. With the presidential election long since safely over and "the sensitive consciences of fortunate office holders" spared the pain of publicly admitting their own mismanagement, the court recommended and James Madison concurred that the death sentence should be commuted. The stay was granted "in consideration of Brigadier General Hull's revolutionary services, and his advanced age." In convicting Hull of cowardice, while affirming that a "brave" army had been "uselessly sacrificed" to one man's perfidy, the court confirmed that emotion constituted one of the key elements in fighting a war.[94]

Claims that emotion mattered as much as accomplishment, indeed that emotion actually made an important public contribution, opened the way for inhabitants of the country to imagine that their own private feelings, properly monitored, could aid in public efforts. And since so few people could claim the kind of firsthand experience of war that guided Hull's decisions at Detroit, romantic stories about the war and the ardor it inspired could easily sway public opinion about the conflict. Such attitudes encouraged Americans of the early republic to deceive themselves that ardent feelings, the pleasurable passions of patriotism, represented the full experience of war and defined its true moral meaning. A dubious war, deplored by Federalists, could be sold to the populace as an enjoyable indulgence of ardor and an ideal occasion for national regeneration.[95]

Chapter 3

⌒◯⌒

Romantic Stories of Republican Conquest on the Great Lakes

LAKE ERIE, SEPTEMBER 1813

The sky was blue, the wind was light, and the air was clear on the bright September noon in 1813 when Captain Oliver Perry sailed to victory against the British on Lake Erie. In an initial hard-fought encounter lasting some two and a half hours, the British disabled Perry's vessel, the *Lawrence*, and forced him to flee in a rowboat to another ship, the *Niagara*. Then, from the deck of the *Niagara*, Perry directed an assault on the British side that culminated in the capture of the entire royal squadron on the lake. Hours after the action had ended, Perry sent official word to Washington that the United States had won the day: "it has pleased the Almighty to give the arms of the United States a signal victory over their enemies on this lake." Perry confidently characterized the triumph as a "signal" one. And those in the capital indeed hungered for some signal that the U.S. war effort would succeed. Yet although most Republicans in Congress hoped to capitalize on the publicity value of Perry's feat, others were wary of puffing up the significance of the battle when so much about the war remained uncertain. News of Perry's naval maneuvers soon gave rise to a round of rhetorical skirmishing, one that pitted Senate opponents against one another while exposing the essential political effects of the nation's deep cultural preoc-cupation with linkages of love, liberty, and victory.[1]

The Senate Committee on Naval Affairs met to draft a congressional reso-lution of thanks to Perry in late December 1813. The first version of the pro-posed resolution contained the claim that Perry's success represented "a vic-tory as decisive and glorious as any ever recorded on the page of history." But some observers objected that this assertion was more than a bit overblown. Commanding the lake was one thing. Achieving the overall goal of conquering Canada was quite another. Senator Eligius Fromentin, then a brand-new legislator from the brand-new state of Louisiana, ventured to remark that, however splendid, the victory represented at best a strategic stepping-stone. Risking the ridicule of the rest of the chamber, Fromentin cautioned, "it may not be true, according to the phraseology of this resolution, that the *glorious* victory on Lake Erie has been *decisive*. It is my wish that in our national acts we shall not appear to vapour, or boast our success too highly." These reservations met swift rejection from his fellow Republican legislators.[2]

Senator Charles Tait, of Georgia, a well-known war hawk who used his seat on the Senate Committee on Naval Affairs to try to encourage Republicans to strengthen the U.S. Navy, countered immediately that he could not accept Fromentin's criticism. "I, sir," he exclaimed, "am very far from cherishing a disposition to light up a glare to dazzle the perception of the American people, or the people of any other nation, by a false description of this glorious victory." He proclaimed it a simple matter of fact that "the victory on Lake Erie was decisive, as the enemy was entirely defeated; his squadron captured, not even one of his vessels having escaped." No oratorical fireworks whatsoever were needed to prove the importance of the moment. To the contrary, Tait insisted, "Nor would I prefer, in our public or official proceedings, a language savouring of vanity or hyperbole. Indeed, the action of which I speak, stands in need of no such aid. A narration, in the simplest terms, of its true incidents creates admiration and gratitude."[3]

It may have come as some surprise to Fromentin, therefore, that when Tait proceeded to offer a simple narrative of Perry's deeds of the day, he cast his naval triumph as a successful romantic courtship. Recounting Perry's move from the *Lawrence* to the *Niagara*, Tait exclaimed, "even after victory had perched on the standard of the enemy, awarding her favor to superior force, Captain Perry, by the gallantry of his continued perseverance, enticed her back into his arms." Victory, in the form of the winged goddess Nike, had perched for a time on the British flag mast. But the "gallant" Perry had successfully wooed the lovely lady and won "her" feminine favor. Politicians portrayed Perry's action as the successful suit of a godly lover, one who lured victory away from his rival and into his own embrace. This evocative language of romantic seduction became key to crystallizing the meaning of Perry's naval actions because it echoed the themes and concerns that had first been proposed in the Republican case for war and that resonated strongly with contemporary popular culture.[4]

The image of the sailor as romantic American hero stirred the public imagination on a number of important levels. From the outbreak of the conflict, American belligerents had insisted that British impressment practices were the provocation that had forced the nation into open confrontation. Portraits of gallant husbands and dedicated fathers severed from their families and compelled to miserable toil in the floating dungeons of an enemy nation proved highly effective in American efforts to dramatize the issue of British impressment. Americans and Britons were warring over which nation could lay the greatest claim to loving liberty. Each side sought as its prize the moral right to imperial expansion—Britain in India, the United States in North America. Despite the fight for freedom that had once framed the American independence movement, the United States' continuing and deepening investment in slavery as well as its territorial designs on Native American lands had compromised newer American pronouncements in favor of liberty. When politicians and popular polemicists used the issue of lost love to emphasize the tyrannical side of the Royal Navy, they did much to tip the scales of virtue back toward the United States.[5]

Sailors pressed into serving the British lost not only their physical freedom but also the right to choose the nation to which they would swear allegiance. In portraying the plight of such involuntary recruits, tableaus of husbands and wives torn apart by British press gangs proved a highly effective way to dramatize the problem. Severing the bonds of love amounted to slashing the basis of liberty. Americans of 1812 equated chosen love with liberty and loyal love with fidelity. Selecting a spouse correlated with the exercise of democratic self-determination, while remaining faithful to the beloved primed people for patriotic allegiance.[6]

Presenting Perry as a gallant lover who freely won the affections of Victory implied that his triumph was as righteous as it was momentous. The operation on Lake Erie did represent a remarkable win for the usually overmatched forces of the small U.S. Navy. Any American naval victory, regardless of its actual strategic impact, gained added significance simply because success against the storied Royal Navy seemed so unlikely. But more than that, in the mouths of Republicans like Charles Tait, Perry's conduct proved that America's fighting men were inflamed by the kind of virtuous love that fed the fires of true liberty.

Unfortunately, by the time the U.S. Senate Committee on Naval Affairs could gather on December 27 to debate the question of whether Perry's victory had been completely decisive, or simply very glorious, new disastrous news had begun to flare. Senator Fromentin raised his objection to the excesses of the Senate celebrations in reference to this reality. Explaining why he did not want to overstate the importance of Perry's action, he asked delicately to "be permitted to advert to the intelligence received from the Niagara." To what did he make reference? Word was then arriving in the capital that the British had seized the American Fort Niagara on December 18, and that combined British and Indian forces were launching attacks across the Niagara Valley.[7]

Worst of all, the American militia had refused to rally in response, either ignoring calls to arms altogether or joining the army march only as a means of fleeing to protection. Their commanding general, George McClure, complained that the few men who volunteered did so with the goal "of taking care of their own families and property by carrying them into the interior" away from the Canadian border. By December 30, the British would burn Buffalo and, in consequence, the United States would lose all control of the crucial western frontier between New York and Canada on the east side of Lake Erie. The lived experience of war, in which flesh-and-blood wives and children faced mortal danger, far overshadowed romantic images of fighting men as carefree cupids.[8]

Yet if romantic rhetoric was useless in the reality of combat, it could still play a crucial part in shaping public perceptions of the war. For politicians determined to maintain power, this consideration mattered most. For this reason, Charles Tait could not bear Eligius Fromentin's efforts to temper the tone of the Senate's celebrations. Tait might insist that he had no intention to "light up a glare to dazzle the perception of the American people," yet he had great need to do exactly that. If American fighting forces could make little headway against the Canadians, their British defenders, and their Indian allies, that need not stop political orators from gaining ground with the American public.[9]

Faced with Fromentin's objectionable facts, Tait successfully countered with compelling visions of Perry's military heroism and romantic powers of seduction. No matter the factual strength of his case, Fromentin gave way before Tait's superior oratory. Withdrawing his previous critique of the meaning of "decisive," he conceded, "I am disposed to accept, as more pertinent than my own, the definition which has been offered by the honorable gentlemen from Georgia." The full resolution citing Perry's "decisive and glorious" victory passed both houses of Congress unanimously and was approved and signed into law by President James Madison on January 6, 1814. Dazzling perceptions were everything.[10]

⚬◇⚬

The first chroniclers of the Battle of Lake Erie emphasized that Perry's romantic sensitivities were key to understanding the nature of his victory. In contrast to the British, whose moral position was supposedly undermined by bloodthirsty barbarity, Perry gained fame for the care he showed his own officers and crew as well as the respect he displayed for the marriage obligations of the Canadian men who fell into his hands.

When a New York volunteer by the name of Samuel R. Brown wrote an account of the action called *Views on Lake Erie*, he had his pick of dramatic details. His highly popular book, reprinted three more times under various editions and titles from Vermont to Pennsylvania in 1814 and 1815, emphasized that Perry's victory came at the cost of "prodigious carnage." On board the *Lawrence* "the morning after the conflict," Brown asserted, the ship's deck "exhibited a scene that defies description." He offered the readers his best observations anyway, describing how "it was literally covered with blood, which still adhered to the plank in clots—brains, hair and fragments of bones were still sticking to the rigging and sides." Brown dwelled on how "the horror appalled my senses," the better to impress his readers with the contrasting "affecting spectacle" of "Perry supporting the wounded British."[11]

Brown most wanted readers to know that, despite the damage the British inflicted, the victorious "Perry treated the prisoners with humanity and indulgence." Some of the fullest proof of this came when "several Canadians, having wives at Malden, were permitted to visit their families on parole." The pens of American war supporters flowed with the idea that romantic love was the basis of virtue and the essence of liberty. The first and finest test of political independence came with the matter of marriage choice. Only if men and women were free to choose their own marriage partners, and only when their marriage bonds were treated as sacred, could legal freedom flourish. By painting Perry as deeply concerned about reuniting Canadian sailor-husbands with their wives, Brown presented a sharp contrast between the American naval hero and the standard procedures of the British press gang.[12]

Sailors portrayed as loving husbands and fathers became important figures for American propagandists. From the moment war broke out, Republican politicians from Washington to Massachusetts challenged their Federalist opponents to imagine the pain of families separated when the British illegally forced men to a lifetime at sea. When British press gangs seized a man, declared one anti-Federalist diatribe, "the agony of a wife and children in his native land may be left to conjecture." As a Maryland writer signing himself as "Publius" argued, "the impressment of our sailors was one of those outrages which might have been expected to unite against it all the softer emotions of the heart, all the loftier passions that sympathise with our country." Waging war against Britain became a means of reuniting lost lovers.[13]

Numerous popular poems and songs, published in songster books and broadside posters, used the tale of an impressed sailor torn from his true love to vivify the links between love and liberty. One such tune, narrated in the voice of an impressed man forced to row aboard a British ship, recounted:

> I was ta'en [taken] by the foe, 'twas the fiat of fate,
> To tare [tear] me from her I adore;
> When thought brings to my mind my once happier state,
> I sigh—I sigh as I tug at the oar.

To heighten the drama, this song presented the sailor not only as a forlorn lover but also as a betrothed man seized and forced into shipboard service on the very morning that should have brought his wedding service. Addressing imaginary lines to "Anna," his fiancée, he laments:

> How fortune deceives! I had pleasure in tow,
> The port where she dwelt was in view,
> But the wish'd nuptial morn was o'er clouded with woe,
> I was hurried, dear Anna, from you.
>   Our shallop was boarded, and I torn away,
> To behold that dear ANNA no more.

The song ends, and the sailor finds relief only when he dies of a broken heart. Titled "The Galley Slave," this song implied that naval impressment was no different than chattel slavery. And the sharpest pain of enslavement came with the loss of love.[14]

Women played integral parts in such stories, suggesting that the emotional contribution they could make to patriotism was as significant as that of men. Popular ballads making this point were often sung in the voice of a woman. One such song, called "Oh Cruel," related by a character named Mary, declared: "Oh! Cruel were my parents as tore my love from me / And cruel was the press gang who took him off to sea." These lines condemned Mary's parents for thwarting her free choice in love as much as they criticized the press gang who forced her beloved to sea. In the tally of rights, choice in the matter of marriage counted as much as the ability to pick occupation or national allegiance. For both men and women alike, freedom of feeling served as the foundation of every other right.[15]

In imagining the frustrated love of impressed seamen, Americans were supposed to find their own love of country. And that love was to be their spur to action. If common tavern goers sang songs that introduced these kinds of scenes, Republican politicians at the highest levels of government also wove them into official speeches. Portrayals of the British as a hard-hearted lot inured by tyranny to the tragedy of broken love shaped formal prowar rhetoric as much as popular culture. Federalists were warned that similar failures of feeling on their part would be tantamount to final proof that they lacked patriotism.

Henry Clay of Kentucky, among the most dedicated of the war's supporters in Congress, drew on just such imagery to argue in favor of legislation to expand the nation's armed forces in January 1813. Conjuring an elaborate fantasy for his audience in the capital and beyond, Clay demanded in one speech that his fellow lawmakers picture a conversation between an impressed American sailor, one of the nation's "gallant tars," and his country, embodied as the Goddess Columbia. "Let me suppose that the Genius of Columbia should visit one of them in his oppressor's prison," Clay suggested. The imprisoned sailor would implore her to fight for him by "appealing to her passions." He would tell her, "'I am no British subject, I am a native of old Massachusetts, where lived my aged father, my wife, my children. I have faithfully discharged my duty. Will you refuse to do yours?'" In Clay's imagined scene, the hardship and injustice of forced service in the Royal Navy lay as much in broken bonds of family love as in impressed labor itself.[16]

Henry Clay's speech proved immensely popular. The fanciful dialogue between the "Genius of Columbia" and the "gallant tar" was quickly reprinted as a stand-alone pamphlet that went through several editions. This "most beautiful effusion from an eloquent speech by Mr. Clay" also featured in a book-length compilation reprinted ten times between 1814 and 1818.[17]

Clay had made deliberate choices in describing his fictional sailor as "a native of Massachusetts" and in having him make his case for war with an appeal to the passions. Massachusetts figured largely in political discussion of impressment for two important reasons. First of all, Boston remained one of the largest port cities in the early United States and a key center of transatlantic trade. If the inhabitants of any state suffered from British impressments, it should have been those of Massachusetts. Yet, in fact, sailors and ship captains from the Bay State vigorously denied that impressments occurred with any frequency. And Massachusetts led the pack in opposition to the war, insisting that runaway passions were no basis for sound national decisions.

In April 1813, no doubt in response to Clay's well-publicized speech, a Federalist newspaper in Salem, Massachusetts, undertook what we would now call a "fact checking" mission to evaluate claimed cases of impressment one by one. The *Salem Gazette*'s findings were published in poster form with twenty-five supposed local cases of impressment debunked one by one on the basis of evidentiary issues such as mistaken identities. The poster proclaimed that the "gross and abominable frauds, practiced upon the public by the democratic papers, in relation to the subject of impressments, furnish conclusive evidence, that the alleged *cause* for continuing the war is only a hollow and unfounded *pretext*." Federalists, of course, believed that a central reason for waging the war was the desire to advance the rise of the Republican Party and the most riotous democratic elements within it. Nothing could better prove this truth than exposing the impressment issue as a sham.[18]

Meanwhile, Federalists refused to be baited on the issue of emotion. They could not be lured into supporting the war simply on the basis of affecting love stories. In direct contrast to Clay's claims that appeals to passion were the best means of stirring people to action, the Salem poster asserted, "we trust, that the people are not to be deluded by the flagitious arts of men, whose corrupt views and whose furious passions lead them to *wish* for a continuation of this unjust, unnecessary, and ruinous contest." For Federalists, passions were the problem, not the idealized basis of a patriotic nation.

Yet however hazy the facts on impressment, nothing stirred war supporters quite like the idea that press gangs were forcing American husbands away from their wives. Stories of lovers crossed not by the stars but by the Royal Navy proved irresistible even in Massachusetts. For every journalistic critique like the one launched in Salem there could be found numerous countering popular tales like that of "Sweet Poll of Plymouth." This broadside ballad was narrated in the voice of a sailor pleading with a press gang for the right to see his wife:

> The press-gang bold I ask'd in vain,
> To let me go on shore,
> Long'd to see my Poll again,
> But saw my Poll no more.

Though this man lamented that his "heart would break," the British simply would not relent. He exclaimed:

> We plow'd the deep, and now between,
> Us lay the ocean wide;
> For five long years I have not seen
> My sweet, my charming bride.

Such lines made wedded love the very face of freedom, endowing domestic life with national significance.[19]

Much the same message was conveyed in another contemporary poem, "The American Patriot's War Song; or, An Appeal to Free Men." This broadside ballad, cast as a call to "those who feel," declared:

> Britain still our sons impressing,
> Tyrannizes o'er the main.
> Thousands, doom'd to base employments,
> Spend in chains their hopeless lives:
> Torn from all their dear enjoyments,
> Parents, children, friends and wives.

Life on a British ship amounted to little better than slavery, the ties of family traded for the chains of the galley. Meanwhile, the American husbands and fathers torn from their homes could only imagine the fate being suffered by those left behind to face the attacks of the British and their Indian allies, "a band let loose from hell." The ballad demanded:

> Freemen can you bear such slaughter?
> Will you drain the cup of woe?

Rouse to save your wives and daughters,
Rouse to conquer every foe!

A man's family obligations were what drove him to serve his country. The ballad drew explicit links between family feelings and national affections, explaining:

Danger binds us all together,
Union is our surest *rock*;
One defense in stormy weather,
But secures the chosen *flock*;
All in bonds of love united,
Safe beneath the eagle's wings

Americans were a "chosen" people. The poem promised them that they could preserve "true liberty" and break the "chains" of the British press gang only if they strengthened their own "bonds of love."[20]

While popular depictions of the emotional stress of impressment could also mention the pangs of parted friends, tales of broken families featured most frequently and carried extra freight. Whereas Commodore Perry was celebrated for enticing victory into his arms, British sea captains were portrayed as dangerous plotters, determined to interrupt the love of American husbands and wives for each other and, laterally, for their country.[21]

⁕

Flags and feelings. If the white flag of surrender that General William Hull had raised at Detroit reportedly affected men's emotions "beyond expression," Commodore Oliver Perry aimed at a very different effect with an "elegant flag" that he hoisted on the mast of the ship the *Lawrence* on Lake Erie in September 1813. Perry's pennant, which he had personally commissioned, was inscribed: "Don't Give Up the Ship." The words referred directly to the dying order given by his fallen friend and colleague Captain James Lawrence, who had lost his life and ship to the British the previous June. But they also might have been applied more generally to the whole American war effort.[22]

When Perry flew his custom blue-and-white banner above the *Lawrence* that day, he meant, literally and figuratively, to raise a standard. According to reports, he created an impression that was "not to be described—every heart was electrified. The crews cheered." If much of the American war effort to that point had been desultory and inconclusive, Perry was determined to hand the nation a signal victory and decided in his efforts to stir emotion.[23]

Perry credited his men with rising to the occasion. In his official report, sent to Secretary of the Navy William Jones, he recorded that "those officers and men who were immediately under my observation evinced the greatest gallantry." Perry's emphasis on "gallantry" gained great appreciation from the public—to the point that when Senator Charles Tait argued in favor of Perry's congressional citation, he did so expressly because of his "gallantry."[24]

A popular account of the war by an amateur writer in Philadelphia named John Lewis Thomson noted approvingly that Perry "attributed the [victory] to the gallant conduct of his officers, his men, and the volunteers on board." Thomson in turn described Perry in similar terms. Thomson had to rely on secondhand accounts, not having served in the war himself, and admitted that the "many contradictory accounts of the war with which he ha[d] been supplied ha[d] not unseldom thrown him into perplexing embarrassments" as an author. Nevertheless, he was confident enough to describe Perry as gallant. He specified that "in passing from the Lawrence to the Niagara," Perry, "stood up, waving his sword, and gallantly cheering his men under a shower of balls and bullets." Though Thomson seems never to have written any other book before or after this one, his *Historical Sketches* of the war sold so briskly that it went through five editions in three years.[25]

Thomson could refer to Perry's gallantry without hesitation because readers would hardly have expected anything else. As the current *Oxford English Dictionary* notes, "gallant" was "the conventional epithet of a military or naval officer." Yet "gallant" and "gallantry" were words richly layered with meaning at the outset of the nineteenth century. For "gallant" was also a word "pertaining to (sexual) love, amorous, amatory." Noah Webster, in his *Compendious Dictionary of the English Language* published in New Haven in 1806, defined "gallantry" as "bravery, generosity, shew, courtship." Links between love, marriage, brave seamanship, and duty to country were literally forged by the very language used to describe Perry's victory on Lake Erie.[26]

In the United States of 1812, connubial love, naval service, and national loyalty not only made for an evocative symbolic configuration but also existed in a concrete legal and political matrix. In traditional English society, subjects owed obedience to the king in the same way that children owed loyalty to their parents. The tie between king and subject was a natural relationship that began at birth and could never be severed. It continued unchanged until the subject's death. In the new United States, by contrast, legal members of the nation were considered citizens, not subjects. And while subjectship was supposed to be natural and perpetual, citizenship was supposed to be contractual and volitional. Indeed, if the best metaphor for subjectship was the relationship between father and child, a closer model for citizenship could be found in the marriage vows between husbands and wives.[27]

Alexander McLeod, a Presbyterian minister and war partisan in New York, preached from the pulpit about the linkages between love, loyalty, and nation. The issue was personal for McLeod in more ways than one. He had arrived in New York from Scotland in 1792 at the age of eighteen and spent the next couple of decades building a life for himself in the United States that included an education at Union College, a call to the ministry, and, in 1805, marriage to one Mary Anne Agnew, the Irish-American daughter of one of his immigrant congregants. Faced with Federalist objections to the war, and in particular with the claims of members of the New England clergy that the war arose from the indulgence of sin, McLeod countered that the war reflected divine will. He argued that the contest was being waged "in order to make it appear whether . . . party distinctions, which have so long and unhappily existed, can be made to yield to Christian attachments." McLeod had a specific kind of attachment in mind.[28]

Marital love was the root of loyalty as well as the flower of liberty. In a sermon that Reverend McLeod called "A Scriptural View of the Character, Causes, and Ends of the Present War," he promised that "the love of country" would be "revived by this second war of independence." He declared: "it is not merely for *Free trade and sailors' rights*," that this contest was intended by the Governor of the world: it was to illustrate . . . the true nature of allegiance." According to McLeod, the war was being fought to "maintain the idea that man is as free to choose his residence as his employment, his country as his wife, his ruler as his servant." Choosing a wife and choosing a country were paired pursuits that together formed the basis of freedom.[29]

Choice of spouse and choice of nation. The "true nature of allegiance" could only be understood through the medium of marital love. Reverend McLeod was so pleased with this formulation that he not only published his sermon in pamphlet form in January 1815 for the enjoyment of the wider reading public, but also forwarded a copy to Congressman Peter Wendover of New York, who in turn sent the sermon with his compliments to former president Thomas Jefferson.[30]

Beyond the metaphoric resonance of love and loyalty, marriages had actual legal ramifications for U.S. citizenship status. For women, citizenship literally followed from marriage decisions. An American-born woman who married a foreigner became an instant expatriate, while an immigrant woman gained naturalized status automatically whenever her husband did. Men's citizenship status was not directly affected by their marital status, yet even for men marriage could have a significant indirect impact. Following congressional reforms in 1802, a foreign-born man wishing to become a naturalized U.S. citizen had only to live in the United States for five years, swear to uphold the U.S. Constitution, and renounce all foreign allegiances. The law had nothing official to say about a man's marital status. Yet the residency requirement indirectly raised the issue of marriage—especially for men who spent the vast majority of their days at sea.[31]

For sailors working on shipboard, verifying residence in any particular country could prove problematic. In such cases, marriage patterns did matter for establishing the place of abode. Since husbands usually lived in one household with their wives, a wife who stayed ashore and maintained a home in the United States could help prove that her husband's legal residence was located there also. Conversely, a wife settled in a foreign land undermined a man's claim to U.S. residency.

As a practical matter, Atlantic shipping lanes were awash with British and Irish-born men hoping to use U.S. naturalization as a means to escape service in the Royal Navy and obtain far more lucrative voluntary work aboard U.S. merchant ships. When Americans protested British impressment, their objections exceeded the violation of an individual man's freedom to encompass concerns about whether the British recognized and respected American power to admit naturalized citizens. By rights the Crown could not commandeer the labor of citizens of a foreign nation. And yet the Royal Navy seemed prepared to do just that. Anxiety about sailors' lost and stolen love and broken marriages thus arose from the importance of chosen love *both* as a symbol of voluntary national allegiance and as a vehicle for creating legal citizenship status. The intersections of love, marriage, locality, and citizenship created considerable confusion about how a man's marriage might or might not change his nationality.[32]

Both partisans in favor of the war and those opposed to it, both observers who deplored the problem of impressment and those who denied its prevalence, displayed uncertainty about how marriages might be manipulated to alter a man's legal rights. John Quincy Adams was the writer who had first complained that British press gangs paid so little heed to a man's family status when forcing him to sea that "the agony of a wife and children in his native land may be left to conjecture." Then-senator Adams, already allied with the Republican Party at the time he made this remark in a private letter in 1808, soon decided to publish it. Yet even Adams was not quite sure of the international political implications of the marriage issue. With some inconsistency, he contended in the same letter that the British Lords of the Admiralty often refused to free impressed sailors on the grounds that "they have been married or settled in England." He displayed a degree of incoherence in charging simultaneously that the British counted dubious marital attachments when they wanted to assert a man's British citizenship yet disregarded sacrosanct ties of union when they sent men to sea.[33]

One contemporary found this illogic so risible that he singled it out for mockery in an opposition pamphlet, quoting from these very lines with the sarcastic remark that "a vague and obscure expression is apt to be admired by some, because it conveys the sense they relish most and by others . . . because it suggests various meanings at once." Yet Adams's concerns resonated enough with the public at large to be read and repeated approvingly by men far outside his Boston and Washington orbit. Five years later, in 1813, the year of Perry's triumph, Solomon Aiken, an unabashedly Republican preacher from Dracut, Massachusetts, a small town on the New Hampshire border, would quote these exact lines from Adams with relish in a published sermon he addressed *To Federal Clergymen, on the Subject of the War Proclaimed by the Congress of the United States, June 18, 1812.*[34]

War opponents exhibited equal anxiety on the subject of sailors' marriages and uncertainty about that civil institution's civic implications. A committee in the Massachusetts House of Representatives, determined, like the editor of the *Salem Gazette*, to debunk the notion that the British impressed Americans at all, drew up a complex set of case reports in 1813. The legislators hit on the tactic of taking sworn depositions from dozens of Massachusetts ship captains, each willing to state under oath that he had never had an American sailor seized from one of his ships. In the rare instances when a captain did admit to having witnessed the work of a press gang, he took care to explain the legitimacy of the action. And here marriages once again came into play in ambiguous ways.[35]

A sea captain by the name of William Parsons gave testimony that showed how some sailors tried to treat marriage ties as a functional proxy for national loyalty. Parsons, who sailed from Boston and said he employed about fifty men a year on his merchant vessels, testified to the committee: "I have no recollection of any of my seamen being impressed for the last twenty years, except in one instance." On the one occasion Parsons could recall, the man taken was an Irishman and the ship commander who seized him offered to return him to the American ship on nothing more than the man's own testimony that he was a U.S. citizen. Parsons recalled that the ship captain "said he would deliver up the man, if the man himself would give his word that he was an American, which he would not do; but said he had a wife in America." In Parsons's telling, the sailor seems to have thought that by mentioning his marriage to an American woman he could imply that he too was a U.S. citizen, but that when challenged explicitly about his nationality he stopped short of an outright lie.[36]

In another case, a man named Andrew Harraden provided evidence that, in some cases, marriage actually could be a good measure of a man's national affinities if not of his actual legal status. Harraden, who identified himself as a mariner from Salem, Massachusetts, and reported working as a shipmaster for twenty-two years, testified that he had never known an instance of British impressment. In cases where Americans did serve the British, he assumed the work was legal and contractual. He gave the example of one of his own American-born cousins who "had been in the British navy for as much as sixteen years past, but . . . had entered into British service voluntarily, and . . . was married in England." Clearly a man could neither formally establish nor extinguish his citizenship through marriage. Still, marriage could become a convenient, informal way of complicating, contesting, or even acquiescing to national membership and military obligations.[37]

Folk understandings of the interconnections of marital status and national status gave added weight to the symbolic meanings of love. In often-literal ways, love for wives and love of country could be conflated. Joshua Penny, a seafarer from Long Island, used these themes to spin a long and wandering yarn of his life under the sway of British marine authority. Penny offered *The Life and Adventures of Joshua Penny*—part fact, part exaggeration, and part pure fabrication—to the public in 1815, telling of forced journeys from America to Africa to Britain to the West Indies. The book began and ended with commentary on British interference in American marriages.[38]

By his own account, Penny was a single young man when first captured by a British press gang. Nevertheless, knowing that complaints that impressment interfered with sailors' family lives were an expected convention, he used the opening pages of his memoir to launch just such a critique. Of the British, he declared, "liberty is mocked by that nation." He objected, "compel a man whom you stile free, to abandon his wife, his children, and every thing else he values in this world, to become your slave on shipboard! How dare you call that a land of freedom where this practice prevails." Despite his own status as a bachelor, Penny could not resist the rhetorical leverage offered by the image of the family man denied the basic liberty of living with his beloved.[39]

Penny's tale took him back and forth across the Atlantic many times from his initial capture in the early 1790s till the onset of war in 1812. Along the way he found time to marry a Long Island woman in 1808 and to settle down to the work of raising crops and rearing boys. Then, after he had become father to three sons, he was supposedly seized a final time. While engaging in wartime duty to guard the Long Island Sound, he recounted, he fell into the hands of the British and was shipped off to prison in Britain.[40]

Penny painted his time in the British jail as a story of attempted sexual seduction, potential treason, and heroic resistance. He reported that one day, after he had languished miserably for months in prison, a strange man entered his cell saying he needed to examine him to determine whether he was the missing husband of a local English woman. In an age when legal divorce was rare, common law separations could be easily achieved if a husband simply abandoned his wife, skipping town with no forwarding address. There was nothing especially unusual about authorities seeking to locate a deadbeat husband who owed his wife support. But Penny smelled a plot.[41]

Penny reported, "I told this man my wife was on Long Island." Yet despite his explanation that he was an American and could not possibly be the lost husband, he was "summoned to a house where this woman and [the] . . . examiner were sitting, with a table covered in decanters and glasses." Tempting Penny with liquor, the strange man asked the woman if she could positively identify Penny as her husband. Penny said, "she answered that she 'could not but that I looked much like him.' Then turning to me, asked, 'if that was my wife?' No, I answered, I would not give my wife for ten thousand of her. This created a laugh and ended in drinking." Despite being willing to raise a glass with these people, Penny related the incident with disgust. However lonely he might have been after months of imprisonment, he asserted that the American wife waiting for him thousands of miles away was far superior to the English woman in front of him.[42]

Penny concluded by explaining the moral of the story: fidelity to wife preserved loyalty to country. He said, "I satisfied myself that this woman was a common prostitute, and my examiner a justice of the peace. But they were unable to make a British subject of me by this or any other stratagem." Penny was sure that he had been offered a sexual bribe in return for national betrayal. He closed his story with one more humorous dig at the British, explaining that although the prostitute "requested the company to leave the room to herself and me," he "refused and retired with the others—one of whom laughing said, 'I believe you don't like our English women very well.'" Affections for women tracked affiliations to nation. At least in popular understanding, union with a foreign woman could be enough to transfer a man's citizenship away from his own native land. Conversely, faithfulness to wife averted treason to country.[43]

⌘

If Senator Charles Tait exercised little subtlety when he portrayed Commodore Oliver Perry as a successful ladies' man who lured Victory away from the British, popular depictions of the Battle of Lake Erie could wield such imagery with blunt force. One broadside poem marking the triumph of Perry's *Niagara* over the opposing British ship the *Queen Charlotte* celebrated:

> With *boldness Perry* strides the Lakes,
> His *Foe* in daring *Combat* stakes,
> . . . .
> His cannon makes Queen Charlotte crack,
> And lays her prostrate on her back.

In contrast to American women, and especially American wives, who were idealized as the virtuous partners of men who engaged in democratic rituals of consent, the British nation could be effectively satirized as a wanton woman who deserved sexual domination and degradation.[44]

Given the complex associations between sexual ardor and patriotic fervor that pervaded American culture in the era of 1812, American women faced complicated stresses in negotiating their own sexuality. Of course, caricatures of the enemy as a weak woman of loose morals increased the political as well as personal pressure on women to maintain reputations for sexual morality. From church pulpits to pulp novels came advice to American women to safeguard their sexual purity in support of patriotism.[45]

Nevertheless, modesty and chastity were *not* the same thing. The overall trend in nineteenth-century ideals was toward images of lower-class women as sexual sinners and middle- and upper-class women as passionless paragons. However, this extreme had not yet been reached in the era of 1812. On the contrary, respectable public-minded women could rouse the patriotic passions of men by presenting themselves as objects of desire. So long as the gratification of such yearnings came within the confines of marriage, women could and should serve the country by awakening men's sexuality.[46]

Not surprisingly, men enjoyed still wider symbolic latitude for indulging sexual desires in the service of country. Even as American sailors were urged to draw on righteous passions to spur their love of country, the baser side of lust could be metaphorically indulged in fantasies of war as sexual conquest. Many wartime metaphors for naval combat encouraged navy tars to imagine themselves as ladykillers who dallied with the susceptible British in battle but ultimately returned to settle down to patriotic marriages with American wives.

Sexualized images of the vanquished British titillated men and remonstrated with women at the same time. A broadside ballad celebrating the win of the U.S. frigate USS *Constitution* over the British frigate HMS *Java* in December of 1812 portrayed battle as courtship and the British frigate as a fallen woman. The song began: "The JAVA our seamen exultingly spied / And as usual all strangers to cowardly fear / To the Brazen-fac'd hussey we quickly drew near." Having rhetorically positioned the British ship as a brazen hussy, a woman who indiscriminately invited the sexual advances of men, the poem moved easily to describing the British defeat as an instance of defilement. It concluded: "sure Miss Java she never met such a deuced rough spark / For we tore her fine rigging and cut up her dress." Released from the required gentlemanly self-restraint of the polite suitor, American sailors—and, perhaps more importantly, the wider reading public—could imagine themselves as "rough sparks" tearing a ship's sails and rigging as if it were a strumpet's dress and corset.[47]

American seafarers paired their rhetorical heterosexual swagger with claims that British sailors were either effeminate scoundrels ripe for sodomy, or, at best, asexual fops who feared women. One graphic broadside satire punned on the names of the American ships USS *Hornet* and USS *Wasp* to suggest that American naval victories gave the British a sexual sting (Figure

Figure 6. A series of Atlantic encounters from Brazil to the Virginia coast under Commodore William Bainbridge, Captain Isaac Hull, and others suggested more of this cartoon's multiple plays on words. When Bainbridge, commander of the USS *Constitution*, sank the HMS *Java*, he first removed passengers, including Lieutenant General Thomas Hislop, governor of India (the probable point of reference for the comment on Bombay). "John Bull stung to Agony by Insects," Philadelphia, March 1, 1813, Collections of the American Antiquarian Society.

6). The cartoon caricatured the Royal Navy as John Bull, a grotesque figure with a stupefied grimace, bulging stomach, and enormous hindquarters being attacked by insects with American flags for wings and unusually long stingers. One annoyed "Johnny" by piercing his middle, the other attacked his rear end. Leaving little to the imagination, the second pest demanded, "How comes on your Copper bottom . . . damn me, but you shall have it between Wind & Water." This winking reference to flatulence and urination—the scatological lightly disguised as the nautical—left little doubt as to the sort of anthropomorphic humiliation Americans intended to deliver to the British. Yet, ironically, the American naval record itself was at best mixed. Though the *Hornet* won a clear victory, the British actually captured the *Wasp* after a long and costly battle. The popular taste for bawdy fun proved especially useful to prowar propagandists when there was the need to distract from the true difficulties of the American effort.[48]

A broadside poem titled "The Uncourteous Knight or Flying Gallant" also documents how sexual metaphors could help put a positive spin on unsuccessful or indeterminate encounters. The factual impetus for the piece came from the conduct of the war on the Great Lakes. Throughout the early years of the war, in 1812 and 1813, both Britain and the United States regarded control of the lakes as essential for deciding the fate of Canada. On Lake Ontario, Sir James Yeo headed the royal squadron, while Isaac Chauncey led the Americans. Yet despite a number of near misses, the two navies on Lake Ontario never engaged in direct battle, a fact that Americans blamed on British unwillingness to enter a fair fight. The poem cast this entirely inconclusive episode as evidence of superior Yankee sexual prowess and military muscle.[49]

In the elaborate allegory of the poem, the British frigate (commanded by Yeo) figured as a "*faithless perjured lover*" who was too timid to return the "amorous fire" of the allegorically female American ship (commanded by Chauncey). As the song told it:

> From Ontario's margin, the Lady set sail,
> Expecting the Knight on that sea;
> She dreamt not that his promise would fail,
> And from a fair lady unmanlike turn tail;
> . . . .
> He fear'd to embrace her—he'd promis'd to woo:
> She'd hail'd him—'Sir James, charming fellow, heave too![']
> . . . .
> At length, from love's fervor, the recreant got clear,
> And may have, for a season, some rest;
> But if this fair lady he ever comes near,
> For breaking his promise he'll pay very dear;
> The price, valiant CHAUNCEY knows best.

In contrast to the figure of the loyal and loving American sailor, whose courtly gallantry showed his devotion to freedom, this poem positioned the British commander as an "unmanlike" and untrustworthy rake—one with no feeling for either ladies or liberty.

Poems like this one targeted female audiences as well as male ones. Though not entitled to vote or fight, women followed the progress of the war closely enough to understand the analogies and allusions presented in broadside posters. "The Flying Gallant" expressly included women among the "public" when it declared that *the public will hear with astonishment that a British Knight, of high reputation, should have declined the advances of an American Lady.* The poem's introduction advised that *all true hearted maidens ought without the least hesitation to set him down for a faithless perjured lover.* The message for American women was clear: their romantic choices could have patriotic effects. Being a "true hearted maiden" who loved her country required that a woman allow the attentions only of valiant fighters and faithful lovers. When women joined in mocking any man who failed in his "fervor" for love or for war, they helped support the culture of ardor.

The wartime conceit of the patriotic and amorous sailor whose admirable fervor for war flowed from his faithful ardor for women defied considerable conventional wisdom. The traditional view of the feckless sailor is captured in the broadside poem "The Yankee Sailor," which portrayed typical shipmen as fellows who dallied "with pretty girls on shore," leaving only "when their cash is gone, and not before." Such ribald rhymes implied that sailors literally bought time with women, hardly an image made for promoting ideals of patriotic virtue in either sex.[50]

Yet much more common in the immediate years of the war was the kind of message delivered by the poem "Black-Ey'd Susan," which promised both that servicemen were to be trusted and that women's love was a crucial element of the war effort. These verses addressed to "Susan" reassured all women:

Believe not what the landmen say,
Who tempt with doubts thy constant mind,
They'll tell th[at] sailors when away,
In every port a mistress find.
Yes, yes, believe them when I tell thee so,
For thou art present whereso'er I go.

Far from having a woman in every port, these lines pledged that wherever he went a sailor thought only of his one true love. The poem ended by invoking a woman's love as a shield from danger, declaring:

Though battle calls me from thy arms,
Let not my pretty Susan mourn;
Though canons roar, yet safe from harms,
William shall to his dear return.
Love turns aside the balls that round me fly,
Lest precious tears should drop from Susan's eye.

If only "pretty Susan" would offer "constant" love to her sailor, not even cannon balls could bring him to harm. This popular poem, which was sometimes published on its own, also appeared on the opposite side of the poster containing the verses on "The Uncourteous Knight." If the first poem called on "true-hearted maidens" to resist British rakes as a matter of patriotic principle, the second specified exactly how romantic love could serve men, women, and country at once.[51]

In very similar terms, a ballad called "Tom Starboard" presented the tale of Tom and Nan to reinforce the idea that when a sailor offered faithful love to one woman, he became a better fighter for his country. The song began by claiming:

Tom Starboard was a lover true,
As brave a tar as ever sail'd
The duties ablest seamen do,
Tom did—and never yet had fail'd.

Tom credited his love for Nan with protecting as well as inspiring him, and "said love for Nan, his only dear, had sav'd his life." The poem went so far as to claim, "love sav'd him sure from being drown'd." Ever-present in the mind of her man, a woman's love was a sailor's life preserver (Figure 7).[52]

If fictional scenarios like the lines addressed to "Nan" and to "Black-Ey'd Susan" dramatized the working of patriotic love in vivid strokes, the same symbols also animated accounts of specific naval encounters. When Captain Isaac Hull took the British frigate HMS *Guerrière* in August 1812, a broadside poem commemorating the battle celebrated, "Now safe in Boston port we're moor'd, Our girls with smiles shall meet us / And every true American,' With loud huzzas shall greet us." Nothing marked a naval triumph like an adoring audience of women.[53]

Figure 7. The image is framed by the shape of a shield, while the "true love" ribbon draped over it changes the overall frame into the shape of a heart, graphically emphasizing the poem's claim that a woman's love is a sailor's shield. "The Sailor's Departure from His True Love Susan," n.d., Collections of the American Antiquarian Society.

Likewise, when James Campbell, "a boatswain's mate on board the *Constitution*," wrote verses to commemorate Bainbridge's December 1812 triumph over the *Java*, he declared:

Here's to our wives and sweethearts, for whom we fought for fame,
And when the lisping children shall sing forth their father's name,

And the pretty girls of every stamp, what more can we do?
So may success attend those heroes of the Constitution's crew.

Not only did men fight in the service of wives and sweethearts, but they also expected that "pretty girls of every stamp" would greet returning heroes with song. Published as a poster, this song broadcast the message that women had crucial parts to play in any patriotic tableau.[54]

⁕

Members of Perry's squadron on the Great Lakes knew how little amorous feelings actually shaped men's experiences in the midst of battle—Samuel Brown's lingering description of Perry's blood-clotted ship deck comes to mind. Yet in popular depictions of the war, the feelings and motivations of real sailors who fought in particular engagements could be blended together with more romance-laden stylized accounts. A broadside made to commemorate "Perry's Victory," for example, presented the public with two poems on one poster: detailed verses on the events of the Battle of Lake Erie on one side and more generic rhymes on "The Question" on the other. This one demanded,

Shall *chains* be the lot of American seamen?
No, no, we will never submit to be prest,
Unless sweet reward to American freemen,
To woman's warm soothing, affectionate breast.

Playing with double meanings of "pressed," these lines underscored yet again the effectiveness of viewing liberty through the prism of love. Here women appeared literally as the "reward" of "freemen." When American wives gave themselves to their husbands, they vivified democratic consent. When they offered up a "warm, soothing, affectionate breast," they both stirred the love of American men and spurred military action.[55]

If "The Question" for men in 1812 was supposed to be whether they could be forced into serving the British, the question for contemporary women was how they would respond to the patriotic politics of marriage. Women were told repeatedly that they could contribute in key ways to the nation when they made sexual and emotional commitments to men. The important historical point here is *not* that the patriotic symbolism of love and marriage "allowed" women an indirect means of political involvement. Clearly, a woman's informal political "participation" in this sense in no way compensated for her lack of formal political rights. On the contrary, the point is that to a real degree women were required to do unremunerated sexual and emotional work for the country, to offer themselves and their love on the altar of patriotism without any recompense of legal rights. While women were positioned to serve as the fighting man's highest prize, for them love was supposed to be its own reward. With the United States claiming that American opportunities for marriage eclipsed those in Britain—and that liberty itself shone brighter in the republic than in the royal empire—women's transformation into wives carried considerable public weight.[56]

The invented tale of "William" and "Black-Ey'd Susan" captures the way marriage could be presented as both women's privilege and women's duty. If the verses of "Black-Ey'd Susan" urged women to offer their love as a means of assuring a man's protection, a sequel song called "Susan's Lamentation" described what Susan could expect once William returned from his long absence at sea. All her lamentations ended at his safe homecoming from the war. Then, "William and Susan sweetly march'd along / To Plymouth church, to Plymouth church / Where multitudes did throng." The inclusion of a new detail—the suggestion that William and Susan, like "Sweet Poll," hailed from Plymouth—underscores the political significance attached to even the blandest-seeming romantic ditties. The figure of a Plymouth, Massachusetts, sailor burdened with impressment but saved by the constant love of his betrothed imaginatively contradicted the factual protestations of Massachusetts Federalists that sailors from the region reported no such problems with the Royal Navy. Meanwhile, the message for women was clear: they were to enter marriages as men entered military service.[57]

Recognizing that popular romantic ballads could encode political commentary on everything from impressment as a pretext for war to men's and women's practical and emotional obligations to the nation invites us to take a new look at other seemingly apolitical wartime cultural productions. One of the best-known "women's novels" of this period, Susannah Rowson's *Sarah; or, The Exemplary Wife*, has often been mined for insights into women's views on marriage, yet it has seldom if ever been considered as a commentary on the War of 1812. Still, the book was published in 1813, in the very midst of the war. Its author, Susannah Rowson, was one of the best-selling novelists of her day as well as the owner of a successful girls school. Rowson steered clear of making explicit political comments in the novel, but enjoyed debating politics in her private correspondence. In the years leading up to the war she declared that although she was "by birth a Briton," she possessed a "heart that clings to America." Once in the United States, Rowson offered her devoted support to the Federalist Party. In the pages of her 1813 novel, her political affiliations come through in veiled critiques. True, Rowson's obvious aim in writing the novel had more to do with promoting women's economic independence than with commenting on geopolitics per se. Yet, when she presented a book that meditated on the question of free choice in marriage in the midst of a war being fought on the premise that American liberty began and ended with conjugal love, Rowson could not avoid creating an element of political allegory.[58]

On examination, *The Exemplary Wife* proves able to shed interesting light not only on women's general views of matrimony but also on their skeptical objections to the notion that marital love embodied American liberty. Rowson presented her readers with the tragic tale of a motherless English girl named Sarah Osborne who, abandoned by her father and "finding her finances reduced to a very small portion," consented to marry a man named George Darnley even "though [her] heart felt no strong emotions in his favor." Honest to a fault, the virtuous Sarah informed her fiancé at the very beginning that she did not love him, but promised that she would strictly observe her wifely duties out of principle. As the story unfolded, Sarah found her virtue tried repeatedly. George promptly took up drinking, racked up debts, took a mistress named Jessey Romain, and cast Sarah out of their home. For hundreds of pages, Sarah then wandered forlornly, trying in vain to find work with which to support herself, harried at every turn by the wiles of unprincipled women and the exploitations of profligate men. No matter her trials and temptations, Sarah maintained perfect virtue and propriety, surviving to achieve reconciliation with her husband. George then repaid her by renewing his dalliance with Jessey, fathering an illegitimate son with her, and leaving Sarah to raise the child. Finally, when Sarah at last died of a broken heart, George married his mistress. The only break in the clouds came when, at the end of her life, Sarah made the acquaintance of a minister who valued her virtue and offered her a chaste friendship. And the reader had the small satisfaction of being told on the final page that George ultimately suffered as much from Jessey as Sarah did from him.[59]

What political messages accompanied this tale of marriage without love? First of all, Rowson set all the action of her story in Britain. Given the extent of contemporary commentary about English failures to respect romantic love, it seems significant that Rowson did not locate her characters in America. Back in 1791, Rowson's most famous heroine, the English-born Charlotte Temple of the novel *Charlotte, A Tale of Truth*, had met seduction and death in the United States. Yet by 1813, Rowson's own affiliations had changed. If America, the self-declared land of the free, was also the land of feeling, then a plot based on the absence of love could best be set in Britain, a place U.S. contemporaries symbolically associated with romantic lack. Rowson dwelt on this theme extensively at the start of the novel. Sarah declared outright to the aunt who raised her in her mother's stead, "I do not love this man." But her aunt only replied, "marry him first, you will learn to love him afterwards." Unlike vociferous American celebrations of true love and free choice, the English advisers surrounding Sarah insisted that love had little to do with marriage and less to do with consent. By 1813, Rowson's U.S. audience would have been primed to expect such disregard for freedom and for feeling from the British.[60]

Another key plot point reinforced the idea that love matches were unlikely to flourish in Britain because of that nation's lack of respect for liberty. Sarah was "cast unprotected on the world" because her "dissipated" father—like her husband after him, a man who gambled away his fortune, consorted with a mistress, and sired a "natural son"—fled his debts in England to go seek better fortune in India. Sarah's father played a key role in sustaining her misery because, late in the novel, just when Sarah was working to achieve reconciliation with George, "her father returned from India with a broken constitution," but with his "loose morals and dissipated habits" firmly intact. He soon succeeded in luring George away from his repentant resolutions with regard to Sarah and ultimately hastened her broken-hearted death. Positioned as a harbor for English scoundrels, Britain's Indian empire was portrayed directly as a haven for paternal vice and, indirectly, as a port for the political variety as well.[61]

Rowson linked the British lack of romantic feeling with that nation's imperial activities in India in a way that would have been clear to readers in the 1812 era, however tenuous the association may seem today. What Rowson implied obliquely through narrative devices other commentators communicated openly. Alexander McLeod, for example, the New York Presbyterian minister who argued explicitly that the United States had gone to war in order to "maintain the idea that man is as free to choose . . . his country as his wife," offered extended commentary on British activities in India in his

Scriptural View of War. In this widely circulated and often-republished volume of essays, McLeod proclaimed that "the rapacity, and cruelty ascribed to the late Emperor of France, are exceeded by degree and permanence by the British government of India." In contrast to the virtuous feelings of connubial love that McLeod claimed motivated Americans, he insisted that the Royal Navy from India to America was motivated by far baser passions: "These are not *defensive wars.* They are the offspring of the lust of power and wealth."[62]

Crucially, McLeod did not condemn the idea of empire itself. Prowar Americans with one eye on Canada and the other on the trans-Mississippi West certainly did not wish to argue against the ethics of territorial expansion. What McLeod and those of his ilk hoped to establish was that the U.S. love of liberty made it uniquely justified in pursuing territorial acquisitions. If Americans' emotions were virtuous, who could condemn their consequent actions? As McLeod temporized in critiquing the British in India: "in a political point of view, the miseries of Asia are not immediately interesting; but in the estimate of moral character, the remoteness of us from the scene of action, must not prevent our taking these enormities into account." In other words, McLeod wanted to make clear that he had no *political* objection to Britain's imperial expansion, only reservations about whether Britain, burdened by "the debauchery, and the licentiousness of the great; and the misery, the baseness, the wickedness of the rabble," could claim the "moral character" needed to justify its ambitions.[63]

McLeod winked at the idea of empire even as he raised his eyebrow at Britain's activities in India. Such contortions were common among Republican commentators of the day. When a group calling itself the "Washington Republicans of Philadelphia" published a wartime address "to the People of Pennsylvania," it declared, "we shall not examine the means by which she [Britain] has acquired her empire in India because . . . it is certain that we are not bound to remedy the injustice and that our present operations can have no operation in avenging or terminating it." Mentioning India while claiming not to, the Philadelphians criticized not the institution of empire itself but the "means" by which Britain acquired one.[64]

Likewise, when Charles Glidden Haines—a New York lawyer soon to become a major backer of the westward settlement that would be enabled by the Erie Canal—delivered an oration to "republican citizens" in New Hampshire in 1812, he declared that, as the "only Republic now in existence," the United States was engaged in a fight to determine "whether the last sanctuary of national freedom shall be destroyed." In this case, Britain came in for the critique that, "abroad she scatters pestilence and death; at home she acts the finished tyrant . . . in Scotland she enforces obedience at the point of the bayonet; in India she renews the slaughters." Again, as a democratic republic that loudly proclaimed its devotion to liberty, the United States claimed a degree of moral latitude in relation to empire that it forcefully denied to Britain.[65]

Ultimately, McLeod, too, brought his argument back around to the fact that Britain's imperial wars were fought at the behest of a tyrannical government, while American ones were, by definition, waged to advance the interests of republicanism. Denouncing the British government as inherently warlike, he declared, "during the last fifty years, she has shed more blood in India than has been shed in Europe: and in all the wars of Europe she is a party." Finally, he railed against Federalists who "reprobat[ed] this contest" not as a matter of "pure conscience" but rather out of "political bias against this republican country, the least guilty in the crime of war." Ironically, then, one of the primary political advantages of the American principle of democratic consent lay in the way it allowed the creation of an artificial contrast between the tyranny of British imperialism and the American empire of liberty.

Logical breaks rent this definition of American liberty at many points. British commentators, of course, were only too happy to emphasize that, in the United States, the grand principle of democratic self-determination applied neither to enslaved blacks nor to invaded Indians. But such objections could also be lobbed from the pit of women's political and economic oppression. This is just the place where Susannah Rowson entered the argument.

Despite its seemingly exclusive emphasis on private life, Susannah Rowson's *Exemplary Wife* helped dramatize the ways in which women's inequalities undermined claims to liberty on both sides of the Atlantic. If Americans regarded marriage as the ultimate ritual of voluntary consent, Rowson set out to demonstrate the hollow core of American beliefs about matrimony. Technically, of course, Sarah did choose her husband herself and therefore was liable to uphold the bad bargain she had made. Yet Rowson argued implicitly that women's economic dependence robbed them of any true capacity to give free and independent consent. And while many an American moralist could have been counted on to argue that if only virtuous wives would school their husbands in moral habits both could enjoy peace and prosperity, Rowson systematically punctured this delusion. Sarah's very "exemplary" behavior did nothing to alter her tragic fate. Setting the scene in England may have softened this critique of American republican ideals to some degree, but Rowson's message could not have been missed. Without the economic means to make truly free and independent decisions, women's marriage compacts could be only empty rituals, not effective enactments of the democratic social contract.

American commentators claimed repeatedly that the unfettered choice of marriage partner was both the base and summit of freedom. Rowson did not challenge this almost canonical American insistence on the connections of love, liberty, and virtue. Rather, she argued that without true economic independence, liberty was false and love could never be true. In one of the last letters she wrote before her death, Rowson's heroine Sarah complained of the "solicitude and anxiety" felt by a wife "obliged to apply to her husband for every shilling she expends." Indeed, Sarah theorized that "the state of total dependence in which women in general are, must tend to weaken that affection, that confidence, which should subsist between married persons."[66]

By setting her political and cultural critique of free choice in Britain rather than in the United States, Rowson held out the possibility of moral deliverance for America. For Rowson's English heroine, there could be no such thing as romantic love. Toward the end of the novel, Sarah exclaimed, "Connubial love! Domestic felicity! . . . Alas to me ye have been like fairy tales!" Yet Rowson took care to show that the love lacking in Britain could still be found in the United States.[67]

Although the United States, as much as Britain, had far to go in granting women true liberty by recognizing their economic rights, Rowson gave the United States an ethical edge by painting it as a place that genuinely did value love. Here again, the particularities of the plot speak volumes. Rowson described Sarah's "natural" brother, Frederic, as having "felt all the fraternal love for her, which a man of sense might be supposed to feel for a sister." Yet she eliminated him from most of the action of the novel by sending him off on repeated tours with the Royal Navy (in itself a suggestive echo of American rhetoric claiming that the Royal Navy regularly interrupted bonds of love). Then, in the book's final pages, Rowson had Frederic "return from America . . . [with] an amiable wife and lovely children." Sarah greeted his arrival with delight, writing to tell him, "you are returned to your native land, my dearest brother, and have brought with you love and peace." The Englishman had to import "love and peace" from the United States in the person of his American wife. In the politics of Rowson's novel, America was indeed the last bastion of love—and possibly of liberty as well.[68]

Yet Rowson's book was as much a warning and a challenge to her adopted land as it was any kind of celebration of American freedom. Back in 1791, when she was still a British subject and when she first published the most celebrated of all her novels, *Charlotte Temple*, Rowson had portrayed the United States as a place of debauchery and misery. By making the America of 1813 a land of love, Rowson essentially dared U.S. policymakers, and especially those Republican politicians so eager to claim their devotion to democratic equality, to make good on the country's boasts. Through its narrative, her book made America's national redemption, its rightful claim to stand at the forefront of the progress of freedom, contingent on improved economic rights for women.[69]

Shortly after Susannah Rowson published *The Exemplary Wife*, a fellow Boston schoolteacher, a single woman by the name of Sarah Savage, published a sort of mirror-image novella called *The Factory Girl* that effectively applied many of Rowson's ideas. As an educated New England woman, Savage was probably well aware of the contemporary literary scene. Whether or not she read Rowson is hard to know, but Savage's novella did neatly invert Rowson's plot, providing a companion narrative that illustrated how much different and how much better women's lives might look if they actually enjoyed the kind of economic independence Rowson advocated.[70]

The Savage story, published in 1814, presented the tale of Mary, an orphan girl who took up work in a textile mill in order to support herself and her ailing grandmother. Savage took care to portray Mary as a spotless model of moral rectitude who impressed all who met her, from church members to factory workers, with her piety and virtue. Entry into the world of work required no moral compromises of any kind.

At first the reader was led to expect the tale to unfold as a predictable parable of republican womanhood, albeit with the twist that it featured a working woman rather than one who remained at home. Over the course of the narrative, Mary met and became engaged to a fellow worker named William Raymond, an unsteady young man who was endeared to Mary by her friendship with his sister. The more time William spent exposed to Mary's shining example, the stronger his virtue seemed to become: "Mary would spend hours in talking with animated delight of the change in William's character and of their pleasing prospects of future comfort."[71]

Yet this novel then took an innovative political turn. For William, "the novelty of being good soon ceased" and his attention wandered to another young woman named Lucy. William proceeded to marry Lucy without any word to

Mary—a course of action that closely paralleled the early infatuation and quick dissipation of Rowson's character George Darnley. But the similarity of the two stories stopped there. Unlike Sarah, Mary had not married her undeserving suitor because no economic necessity had driven her to a hasty marriage decision. Having been jilted, Mary was quite able to support herself by continuing her factory work. And Mary "rejoiced that she had not been united to a man from whom she must have been estranged." While Mary did achieve a conventional happy ending as wife and mother by the end of the book, this transpired only after she had lived and worked independently for several more years, all the while waiting for a suitor of "piety and exemplary character" to present himself. With this ending, author Sarah Savage sent a clear message: only when women were allowed economic independence could their marriage contracts truly epitomize the American ideal of free consent (Figure 8).[72]

Meanwhile, Savage used the interlude before the appearance of a suitable husband for Mary to introduce a few quick plot twists that greatly amplified the political content of the novel. Mary quit factory life and opened a school in order to support the helpless wife and children of one of her cousins, a man named George Holden who was a sailor feared lost at sea. When George's wife died, Mary was left as the sole support of his four children. Once George finally returned, distraught to find "my poor wife is not here to greet me," he explained that he had been so long absent because he had been taken captive by pirates in Algiers. Here, then, virtual slavery in a tyrannical land cost a man his marriage as well as his physical freedom, while American liberty allowed Mary the economic freedom to support children even in the absence of their father. Savage's novel made the case that American liberty contrasted best with foreign tyranny when women's rights were recognized. In reality, few single American women of this period were or could be economically self-supporting, while no married women enjoyed economic equality. Yet Savage's novel tried to show the way to future progress.[73]

When U.S. polemicists seized on the issue of marriage choice as way to distinguish American freedom from British fetters, they claimed that loving and wedding a woman trained a man's passions toward patriotic love and loyalty. Glorifying love and marriage as the heart of nationalism, they counted on women to play the part of patriots and consent to become wives. Yet female writers like Rowson and Savage argued that love could not stand as the symbol of liberty if U.S. men could still exercise domestic tyranny. They drove home the point that the transubstantiation of conjugal bliss into national feeling

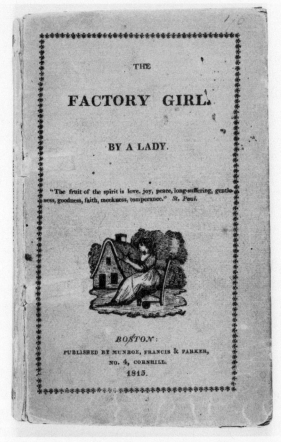

Figure 8. This portrait of Mary seated in front of her cottage visually emphasizes the author's decision to center her novel on a female heroine and her desire to place women at the forefront of society. Sarah Savage, *The Factory Girl* (Boston: Munroe, Francis, & Parker, 1815), title page, Collections of the American Antiquarian Society.

could occur only in marriages based on the free exchange of love, never in those contracted through economic coercion. If male writers hoped that they could encourage women to accept private happiness instead of public rights, leading female writers dashed these expectations. Not only did they insist that women should be compensated for their emotional labor with economic rights, but they also posed some politically damaging questions. Could wedding ceremonies serve as symbolic enactments of consent if not all parties to the marriage contract could act as free agents? Could feeling provide a basis for freedom even in the presence of legal and material constraints?

⤳∞↶

Writing an official report back to William Jones, secretary of the navy, at 4 PM on September 10, 1813, the day of the Battle of Lake Erie, Commodore Oliver Perry had little time to shape a story about the day's endeavors. He knew the encounter had been important strategically and that it could be even more significant politically. He did have the presence of mind to describe the battle as a "signal victory." But he could hardly be expected to craft an eloquent narrative in the first exhausted hours after the fight and he sent only a few scant lines to the capital. Three days later, however, Perry took the opportunity to paint the battle in vivid colors.[74]

In contrast to General William Hull who, deaf to the tenor of his times, claimed that enduring character mattered more than transient feeling, Perry deliberately portrayed himself as a man whose emotional sensitivities spurred him to action. Describing how he left the *Lawrence* for lost and jumped ship to the *Niagara* in a lengthy official letter sent to Washington on September 13, Perry confided that "it was with unspeakable pain that I saw, soon after I got on board the *Niagara*, the flag of the *Lawrence* come down; although I was perfectly sensible that she had been defended to the last." His self-presentation as a "sensible" sailor, pained by events yet powering through to victory, proved incredibly effective. His letter was immediately reprinted for public enjoyment in newspapers across the country and included in numerous documentary records of the war.[75]

Perry's depiction of his emotional departure from the *Lawrence* soon earned him popular acclaim as a man who "though [a] *warrior* had not ceased to *feel*." A New York newspaper editor, committed nationalist, and aspiring literary wit named Samuel Woodworth readied his press and self-published a poem in Perry's honor "written in the autumn of 1813" as soon as word of the victory arrived in the east. Woodworth's 108-page poem, "The Heroes of the Lake," presented Perry as classical hero at epic length.[76]

Perry won Woodworth's admiration by claiming the ability to maintain fine feelings even when fighting. In deliberate contrast to Federalist claims that warfare rose only from insensate anger, Woodworth promoted the idea that Perry's sensibilities prompted him to battle:

There are, [those] who say the hero never *feels*,
That Valour's rage *alone* his breast impels—

. . . .
Rashness the *deed*! The *sentiment* untrue!
And such, my country's hero! As not thou.

Perry was not impelled by rage, he was moved by emotion. The "country's hero" was a man of feeling.[77]

Woodworth invented one highly dramatic scene in which he pictured Perry aboard the *Lawrence* nearly brimming with tears while surveying "the marks of desolating war" along Erie's shores: "a tear-drop, stealing down that manly cheek / in pity shed, had wet the LAWRENCE' deck." In claiming that Perry cried inwardly, producing a kind of "inland flood," he argued that the commodore's ability to feel was what made him an effective fighter as well as an admirable leader.[78]

Woodworth capped his special claims for Perry's flights of feeling with a sustained poetic meditation on the uniquely American capacity for emotion. For Woodworth, the highest emotion was love and its best defenders were the heroes of Lake Erie. He closed the first book of his poem by declaring:

Let Europe boast her sons of iron mould:
Let Asia sell her sympathies for gold;
Afric may glory in her serpent guile,
And 'on for vengeance' . . . 'toil;'
Be it my country's richer glory far,
With deeds of love to blunt the rage of war.

Again and again, emotion was proclaimed to be the source of American exceptionalism. Alone of all the dwellers of the earth, said Woodworth, the people of the United States embodied the ideal of love.[79]

If Perry's victory gained symbolic luster by being cast as the romantic conquest of a sensitive man, it gained practical significance when credited with bringing new security to the lives of actual American couples across the Great Lakes region. When a 24-year-old New York poet named Benjamin Allen published his own epic verses, *Columbia's Naval Triumphs*, in 1813, he played with the theme of Indian menace to proclaim that Perry's victory over the British had saved American husbands from the anguish of seeing their wives killed by Indians. He wrote:

No more with mute, and suicide despair,
The tender partner sees his early fair,
Torn by the rude and iron son of death,
Who laughs, exulting, o'er her parting breath.
. . . .
Twas thou . . . gallant Perry! To whose arm 'twas giv'n
To sweep away the clouds of wo and night,
Which fill'd a tortur'd region with affright.

Evoking the poignancy of young love, of the "tender partner" and "his early fair," Allen drew a dramatic emotional picture. War was a romantic contest in which a husband's ability to protect his wife both was both the requirement and the reward of military service.[80]

From depictions of Commodore Perry as romantic hero to novelistic treatments of the United States as the land of connubial bliss, from broadside ballads featuring amorous American sailor-husbands to formal epic poems claiming that Europe, Asia, and Africa were all dead to love, U.S. liberty often seemed to positively depend on the matrimonial love of the country's men and women.

Yet in many cases, the reality of marriage as an institution failed to match the rhetoric that nationalists relied on. Not only was this true in the case of women—whose secondary status as citizens burdened them with unequal pressures in making marriage decisions—but it also factored importantly for perpetual noncitizens. For Native Americans, as for enslaved Africans and their descendants, the Christian monogamous marriages Americans so often boasted about conferred little tangible liberty.[81]

Indians who practiced other kinds of matrimony, from plural marriage to simple divorce, could expect rigid criticism for their failure to meet what Euro-Americans defined as a civilized standard of behavior. Yet in a period in which the Euro-American right to take over Indian lands rested in large part on the idea that only whites could tame the wilderness and promote civilization, any time Indians attempted to conform to U.S. marriage practices they risked being met with resentment.

A Boston broadside about a "Trial for Murder!" that occurred on December 18, 1813, the very same month in which senators made speeches about

Perry's romantic gallantry, exposes the kind of double standard faced even by Indians who attempted to conform to U.S. norms. The broadside related that an Indian man named Nicholas John Crevay, who lived in Malden, Massachusetts, near a nail factory, angered several white factory workers by beating them one by one in a wrestling match. Crevay's masterful show of strength intimidated his neighbors enough that they felt the need to unman him. How better to do it than by killing not only him but also his defenseless wife?[82]

The workers took their revenge by murdering Crevay and his wife, Sally, "by shooting them while in their beds with muskets loaded with balls and ten-penny nails." The poster specified that "the arms and bodies of these poor creatures were lacerated in a shocking manner; the condition of the woman rendered the deed still more deplorable." Anti-Indian rhetoric routinely claimed that Indians were savage because they attacked white married couples at home in their beds. Yet these Indians suffered just such an assault. The broadside poster, which strongly condemned these actions, dwelled repeatedly on the fact that the murders occurred in bed. Noting that the killers had received the death penalty, the poster declared: "it is a melancholy thing to see two such young men perish at the gallows, but it is not so dreadful as the idea of a man and wife being shot in their beds." To the poster's author, Crevay's marriage to his wife helped mark him as a man of worth and his life as worthy of preservation. To the two "young men" convicted of the murder (who appear to have been unmarried), Crevay's marriage was just one more unsettling mark of his competitive success.

One fundamental lesson of the story is that Indians threatened whites' sense of order just as much when they organized their lives according to Christian patterns as when they followed divergent practices. White self-image relied on the notion that U.S. marriages were a special sign of U.S. liberty. In the view of the murderers, the Indian Nicholas Crevay and his wife deserved to be defiled because they undermined white working-class dignity. In a sense, nothing imperiled U.S. patriotic ideals for marriage more than the possibility that Indians could attain them.

It would be easy to dismiss the Crevay killers' attitude as that of only the most economically marginal Americans. Yet these murders occurred in the same year that the genteel students of Middlebury College used their commencement exercises to "Dispute on the Question, *Would it be just for the U.S. to exterminate the Western Indians?*" The title of this debate was publicized in a commencement broadside poster along with the names of the two speakers arguing for and against the proposition. No specific mention was made of which of the two students advocated the position, nor of which side won. Still, one of the two debaters who argued this question, the Connecticut-born Horatio Conant, moved to Maumee, Ohio, shortly after his Middlebury graduation, where he married in 1817, raised four children with two successive wives, and finally died in 1879 after a long and prosperous life in what had only recently been Indian territory. Meanwhile, Conant's opponent, Samuel Nelson, actually served in the War of 1812 before eventually going on to two marriages of his own, many children, and a career capped by his appointment as a justice of the Supreme Court of the United States. Pro or con on the question of Indian "extermination," neither young man had any apparent qualms about the nation's western expansion.[83]

Given how much symbolic importance U.S. war supporters attached to marriage as a mark of American freedom, the wanton murder of an Indian man and woman living peaceably as husband and wife had explosive implications. The Boston poster asserted directly that the murder case had national significance too important to ignore. It declared that "the cause of humanity and the character of our country are too much concerned to cover over an atrocious deed of this nature." At a time when U.S. fighting men campaigned actively for control of Indian territory in part on the premise that Euro-Americans living in conventional marriages could best use the land, the murder of two Indians who conformed to that standard had the potential to expose American hypocrisy in harsh light. The only saving grace, from a political standpoint, was that the double murder did not go unpunished. Little wonder, then, that the trial and conviction merited the widest possible publication through the creation of a dramatic broadside poster.[84]

Even some of the most vocal proponents of linking love and liberty admitted the problems of treating marriage as a living model of American freedom. Consider, for example, an epilogue to the story of the Reverend Alexander McLeod, the New York minister whose forceful claim that "a man should be as free to choose his country as his wife" reached the eyes of former president Thomas Jefferson. McLeod's equation of marriage vows, that most basic of human contracts, and naturalization ceremonies advanced Jefferson's claim that voluntary national allegiance was a natural right. Yet although McLeod bolstered Jefferson's opinions on war, patriotism, and the right of expatriation, he differed sharply from Jefferson on another key issue: slavery. The New York minister was the author of only five other publications at the time that his

Scriptural View of War came out in 1815. The first of these was the pamphlet *Negro Slavery Unjustifiable*, published in 1802 when McLeod was only twenty-eight years old. McLeod's antislavery activism arose specifically from his concern for the way the institution of slavery interfered with another institution: marriage.[85]

While some proslavery apologists claimed that because American slaves could marry informally they enjoyed a crucial form of basic liberty, critics like McLeod exposed the absurdity of such assertions. Denouncing slavery as a "national evil," he called it "treason against Heaven—a conspiracy against the liberties of his subjects." He based this critique in part on the fact that "among the slaves . . . marriage is a slender tie. The master sells the husband at a distance from his wife and the mother is separated from her infant children. This is a common thing. It must destroy, in great measure, natural affection." If ability to choose one's spouse was a key enactment of liberty, if the natural affection of husbands and wives created the political feelings of patriotic love, then the denial of full marriage rights to the enslaved fundamentally undermined American claims to champion freedom. Disrespect for slave marriages deeply compromised the efforts of American propagandists to use the marriage issue as a means of dramatizing the evils of British impressment tactics. McLeod recognized this moral, political, and rhetorical problem directly. For him, the obvious solution was to put an end to slavery. For others, the inferior status of black and Indian marital ties proved politically convenient.[86]

When prowar writers praised marital desires as a wellspring of patriotism, they offered women as well as men an invitation to civic participation and obligation. In this way they greatly expanded the rolls of the nation's patriots. Yet at the same time, many in this latest generation of American "republicans" embraced a new and newly exclusionary standard of civic virtue. While any man could desire and any woman could reproduce, not all men and women could marry. In an era when the marriages of blacks and Indians enjoyed limited legal respect, white men's marriages enjoyed special status and their legitimate offspring privileged sanction.[87]

Proponents of the war appealed to national "ardor" in the effort to rouse the populace to support the war. Pamphleteers addressing themselves "To the Fair Daughters of the United States" boasted, "we have seen female energy rousing manly vigour, to assert the cause of their common country. . . . Exultingly we reflect on the sincere patriotism that pervades the breasts of the American fair . . . generous, ardent, and impassioned." Men and women alike were urged to aid the new nation's efforts. Yet when prowar writers urged the "fair daughters" of the United States to use "female energy" to "rous[e] manly vigor," they not only invited women as well as men to contribute to militarism but also insinuated through the use of the adjective "fair" that only *fair-skinned* white women had the ability to excite virtuous brands of ardor. Any emphasis on conjugal love over fraternal affection implicitly privileged the patriotism of the men and women whose romances could be most easily ratified.[88]

⌘

American war supporters of the 1812 era repeatedly turned to images of love and marriage to blur the realties of war and burnish the appeal of patriotism. Understood as a natural right, conjugal love formed the bedrock of freedom, one of the most basic benefits enjoyed by every American. Considered as a national duty, marital love became the molten fire of liberty, arousing ardor for service to country. Symbolic of loyalty, wedding rites became important rituals of consent, vivifying the American approach to citizenship and dramatizing democracy. Private lovers became public patriots and vice versa. Men and women alike contributed to the cause of the country and the success of the war with every loving word and look they exchanged, with every lusty verse they sang or romantic line they read.

Yet if romantic rhetoric failed to fully mask certain enduring limitations on American liberty, it proved still less effective as an actual element of military preparedness. When the time arrived to put the culture of ardor to test on the battlefield, U.S. men proved again and again to be better lovers than fighters. The desertions of the militia members who ceded control of the Niagara Valley back to the British just weeks after Perry's dramatic action on Lake Erie proved to be just such a case.

Even some of the war's most committed supporters were dismayed by the way the language of love seemed to be leaving people unprepared for the realities of war. Taking literally General George McClure's complaint that his men's only interest was in carrying their families to safety, the Philadelphia satirist and staunch member of the Democratic-Republican Party William Charles produced a cartoon that neatly captured the prevalence and problems of American ardor.

In an 1814 engraving, Charles portrayed "Soldiers on a March to Buffalo" accompanied by a grotesque coterie of women and children (Figure 9). In the Charles print, some lewd ladies hitched their skirts to their thighs and

Figure 9. William Charles, "Soldiers on a March to Buffalo" ([Philadelphia], c. 1814), Library Company of Philadelphia.

hauled soldiers on their shoulders, while others straddled leering fighters on their backs. The dubious status of the women in question was amplified by the remarks they made on the march, one vowing, "a Soldier I'll marry and carry his Wallet." Meanwhile, the priorities of the men were betrayed by the young recruit who fantasized about settling down with a sexually experienced older woman, saying, "if ever I marry, I'll marry a widow for fun."

Still, though Charles lampooned the idea that sexual lust was an effective prod to military ardor, he nevertheless left the door cracked to the idea that moral marital affections could ground patriotic love. Unlike McClure's flesh-and-blood militiamen, who struggled to save their families, Charles's pen and ink soldiers consorted only with women of ill repute. The possibility remained open, even in the eyes of satirists, that marital love could be the font of republican virtue and the spring of American freedom.

As demonstrated by the Fromentin-Tait debate in the Senate, American investment in the political culture of popular ardor was simply too great to dispense with. Rather than turn to a more sober analysis of the war's ethical and practical problems, supporters of the war retrenched their rhetoric and pushed even harder the idea that American patriots were enflamed by a unique brand of ardor. With bad news coming fast on the heels of the good, the best

Madison and the Republican-dominated Congress could do was trumpet the image of Perry as a successful romantic suitor even as they denied engaging in an effort to "light up a glare to dazzle the perception of the American people."

To the degree that the autumn of 1813 has been remembered for the triumph of American sailors over the celebrated tars of the Royal Navy and not for the desertions of militiamen in the Niagara Valley that foretold the ultimate failure of U.S designs on Canada, Senator Tait succeeded. By the logic of American ardor, romantic love fostered patriotic virtue, ensuring that U.S. soldiers and sailors would act from entirely different motives than those that drove agents of the tyrannical British Empire from America to India. Meanwhile, stories of lovelorn sailors torn from their wives and families helped entrench claims that the United States fought the War of 1812 for liberty on the seas, not for dominion over Indian lands.

Chapter 4

❧❧

Demographic Strategies and the Defeat of Tecumseh
MORAVIANTOWN, CANADA, OCTOBER 1813

The progress of war can be tracked on a map or tabulated in body counts. When General William Henry Harrison's troops confronted the British forces of General Henry Proctor on the River Thames in Upper Canada (present-day Ontario) on October 5, 1813, they made good on the promise of Perry's victory on Lake Erie. They consolidated late September gains made by retaking Detroit from the British and seizing the British Fort at Malden on the opposite bank of the Detroit River. And they eliminated the Shawnee leader Tecumseh, one of the staunchest Indian opponents of the United States. According to American and British formal statements on the war, the body count, while a convenient means of score keeping, was hardly the aim of the conflict. The purpose of any given battle was to take and hold ground. Once that work was done, any survivors of the conflict were to be treated not as prizes but simply as people in need of care. The eventual "parole" and return of prisoners from each side was a routine, even ritual, element in the aftermath of battle.[1]

General Proctor must have regarded it as an almost mundane matter, when, ten days after the battle, he sent a letter to General Harrison "requesting humane treatment for the prisoners" in the blandest formal terms. But Harrison did not respond in kind. Instead, he chose that moment to rail against the British for "horrible depredations against the peaceful inhabitants of our frontiers." On November 3, a month after the action, he penned a stirring letter of outrage that spared no literary flourish in accusing the British, in concert with their Indian allies, of violating every possible rule of humane conduct, most especially in the matter of prisoners.[2]

The centerpiece of General Harrison's gothic account of atrocities was the story of an expectant mother taken prisoner by British-allied Indians at Cold Creek near Lake Erie the previous spring. Captured "in an advanced state of pregnancy—she was immediately tomahawked, stripped naked, her womb ripped open, and the child taken out!" Despite the more than six hundred British prisoners taken in the Battle of Thames, for Harrison, the story of this single feticide was the casualty that counted most.[3]

Unlike Europeans and Euro-Americans, Indians regarded the taking of captives as one of the primary rewards of war. Sometimes tortured, sometimes adopted, people taken in battle played important symbolic and practical roles in Indian communities. And whereas Europeans and Euro-Americans claimed that only soldiers could ever be made prisoners of war, Indians deliberately included men and women, adults and children alike among their captives. With the British fighting alongside Indians, two very different approaches to war coincided in ways that the United States portrayed as deeply alarming. Urging the British not to accept aid from their Indian allies, Harrison charged them to "stop that dreadful effusion of innocent blood which proceeds from the employment of those savage monsters."[4]

From that day to this, Americans have usually assumed that it is armies that take and hold land. But General Harrison and his Indian antagonists were battling over a deeper truth. The ground is controlled by those who populate it.[5]

U.S. tradition said that access to more acreage allowed families to grow larger. But the reverse proposition also applied. The bigger the nation's population, the more numerous were the claimants available to seize the land through settlement. In an era when inhabitants of the United States sought eagerly to spread their habitations ever westward to the farthest horizon, Indians and Americans alike understood the key relationship between population expansion and territorial extension.[5]

Despite U.S. claims that women and children had no role to play in battles and should never be taken prisoner by Indians, all antagonists in the era of 1812 understood at some fundamental level that reproduction was a tool of war. Whether the Cold Creek maternal-fetal massacre really occurred—and General Harrison swore in the very last line of his letter, "I pledge myself for the truth of the above statement in relation to the murders committed by Indians"—or whether the story simply echoed the sort of penny-dreadful atrocity tales Americans had read recreationally for decades, the story illuminated a larger fact. In the competition for control of the North American continent, every body counted.[6]

And in the contest to frame the public attitudes toward the war effort, storytellers from military and political leaders down to amateur scribblers could be counted on to cater to the popular taste for captivity narratives. Harrison's letter to Proctor caused a sensation. Quickly leaked to the popular press, his charges were published and republished more than two dozen times in northeastern newspapers from Maine to what is now West Virginia in the three months after it was written. At that point, a year and a half into the war, when so many official communiqués had found print, Harrison had to have anticipated that his letter would reach the reading public. It was a mini literary masterpiece and he likely intended it as such.[7]

Captivity narratives have long been acknowledged as the first Anglophone American literary form. Part of what made such tales so quintessentially American, of course, were the ruggedly beautiful landscapes they evoked and the epic characters they channeled: noble, fearsome, doomed Indians versus intrepid, virtuous, and determined settlers. In these books, the murmuring hemlocks of the forest primeval rustle pages scented by leather and wood smoke. But more than that, captivity narratives were a genre that could be penned by anyone, from barely literate frontier folk to New England ministers, from literary giants like Henry Wadsworth Longfellow to military men and future presidents like William Henry Harrison.[8]

In the era of 1812, no bright line divided formal literature, political propaganda, and popular culture. Instead, all worked in tandem to advance American expansionism. Accounts of captivity focused public attention on the problem of population in gripping fashion. Such tales emphasized the power of ordinary people to advance the progress of the U.S. nation through the simple acts of migration and procreation. And they offered dire warnings to people who might imperil the body politic by allowing themselves or their families to be absorbed into the body of the enemy.

Combining alluring visions of fertile families and fecund land with repellent images of suffering, slavery, and death at enemy hands, captivity and atrocity tales aimed to create a kind of sensory flooding. Desire and disgust alternated in emotionally compelling ways. The best means of both achieving sensual delights and avoiding revolting horrors seemed to be support for war.[9]

More than a dozen book-length captivity narratives appeared from U.S. presses between 1812 and 1815, during the active years of the war. Taken together, these recreational literary productions advanced deadly serious goals. Some wartime publications presented new captivity tales, never before invented or recounted. Others reprinted much older works, repurposed with decidedly contemporary revisions. Most contained references to current events and many to William Henry Harrison, the man of the hour. Central to the drama of these narratives were questions of population and procreation. Should captive white women expect to face forced sex and marriage among Indians? Would white male prisoners acknowledge adoptive Indian mothers, take Indian wives, or sire Indian children? Could captive white women give birth or nurse infants in the wilderness? In these stories, the contest between white efforts at reproduction and Indian practices of adoption became the most primal of all struggles. Who would people the land and claim the continent?[10]

In the era of 1812, fireside fictional tales and formal military correspondence blurred together. Products of the financially lucrative literary marketplace and those of the politically profitable trade in public prints overlapped in ways that are worth pausing over. Far from innocent coincidence, this blending of genres allowed the power of narrative, the emotional compulsion of a tale well told, to reframe popular understandings of the war.

⌇∞⌇

The Cold Creek murders that Harrison etched in the minds of the U.S. public had been organized from the British Fort Malden, located near the mouth of the Detroit River, on the British side just north of Lake Erie. The United States claimed that British Regulars and their Indian allies packed the fort, just waiting for a chance to wreak havoc in the United States. Destroying Malden, therefore, had been a first crucial step in cementing Perry's gains at Erie and orchestrating Proctor's full defeat.[11]

Samuel R. Brown, the New York volunteer who fought in the Northwest campaign, gave firsthand testimony that as U.S. troops approached Malden that September, they fully expected to encounter "the red coats and [the] war whoop of the Indians." He was shocked, then, when "a group of well dressed ladies advanced to meet" them instead. This greeting committee of finely attired women had organized itself "to implore mercy and protection" from the U.S troops about to fire on the fort. Brown boasted that his commander "soon quieted their fears by assuring them we came not to make war on women and children but to protect them." War stories like this one reinforced the preferred U.S. narrative: civilized fighters never made war on women and children and virtuous U.S. soldiers could always be counted on to act in civilized fashion.[12]

If Brown claimed to be surprised by the presence of families at Fort Malden, he should not have been. In the era of 1812, the U.S. Army practice of segregating women and children applied only to active combat areas, not to military fortifications. Men commonly brought their wives with them on long campaigns, the better to provide the support services, like laundry and cooking, left unorganized by each country's war department. And during times of danger, civilian families living in the surrounding countryside crowded into forts for protection. Nonetheless, Brown relished the picture of Canadians so cowed by U.S. might that the men hid while the women advanced. And he cherished the chance to stage American civility by replaying his unit's courtly assurances to the "well dressed ladies" of Canada.

Brown apparently saw little irony in the fact that no such guarantees were given to Indian women. On the contrary, as General William Henry Harrison reported in an official letter to the War Department in October 1813, when Indian groups like the Ottawa and Chippewa left the British side and sued for peace in the wake of Proctor's defeat, U.S. commanders agreed to accept their overtures only "upon condition of their giving hostages for their fidelity and immediately joining us with all their warriors." This news was quickly reported in U.S. newspapers and Samuel Brown included the detail when he wrote his war memoirs.[13]

Brown betrayed no sense of contradiction when he relayed that the Indians "brought in their women and children and offered them as hostages for their good behavior." By U.S. definition, this did not amount to the "savage" practice of subjecting women and children to captivity, since neither torture nor adoption had any place in U.S. plans for their Indian prisoners. Nevertheless, the reverse situation was a sheer impossibility. Under no circumstances would the United States ever have been willing to send any of its women and children to live alone among Indian allies, no matter the assurances of favorable treatment. In a war in which Indians played for control of population, nothing could send a stronger signal of dominance than this U.S. demand to hold Indian women and children.[14]

When Samuel Brown returned from the war, these tales of U.S. soldiery made up his bread and butter. He included the two anecdotes about "ladies" of Malden and the "women" of the Indians in two different books he published in 1814, one called *Views of the Campaigns of the North-Western Army* and another shorter book of excerpts called *Views on Lake Erie*. The books sold well. *Views of the Campaigns* went through two editions in 1814 and a third in 1815. Brown built on the success of these books to offer *An Authentic History of the Second War for Independence* (among the first times the war was ever referred to with this title), then capped off his efforts with a final title in 1817, *The Western Gazetteer; or, Emigrant's Directory Containing a Geographical Description of the Western States and Territories*. For Brown, as for so many of his contemporaries, U.S. independence required Indian territory, while civilized treatment of Euro-American women and children necessitated protections to which Indian women and children were not entitled.[15]

Married U.S. women enjoyed only limited legal rights in the era of 1812, but on two points their privileges could not easily be denied: their right to choose a marriage partner and their right to expect their husbands' and nation's physical and legal protection. They could claim these benefits by virtue of their sex and by dint of their civility. Wartime reports that U.S. troops automatically extended gentle treatment to Euro-American women that they did not necessarily provide to Indian women helped to forefront the advantages associated with U.S. residency even for those not fully admitted to the citizenry. Meanwhile, captivity narratives that detailed Indian violations of "civilized" standards for feminine treatment helped make the case not only for the relatively fortunate position of U.S. women but also for the broad superiority of U.S. liberty.

Much of the drama in captivity tales swirled around the question of when and whether captives could be pressured or tempted into entering into sexual unions with Indians. In a war for population domination, consorting with the enemy posed grave risks. Captivity tales that titillated with opportunities for illicit love between the politically distinct populations of the United States and Indian nations courted great danger.

Since romantic ardor formed an important basis for U.S. patriotism, any diversion of desire onto Indians carried potentially disastrous consequences for the nation. From political rhetoric to broadside poems, romantic longing provided an important emotional prop to the U.S. war effort. Images of lusty and loving ties between brave soldiers and sailors and caring wives and sweethearts helped prime the U.S. public to stand behind the nation. Freemen and fair women who pledged their troth to each other likewise promised faithfulness to country. The combined possibility of personal debauchery and national treachery created sustained narrative tension.

As in the United States, Indian peoples adhered to the ideal of free personal choice in the matter of marriage. Consent, that most vaunted of U.S. romantic and political principles, had a firm place in Indian practice. While this fact might have been expected to reassure U.S. readers of captivity tales of their personal safety, it actually seems only to have increased concern. Because Indians respected the right of free choice in marriage, any liaisons that occurred in captivity could be regarded as consensual.

Efforts to dehumanize the enemy are characteristic of many wars. Yet the two-pronged literary initiatives of the War of 1812 present an especially instructive historical case. Writers of wartime captivity narratives sought to provoke patriotism by stirring domestic desires at the very same time that Indians were positioned to evoke maximum loathing. If emotions can be aroused to stimulate either avoidance or approach, prowar provocateurs needed to pay as much attention to eliciting feelings of repulsion toward Indians as they did in exciting feelings of attraction toward the United States.[16]

Captivity narratives published during the years of active conflict went to great lengths to deny the sexual attractiveness of Indian men and women. One surviving captive, a soldier called Elias Darnell, returned to Kentucky to publish his own and two of his fellow soldiers' narratives in an 1813 book he called *A Journal Containing an Accurate and Interesting Account of the Hardships, Sufferings, Battles, Defeat, and Captivity of Those Heroic Kentucky Volunteers and Regulars . . . Taken Captive by the Indians*. In these tales, Darnell and his comrades in arms recounted in great detail their visceral refusals to take Indian wives.[17]

Darnell reported that when an Indian man asked if he "had a squaw," the women responded to his response that he was unmarried by "twittering and grinning." He signaled his revulsion immediately by mocking the women in question as old and ugly: "one I observed had a great desire to express her joy by shewing her teeth, but the length of time she had lived in this world put it out of her power." Confiding in the reader his fear that he would be forced to undergo a "disagreeable adoption" he added that he dreaded a possibility "still more unpleasant": that he would "be united in the conjugal band to one of these swarthy, disgustful animals." The language of dehumanizing avoidance could not have been more direct.[18]

Darnell's cowriters expressed for themselves and evoked for readers the same high levels of inner prohibition. The second account Darnell attached to his own memoir, "The Narrative of Timothy Mallory," confirmed the prevalence of Indian efforts to integrate U.S. captives into Indian populations. Not only was he made an adoptive son, but his captors also "brought [him] a squaw, urging [him] to marry her." Mallory claimed that when he adamantly refused, "this they took as a great offence." Stories of prisoners who rebuffed Indians' offers of marriage even while caught in the grasp of captivity were a staple of wartime tales.[19]

Meanwhile, the third narrative Darnell included in his book took derogatory rhetoric to new heights. According to Darnell, John Davenport alleged that the Indians boasted to him, "*we make an Indian of you, and by'n by you have a squaw.*" Davenport asserted that he was presented to an old "squaw" and forced to call "the old witch" mother. He complained that he "thus had to become the adopted son of the most hideous of all animals that ever roamed over the forests of North America." But worse was still to come. "In a few days after, the Indians presented a squaw" for him to marry, a woman who he said "appeared to have little more of humanity than the form, [and was] equally as detestable as my MOTHER." Davenport refused this first proposed marriage, saying "I confess I never was so shocked at the thoughts of matrimony in my life! I told them, 'NO GOOD SQUAW.'" He rejected every other option, even though they pestered him with possible partners: "they then brought several more of those inhuman looking creatures, whom I understood were also candidates for conjugal felicity. . . . I frequently had to put them off." Hideous animals and inhuman creatures. The dissonance between this language of revulsion and the usual pleasurable emotions associated with courtship was deliberate. Davenport designed his memoir to "shock" his readers into the same feelings of deep distaste he claimed to experience.[20]

These men avoided marriage by timely escape. For women captives, the drama was heighted still further by claims that they could only avoid being forced into matrimony by murdering their captors. *An Affecting Narrative of the Captivity and Sufferings of Mrs. Mary Smith*, published in 1815, announced its pretensions to contemporary relevance by asserting, in an extended subtitle, that she had been "*Taken Prisoner in August Last (1814)*" and that she had only been "*Rescued from the Merciless Hands of the Savages by a Detached Party from the Brave Army of General Jackson.*" In reality, key sections of the Smith account were lifted verbatim from earlier eighteenth-century captivity narratives. There is little to suggest any authentic basis even for the apparently original sections of her account. Nor can we judge accurately whether the unknown author was actually male or female. But like the generic name "Mary Smith," the narrative itself typified a war-era genre with the story of a narrowly avoided forced marriage to an inhuman enemy.[21]

Smith claimed to have been captured along with her two teenaged daughters after the murder of her husband, to have witnessed their extensive torture and subsequent deaths, and to have been spared herself only because an "old Indian," sometimes described as an "old chief," wanted "to adopt her to supply the place of his squaw, who with his two children had been killed by the whites." Ridiculing the idea that a Euro-American marriage to an Indian could ever have been made on the basis of free consent, Smith was given only the "choice whether she would succede to the proposals of the old chief, or would rather resign herself up a victim to savage barbarity." Here the narrative switched from the third person to the first.[22]

Speaking directly to her readers, Smith exclaimed, "I heartily wished to be delivered from such merciless cannibals! But . . . I was reduced to the necessity of becoming a prostitute in order to prevent the most cruel death." Smith insisted that Indian "marriage" represented nothing more than prostitution, with wages to be paid in the form of her very life. She declared that "to gratify the wishes of these vile monsters, was as I conceived, although shocking in the extreme, not quite so bad as to endure their savage torture." Savage barbarians, merciless cannibals, and vile monsters. Smith killed the inhuman being that held her captive before their pact could be consummated. Readers, were, by implication, asked to do likewise, to act on the feelings of disgust that such writing invoked by supporting the war action.[23]

U.S. writers took the superiority of Christian marriage over the pagan Indian variety as an article of faith. In John Finch's 1812 novel *The Soldier's Orphan*, a minister told the book's heroine, Emily Thompson, that marriage served the country by encouraging reproduction. Finch's minister used deliberate care to distinguish Christian marriage from the savage kind. He lectured her that "in a savage state, instinct . . . was possibly the only . . . inducement to the union of the sexes." By "instinct," he apparently meant the sexual instinct because he continued, "in society, other objects are pursued than mere sensual indulgence." According to the minister, procreation for the good of the nation, not primitive personal pleasure, was the point of marital relations. Indians, however, pursued the simple "indulgence" of lust.[24]

Wartime captivity accounts painted Indians as sexually voracious beings with difficult-to-"gratify" wishes and hideous sexual demands. In many respects, these personal memoirs and sensational fictions simply echoed sober conventional wisdom of the day. Isaiah Thomas, for example, that enterprising Massachusetts printer and compiler of many a war-boosting broadside song and story, chose the year 1813 to reprint a book by one Jonathan Carver called *Travels Through the Interior Parts of North America in the Years 1766, 1767, and 1768* that had first been published in London in the eighteenth century. Carver's book evidently contained a patchwork of his own observations and unattributed quotations from earlier colonial accounts. Its most recent prior publication in the United States had been back in 1797. Nevertheless, Thomas suddenly saw a useful opportunity in bringing it to print again after a sixteen-year lapse. Carver reaffirmed what Americans had long claimed, that "Indian women in general are of an amorous temperature and before they are married are not in the less esteemed for the indulgence of their passions." Despite lingering traditions of "bundling" among U.S. courting couples that bedded down before marriage, Carver's discussion of the lax sexual standards of Indian women clearly suggested that white women did and should demonstrate greater purity.[25]

Carver did not portray Indian men as sexual fiends, taking care to assure readers that many were "remarkable for their moderation to . . . female prisoners" and that "women of great beauty . . . have lain by their sides without receiving any insult and their chastity has remained inviolate." Nevertheless, he reinforced the overall picture of Indian lewdness by affirming that "the Indians allow of polygamy and persons of every rank indulge themselves in this point. The chiefs in particular have a seralgio." Over and over again "Indian" stood for "indulgence."[26]

The War of 1812 prodded writers, editors, and publishers to harness the narrative power of captivity tales featuring female exploitation for political and military advantage. In 1815 *The Analectic Magazine*, published in Philadelphia, presented a story of U.S. wives and mothers oppressed by Indians in the *Narrative of Henry Bird*. First published in that periodical and then reprinted as a stand-alone pamphlet in Connecticut the same year, the very wordy full title of the book version conveyed both the work's factual improbability and its political efficacy: *The Narrative of Henry Bird, Who Was Carried Away by the Indians, After the Murder of His Whole Family in 1811, and Held in Captivity: His Sufferings, and Rescue from the Savage Monsters, in 1815, While Burning at the Stake.* Was there really a man who was captured but spared after his "whole family" was murdered by "savage monsters" only to be tortured nearly to death a full four years later and then rescued "while burning at the stake"? The story defies belief; a set of inconsistent dates within the text does little to shore up its credibility. Nevertheless, "Bird" knew the value of a story that helped define the war as a death struggle over population.[27]

The author of the Bird narrative set the action of the story directly in the neighborhood of General William Henry Harrison and centered it on the problem of Indian seizures of U.S. women. The tale began in 1811, when "after the battle of Tippecanoe," the Indians among whom Bird lived in Ohio "all disappeared, a signal that they meditated revenge." According to the story, members of the "Shawanese tribe" massacred eighteen of Bird's family and friends but spared him and took him into captivity, where he acted as a personal servant to an Indian called "Big Captain," fetching his water and lighting his pipe. At a mere eight pages long, the story had room to offer few details, making those that were included stand out all the more clearly. Bird built drama by relating that, while carrying water to the captain, "he sometimes met at the spring American white women, whose families mostly had been murdered and who were now slaves to the Shawanese." Bird's role was to play the heroic rescuer of these American women, carefully specified as "white," lest there be any confusion about who should be counted among "American women" and who were worthy objects of the efforts of a white male savior.[28]

As the tale unfolded, Bird recognized a woman he knew from his former home in Ohio. He asserted that "her story was that of hundreds of others, whose husbands and children had been surprised at their firesides and murdered." Women interrupted in the midst of performing their proper roles as white mothers lent the story narrative tension while the question of whether they would continue to serve as "slaves to the Shawanese" or be repatriated to labor as the wives and mothers of U.S. citizens provided the narrative suspense. "Bird promised should he ever live to escape, that he would give information of the fate of these unhappy women, whose number in this single village was fifty-eight."[29]

The narrative left some confusion about how and when Bird escaped, claiming both that he was tortured under the direction of the Shawnee Prophet, brother to Tecumseh, in February 1815 *and* that he had arrived safely in Washington, D.C., by the "6th day of January 1815" (Figure 10). But the moral of the story was clear: Bird's "object" in going to Washington "was

NARRATIVE

OF

HENRY BIRD,

Who was carried away by the Indians, after the murder of his whole family, in 1811, and held in Captivity :—His sufferings, and rescue from the Savage Monsters, in 1815, while burning at the stake.

PRINTED AT BRIDGEPORT, NOVEMBER 1815.

Figure 10. Note the crude image of a skeletal figure surrounded by upright tree limbs in the background, right, presumably a representation of Bird at the stake, while the bearded figure in the foreground shows Bird as he appeared when in full health and strength. Title Page, *The Narrative of Henry Bird*, Bridgeport, 1815, New York Public Library.

to fulfill his promise to the poor woman of the old Shawanese Town." The anonymous narrator concluded the tale by saying, "it is with pleasure I add, that he was admitted to an audience of the President, and that measures have been taken, by the proper authority, to recover these unfortunate captives, should they still be alive." As in so many other tales, Indians appeared not as people, but as "savage monsters," with claims that they enslaved white women offered as special proof of their depravity. Bird modeled the proper response to the gut feelings of disgust they generated: armed aggression organized from Washington.[30]

The happiest possible ending envisioned in wartime captivity tales came with the marriage of a returning captive and another Euro-American. When an often-excerpted narrative first published in Britain in the 1750s, *The Life and Adventures of Peter Williamson*, was retooled for the release of an expanded U.S. edition in 1807, the inclusion of the story of a successful "white wedding" between a rescued captive named Miss Long and her redeemer, Captain Crawford (omitted from earlier American editions), marked the most important change.[31]

In the basic narrative featured in all the editions from the 1750s forward, Peter Williamson claimed to have been living "on the frontiers of the province of Philadelphia," married to "a wealthy planters daughter," when, alone in the house one day, he was "surprised with [the] fearful war-whoop . . . of merciless monsters." Following this announcement, Williamson heaved forth twenty pages of extraordinarily graphic atrocity tales, one flowing into the next in a foul torrent. In one, a man's "unhappy family, consisting of a wife and five small children [was] . . . scalped and robbed without remorse" by Indians. In another, almost identically worded account, "they scalped the unhappy wife and children." In that case Williamson added the detail that "when they had murdered the poor woman, they acted with her in such a brutal manner as decency will not permit me to mention; and this even before the unhappy husband." The implication that this wife's corpse was sexually defiled took the erotic tension of atrocity tales to absurdist heights, purposefully arousing readers to bay for the blood of Indians.[32]

Through it all, Williamson thought of his own wife, who he "feared would . . . become another prey to their fury." She did not. Instead, she simply succumbed to an early death, "occasioned by her grief and fears of another visit from the inhuman monsters." Adding to the sense of unreality of this litany of horror, Williamson offered no other comment on her loss beyond that it was "unwelcome news." In fact, the reader was left to conclude that his wife had simply done her female duty by dying during his captivity. In this way, she avoided becoming involved with another white man (on the presumption that she was widowed) or, worse still, being "violated" by an Indian. Instead, she chastely faded away, preserving her own virtue and Williamson's masculinity. Patriotic white women did *not* have to avoid sexuality altogether; but their sole focus was to be on forming a fruitful and faithful relationship with a white husband.[33]

Until 1807, American editions of Williamson's narrative ended on the off-note of his wife's death. Like a number of other captivity narratives of the 1812 era, this one had first been produced in the midst of the French and Indian War as a means of discrediting French-allied Indians. But in 1807, a full fifteen years after Williamson's death, someone decided to give the story some strategic tweaking. With U.S.-Indian tensions building up, the story needed only a little adjusting to serve well as a vehicle for discrediting British-allied Indians. The New York and Connecticut publishers who resurrected the story for the 1807, 1809, and two wartime 1813 editions decided that a more celebratory climax was in order. The expanded version restored a key story-within-the-story that had appeared in the English original of Williamson's narrative, but that had been omitted in all American editions before 1807. In this episode, Williamson regaled the reader with one last tale of a family scalping, but this time the story ended with the successful Euro-American marriage of a repatriated U.S. woman.[34]

No sooner did Peter Williamson return from captivity, in the 1807-1809-1813 version, than he heard bad news about a family of his acquaintance, the Longs. Indians "plundered and massacred J. Long's family" and took his daughter, "Miss Long," and her brother captive. Miss Long, it emerged, was engaged to be married to one Captain James Crawford, who appealed to "Williamson" to aid him "to go in quest of the villains" along with a party of one hundred volunteers.[35]

The men quickly found Miss Long, "naked and tied to a tree." Williamson claimed that they had arrived too late to save the brother and just in the nick of time for Miss Long, as "the next day was to have seen her perish . . . after suffering worse than even such a terrible death, the satisfying these diabolical miscreants in their brutal lust." Crawford and Williamson were able to "extirpate this crew of devils" and "in about a fortnight afterwards . . . Miss Long got to church with her deliverer, and they became as happy a pair, as any to be found in that part of the world." The story ended in victory because although J. Long, his wife, and their whole household were killed, although his son and heir died, his daughter lived.[36]

Crucially, even in the 1757 British edition that *did* include the Long-Crawford wedding story, the Crawfords were not described as a "happy pair." Instead, that account related that at the wedding "no riotous or noisy Mirth was allowed, the young Lady, as we may well imagine, being still under great Affliction." The American revisions of 1807–1813, then, literally created a happy ending that had not been there before.[37]

Though threatened with rape, Miss Long survived as a virgin who could then go on to a church marriage with a white man. All the drama of the tale revolved around the right of access to Miss Long's reproductive capacity, whether it would be appropriated by Indians or reserved for whites. A "Christian marriage," of course, meant procreation; the happy ending for Captain Crawford and Miss Long brought excellent news for a country at war. Just as he lived to fight another day, she survived to bear children for the nation.[38]

Appending the Long-Crawford story to the Williamson narrative apportioned readers an emotional double dose. The feelings of revulsion provoked by Williamson's generous helping of atrocity tales primed people to support action against Indians. The sensations of delight and desire at the imagined wedding of Long and Crawford stirred a pride that shaded easily into patriotism. Together, both whet the appetite for war.

⌒∞⌒

Captivity tales captured the public attention so effectively that General Harrison made them the centerpiece of his critique of British conduct. The full text of his letter to General Proctor mentioned more than a dozen different murders of child captives by Indians. His communiqué to the opposing commander warned the British that the "effect of their barbarities will not be confined to the present generation. Ages yet to come will feel the deep rooted hatred and enmity which they must produce between the two nations." If stories of marital disruption through captivity had proved popular, Indian atrocity tales focused on the mistreatment of children, from infanticide to captive prisoner adoption, appeared riveting. As it turned out, General Harrison needed every rhetorical weapon at his disposal.[39]

Though General Harrison tried to paint British and Indian actions against American women and children as uniquely cruel and unprecedented, his antagonists easily countered that American war efforts fell into similar patterns. In fact, on December 10, 1814, just two months after Harrison defeated Proctor on the Thames, American forces burned the Canadian town of Newark to the ground, an action that destroyed military installations and ordinary houses alike. When the British commander in the region, General George Prevost, issued an open proclamation condemning the action, American newspapers reprinted it. He deplored the fact "that in the enlightened era of the 19th century, and in the inclemency of a Canadian winter, the troops of a nation calling itself civilized and Christian, had wantonly and without the shadow of a pretext, forced 400 helpless women and children to quit their dwellings, and to be mournful spectators of the conflagration and total destruction of all that belonged to them." Prevost implied that the United States had no rightful claim to modernity, Christianity, or civility. The nation had forfeited this claim by subjecting "400 helpless women and children" to near certain death by exposure. The British general's charges were duly reported in newspapers from Lexington, Kentucky, to Windsor, Vermont.[40]

Still more damaging than the British critique itself were the confirmations added by some war opponents within the United States. When the *Boston Gazette* reprinted this speech, it offered a full endorsement of the contents. The editors affirmed that "the avowals in this proclamation are corroborated by facts, within our own knowledge." Worst of all, the editors of the *Boston Gazette* opined, "the arguments which are adduced in their support are expressed in language not more indignant than what becomes the spirit of a soldier, who is conscious of the rectitude of his cause, and the sacred trust deposited in his hands." In such a climate of debate, captivity tales documenting Indian depredations versus U.S resilience carried urgent political value as well as narrative power.[41]

Susannah Willard Johnson was twenty-four years old when as a nine-months-pregnant New Hampshire farm wife, she was captured by Indians along with her husband and marched off to Canada. The year was 1754 and the British Empire was at war with the French and their Indian allies. According to the first-person account credited to Johnson and published in 1796, she struggled mightily through the dark and brambly woods before lying down by the banks of a rocky stream and giving birth to a daughter, with no one but her husband to assist her. They named the baby Captive. In time, the family made its way back to New Hampshire and the "warm sunshine" of Anglo-American rule. Ultimately, Susannah Johnson died a proud American in 1810, at the ripe old age of eighty, having seen her account reprinted in a second edition in 1807. Curiously, however, this was *not* the end of her story.[42]

In 1814, four years *after* Susannah Willard Johnson's death and in the midst of another transatlantic conflict with continental implications, a new edition of her tale, *A Narrative of the Captivity of Mrs. Johnson*, appeared interlaced "with sundry other interesting articles." In this version, expanded by over thirty pages of new material, Johnson was still the only acknowledged author. It seems clear, however, that the book was literally ghost written. In any case, for the wartime 1814 edition "Johnson" introduced her popular account of giving birth while under Indian captivity with a new and explicit claim that population determined the fortune of nations.[43]

For any reader who doubted that Johnson's reproductive feat in the wilderness was the most important event of her captivity tale (that anecdote, after all, had taken up only a few pages of the original book), the new edition put procreation front and center. The 1814 introduction started off by providing an almost biblical recital of the generations of the Willard family, beginning with Susannah's great-grandfather, who had two sons, and continuing to her grandfather, who had nine sons, including her father (named Moses!), who was purported to have had twelve children and eventually "ninety-two grand-children, one hundred and twenty-three great grand-children and four great-great-grand-children." If Christianity's sacred text told people to be fruitful and multiply, then Johnson's maternal accomplishments were religious acts. They were also presented as national achievements.[44]

This new genealogical material was capped off with deliberate comments on population: "It is an old maxim, that after a man is in possession of a small independent property, it is easy for him to acquire a great fortune; just so with countries; possess them of a few inhabitants, and let those be unmolested by Indians and enemies, the land will soon swarm with inhabitants." In the somewhat circular reasoning of this analysis, landed property brought a man fortune, while plentiful inhabitants brought prosperity to countries. Land was good for people and people were good for the land. Only the molestations of "Indians and enemies" might interrupt this fruitful cycle.[45]

Together, Johnson's biblical-style recounting of the hundreds of children begotten by generations of patriarchs and her assertions that only a land "unmolested by Indians" could flourish also suggested that white people were divinely directed to populate the lands of America. This was a common attitude in the United States at the time. In New London, Connecticut, in 1812, for example, the townspeople who gathered on July 4 to celebrate the anniversary of American Independence appropriated a psalm for contemporary needs. They prayed:

O Lord, our Fathers oft have told,
    In our attentive ears,
Thy wonders in their days perform'd,
    And elder times than theirs;
How thou to plant them here didst drive
    The heathen from this land,
Dispeopled by repeated strokes
    Of thy avenging hand.
    Whose succor they implor'd;
Thy presence with the chosen race,
    Who thy great name ador'd.

War supporters cast the confrontation with Britain as the continuation of a divine mission to populate North America with European-descended peoples, purportedly the "chosen race" of God. If heathen Indians were "dispeopled" in the course of U.S. progress, this was only what God would have wanted, indeed what God himself had wrought with his "avenging hand." This use of the psalm pleased people so much that an enterprising printer prepared a broadside edition of this version of the psalm, the better for purchasers to display and enjoy.[46]

The nationalist implications of a July 4 recitation of a psalm praising God for enabling his chosen race to dispeople heathens are almost impossible to miss, even a couple of hundred years after the fact. Less obviously, but no less certainly, such thinking permeated many productions of popular culture that we might not initially identify as having geopolitical implications. When an author by the name of George Fowler convinced a Baltimore printer to publish and sell a story he called *A Flight to the Moon; or, The Vision of Randalthus* in 1813, he counted on his contemporary readers to recognize what many later ones have not. His fanciful description of a mystical trip to the moon was a conduit for political commentary.[47]

Fowler's narrator, Randalthus, fell asleep beneath a full moon and dreamed that he was granted the ability to fly there. He spent his time in outer space lecturing the moon-dwelling "Lunarians" at length about conditions on earth. In the midst of the meandering and nearly plotless piece of pedantry that Fowler produced, population concerns took a prominent place. Randalthus remarked early to his lunar audience that "some regions of the earth support a numerous population; in other tracts a human footprint scarcely ever pressed." This was not an innocuous observation. Rather, it was a prelude to arguing that "some parts" of the earth were "fruitful," others "barren" because some "some regions display all the luxuriance of human cultivation; others remain in the wild original state of nature." From a celestial perspective, only civilization could bring land under proper cultivation and allow a desirable maximization of population.[48]

Anyone who persevered to page 144 of the narrative would be rewarded by Fowler's explicit comments on the problems of the War of 1812, then in progress. Randalthus revealed to the Lunarians that to the "eternal disgrace" of the British, they were plunging the world into "a scene of slaughter and rapine." *A Flight to the Moon* became an all too terrestrial vehicle for Fowler to advance ideas and political positions supportive of the American war effort and critical of Indians and British alike.[49]

As the War of 1812 heated up and the conflict with Britain and British-allied Indians intensified, links between reproduction and war gave ordinary Americans a direct stake in events. The commonplace choice to raise a family became fraught with political and military meaning. In a very real sense, women's work in childbed mattered as much as men's efforts on the battlefield. Susannah Willard Johnson rose from the grave to assert this very point.[50]

In a plot twist new to the 1814 edition of *A Narrative of the Captivity of Mrs. Johnson*, the author recounted in riveting (if somewhat improbable) detail how, in 1797, forty-three years after being captured and at the advanced age of sixty-seven, she had trudged again—voluntarily this time—on a long march to return to the very place of her travail to "find the spot of ground where my daughter was born." She did not find it on that trip, but searched again in 1798 and 1799 until she was sure she had located it. (Why these deeply important return journeys had received no mention in the 1807 version of her narrative, the last published in her lifetime, was never explained.) Once "Johnson" had found "the identical spot of ground,

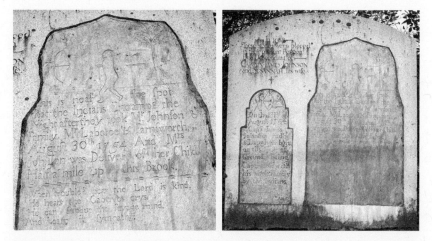

Figure 11. The Susannah Willard Johnson monuments, now known as the "Indian Stones," were mounted in granite and placed by the roadside in Reading, Vt., at the turn of the twentieth century, where they can still be seen today. "Indian Stones," Reading, Vt. Photo: Jay Klancnik.

even within a few feet," by recognizing the exact rocks she had lain among as she labored, she "proposed to have a monument erected on the spot." Military monuments to commemorate major moments of the War of 1812 now grace forts and battlefields across the country. But "Johnson's" decision to have a "monument . . . erected on the spot of ground where the child was born" must be unique (Figure 11).[51]

Nothing could better symbolize the equivalence that U.S. war-supporters of the 1812 era accorded to warfare and reproduction than a military-style monument erected to commemorate a birth in captivity. Population increases brought a source of national strength, an element of military strategy, and an essential means of wresting territory away from Indians. The creation of a monument honoring Susannah Willard Johnson for her maternity did more than make her the protagonist of a captivity tale. It offered her up as a national hero. "Johnson's" 1814 *Narrative* treated readers to the exact inscription featured on the monument: "On the 31st of August, A.D. 1754, Capt. James Johnson had a daughter born on this spot of ground; being captivated with his whole family by the Indians." While her name was omitted here, it was included on a smaller stone guidepost pointing the way up the stream. That marker included the information that

"Mrs. Johnson was delivered of her child half a mile up this brook." In the era of 1812, demonstrating love of country required giving birth as much as giving battle.[52]

Fertile women figured as the natural companions of virile male warriors in many literary works of the day. In fact, Johnson's maternal monument shared many features with a purely fictional marker featured in a novel published in New York in 1812, *The Soldier's Orphan*. A sentimental tale of a beautiful, virtuous, and cultured young orphan by the name of Emily Thompson, *The Soldier's Orphan* followed Emily's trials as she came of age and sought to find a suitable marriage partner. It featured a dramatic climax in which Emily and her new husband erected a monument to the memory of her parents: to her father, George Thompson, who died fighting the British in the American Revolution on the last day of 1775 and to her mother, also named Emily, who died while giving birth to her one day later, on January 1, 1776.[53]

This was no ordinary monument. "A quadrangle at its base," with "a pedestal three feet high, ornamented at its sides," the monument merited five pages of description. Most significant were the monument's inscriptions. The first was:

> To the memory of George Thompson . . . Who, fir'd with love of glory
> And the liberty of his country . . . Lived . . . not for himself
> But for his country.

The second inscription was:

> To Emily . . . who equaled her husband's fortitude. . . . For her country she was willing
> To bear every hardship:
> In giving the world a daughter
> Like herself
> She died.

Husband and wife were celebrated equally for service to country, he for serving as a soldier, she for bearing a child. According to the pronatalist ideas of the 1812 era, this was a natural equivalence. The nation needed men to win the land and women to populate it.[54]

The Soldier's Orphan addressed the patriotic importance of reproduction explicitly. Emily and her future husband, Mr. Center, were guided in their courtship by a minister named Mr. Young. On one occasion, Mr. Young advised them, "let us briefly consider the motives, the designs of matrimony." He argued that a "laudable motive to marry" was the creation of new offspring to serve the nation. He told them: "it is not only our duty to do all the good we can to ourselves, but to present our country, which cannot long enjoy our personal services, those who will at last fill our places with respectability." People were a national resource and marriage, the first step for "respectable" reproduction, was a patriotic duty.[55]

In this novel, as in *A Flight to the Moon*, the land itself desired habitation and cultivation by Euro-Americans. The minister continued, "in a country where . . . an extensive territory requires a large increase of population to clear up its forests, and extend the blessings of agriculture and the arts, to its distant bounds, what greater legacy can a man bequeath his native land, than a rising family of freemen?" The idea that Indians were to be displaced from *their* native ground hardly merited attention in light of the importance of extending the "blessings" of civilization to "distant grounds." Still, it was perfectly clear that procreation directly advanced the aggressive geographic expansion of the nation. In fact, Mr. Young told Emily and Center, by raising a "family of freemen . . . to subdue [the] unbroken soil," married couples could "lay open to the state . . . immense resources of wealth and greatness."[56]

The Captivity of Mrs. Johnson conveyed an equally clear message about the links between extensive family lineages and an enhanced national power. In the 1814 edition, the author added to the story of her prior anniversary trips to Captive's place of birth one last odyssey tale that reasserted the relationship between fertility and freedom. The narrator stated that once more, "in June 1808, I for the last time visited the place where almost fifty-four years before I had experienced the keenest sorrow . . . I was accompanied by . . . my daughter, E. Captive." Leaving aside the suspicion that this could not easily have occurred, that Johnson could never have made such a rugged journey at the age of seventy-eight and a mere two years before her death, it remains fascinating that Captive's birthplace became ground zero for the 1814 version of the Johnson narrative, the place purportedly visited over and over again in 1754, 1797, 1798, 1799, and 1808.[57]

The last image "Johnson" wished to convey was that of herself and her grown daughter regaling themselves beside waters that had once offered only bitter draught. Johnson struggled to describe how "wildly different" the place of Captive's birth was fifty-four years later. "It was then a dreary wilderness; now the wilderness was turned into fruitful fields, dressed in verdure, which richly repaid the labors of the husbandman." Agriculture had improved the land, while Euro-Americans had replaced the former population: "it was then a dwelling for savages and wild beasts of the forest; now a habitation of good citizens." The final piece of the U.S. rationale for its territorial aggression lay with the ideal of good citizenship.[58]

The United States vowed to claim land for liberty and to settle it with—in the words of *Soldier's Orphan* author John Finch—rising families of freemen. No matter how the land was taken, its occupation by free citizens made it free. Only the children of marriage unions between white male citizens and their wives could effect this population transformation. There was nothing—short of full assimilation into Christian monogamous marriages and the adoption of settled agriculture under U.S. jurisdiction—that any Indian could do to add to the body of free citizens and that in itself proved a politically satisfactory fact.

Did women themselves embrace this pronatalist vision? Did Susannah Willard Johnson have any part in writing the words published posthumously in her name? We do not know for sure who produced these ideas, but it is abundantly clear who was supposed to consume them. Again and again the "Johnson" of 1814 addressed herself to an explicitly female intended audience. She appealed to mothers to envision the wonderful changes accomplished by white settlers in the days since she had been taken captive, saying, "the contrast is too great for pen to describe. My female readers, who are mothers, may in some degree conceive of it." Though women could not vote for or against the war and the politicians who promoted it, mothers supposedly had special emotional access to Johnson's experiences and to her celebration of U.S. control of the land.[59]

Detailing the inscription on the "Mrs. Johnson" guidepost stone, the 1814 edition of the *Narrative* quoted a poem directed especially to mothers that said:

> If mothers e'er should wander here,
> They'll drop a sympathetic tear
> For her, who in the howling wild,
> Was safe deliver'd of a child.

The only trouble is, as anyone able to inspect the stone tablet itself could easily see, this poem does *not* appear anywhere on either of the Johnson stones (see, again, Figure 11). Indeed, the guidepost stone is much too small to contain these lines. What could account for such a discrepancy?[60]

Traditionally, Susannah Willard Johnson herself has been credited with having the monument created. Yet the *Narrative* does not claim this explicitly. It coyly employs the passive voice when describing the spot "where is erected a monument." This hedge, together with the significant inconsistency between the actual inscription on the surviving monument and the more extensive text quoted in the *Narrative*, hints that the monument may actually have been raised only after Johnson's death. This possibility is, of course, also supported by the odd fact that Johnson made no mention of this seemingly profound memorial in 1807, in the last version of the *Narrative* published in her lifetime, despite the strong implication in the 1814 edition that the monument had been erected in 1799.[61]

Perhaps Johnson herself truly did erect the monument before her death, but the editor or publisher of the 1814 edition—bringing the book to print again in the midst of the war—decided that its message needed to be amplified with the addition of verses addressed directly to mothers. Or perhaps the monument began as a complete fabrication by the 1814 editor and someone later came along and created an approximation of the stones described in the book as a way to try to bring fiction to life. If the monument *was* created sometime after Johnson's death in 1810, this timing would tie the physical monument, like the literary description of its existence, all the more closely to the War of 1812.[62]

No matter the true story behind the monument, the obvious intention of the verses addressed to mothers was to invite female readers to enter emotionally into the drama of the Johnson story. A military-style monument inscribed with a poem for mothers clearly aimed to convey that giving birth was a noble act for the nation as much as a duty women owed to their own families. Each woman could enjoy the idea that her ordinary maternal efforts made her a patriotic heroine.[63]

Bathed in the imagined joy of a safely delivered new baby, dropping sympathetic tears for the captive mother and child, who could pause for dry calculations of the justice of invading Indian territory? Whether trumpeting the spread of Christianity, civility, or liberty, U.S. expansionists betrayed few qualms of any kind about their right to seize and hold Indian lands. The question was not whether to do so, but how. In the era of 1812, the answer involved women as much as men, bearing children as well as bearing arms.

⟡

Flags and drums. Precision rows of marching men in uniform. Generals directing organized flanks of soldiers from on horseback. In the United States as in Britain, all insisted that there was such a thing as civilized war. Some means of killing were more righteous than others. Some objects of slaughter made deserving targets, while others should be immune from assault. According to the formal logic of U.S. war, only men who had volunteered for combat and were outfitted in military garb should ever be involved in armed battles. Women and children must always be shielded from sight of steel and smell of gun smoke.

Never mind that no sooner did U.S. soldiers quit the field than U.S. women and children arrived to help settle homesteads and populate the ground. Never mind that Indians well understood this process and expressed their dismay with symbolically laden acts such as feticide. In the eyes of the United States, the mere fact that Indians involved women and children in their mode of war conveniently invalidated any other moral claim they might assert to the lands of North America.

As the United States and Britain squared off, each enjoyed lobbing charges of incivility against the other (Figure 12). Since many Americans, even after the Revolution, remained in thrall to the idea that Britain epitomized civilized ideals, British critiques like General Prevost's claim that American soldiers "wantonly" endangered Canadian women and children could sting sharply. Yet such accusations could also serve as a useful rallying point, and General William Henry Harrison understood this well.[64]

The final flourish of General Harrison's reply to General Proctor in November in 1813 came with a pointed rebuke of British efforts to impute incivility to the United States. Harrison seethed, "I have never heard a single excuse for the employment of the savages by your government, unless we can credit the story of some British officer having dared to assert that 'as we employed the Kentuckians you had a right to make use of the Indians.'" Harrison boasted that his soldiers displayed more civility in their treatment of British soldier-prisoners than Proctor had any reason to imagine or right to expect. Feigning disbelief that a Briton would dare to accuse Kentucky militiamen of behaving like Indian fighters, he asserted, "if such injurious

Figure 12. Note the sarcastic references to the British as "humane" and to Indians as "worthy allies." Again and again, U.S. commentators tried to use the British association with Indians as a means of critiquing their claims to uphold liberty and civility. "A Scene on the FRONTIERS as Practiced by the HUMANE BRITISH and their WORTHY ALLIES," William Charles, [Philadelphia], c. 1813, Collections of the American Antiquarian Society.

sentiments have really prevailed, to the prejudice of a brave, well informed, and virtuous people, it will be removed by the representations of your officers who were lately taken upon the river Thames." Harrison vouched that British prisoners would have nothing but humane treatment to report.[65]

Kentuckians were virtuous, brave, and so gentle and refined in their behavior that "far from offering any violence to the persons of their prisoners, *these savages* would not permit a word to escape them which was calculated to wound or insult their feelings." Harrison pointedly reused the word "savages" to underscore the absurdity of associating the word with members of the United States. Every U.S. victory was ipso facto a triumph of civility and liberty over Indian savagery and British tyranny. He painted his victory primarily as a strike against captive takers and portrayed continuing British-Indian alliances as the main menace to American freedom.[66]

Harrison sought to paint Indian captivity practices as the sole interruption in this triumphal story of progress. Official and popular celebrations of Harrison's victory alike focused on its effect on frontier settlements and the added security it would provide to families living there. U.S. chroniclers rejoiced that Harrison's success was complete. One man, a prolific author named Michael Smith who published a remarkable print run of twenty-five hundred copies of a book of travel and war reportage in 1814, cheered that "in this memorable victory, which was of infinite benefit to the inhabitants of an extensive frontier, the celebrated warrior *Tecumseh*, was killed." The footnote Smith attached to this statement quoted an official proclamation by the mayor of Philadelphia that "by this victory, the wives, maids, and infants on our frontiers will be preserved from British and Indian scalping knives and tomahawks." From Michigan to Kentucky to Pennsylvania, the image of women and children suffering at the hands of Indians held great rhetorical power.[67]

If the British said the Kentuckians were savage in their prosecution of the war, Kentucky volunteers themselves argued that British tolerance for Indian attacks on women and children proved that they were the ones who should be blamed for perversion. U.S. soldiers taken captive on the River Raisin in the early days of Harrison's efforts to retake Detroit helped stoke prevailing national prejudices by penning a brand new set of captivity tales, published in Kentucky in 1813, recounting their experiences. These were none other than the stories of hideous would-be Indian wives compiled by Elias Darnell, author and editor of the 1813 *Journal Containing an Accurate and Interesting Account*. Darnell capped off his efforts by addressing the issue of competitive civility directly.

The climax of Darnell's tale came when, finally making his way toward home from Canada after months of Indian captivity and fifty pages of narrative, he and a fellow parolee sheltered for the night in the home of an old Canadian farmer. He reported in detail a debate with the farmer, a "Tory General," who had fled the United States for Canada after the British loss in the American Revolution. When the Canadian old man insulted the U.S. soldiers by calling them "bloody dogs," Darnell proudly reported their sarcastic retort: "You might say so if we had hired the savages *to kill* your women and children." Exactly as their commanding general, William Henry Harrison, would assert in his formal correspondence at the end of that same year, these soldiers claimed the British deserved extra opprobrium for allowing Indians to attack families.[68]

Darnell supplied the old Canadian's rejoinder—"the *British* had never *hired* the *Indians* to kill women and children, they were too *humane* a people to *do so*."—the better to allow readers to appreciate the blunt force of the American reply. Darnell's fellow parolee said: "Yes ... they shewed humanity ... when they paid the Indians for infants' scalps that were taken out of their mothers' wombs;—they call themselves Christians—and when the Indians sent home to them scalps from the unborn infant to the grey hairs in bales, like goods." Infants torn from the womb, scalps turned into trade goods. Nothing more fully symbolized Americans' mortal fears—nor more fully realized their moral hopes of turning the tables on their opponents.[69]

According to Darnell's tale, "a young woman who was in the house" then brought the hidden motives of the United States out into the open with an accusation of her own. She said, he recalled, "we were only coming to drive them off their lands." When Darnell's friend tried to reassure her that "'we were only coming to set them *free*, so that these lands might be their OWN not King George's.'—She said, 'the Americans that were killed at Queenstown had deeds in their pockets for all their best plantations.'" In answer to this, Darnell and his fellow soldier had little to offer. His friend said, "I must believe it because you say so, but if I had seen it myself, I would not." Darnell recounted that after all this the debaters' "passion subsided" and all "were friendly" until the parolees left the house the next day. He clearly believed that he and his companions had gotten the best of the dispute, that he had established liberty, not land acquisition, as the sole U.S. motive for war.[70]

It is all the more ironic, then, that when Darnell's successful book went into a second printing in Kentucky the following year in 1814, it boasted a new subtitle tacked onto the original: *To Which Is Added a Geographical Description of the North-Western Section of the State of Ohio, or That Part to Which the Indian Title Has Not Been Extinguished.* If Anglo-Canadians deserved Darnell's best assurances that the United States did not covet their lands, exactly the opposite message was intended for the Canadians' Indian allies.[71]

Darnell, or perhaps his publisher, apparently enjoyed reading the *Niles Weekly Register*—itself, of course, the source of many anti-Malthusian musings about the geopolitical value of a growing population. Darnell credited his new "Geographical Description" of Ohio directly to the *Niles Weekly*. The opening lines of the new essay selection read: "As there is great probability, from the present state of our relations with the Indian tribes, that their right to the soil will be forfeited to the United States ... a brief geographical sketch may in some degree, be interesting." There could be no fuller admission that, whatever its protestations to the contrary, the United States had entered the War of 1812 with the express goal of expanding its territories.[72]

The concluding lines of the *Niles Weekly* essay quoted by Darnell once more asserted the importance of population expansion for the establishment of property rights: "Such is the tide of popular opinion in favor of the lake side of this state, that there is every reason to believe, if, at the close of the war, these lands should fall into the hands of our government and be offered for sale, that the country will be settled with a rapidity unparalleled in the history of the western world." Long before they began using the phrase "manifest destiny," U.S. residents believed that gaining control of North America would give them a celebrated place in "the history of the western world," the only history that counted as far as they were concerned. The *Register* insisted that Indian rights were "forfeited" *to*, not violated *by*, the United States, implying that Indians deserved to have their lands confiscated in retaliation for crimes against humanity.[73]

Only in New England, seat of Federalist opposition to the war, did writers make any attempt to advance an argument different from the standard one that Indians were savages whose depredations against U.S. families made them worthy of eradication. In Boston, in February 1814, a Dartmouth College graduate by the name of Caleb Bingham published a wilderness narrative that diverged in remarkable ways from the common run of Indian atrocity tales. At that point, people around the country were embracing the idea that Indian captives endured unspeakable horror, while the United States' prisoners of war never suffered so much as hurt feelings before being speedily paroled. Yet Bingham chose precisely that moment, fast on the heels of Harrison's victory, to publish for the first time the story of a European-Indian friendship that he said he had witnessed blossoming back in 1776, nearly forty years before.[74]

Bingham offered the story of two Dartmouth students, Hugh and Francis, one a French Canadian merchant's son from Montreal, the other "an Indian youth from the tribe of St. Francis in Canada," who forged a faithful bond while lost together in the forest. He called his tale *The Hunters; or, The Sufferings of Hugh and Francis, in the Wilderness, a True Story*, and he minced no words about the intended moral. He challenged "those who are accustomed to depreciate the character of Indians, and who are more disposed to extirpate them from the face of the earth, than to civilize and Christianize them," not to change their minds after reading his tale of the "heroic and benevolent Francis."[75]

Bingham rowed against a fierce cultural current by insisting that Francis exemplified the general benevolence of the "Indian character." By the time he published in early 1814, conventional wisdom held just the opposite: that the distinguishing trait of Indians was their brutal tendency to subject "wives, maids, and infants" to captivity if not "scalping knives and tomahawks." In case anyone needed reminding that this was the traditional rap against Indians, plenty of publishers stepped up to their presses during the war years to prod people's memories by printing new and classic commentaries on Indian warfare.

Writers such as Jonathan Carver, whose descriptions of *Travels Through the Interior Parts of North America* were reprinted by Isaiah Thomas in 1813, offered the caustic observation that "the Indians have no idea of moderating the ravages of war, by sparing their prisoners. . . . All that are captivated . . . are either put to death, adopted, or made slaves of." Whereas "civilized" war was defined by the lenient treatment and quick return of prisoners, "savage" war deserved strict censure for the way it made people into objects of prey. If the prospect of a prisoner's physical suffering alarmed Euro-Americans, the idea that their population could be put at the service of an opposing people's agenda was still more disturbing.[76]

U.S. commentators argued regularly that the single most troubling element of Indian war was the way it targeted women and children. George Fowler's narrator, Randalthus the visionary, took that question up directly with the Lunarians he lectured in his *Flight to the Moon*. When one Lunarian observed "that the disputes between hostile nations were among the greatest sources of earthly calamities," and demanded to know "is there no law, no power, to decide on these contests and stop the effusion of human blood," Randalthus had a ready answer. The problem, he replied, was not with the practices of civilized nations, but rather with the savage sort. He denied that "civilized nations in respect to their intercourse in war or peace are yet in the same condition of barbarian tribes, among whom the mangled carcasses and dying shrieks of the smiling infant or helpless female serve to glut the savage revenge." By U.S. logic, attacks aimed at defenseless women and children exhibited an egregious degree of cruelty and highlighted the supposedly more humane outcomes of European forms of war.[77]

When U.S. critics appraised Indian tactics, the notion that Indians were motivated by bloodlust, by gluttonous desires for violent revenge, proved central to their arguments. The point of these condemnations was to convey that the Indians' focus on people lacked any rational explanation. In actuality, however, Indian captive taking had always served logical aims, and perhaps never more so than in the era of 1812.[78]

Traditionally, Indians had taken captives to fill ritual roles and to augment families shrunken by the ravages of war or disease. With famously low birthrates among Indian women, the practices of captive taking and adoption allowed Indian men to contribute actively to the social reproduction of their peoples in ways far more extensive than the limited labor that white men contributed to sexual reproduction within their own societies. The advent of Euro-American markets for slaves, in which captives became cash commodities, only added to the array of reasons why Indians might regard women and children as the most desirable trophies of battle.[79]

Euro-Americans recognized population as an important resource every bit as much as Indians did. They proved it not only with their many comments about the connections between population size and national strength in the abstract but also with their quite concrete remarks about the usefulness of a rising populace for the settlement of land. And, of course, they demonstrated this understanding by deed as well as by word every time they acted as purchasers in the burgeoning North American slave trade in Indians and African Americans alike. Yet while many a U.S. citizen participated eagerly in the slave trade, they recoiled at the notion that they themselves could become objects of trade. The threat of forced labor and forced affiliation repelled those who styled themselves as "freemen."[80]

Perhaps most devastating of all, though, was the knowledge that some Euro-American women and children did *not* regard adoption by Indians as a hideous fate. Some actually found life among Indians preferable to that passed among Euro-Americans. When Caleb Bingham wrote up his thoughts in his parable-like tale, *The Sufferings of Hugh and Francis*, he had these issues directly in mind. He signaled as much by bringing up the all-too-real story of the most famous Anglo-American captive ever to be taken into captivity and then to refuse repatriation: Eunice Williams, taken at Deerfield, Massachusetts, in 1704.[81]

Bingham asserted that the Indian hero of his tale, Francis, "was a descendent from Mrs. Williams, who was captivated in her childhood, at Deerfield, Massachusetts, in 1704, and was married and spent her days among the Indians." Eunice's preacher-father John had also been captured and he had published a famous account of his return, *The Redeemed Captive Returning to Zion*.

Nonetheless, everyone knew the dark underside of his tale: all the efforts he made to persuade his daughter to resume life among Anglo-Americans failed. Even a century after the fact, the case of Eunice Williams remained current. Her father's book had been republished as recently as 1811 in Brookfield, Massachusetts. So when Bingham brought up "Mrs. Williams," he knew he was touching a raw nerve.[82]

At a time when many in the prowar camp sought to portray Indian captivity as a fate worse than death and Indians as amoral monsters for their mistreatment of women and children, Bingham mildly pointed out that many captive adoptions went smoothly and resulted in the creation of new family ties between Indians and whites. In an era when population mattered much to the fortunes of nations, and when the United States had staked its moral right to empire on the idea that Indian seizures of women and children proved their depravity, this amounted to an inconvenient observation at best.

As if to rub salt in the rhetorical wound, Bingham even went so far as to report that Francis, upon leaving Dartmouth College, returned to Canada and received a "lieutenant's commission" from the British. And though he "made some depredations upon the frontiers, . . . he always spared to shed blood and treated his prisoners with humanity." With a knowing wink at the contemporary crisis his tale was intended to influence, Bingham closed his account with the information that the Canadian boy Hugh "acquired a handsome estate, and is now the respectable head of a numerous family, on the river Thames in Upper Canada, near where Gen Harrison captured Gen. Proctor's army, in 1813. THE END." It is hard to imagine Bingham finding an appreciative audience for this sort of tale anywhere outside of Federalist Massachusetts. And, in fact, this counter-captivity story was, more or less, unique.[83]

cωo

When General William Henry Harrison defeated General Henry Proctor's army, he seized Proctor's papers as part of his prize booty. Valued for the insights they gave into enemy motives and enemy strategy, purloined papers also served as a humiliating reminder of the victor's total ground control, including even the flow of information. Among the cache of papers, Harrison discovered a speech by Tecumseh—appealing to the British for arms and ammunition—that he treated as a smoking gun. These diplomatic records provided him with unequivocal documentation of the "unchristian" alliance between Britons and Indians. Harrison forwarded a copy of the speech to

Governor Return Meigs of Ohio; Meigs seems to have lost no time in leaking the speech to the Lexington, Kentucky, newspaper *The Reporter*, in which it was published on November 6, 1813, exactly a month and a day after Harrison's victory.[84]

Today, the copy of Tecumseh's remarks reprinted in the *Reporter* still makes for interesting reading. In the speech, dated September 18, 1813, at Amherstberg, Tecumseh clearly stated the muffled fact of the war: for Indians it was a fight for raw physical survival. Tecumseh feared, all too presciently as the force of events would ultimately prove, that the British had only weak resolve to ensure the rights of Native Americans. Tecumseh beseeched the British general to release arms that the king requisitioned for Indians and thus to give him the power to do what Proctor would not, saying, "*Father!* You have got the arms and ammunition which our great father sent for his red children. If you have an idea of going away, give them to us, and you may go and welcome, for us." He explained the reason for his urgent request in the plainest terms: "Our lives are in the hands of the Great Spirit. We are determined to defend our lands, and if it is his will, we wish to leave our bones upon them." When Tecumseh did soon leave his bones upon the ground, dying in battle a couple of weeks later, people within the United States eagerly agreed that his death had been divinely ordained—and that, by implication, U.S. acquisition of Indian lands had been as well. The speech was so pleasurable to read in the context of the U.S. victory that nearly two dozen newspapers in more than a dozen states in every region of the country reprinted it.[85]

Tecumseh's widely reported speech made no reference to committing reproductive atrocities, only to retaining Indian lands even if it meant dying in the attempt. The Indian leader offered no fuel to fire the gossip that white women and children were always the preferred Indian targets. Yet, as illustrated by books like the travel records of Michael Smith, U.S. citizens clung to this story line, insisting that with Tecumseh's death "the wives, maids, and infants on our frontiers will be preserved." As they sought to define the war, Americans scrabbled for the moral clarity that came with blaming Indians for attacking the innocent. Even if Tecumseh never declared any intent to do so, many in the United States were determined to associate Tecumseh with those actions. After his death, Tecumseh would be remembered equally for the majesty of his oratory and the strength of his ferocity.

Stories of infanticide and feticide worked an incantation, casting such a spell of disgust on Indians that all moral claims they might make to their own lands were extinguished in the minds of U.S. readers. The tale of Tecumseh's threat to white families mattered so much to American nationalist narratives that, by the mid-nineteenth century, a Mississippi plantation owner, newspaper editor, and eager amateur historian by the name of John Francis Hamtramck Claiborne took the step of inventing a speech for Tecumseh in which he put words to that effect in his mouth. Resurrected in 1860, Claiborne's Tecumseh stormed, "tears drop from the weeping skies. Let the white race perish. . . . Slay their wives and children! The red man must own the country and the pale face must never enjoy it!" Claiborne, who was born in 1809, was two years old at the time that Tecumseh supposedly made this speech to Creek Indians to motivate them to join a pan-Indian alliance. He pretended no firsthand knowledge. But he was a talented ventriloquist. Claiming to be transcribing the words of an informant who supposedly truly had heard Tecumseh, he wrote his account of Tecumseh in the first person as if he were an eyewitness.[86]

Claiborne's purported source was Samuel Dale, an aide to the U.S. Indian agent Benjamin Hawkins, who was present at the treaty council in which Tecumseh appeared. (Claiborne first recounted Dale's supposed experience in a biography of him.) However, Tecumseh had addressed the Creeks in a private session to which no U.S. official was privy and of which no record was made. Neither Hawkins (who himself used an interpreter) nor Dale (who spoke no Indian languages at all) could possibly have had any precise information about the speech. Whatever Dale may have told Claiborne about it, he had been dead for nearly twenty years by the time Claiborne, writing in his voice, declared of Tecumseh's oration, "I have heard many great orators, but I never saw one with the vocal powers of Tecumseh. . . . Had I been deaf, the play of his countenance would have told me what he said. . . . I think I can repeat the substance of what he said, and, indeed, his very words." No one in the United States needed to understand or even to hear Tecumseh's words in order to use them against him.[87]

The tale of the bloodthirsty savage bent on violating women and children in the pursuit of a population competition that bordered on genocide usefully projected U.S. goals and tactics onto the nation's enemies. Claiborne, for one, could not keep himself from continuing to riff on a theme he found so satisfying. By the time he incorporated the anecdote from Dale's biography into his 1880 masterwork, *Mississippi as Province, Territory, and State*, Tecumseh had grown more vicious than ever. This time he intoned, "Let the white race perish. . . . Slay their wives and children that the very breed may perish!" In this war story, the 1812 era emerged as the turning point in a mortal contest to see which "breed" of people would populate the continent. Claiborne's creative invention has continued to be attributed to Tecumseh down to the present day, despite the fact that the first and only record of his threats was not made until a half century after his death. When it comes to Native American history, those in the United States often hear what they want to, whether or not any Indian has actually said it.[88]

No matter whether Indians challenged the U.S. right to take their lands with words or with muskets, expansionists within the United States always tried to turn attention back to the inverse issue of Indian aggression in menacing the reproductive potential of the people of the United States. No cultural inventions could accomplish this more effectively than the captivity tale, no doubt the reason so many were produced and revised during the war. Many of these tales rounded out their descriptions of Indian infant maulings and child murders with discussions of the tradition of Indian adoption of U.S. residents and the resultant threat to the nation's strength in population.

The town of Paris, Kentucky, announced its staunch Republican sympathies with its very name. Located in Bourbon County (so named in 1785 in a flush of gratitude for the French royal family's assistance in the American Revolution), the town itself had been renamed from Hopewell to Paris in 1790, just months after the outbreak of the French Revolution. Paris was known as an anti-Federalist town. Its newspaper was the *Western Citizen*, another title with clear political implications, a signal that the male residents of the town took special pride in contrasting their free citizenship with the lesser status of the enslaved Africans and displaced Indians in their environs. During the War of 1812, the *Western Citizen* was owned and edited by the father-son team of Joel R. and William C. Lyle. Joel had a minor profitable sideline in publishing captivity tales. He would soon emerge as the printer of Elias Darnell's 1813 *Journal*. But in 1812, the year the war broke out, he was still putting his efforts behind another tract by a former soldier, this one by the name of James Smith.[89]

James Smith had been born in 1737 and died in 1812. He had first published his narrative in 1799, under the title *An Account of the Remarkable Occurrences in the Life and Travels of Col. James Smith (Now a Citizen of Bourbon County, Kentucky) During His Captivity with the Indians in the Years*

1755, '56, '57, '58, *and* '59. But by the time Joel Lyle prepared a new edition for press in 1812, that title would be jettisoned in favor of one with a more overtly martial tone. The newly revised volume, which must have been among the 75-year-old Smith's final accomplishments, promised to discuss many events since 1755, "Gov. Harrison's included." The new title, *A Treatise on the Mode and Manner of Indian War . . . Ways and Means Proposed to Prevent the Indians from Obtaining the Advantage*, aggressively repositioned Smith's work not as a literary diversion but as a military manual.[90]

In a crucial sense, all captivity tales were war stories—intended not only to entertain but also to inspire and instruct those who ranged themselves in opposition to Indians. But the Smith volume—released in April 1812, just six months after William Henry Harrison's first major victory against the forces of Tecumseh at Tippecanoe in November 1811 and a mere two months before the first-ever congressional declaration of war in June—pivoted in an important way. The new book on the "mode and manner of Indian war" made explicit what had often before been only implicit. Captivity narratives were war propaganda. They incited U.S. hostility by describing Indian atrocity. And although Congress would formally declare war against the British, in Kentucky rifles were already trained on Indians.

Despite Smith's promise to offer new information on Indian "tactics, discipline and encampments, the various methods they practice in order to gain the advantage," his 1812 volume still devoted considerable space to documenting his experience of captivity in the 1750s. Smith recounted that he was adopted in a formal ceremony as a member of the Caughnewag nation (presumably a reference to the Montreal-area Mohawk nation, the Kahnawake or Caughnawaga). He claimed to recall (with a suspicious degree of perfection) the ceremonial speech with which he was inducted. He reported being told: "You are adopted into a great family, and now received with great seriousness and solemnity in the place of a great man; after what has passed this day, you are now one of us by an old strong law and custom." Smith's recital focused less on the "mode and manner of Indian war" than on the *motives*: on the Indian aim of strengthening their population by augmenting biological reproduction with captive adoption.[91]

Indeed, when it came to taking male captives, family building and military staffing became one and the same. In effect, Smith was being forced to provide added manpower for enemy fighters. The Indians addressed the martial implications of his adoption overtly by telling him, "You are now flesh of our flesh, and bone of our bone. . . . Every drop of white blood is washed from your veins; you are taken into the Caughnewag nation and initiated into a war-like tribe." Smith's experience would be echoed in Joel Lyle's 1813 edition of Darnell's *Journal*, which would include a narrative in which a soldier captured on the River Raisin reported that he literally provided a one-to-one replacement for a dead Indian warrior. This captured serviceman was "adopted into a Potawatamie family that had lost a son in the battle at the river Raisin." If the U.S. mode of war in the era of 1812 was to take land and then settle it with people, the Indian one was to take people and then use them to defend land. Fundamentally, the struggle was always over population, yet Euro-American emphasis on the importance of sexual reproduction in this process diverged greatly from the more flexible Indian attitude.[92]

Authors could also highlight the population competition inherent in Indian captivity practices by focusing attention on the frequent Indian practice of adopting children. In a book called *A Topographical Description of the State of Ohio, Indiana Territory, and Louisiana*, published in Boston in 1812, author Jervis Cutler smoothly combined critiques of Indian captivity with avid descriptions of Indian lands. He explained at the outset that he believed his book "would be acceptable to the public" precisely because the issue of U.S. population expansion was garnering so much current attention. He expected his book to appeal "especially to those interested, or who wish to become interested, in a country so rapidly increasing in population." In the era of 1812, it was a fair bet that many people, even in Federalist centers like Massachusetts, took interest in increasing the Euro-American population in Indian country. But Cutler warned his readers to beware that Indians themselves were interested in population expansion. In a discussion of the Osage nation, for example, Cutler informed his readers flatly that "they generally kill all their prisoners, except the children; and these they will sometimes adopt as their own." To the menace of scalping could be added the threat of kidnapping.[93]

Euro-Americans hardly considered countering Indians tit for tat by attempting to incorporate Indian populations within that of the United States. Yet however unlikely such a proceeding might have been in actuality, it proved irresistible as a narrative possibility. Two versions of the captivity story of a man named John R. Jewitt (a blacksmith and crew member of the oceangoing vessel *Boston* who was ambushed in the Pacific Northwest in 1803), the first published in 1807, the second in 1815, highlight how quickly the war elevated population competition to the forefront of political and cultural concerns.[94]

Jewitt was captured at Nootka Sound (on the coast of present-day British Columbia), adopted by a local tribe of Indians, rescued years later by another ship, and returned to New England, where he published a forty-eight-page account of his experiences as *A Journal Kept at Nootka Sound* in Boston in 1807. The *Journal* presented an apparently forthright account of Jewitt's captivity. He and a fellow captive named Thompson, the sailmaker on the *Boston*, largely spent their time "employed at slavery." Jewitt made harpoons, copper rings, and other metal implements and ornaments for the chief, fished often for salmon, and recorded the weather. The dull routine of his days was interrupted only occasionally by events such as his compulsory marriage to an Indian woman. He claimed reluctance to enter the union, but appreciated that since she had "a father who always goes fishing," partnering with her allowed him to "live much better" than he had before. The book enjoyed little initial success in the years before the outbreak of war.[95]

But then Jewitt's fortunes changed. In the midst of the War of 1812, he teamed with an enterprising coauthor by the name of Richard Alsop, a writer who quadrupled the length of the book, retitled it *A Narrative of the Adventures and Sufferings, of John R. Jewitt*, and reissued it in Connecticut in 1815. Alsop's *Narrative* contained a novel narrative arc: he made Jewitt not only the husband of an Indian wife but also the adoptive father of an Indian boy. This version of Jewitt's story went through two editions in 1815 and a third in 1816 and was further memorialized in an 1815 broadside song.[96]

By revising the Jewitt text as he did, Alsop tried to eliminate the uncomfortable reversals of status and culture that Jewitt had actually experienced. If Jewitt's straightforward and unassuming *Journal* was accurate, forced labor had taken up most of his time. An account of his work, together with his daily observations of Indian life—from cooking salmon in pots brought to boil with hot stones to dining on whale blubber—was all he had offered the reader. Alsop, however, was determined to spin gold from Jewitt's straw.[97]

Alsop's version of Jewitt's story introduced a startling contemporary turn: Jewitt supposedly took charge of "Sat-sat-sak-sis, the king's son." The Nootka chief then assigned him his own apartment within the chief's house. In this edition, "Jewitt" declared, "Here I established myself with my family, consisting of myself and wife, Thompson, and the little Sat-sat-sak-sis, who had always been strongly attached to me, and now solicited his father to let him live with me, to which he consented." Even taking into consideration that in nineteenth-century usage the word "family" often simply applied to all resident members of a household, whether kin, guest, servant, or slave, the claim that the king's son lived as part of Jewitt's family was an extraordinary one. In the 1807 *Journal*, Jewitt did mention the king's son several times, but only in describing his leading role in ceremonial dances. He never named him in the 1807 version and he certainly never described personal contact, much less an adoptive relationship. Alsop's 1815 story dramatically reversed the usual anxieties provoked by captivity tales; an Indian chose a U.S. man as a father figure, preferring life with the captive Euro-American to that as the son of an Indian chief.[98]

In effect, the 1815 Jewitt transposed the usual cross-cultural adoption process, taking an Indian child and making him Euro-American, rather than himself being made Indian. Jewitt lingered long over this scene, recounting that "in making my domestic establishment, I determined, as far as possible, to live in a more comfortable and cleanly manner than the others." Even in captivity, possessed of nothing but the gifts of the chief, Jewitt's European habits of cleanliness supposedly set him above and made his home appealing to Sat-sat-sak-sis. Jewitt lavished paternal care on the boy. The *Narrative* reported: "This boy was handsome, extremely well formed, amiable, and of a pleasant sprightly disposition. I used to take pleasure in decorating him with rings, bracelets, ear jewels &c. which I made for him of copper. . . . I was also very careful to keep him free of vermin of every kind, washing him and combing his hair every day." The author lingered pleasurably over the intimate scene, declaring that "these marks of attention were . . . very pleasing to the child, who delighted in being kept neat and clean." Here the chief's son, who in the Jewitt *Journal* had been a central figure in tribal rituals, became infantilized, even domesticated like a pet animal, an object to be "decorated" and "combed" and certainly no kind of threat.[99]

It must be significant that this idealized scene took place on the Pacific Coast, where few U.S. citizens were yet attempting to settle, and that it appeared after the war's close, in 1815. By then, relatively benign images of Indians would have been more palatable than they were in the midst of wartime crisis. Still, there were stark limits to the extent of familial blending Alsop presented as possible. While a truly radical vision could have presented Jewitt as the acknowledged father of an adopted or mixed-race child, one he named, supported, educated, and brought up to enjoy U.S. citizenship, nothing of the kind was contemplated. In fact, when "Jewitt" had the opportunity to depart on a new ship, he jumped at the chance to return to life in the United

States without so much as a backward glance at the son of the chief he had once taken as his own, though he noted pointedly that "the boy could not bear to part with me."[100]

"Sat-sat-sak-sis" served not as the representative of any bold new vision of pan-American unity, but simply as a symbol of the Indian pacification the United States hoped it had advanced with the war. Ultimately, the 1815 version of Jewitt's captivity story—highly unusual in imagining an Indian child adoption—simply helped to relieve U.S. anxiety about population competition with Indians through the effective literary device of comic inversion.

Far more typical of the tone and concerns of wartime captivity narratives were the 1812 comments of James Smith of Paris, Kentucky, who could never even have conceived of the idea of U.S.-Indian family alliances. For Smith, as for most war supporters, the unholy combination of British and Indians could only be overcome by military means. Smith offered "the opinion that nothing but fear will cause the Shawanees and their confederates to stand a treaty, while they have the British to supply and encourage them." And he sounded the theme that was the U.S. refrain, demanding, "Is it not high time that we should learn wisdom by long repeated experience? The Shawanoe Prophet and his brother after repeated, unsufferable insolence killed and scalped in several places, took a young woman prisoner." Smith was only too happy to report that his story differed from the common tale of callous government neglect for settlers because "Governor Harrison on this situation of things did not, as usual, suffer the frontiers to be exposed to savage cruelty for several years: But immediately marched an army into their country." From Tippecanoe to the Thames, the United States generally and General Harrison specifically insisted that Indians should be the target of U.S. arms because of the way they attacked those women and children who should rightfully have been regarded as noncombatants.[101]

⟨∞⟩

Following their victory on the Thames, Harrison's troops set out to destroy Indian strength in the area. They marched along the river into the nearby settlement at Moraviantown, where Christian Indian converts living under the tutelage of a Pennsylvania missionary, the Reverend John Scoll, had established a flourishing village of about one hundred houses, a schoolhouse, and a chapel, all surrounded by extensive fields of green corn and garden vegetables in abundance. New York volunteer and memoirist Samuel R. Brown

reported these facts along with the information that most Indians at Moraviantown spoke English. In his judgment, "the gardens were luxuriant and cultivated with taste." Nevertheless, despite the success these Indians had achieved
in creating a settlement that met the highest standards of Christianity and
civility, "the town was destroyed as well as the cornfields in its vicinity, by the
troops."[102]

The Indians of Moraviantown, knowing of the disastrous loss on the
Thames, had fled the town in advance of the U.S. Army approach, so that
when Brown and his compatriots arrived, the "town was deserted." Marks of
desperate departure were everywhere to be seen and Brown exclaimed, "so
panic struck were some of the women in their flight, that they are said to have
thrown their children into the Thames, to prevent their being butchered by the
Americans!" Soldiers who sent home reports like this one intended to make
the point that, whatever their achievements, the Indians at Moraviantown
still did not understand the civilized values that guided U.S. policy. Indian
women, ignorant of the humane restraints of civilized warfare, inflicted their
greatest sufferings on themselves.[103]

Brown did not claim to have witnessed this action firsthand. Rather, it was
a story making the rounds among the men. He added a footnote explaining
that he "had this fact from an American gentlemen" who had seen Proctor
and the Indians passing out of town and who said that "the Squaws were then
lamenting the loss of their children." The anecdote does not seem to have been
recounted in other publications and cannot be corroborated.[104]

Yet the story gained what currency it did—and Brown's work did circu-
late widely—because it worked to affirm popular beliefs. What mother worth
the name would kill her children on the mere chance that an invading army
might? Everything from captivity narratives to anthropological treatises to
travelers' accounts could be found arguing that Indian women lacked some
essential maternal quality needed to bear and rear large families of children
to adulthood. U.S. claims to superior civility rested in part on comparative
fecundity, while the country's hopes for expansion also rested on its ability to
produce a growing settler population.

For his part, Brown remained conflicted. Foolish and deluded though the
Indian women might have been in supposedly sacrificing their own children, it
could not be denied that such fears had some basis in fact. Brown complained,
"I have yet to learn that it is either good policy or justice, for the American
troops, in every instance, to burn the Indian towns that fall in their power.

Are the Indians to be reclaimed by fire?" The answer, of course, was that for many in the United States, Indian decimation—not reclamation—remained the goal.[105]

If population competition with Indians provided an important element of U.S. strategy, mothers had both a crucial practical role to play and an essential symbolic part to embody. Reproductive work represented a critical stage in the Euro-American cycle of continental warfare. From the beginning of the War of 1812 to the end, from high politics to popular literature, the image of the virtuous mother menaced by savages provided an irresistible rallying point for prowar forces.

When Governor Willie Blount of Tennessee wanted to make demands on the Madison administration, urging it to amplify its military efforts against the Creek nation, nothing served to make his case like the specter of an abused mother and midwife. In June 1812, the very month that war was declared against Britain, Blount began lobbying Secretary of War William Eustis with reports of Creek aggression against frontier families. In formal correspondence with the War Department, he asserted that the Creeks were staging an exhibition in which they took one "poor woman from town to town in their nation, naked, and exultingly dance[d] around her as their captive." The woman in question, one "Mrs. Crawley," was not only a mother, but also an obstetric practitioner. According to Blount's recital, a group of Creek Indians had seized her in the midst of performing her professional duties, offering postpartum care to a new mother and baby.[106]

Demographic efforts furthered geographic designs and vice versa. In the words of the account Blount forwarded to Washington, Mrs. Crawley "was in her own house and her husband absent, when eleven of those monsters attacked her." At that very moment, she had been busily tending to "another woman, Mrs. Manley, who had come to her house, Mrs. Crawley's to lie in, and whose babe was only seven days old." Despite Crawley's efforts to bar the door, it "was burst open upon her, and . . . Indians immediately rushed in, and the poor woman and her babe were the first victims." Witnessing the murder of her patients was only the beginning of Mrs. Crawley's troubles as she soon "saw them kill one of her own children in the house, shoot another in the yard, and two others of Mrs. Manley's," before "they then plundered the house, and brought her off to a village on the Black Warrior River." Blount declared that "the spirit of the people" of his state was so "roused" by these events that they would be ungovernable unless "the government would order a campaign to be carried to the Creek nation." Blount's story of the captive midwife twined the issues of natal contests and martial conquests too tightly to be disentangled.[107]

Secretary Eustis declined to follow Blout's prescribed course of action at his own peril. He replied to Blount that "the prompt manner in which the Indians have administered justice on the offenders, will supersede the necessity of making a campaign against them." Blount begged to disagree, saying, "our opinions as to what amounts to a ready compliance with the demand made in that case, widely differ." Eustis was forced to resign from his position six months later, in December 1812.[108]

However she may have failed Mrs. Manley and her baby, Mrs. Crawley ably midwifed a pronatalist strain of prowar politics. Of course, Eustis's failures in the disastrous opening months of the War of 1812 were legion and his role in the crisis of the captive mother and midwife has long faded from memory, eclipsed by events like Hull's catastrophic failure at Detroit. Yet the story of Mrs. Crawley enjoyed great political prominence at the time. Just weeks after Eustis's December departure from office, on January 11, 1813, President James Madison forwarded the Blount-Eustis correspondence to the Senate and ordered it to be published and distributed by the Congressional Printing Office, whence it appeared as *Message from the President of the United States, Transmitting a Report of the Secretary of War, Relative to Murders Committed by the Indians in the State of Tennessee.* The Creeks, meanwhile, would soon face the opposition of General Andrew Jackson, whose own rise to national prominence began with his successful campaign against them.[109]

Despite their determined martial tactics, U.S. residents preferred to attribute Indian population declines not to military consequences but rather to social and cultural causes. Even in a purported war manual, popular comments on Indian losses focused primarily on Indian moral failings. As James Smith asserted in his 1812 *Treatise on the Mode and Manner of Indian War*: "Some of their ancient laws or customs are very pernicious, and disturb the public weal. Their vague law of marriage is a glaring instance of this, as the man and his wife are under no legal obligation to live together, but part when they please. . . . Their frequent changing of partners prevents propagation." Unlike U.S. citizens, who understood marriage as a key ceremony of national belonging, and children as membership dues to be paid, Indians entered marriages solely at their own pleasure. And unlike monogamous Christian marriages, contracted for life for the express purpose of procreation, Indians' easy divorces hindered the growth of their population.[110]

Another favorite explanation for the rapid declines of Indian populations blamed their alcohol consumption. The scholarly toned *Topographical Description of the State of Ohio* by Jervis Cutler noted curtly that "the greatest enemy to their population has doubtless been the intemperate use of spirituous liquors." Exactly how alcohol did disproportionate damage to Indian fertility—at a time when estimates place U.S. alcohol consumption at something like five to seven gallons of absolute alcohol per person per year—was never precisely explained. But in an era in which temperance movements were hardly yet thought of in the United States, emphasis on Indian alcoholism laid responsibility for their population problems at their own feet.[111]

If neither Smith nor Cutler sensed any paradox in impugning Indians for their population losses within the pages of books that described how to vanquish them in war or navigate their lands once they were acquired, other writers did occasionally tiptoe up to this point. In his 1813 *Flight to the Moon*, George Fowler's narrator, Randalthus, lecturing the Lunarians on North America, told them that "in this continent, there are numerous tribes of Indians, but their number, since the invasion of the whites, has greatly diminished." The word "invasion" might seem to imply that military forces explained Indian losses. But Fowler too turned out to favor a more moralistic rationale. He continued, "while the Europeans have seized their territory, and have rapidly increased, the poor natives . . . have grown dispirited and drop off in a melancholy manner." In the end, Fowler, like many popular prowar writers, backed away from admitting any U.S. guilt. Instead, he emphasized Indian emotional failings. If only they had not given way to melancholy moping, their population might have remained robust. Such a stance was only likely to further fuel U.S. efforts to rouse the nation for expansion and procreation.[112]

If relative rates of population increase contributed both to military conquests and morality contests, the United States came one step closer to final victory every time the white wife of one of its citizens reproduced. Conversely, every mother or child lost to Indians represented a critical threat to the nation. Nothing dramatized—and literalized—this competition like a captivity tale.

And nothing brought the genre to its full potential like the climactic new captivity narrative published in Boston in 1815: *An Affecting Account of the Tragical Death of Major Swan, and of the Captivity of Mrs. Swan and Infant Child, by the Savages.* Based on the true story of Major Caleb Swan, a U.S.

deputy agent to the Creek nation, and his wife, Eliza, this tale was adorned with many a literary flourish and wore its politics proudly. The first edition just happened to be "issued with the reprint of the 1813 ed. of U.S. War Dept. Message from the President Relative to the Murders Committed by the Indians." The function of captivity narratives in stitching together high politics and popular culture in the era of 1812 could hardly have been put on more vivid display.[113]

Major Swan met a swift demise on the second page of the twenty-four-page pamphlet, but his child and his wife, Eliza, survived to star in the tale. The story revolved around a sustained struggle to claim the Swan baby, which was passed back and forth between Eliza and various Indian women multiple times in the drama, each time changing nomenclature from "infant" to "papoose."[114]

Set on a "small river 30 miles southwest of St. Louis" in April 1813, the Swan story centered on Eliza Swan's motherly devotion and the threats to her maternity from female Indian competitors who repeatedly tried to usurp her role. Eliza's torments began from the moment of her capture when, taken naked on a forced march, she was forced to bear a heavy load of Indian packs and "not privileged to embrace or nurse my infant babe, which was but eleven months old, and which was carried in a fur sack by one of their young squaws." Eliza bridled at being forced to haul Indian supplies while a "young squaw" won the right to carry her "infant babe." But the worst of her suffering came because she was not allowed to breast-feed her child while on the march.[115]

Eliza Swan described in sensory detail how "the overflow of milk from my breasts gave me too intolerable pain" and testified, "I intreated my savage masters to permit me, for a few moments, to nurse my poor babe, but my intreaties were productive of nothing but abuse and severe blows!" When not allowed to nourish her child, Eliza begged for death. Her entreaties had the desired effect and after four days she was allowed a "pleasing indulgence" and "permitted . . . for a few moments to nurse [her] babe . . . seated upon a log." The drama of the tale revolved around whether or not Swan could continue to perform her maternal role in the wilderness. Her insistence on nursing became an example of heroism.[116]

Still, neither Eliza Swan nor her baby was out of the woods. Swan described their reunion as sweet, declaring, "with what apparent extacy did my poor little infant view its mother, and receive its natural food, of which it had been deprived for the last four days." Yet the time in captivity separated from its "natural food" (and its natural mother) had already threatened the baby with transformation. Swan exclaimed that "so great was its hunger, that it was with some difficulty that I prevented its biting me!" Denied the mother's care for four days, the baby took on an almost bestial quality, trying to bite the breast that fed it.[117]

Whether or not the published story of the Swan family hewed closely to fact, whether or not it was truly written by Eliza Swan herself, or even by a woman, it, like the memoir of Susannah Willard Johnson, was designed to be emotionally "affecting" and to appeal explicitly to a female audience. No sooner had Swan suckled her baby for a few moments than she was ordered to "deliver it to its savage mistress again." Her distress renewed, Swan said, "it is impossible for me to describe to you the manner in which it clung to its mother's bosom, and the deep and melancholy impression which its screeches made on my half distracted mind! Alas! Mothers only are capable of judging!" Here female readers and especially maternal readers were offered an exalted vantage point from which to appreciate the tale. Motherhood conveyed understanding and insights that could not be gleaned in any other fashion and conferred possibilities for action sorely needed by the nation.[118]

It seems quite clear that many women may have rejected such visions. There is good evidence that U.S. women were beginning to actively seek strategies for family limitation in this period. And there must have been some reason why so many men perceived the need to take on women's voices in print and to express desires and attitudes not often actually conveyed by female writers. Nevertheless, there is also good evidence to show that whatever women's true preferences, men remained staunchly in favor of maximal reproduction, with marital fertility remaining high throughout the coming decades and especially so in frontier areas. As far as men were concerned, women who performed reproductive work for the nation could play a key part in the country's advancement without thereby earning any formal political roles or rights.[119]

At a time when so many literary productions proposed a sort of practical and moral equivalence between warriors and mothers, it is all the more striking that Eliza Swan succeeded where her husband did not. Major Swan, a man with a military appointment, died unable to defend his family, much less his country. Yet his wife exhibited a personal heroism that was positively patriotic by insisting on nursing in the middle of the "pathless wilderness." Eliza herself downplayed her efforts, apologizing for not having "possessed the courage of some of the heroines of my sex, whom history informs us, have

Figure 13. Note that in contradiction to the text, which specifies that Swan did *not* act the historical part of "heroines of my sex" by murdering her captors, this image shows her in active combat with a giant pitch-black Indian while her helpless husband lies bleeding. At the same time, it also portrays her as a woman of goddess-like beauty, whose scoop-necked gown hints at her ample cleavage. Altogether, the illustration elicits both horror and desire. And it presents an indelible image of nursing mother as military heroine. "Eliza Swan, Defending Her Husband," illustration from *An Affecting Account of the Tragical Death of Major Swan* (Boston: H. Trumbull, 1815), American Antiquarian Society.

distinguished themselves" by managing to murder their captors (Figure 13). She reproached herself for failing to "revenge my husband's death." Yet she congratulated herself that when her captors drank themselves into stupors, "I did not, however, let pass this opportunity once more to impart nourishment to my half famished babe!" In some sense, Eliza made the more critical contribution. Fighters could always be replaced, but not without mothers to bear them and nurture them through infancy. One thinks again of Jefferson's 1814 prophecy: "we shall indeed survive the conflict. Breeders enough will remain to carry on population."[120]

Through two dozen pages of trials and tribulations, as Eliza Swan was captured yet again by a rival band of Indians and separated from her baby for a lengthy period, the plot always revolved around nursing. When away from her child, she gratefully accepted the offer of "one of their squaws with a young papoose" who understood the severe discomfort of Swan's engorged breasts: "Perceiving me in a bad situation, in consequence of being deprived of my infant, [she] kindly offered her's to perform the part which nature required." For this mother, being cast back to nature did not result in any loss of civility but only in a deeper devotion to maternity.[121]

Meanwhile, Swan expressed gratitude in turn that while they were parted, "my papoose then had tender care taken of it, and a squaw nurse was procured for it." But lest a reader come away with the mistaken idea that Swan felt any great sororal tie to her "savage" sisters, she asserted that the Indians had kept her baby alive with the sole goal of profiting by selling it into slavery. Swan finally recovered the child only after making a "miraculous escape" and then meeting up with a Spanish trader who, she said, "related to me the particulars relative to my child, which he said he had paid 10 dollars for." A "papoose" when in the arms of a "squaw," her baby was "my infant . . . 'MY CHILD! —MY POOR CHILD!'" in all capital letters when they were finally brought together again for good.[122]

All the interest of the story rested on voluptuous tableaus of nursing mothers and infants. Time and again, the reader was invited to imagine the sight and sensations of breasts full with milk. Eliza Swan recounted in intimate detail every nuance of her nursing sessions, the mother's posture, and the baby's. During her finest hour of maternal heroism, when she crept through the night to fetch her baby from the side of the drunken "squaw" who had taken it, she related that she was "enabled again to nurse the poor little sufferer" only by "prostrating" herself on the ground. She went on to specify that because the baby's "body [was] enclosed in a blanket, [she] could not with safety disengage it, but having its head at liberty, [she] was enabled to nurse it." For all that the Swan story repulsed readers with repeated references to "vile barbarians," "vile savages," and "merciless barbarians," with descriptions of "torments exquisite beyond endurance" and "hellish plans to torment," it also enticed them with a steady stream of sensual images. Horror and pleasure worked together, a front-to-back motivational system prodding men to attack, women to reproduce, and both together to exploit and expand their numerical advantage over Indians.[123]

⌀

General William Henry Harrison had never made any secret of his belief that the United States had a mandate from God to take over Indian lands and fill them with U.S. settlers. Posing a rhetorical question to the territorial legislature of Indiana back in 1810, Harrison had demanded, "Is one of the fairest portions of the globe to remain in a state of nature, the haunt of a few wretched savages, when it seems destined by the Creator to give support to a large population, and to be the seat of civilization, of science, and true religion?" In a few well-considered lines, Harrison summed up every element of the prowar, proexpansionist agenda that would dominate the nation for decades, from the onset of the War of 1812 right through his own presidential election in 1840 and beyond. Population expansion enabled national might and enacted divine intentions. But not just any population would do. Harrison's God wanted the land to be settled by civilized Euro-American Christians. Making good on the nation's divine mission required those loyal to the United States not only to prosecute wars but also to produce the "large population" that was "destined by the Creator."[124]

When General Harrison took Indian women and children into custody in October 1813, he minced no words in calling them "hostages." His fellow commander, General Duncan McArthur, employed nearly the same exact phrasing, reporting back to the War Department that he had agreed to a cessation of hostilities with "five nations of Indians, viz. the Ottoways, Chippeways, Pottewattomies, Miamies and Kickapoos," on the condition that "they are to bring in a number of their women and children, and leave them hostages whilst they accompany us to war." These military leaders acknowledged without apology that they were involving in negotiations a subset of the population that would have been firmly placed off-limits as dependents and noncombatants had they claimed residency in the United States. No U.S. general would ever have given up U.S. women or children as hostages to Indians.[125]

Yet McArthur's letter added a key detail that made the procedure far more defensible in the minds of U.S. readers. He noted that "some of them have already brought in their women and are drawing rations." Feeding Indian women and children provided a humanitarian gesture that belied the country's concerted aggression against them. Like Harrison's letter, McArthur's quickly saw print, appearing in newspapers from Washington, D.C., to Dover, New Hampshire.[126]

Some accounts went still further in their efforts to gloss the U.S. seizure of women and children with the sheen of benevolence. According to a report sent by one "Captain Martin" of Detroit, whose claims appeared in newspapers across Connecticut, New York, New Jersey, and Delaware, Indian representatives actually went so far as to *ask* the U.S. Army to take in their families, not as captives but as objects of charity. Martin related that Indian deputies told McArthur, "Our squaws and children are perishing; we ourselves are perishing." In response, McArthur offered his protection: "they were directed to bring in their squaws and children—and were promised that they and their tribes should be fed at the expence of the U. States." At the end of the day, the United States hoped to project both power invincible and mercy illimitable. Still, the spectacle of Indian women and children held at the pleasure of U.S. soldiers nicely inverted every anxiety of frontier settlers—and of captivity narrative readers.[127]

Neither the defeat of Proctor nor the slaying of Tecumseh would have brought complete victory without the concurrent control of Indian peoples. Winning the population competition was so important to command of the continent that it justified the U.S. military in taking control of Indian women and children. Once turned over as hostages, they owed their very existence to the sufferance of U.S. commanders. They would be allowed to live only so long as their husbands and fathers willingly died for a country not their own, one that offered them limited rewards and fewer rights.

In a nation enraptured by captivity stories that celebrated procreative Christian marriages while denigrating barren Indian unions, that glorified white births while vilifying Indian adoptions, and that idealized white mothers while demonizing Indian ones, it was perhaps inevitable that some promoter would create a spectacle out of Harrison's seizure of Indian families. On November 1, 1813, a Philadelphia theater company produced "A GRAND PRESENTATION OF GENERAL PROCTOR'S DEFEAT BY *General Harrison.*" The advertisement for the "pantomime" detailed for the prospective audience members exactly what they could plan to enjoy at the show. Harrison and Proctor, of course, would both appear. Commodore Perry pledged to stride the stage and Tecumseh promised to fall on it. Lake Erie would feature as would the River Thames. And the public could look forward to "new Scenery, Dresses and Decorations and a new March, composed for the occasion, called Harrison's March." But the climax of the whole tableau would come only when "the Indians with their women and children kneel to Gen. Harrison, offer their services, and leave their wives and children as hostages. The whole form a picture and the Pantomime concludes." For the Pennsylvania theater audience, as for the U.S. readers of wartime captivity narratives, nothing could be more emotionally satisfying or politically stirring than the vivid enactment of population domination.[128]

Chapter 5

Liberty, Slavery, and the Burning of the Capital
WASHINGTON, D.C., AUGUST 1814

Philadelphia physician Jesse Torrey traveled to Washington, D.C., in December 1815 to witness history. Torrey had arrived at the seat of the national government in time to observe the start of a new session of Congress. He wished to see firsthand the determined endurance of a nation literally rising from the ashes. Fifteen months earlier, in August 1814, the British had burned the Capitol, the president's house, and most other major government buildings to cinders. The legislators who gathered in the District of Columbia on the day of Torrey's visit were governing in the aftermath of a foreign conquest. Yet the opening of Congress was not the event that arrested Torrey's attention. As Torrey paused before the Capitol to take in the devastating sight of the once "beautiful white freestone" building reduced to a charred hulk, he faced another nightmare vision. In front of the ruin, iron chains clanking, a file of enslaved people shuffled toward the auction block.[1]

Describing the scene in his book *A Portraiture of Domestic Slavery in the United States*, Torrey drew a direct connection between the destruction of the Capitol building by fire and the human devastation of the slave trade. He demanded of his readers: "would it be superstitious to presume, that the Sovereign Father of all nations, permitted the *perpetration* of this apparently execrable transaction, as a *fiery*, though salutary signal of his displeasure at the conduct of his Columbian children, in erecting and idolizing this splendid . . . temple of freedom, and at the same time oppressing with the yoke of captivity and toilsome bondage twelve or fifteen hundred thousand of their

Figure 14. Torrey's engraving vividly linked the burning of Washington (the roofless Capitol is shown with flames pouring out of the tops of the windows) with the practice of slave trading in the capital. Note the presence of little children in the coffle of enslaved people in chains, a visual representation of Torrey's rhetorical stress on the theme of family rupture. "View of the Capitol of the United States after the Conflagration in 1814," frontispiece, *A Portraiture of Domestic Slavery in the United States* (Philadelphia: J. Biorden, 1817), Collections of the Library Company of Philadelphia.

African *brethren* . . . making merchandize of their *blood*, and dragging their bodies with *iron chains*, even under its towering walls?" (Figure 14).[2]

The British burning of the Capitol was an "execrable transaction." Selling Africans and African Americans into bondage under the "towering walls" of a building better known as a "temple of freedom" was something worse: a sin so grievous God willed the destruction of the false temple. For Torrey, the answer to his rhetorical question was clear. God most certainly had ordained the ruination of the Capitol as a "signal of displeasure at the conduct of his Columbian children" because he condemned U.S. hypocrisy.

If the War of 1812 pitched the United States against the United Kingdom in a battle to claim status as the true land of liberty, then the republic lost significant moral ground to the monarchy whenever anyone raised the issue of slavery. Britain could boast that its powerful navy had forced an end to the Atlantic slave trade, while the United States could only admit that it still allowed a flourishing domestic market in slave labor. Yet Torrey's analysis did not represent anything like an American consensus. While Torrey believed that the United States endangered liberty by its inconsistency on the crucial issue of slavery, there were plenty of Americans who stood ready to invert Torrey's argument exactly. Critics of Britain accused that nation of base hypocrisy for impressing U.S. sailors into the Royal Navy even as it bragged of safeguarding the freedom of the seas.[3]

Ironically, both war boosters and antislavery activists relied on the same set of emotional symbols to make their respective arguments. Each dwelled on the tragedy of family love menaced by violent military action, of private lives destroyed by bad public policy. Torrey devoted many pages of his *Portraiture of Domestic Slavery* to painting individual African American victims of slavery, case studies that featured husbands and wives torn asunder by slave traders, parents and children lost to each other in separate sales. Yet those who made the case for war argued that the British were the main menace to the values of home and hearth, that royal press gangs tore American men from their families illegally and condemned them to near-certain death on the main. Meanwhile, British soldiers and their Indian allies on the North American continent brought death and destruction to many flourishing American families.

Since familial affections—between husbands and wives, parents and children—laid the first foundation for social love, family ties formed the basis for societal bonds. Because love of family provided the platform for love of country and love of liberty, any policy that endangered the family imperiled the nation. Yet the issue of black family love complicated this neat equation. If black husbands and wives could have their marital vows violated by white slavers, and black mothers and fathers could be routinely separated from their children, what did this say about the American commitment to protect liberty by respecting familial love? The continuation of slavery brought a significant problem into sharp relief: not everyone was welcome to claim membership in the wider "American family."[4]

The crisis of war highlighted the nation's complicated relation to its black inhabitants. Much as white U.S. writers and commentators celebrated the growing strength of the U.S. population, many remained ambivalent if not hostile toward the free and enslaved Africans and African Americans who were living—and multiplying—in their midst. On the one hand, wartime mobilization reminded everyone of the basic fact that there was strength in numbers, that free and enslaved blacks contributed much to making the nation robust. On the other hand, the war put patriotic loyalty at a premium, and it was anyone's guess whether free and enslaved blacks, who enjoyed so few rights compared to free whites, could possibly prove devoted to the country. The Atlantic slave trade might have formally ended four years before war broke out, but the millions of blacks already present in the United States could be as much a threat as an asset to the white populace. Even as the conflict with Britain was being fought, slavery debates continued apace.

Though militantly united in their opposition to slavery, African Americans were as divided in their views of the War of 1812 as whites were. Free black writers, those rare few whose written comments survive to provide direct African American perspectives on events, universally condemned the family ruptures and emotional suffering brought about by slavery. But they differed sharply in their preferred response to the immediate war crisis itself. Some asserted that free and enslaved blacks alike made up an essential part of the U.S. population, and that they could and should show their love of country by supporting the war with men and materiel. They urged the nation in turn to recognize the worth of black contributions to America's patriotic population by respecting black family love. African American families could not flourish without the end of slavery, the institution that not only claimed black labor but also denied black men and women the right to legal marriage and made black children the chattel of white owners. Other black writers, however, seized the moment of 1812 to point out the absurdity of a war of liberty championed by proponents of slavery. Some free black war opponents even went so far as to argue that the love of family and love of country—so fatally threatened by slavery—were hopelessly perverted into human hatred on the killing fields of war.

Theorists, theologians, and ordinary people in the United States and Britain alike agreed that family love should always be sacrosanct, that just wars treated women, children, and the aged as noncombatants. Claimed violations of these principles animated the outrage volleyed back and forth between U.S. troops, British soldiers, and Indian fighters. Yet somehow whites never applied this principle to Africans. U.S. slaveholders often tried to depict African slavery as the reasonable result of widely accepted standards of just war—people taken as prisoners of war should regard slavery as a merciful alternative to death. Yet how to explain the mass seizures of African women and children and the continual enslavement of generation after generation of the progeny of those "prisoners of war"—events in direct violation of the most cherished American principles?[5]

For Jesse Torrey, the simultaneous sight of the Capitol in ashes and enslaved people in shackles brought up just these vexed issues. As he told his readers: "Passing by the capitol, I thought Alas! Poor Africa,—*thy cup* is the *essence* of bitterness!—This *solitary* magnificent temple, *dedicated to liberty*— opens its portals to *all* other nations but *thee*, and bids their sons drink *freely* of the cup of *freedom* and happiness:—but when thy unoffending enslaved sons, clank their blood-smeared *chains* under its towers, it sneers at their calamity and mocks their lamentations with the echo of contempt!"[6]

The British burning of Washington brought U.S. military morale to an all-time low. The continuation of domestic slavery marked a moral low point for the country. Making sense of these confounding issues and events was an interrelated exercise for contemporaries both black and white. If the tragedy of family ruptures made great political fodder for attacks on the British and Indians, how could white Americans explain their tolerance for seeing this calamity inflicted regularly on the country's black inhabitants? If love of family built love of country, what did it do to the nation's patriotic foundation to destroy the family bonds of millions? Even as many contemporary war supporters proclaimed the War of 1812 to be a "Second War for Independence," the newest generation of white revolutionaries continued to impose dependence on African Americans.[7]

❧

On August 24, 1814, the day the capital was burned, the city of Washington, D.C., counted about eight thousand usual residents who lived in some nine hundred houses strung out along a two-mile stretch from the navy yard to the White House. The Capitol building was sited halfway along the main avenue, about a mile from the Potomac River. While "the capitol and the president's house" were widely and "deservedly esteemed as the finest specimens of architecture in the United States," the city itself "would elsewhere have been denominated a large village." In comparison to wealthy towns from Charleston to Philadelphia to New York to Boston, urban centers that boasted many more buildings and much larger populations, the newly established capital offered little to look at.[8]

U.S. commentators cringed at the thought of British strategists plotting their triumph. They imagined British planners predicting the "effect in Europe, where the occupation of the capital of their enemy, it was doubtless conceived, would be viewed as a most brilliant exploit." But Americans tried to

mitigate the severity of the national loss by emphasizing that the city had contained only "an inconsiderable population . . . sparsely scattered over an extensive site." Describing the destruction in the *Historical Register of the United
States* (a multivolume annual publication that recorded the events of the war
almost as soon they occurred), T. H. Palmer declared "that in the modern art
of war, *men* are of more importance than fortified places." By this reckoning,
the loss of Washington scarcely mattered at all.[9]

Palmer reassured readers that "the possession of a capital does not decide
the fate of a state," especially when that capital was "a mere open village, of
about 8000 inhabitants, and in a country thinly populated!" Palmer's analysis
rang of the rationalizations of the losing side, yet it also contained an important note of truth. Most of the city's inhabitants, from the president and the
first lady down to ordinary folk, had fled the city well in advance of the British
Army's arrival. The British had come to conquer an empty town and so, in
that sense, the fall of Washington was not as dire as it might have seemed
otherwise.[10]

From the beginning, U.S. Republicans had viewed the War of 1812 as a
struggle over the principle of population. The Royal Navy was so desperate for
manpower that it had to go trawling for deserters aboard American merchant
ships. For U.S. war supporters, this mere fact showed how important population strength was as an index of national might. Whatever the war's detractors might say about the hidden motivations of Republican war boosters, the
war's public proponents routinely insisted that "free trade and sailors rights"
were the primary cause and principle aim of the war. No matter how few the
number of Americans wrongfully compelled to serve aboard British ships, the
important principle was that of forced labor. Free white Americans expected
to labor first for themselves and then for their country, but never for another
nation.

Given British boasts about their nation's devotion to liberty, many white
Americans could not resist pointing out the similarities between impressment and slavery, no matter that this rhetorical move laid bare their moral
flank. If the British were wrong to commandeer American labor, what right
did U.S. slaveholders have to claim the productive—and reproductive—
capacities of Africans? If a loyal population was a nation's finest resource, how
should a potentially rebellious population of enslaved people be regarded?
Should whites view the black population of the United States as a resource
to be exploited, as fellow family members to be protected, or as a peril to

be controlled? These questions shadowed U.S. polemicists every time they equated enslavement and impressment.[11]

In the opening days of the war, President James Madison's chargé d'affaires in Britain, Jonathan Russell, claimed loudly that British impressment compared poorly with American slavery. Russell began by declaring that impressing a sailor into royal service was much like forcing him into perpetual hereditary bondage. Meeting in London with the British foreign minister, Lord Castlereagh, in the summer of 1812, Russell argued that, "in the United States, this practice of impressment was seen as bearing a strong resemblance to the slave trade." In fact, he went on, compared to enslavement in America, impressment aboard a British ship was actually "aggravated indeed in some of its features." How could Russell claim that impressing sailors was even worse in some respects than enslaving men, women, and children?[12]

American slave masters were paragons of virtue compared to British naval officers, according to Russell: "as the negro was purchased already bereft of his liberty . . . his slavery and exile were at least mitigated . . . while the American citizen is torn without price, at once, from all the blessings of freedom." In other words, since U.S. slaveholders made their purchases stateside, they could not be burdened with the guilt of converting people into commodities—only of benefiting from the plight of those who had already lost their freedom on the other side of the ocean. British sea captains, on the other hand, served directly as the awful alchemists who seized freeborn sailors and transformed them into galley lackeys.[13]

Impressed U.S. sailors suffered more than enslaved Africans did, Russell continued, because once Africans had been torn from their homeland they had no chance of ever meeting kith or kin again, whereas American sailors forced into British service might very well be put into the position of having to fight against members of their own families. As Russell put the point to Castlereagh, an enslaved African could enjoy "the consciousness that, if he could no longer associate with those who were dear to him, he was not compelled to do them injury." By contrast, an American tar ran the risk of being "forced, at times, to hazard his life in despoiling or destroying his kindred and countrymen." In this preposterous argument, the social death of Atlantic enslavement compared favorably with a stint of royal naval service.[14]

The extent of family devastation served as the key index of suffering. Even though an enslaved person would never see home or homeland again, he or she did not have to fight and kill those once held close. By this convoluted reasoning, American slavery offered something like liberty and U.S. slave-holders could hold their heads high when calling for confrontation with British tyranny.

Many listeners in the United States lapped up what Russell dished out. Russell offered the synopsis of his conversation with Castlereagh in a formal report prepared for Secretary of State James Monroe. Monroe and Madison made immediate use of his remarks, ordering them to be published by official congressional printer Roger Chew Weightman as *A Message from the President of the United States, Transmitting Copies of a Communication from Mr. Russell to the Secretary of State*. The dateline on Russell's letter read London, September 17, 1812. Madison forwarded it to Congress on November 18, 1812—almost two months to the day after it was sent—something like warp speed in an age when Atlantic crossings took weeks. No sooner did Russell's repartee with Castlereagh appear in print in the capital than it was reprinted in newspapers across the Northeast for the benefit of the general reading public.[15]

Some Federalists, on the other hand, abhorred Russell's analogy. John Lowell of Massachusetts—a lawyer, frequent pamphlet writer, and Harvard man—had opposed President James Madison's policies from the beginning. As far back as 1798 he had begun publishing pamphlets under the sobriquet "The Antigallican; or, The Lover of His Own Country," in which he had warned that the "French influence" was leading American Republicans into Napoleonic-style wars of aggression. He suggested that the average war booster was stirred by "false patriotism," that is by a "meretricious affection" for the French that had "swallowed up his *first* love—*his love of his country*." First among those attached to this improper love object was the president himself. In fact, Lowell came up with the name many contemporary critics used to describe the conflict: "Mr. Madison's War."[16]

Believing that the war could be explained by Madison's emotional foibles, Lowell had little use for Russell's claim that the emotional suffering of impressed seamen had motivated the war. He had no time at all for the assertion that sailors separated from their families suffered more than did enslaved people severed from theirs. In a pamphlet called *Perpetual War the Policy of Mr. Madison*, Lowell complained, "Mr. Russell very offensively, and ... very petulantly and insultingly, compared the British practice of taking their own seamen to the *slave Trade*." In Lowell's eyes, Russell had no grounds for "intimating that a British subject serving his king and country is in the condition of a *West India* or *Virginia* negro." Lowell believed the British Crown enjoyed a legal right to demand the services of its own subjects that had no analogue in the specious claims of American slaveholders to the labor of forced African migrants.[17]

John Lowell did not present himself primarily as an antislavery activist. He objected most strenuously to the military and diplomatic policies of the Madison administration and chose to address the issue of slavery only because Russell raised it first. It is not even altogether clear whether he regarded it as most insulting that Russell equated impressment with slavery or that Russell compared British sailors to "*West India* or *Virginia* negro[es]." Yet other New England Federalists who opposed the war actively regarded slavery as a problem of the first importance and stood ready to link the tragedy of slavery with what they saw as the travesty of war.

Like Lowell, Nathan Perkins was a New England writer with an elite education, a strong Federalist persuasion, and a staunch opposition to the war. (Born in Connecticut in 1748, Perkins had graduated from Princeton and preached in his native state since the age of twenty-four.) But whereas Lowell was a lawyer with only a tangential interest in slavery, Perkins was a Congregationalist minister ready to confront the moral crisis of human bondage directly. Scarcely a month after war broke out, Perkins preached a searching sermon in which he proclaimed, as many others would do after him, that the war came as a heavenly punishment for the nation's transgressions.[18]

Although Congregationalist ministers had been describing wars as a form of divine retribution for centuries, Perkins was contemporary in the sins he singled out for comment. In July 1812, "the Land-defiling crimes of the UNITED STATES" that Perkins identified included "the national crime [of] slaveholding." In the sermon preached in his home church in Hartford that would be "published at the request of the hearers," Perkins pronounced slaveholding to be a "sin attended with awful consequences" and suggested "perhaps we are now punished for this sin, as a nation, by being left of God, to the miseries of war." When Republican politicians compared impressment to slavery, they unintentionally marshaled opposition as much as patriotism. By 1814, Hartford, Connecticut, would emerge as the seat not only of opposition but also of talk of New England's secession from the United States.[19]

For all his antagonism toward what would soon be known as Mr. Madison's War, Nathan Perkins nevertheless shared the central preoccupation of many in the United States at the time: the harmful effects of public policies on family feelings. Yet whereas men like Jonathan Russell decried the impact of impressment on sailors' domestic bonds, Perkins applied these same concerns to the impact of war itself. He demanded to know how the family disruptions created when men were forced to sea on British ships could possibly be improved by sending those same men to die in combat on the American continent. Mincing no words, he reminded his audience, "the purpose of war is to kill and destroy. Fathers and sons, husbands and brothers are led to the field of battle to be slain." If good public policy promoted the stability and growth of families, Perkins could not conceive that a large-scale American war offered any improvement over the small-scale problem of wrongful British impressment.[20]

Perkins dwelt at length on visions of "a father bereaved of a son slaughtered" and of "a widow weeping over a tender husband slain." He could keenly imagine the pain of parents deprived of their adult sons. Only eighteen months earlier, in October 1810, he had enjoyed the satisfaction of preaching at the ordination ceremony of his son and namesake, Nathan Perkins Jr., who had honored his father by following his profession. Now, Perkins Sr. demanded that his listeners too stop to consider the specter of loss. He said: "Only reflect on one instance to affect your minds. Here are tender parents, the prudent father and affectionate mother, they have reared up a promising son; they cherished and watched over him in infancy; his life has been spared; he is grown up to man's state; he has been fed, clothed and educated by them; he goes into the army; he engages in battle, he is killed. How must his parents be affected with the news! They are overwhelmed with sorrow." Republicans based in Washington thought that the best way to engage the populace in support of the war was to paint a moving picture of the experiences of men exiled from their families. Federalists in New England insisted that the annihilation of war brought home a far deeper sadness.[21]

Yet despite his readiness to declare slavery a "land-defiling crime" and to dwell on the emotional costs of warfare, Nathan Perkins did not make the leap to considering the emotional suffering of families severed through slavery. Perkins veered toward a different set of concerns as he developed his linked arguments against war and slavery. Appealing less to his listeners' sympathies than to their fears, he warned that enslaved African Americans had little reason to remain loyal to a nation that denied them their liberty. He predicted that they were likely to use the wartime crisis as an opportunity to stage armed rebellions of their own. He lectured, "Man is born free. Nature will ere long see this. Nature will reason and feel. The day will come when slavery will not be endured." Like many antislavery leaders of the day, Perkins opposed slavery less because of its impact on blacks than because of its effect on whites.[22]

Perkins centered his analysis squarely on the question of population and on the vexed debate over how to situate African Americans within the U.S. populace. Turning to the government's official population tally, cause for such satisfaction in other contexts, Perkins mused, "the black population of the Southern states, as may be seen in the last census, is immense. What according to the course of nature will be the effect, eventually?" Contemplating the census ordinarily brought people in the United States welcome evidence of their nation's growing strength. Yet Perkins saw only cause for alarm in the fact that such a substantial percentage of the U.S. population was of non-European origins. He saw African Americans as a dire threat to the land they inhabited.[23]

Perkins could not imagine a place for African Americans within the United States. At best, enslaved people represented a dormant menace to whites, one that might easily be activated by the onset of war. "In case of war and insurrection," Perkins demanded, "what will become of our dear brethren, the white population? The slave has the same right to make his master a slave, as the master has to make him a slave." Though he insisted on the injustice of slavery, Perkins regarded only white people as his "dear brethren." He did not deem potentially belligerent enslaved people to be his brothers and sisters nor could he contemplate a place for African Americans within the American family.[24]

For all that the ever-growing U.S. population provided a tremendous source of pride for many, for all that the pleasure of family love often stood in for the blessing of liberty itself, black families and black familial affections were seldom respected or protected in either the domestic or the national sense. True, many antislavery activists, like Nathan Perkins, looked at the teetering stack of the nation's social strata and saw disaster waiting to happen. They rejected the notion that blacks could make useful population contributions without being counted among the formal citizenry, arguing that the presence of unfree people fatally destabilized the wider American family, posing dire threats to their "dear brethren, the white population." But rather than making the leap to offering African Americans full citizenship, antislavery whites in this era began to call for African Americans to be removed from the United States entirely. They said that blacks should be transported away, perhaps to Africa or even to somewhere in western North America, anywhere but within the boundaries of the constitutional United States and the bosom of the U.S. family.[25]

White commentators from across the political spectrum and around the country differed in their views of the relationship between slavery and the war. Some blamed the war on God's displeasure with U.S. slaveholding, while others laid responsibility at the feet of British sea captains who behaved worse than slave traders. Yet for everyone, the war—with its demands for labor and calls for demonstrations of loyalty—cast questions about the makeup of the American family into sharp relief.

Who counted as members of the U.S. family and what were the emotional ties that bound them? Whereas Nathan Perkins could not conceive of blacks and whites as "brethren," others found family metaphors far more appealing. Jesse Torrey, for example, freely condemned whites for "making merchandize" of "their African brethren," showing no hesitation about using a familial word for "Africans" that Perkins reserved for "whites." Torrey devoted many pages of his screed against the slave trade to stories of parents and children made miserable through that market. As he surveyed the devastation in Washington, and watched the efforts to rebuild the Capitol, Torrey reported with dismay the "fact that *slaves* are employed in rebuilding this sanctuary of liberty." It seemed he could not reconcile himself to the hypocrisy on display.[26]

Yet Torrey himself did *not* think the slaves should be freed. For all of Torrey's familial feelings for African Americans, for all that catching even "a distant glimpse . . . of a procession of men, women, and children . . . bound . . . with iron chains . . . used only for restraining beasts" caused him to experience "involuntary successive heavings of [his] bosom," Torrey argued only for improving the conditions of slavery, not for ending the institution. Sobbing at the sight of slave markets in the capital city did not equate to supporting the emancipation of slaves. Oh no. Torrey felt himself "constrained to perform the melancholy task of recording my dissent from the sentiments of those who . . . request . . . universal, simultaneous, and *unconditional* emancipation." All that Torrey wished to combat was the slave trade itself—along with the family separations it imposed.[27]

Just because Torrey regarded his "sable heathen neighbors" as proper objects of "religious duty and brotherly love," he did not have to recognize black rights to equal citizenship. He had no desire to live in parity with a people he regarded as beings "enveloped in the fogs of brutal ignorance and debasement." If Torrey felt a familial relationship with his African brethren, it was actually less as brother than as detached foster father. Torrey demanded only that slaveholders perform as the "patrons" of those "whose lot ha[d] been cast under their guardianship." With American family like Torrey, why should African Americans have viewed the British as the enemy?[28]

Ironically, the whites most likely to claim family feelings for blacks and to appreciate black contributions to the U.S. population were the very ones most determined to keep them enslaved. Many white abolitionists who desired a total end to slavery also wanted to sever all ties with blacks, denying them any membership in the nation. In 1812, many of slavery's most vocal white opponents could not regard African Americans as members of the national family, while many whites willing to claim a familial relationship with Africans could not imagine an end to slavery. For enslaved Africans and their descendants, joining the American family meant accepting degraded status as dependent wards, while gaining freedom meant accepting the threat of a new round of exile. Ultimately leading politicians, from Jonathan Russell to President Madison himself, were most likely to make use of the notion of slavery as a philosophical abstraction without much concern at all for the effects of the real institution on actual persons.[29]

cᗡᏆᓚᎧ

No sooner did Congress reconvene after the dramatic fall of the capital than it commissioned a *Report . . . to Inquire into the Causes and Particulars of the Invasion of the City of Washington by the British Forces.* The most salient single fact was that the U.S. troops had fled without offering any resistance. The British had marched into an empty city and no one had raised an arm against them. Try as some writers might to make the British failure to seize prisoners into some sort of backward triumph of population preservation, the fact remained that many regarded the day's events as a complete disgrace for the United States. Admitting that this latest military disaster "intimately concern[ed] the character of the administration [and] the sensibility of the nation," the investigating committee embarked on a by-then familiar quest to pinpoint exactly what logistical problems and emotional proclivities had contributed to the men's failure to fight. Was the loss of the capital a simple matter of failures of courage?[30]

Like General Hull and so many others before him, General William H. Winder, commander of the U.S. forces in D.C., had a lot to answer for. But

Winder had learned from Hull's mistakes and did not wait to be accused either of lacking patriotic ardor himself or of causing the men's ardor to abate. Instead, in explaining the "disasters of the day," he and Secretary of War John Armstrong jointly agreed that "without all doubt the determining cause of these is to be found in that love of life which, in many of the corps, predominated over a love of country and of honor." The ultimate proof of the troops' base self-love came with the fact that they deserted the ranks in order to return to their families in local communities surrounding Washington. As Winder specified, the men "gave themselves up to . . . uncontrouled feelings . . . and many hundreds, in spite of all precautions and efforts, passed on and pursued their way either towards home or in search of refreshments." By their leaders' account, the rank and file was to blame not so much for lack of feeling as for indulging a base and inferior kind of feeling.[31]

Yet according to widely accepted ideas about love and service, there was a flaw in the Armstrong-Winder logic. Subordinate officers who testified against them took care to exploit it. If patriotic love was built pyramid-style on a base of romantic and familial love, then the men could hardly be faulted as selfish for making the defense of home and hearth their first priority. General William Smith, arguing that critiques of the troops were "as unmerited as . . . cruel and wanton," defended his men by saying that they had not gone home until *after* Winder had ordered the retreat and that they had only done so then because their commanding general's decision to fall back meant their families would receive no defense beyond what each man could personally provide: "The idea of leaving their families, their houses, and their homes to the mercy of an enraged enemy was insupportable." In the event, the results of Armstrong and Winder's rationalizations and accusations were mixed; Winder was largely exonerated by a "court of inquiry," while Armstrong was forced to resign.[32]

Left almost, but not entirely, unspoken was another issue: white soldiers in Washington believed that their families could be in danger of attack by blacks. Just months before the August attack on the capital city, on April 2, 1814, the British naval commander, Vice-Admiral Alexander Cochrane, had issued a proclamation offering asylum to anyone, white or black, "disposed to emigrate" and by May he had successfully established a refugee camp for blacks fleeing enslavement on Tangier Island at the mouth of the Potomac River. From there, he organized a black marine corps that in due course served in the invasion of Washington. Moreover, word spread among whites that

American blacks unaffiliated with any army supposedly took advantage of the chaos to threaten the homes and families of whites. According to reports, "nearly the whole of the male population having joined the army, a great number of houses were broken open and plundered by the blacks and a few disorderly inhabitants." Of course, this was not the whole story. In actuality, many free blacks in Washington were among the "whole male population" that joined the ranks of U.S. troops and these black men bore no more responsibility for the British sweep than did their white American counterparts. Nevertheless, the possibility of black-on-white violence proved a useful tool of legal self-defense for deserting white soldiers.[33]

In his testimony before the congressional committee, General Tobias Stansbury of Baltimore took the "black menace" defense for white desertions to its height. "The arms of many of the enemy had fallen into the hands of the blacks," he declared, elaborating that "it was apprehended that they would take advantage of the absence of the men to insult the females and complete the work of destruction commenced by the enemy." Stansbury obviously hoped to send a visceral shock through the investigating members of Congress in confronting them with the most lurid possible picture of sexual disorder, of free white women forced into sex by enslaved black men. If emotions motivated actions, then surely Congress could come to view these troops not as deserters of the nation but as defenders of the patriarchal racial order that formed the very basis of U.S. society. Part of what gave the image such emotive power was the possibility that, if impregnated, such white women would themselves have been forced into reproductive labor for the benefit of enemy-allied former slaves.[34]

Whether or not free and enslaved blacks enjoyed metaphorical membership in the nation, their sheer physical presence as members of the U.S. population could not be ignored. The wartime emergency made manifest the contradictory possibilities for black participation in unfolding public events. Did they threaten dire harm to the whites around them, putting even white women's reproductive lives in peril? Might they be a source of crucial aid, lending their strength to the nation in an hour of need? How would blacks' emotions shape their national loyalty or lack thereof? No matter whether whites welcomed them or not, free and enslaved blacks strode the streets of the war-torn capital. Meanwhile, in the northern states, where educated free blacks could speak out and publish their thoughts in print, African Americans were stepping forward to declare their views on the relationship between black family life and American liberty, between black family love and patriotic feeling.

In Philadelphia in 1814, at the center of free black learning and culture in the early United States, there lived a young black man who was a printer by trade and a preacher by calling, a 21-year-old by the name of Russell Parrott. A member of the city's African Literary Society, Parrott knew his books and was quick with his pen. A leading member of Philadelphia's African Church of St. Thomas, he was a minister-in-training with a finely tuned ear for moral nuance. Though still a young man when the War of 1812 broke out, Parrott understood intricately the symbolic and actual importance of black families to the American family. He demonstrated this understanding by word and deed. Beginning in 1812, Parrott presented a series of orations in celebration of the abolition of the Atlantic slave trade that brought black population questions to the forefront. And in the critical days immediately after the fall of Washington, when every city in the Northeast seemed vulnerable to the next attack, Parrott delivered black people to the bulwarks, organizing twenty-five hundred men of color for two days of voluntary labor in September 1814 to build fortifications for the city of Philadelphia.[35]

Parrott displayed a critical perspective on population questions that showed he was fluent in the theoretical debates of his day. In an *Oration on the Abolition of the Slave Trade* offered at the African Church of St. Thomas on January 1, 1814, he pointed out the contributions of African Americans to the United States' much-boasted strength in population. Taking his audience on a historical tour of the origins of English and Spanish slavery in the Americas, he noted that as British colonial possessions "were not so populous as those of their neighbor" in Latin America, Queen Elizabeth decided "to populate her newly acquired domain by the introduction of Africans." The result, as anyone could see, was that African Americans had played a crucial part in helping to seize and settle the land once claimed by Britain and now governed as the sovereign territory of the United States.[36]

At the same time, Parrott introduced an argument that many white Americans would have preferred to overlook: African American population contributions in British America and later the United States were made possible only by the destruction of black families in Africa. His voice carrying through the Church of St. Thomas, Parrott charged each member of his audience to "fancy yourself on the fertile plains of Africa" where sat a husband

and father "in the midst of his domestic enjoyment" sharing life with "the partner of his affection and the friend of his heart," both of them "surrounded by a flock of innocents," who entertained them with their "endearing, artless prattle." Into this idyllic scene, Parrott continued, "a fiend steals in and mars all his happiness: the slave merchant . . . tears from the bosom of his family the poor African!" African husbands and fathers endured severe emotional suffering as the result of such actions. "What language can tell the feelings of his soul?'" Parrott demanded, "What pen portray the intenseness of his grief?" When one country laid claim to the people of another, dire family ruptures were the painful result.[37]

From Jonathan Russell to Russell Parrott, U.S. public commentators understood the emotional impact and moral power of charging their opponents with destroying families. But whereas Russell's leaky argument equating British impressment and American slavery began to take on water almost the moment he launched it, Parrott's analysis was all but impermeable. For anyone who might have preferred to regard his stories of African family disruptions as tales from the distant past, Parrott offered up the key point that domestic slave sales continued to the present day with the same drastic consequences. Of contemporary slave buyers, he said, "with the purchaser, it is not whether he separates parents and children, or husband and wife; a thought of this kind never enters his cold calculating soul." As a direct result of domestic markets, enslaved family members were forever "forced from each other's embrace, and doomed to disgrace and labour." Finally, of those apologists who insisted that American slavery improved the basic conditions of life for Africans, Parrott said, "they say the slave's situation is more happy, he is better fed and clad, than the poor of civilized Europe. Can he claim the proud privilege of being a citizen of the country in which he resides?" The answer was obviously "no." For Parrott, and for the nation, citizenship was the crux of the matter.[38]

Making his case in the context of the ongoing war, Parrott asserted forthrightly that "if the security of a country should rest within her bosom, then it is necessary that each citizen should be a freeman." Blacks and whites alike agreed in 1812 that the defense of citizenship was the single greatest crisis facing the nation. The narrative prowar whites liked to tell claimed that free American citizens had gone to war to ensure that not one U.S. sailor would ever be forced to relinquish his rights as a U.S. citizen and return to the degraded status of British subject. Their preferred story line told a tale of progress, of the rise of freemen from royal and aristocratic subjugation.

The citizen was a new figure on the world stage, a man who chose his rules and his rulers through a democratic process of consent. Across the Atlantic, republican governments were replacing hereditary monarchies. When the United States went to war, it did so to ensure that this progress could not be reversed.[39]

Yet this story of a triumphal transition from the archetypal figure of the royal subject to that of the democratic citizen left a crucial plot point unresolved. Every inhabitant of the royal kingdom, man, woman, or child, was a subject of the Crown. Yet not every denizen of the new United States was a citizen of the nation. If the natural rights that justified democratic citizenship were universal rights, how could citizenship itself be restricted rather than universal?[40]

For many U.S. observers the notion of "population" provided a useful catchall term that described how all the nation's people could contribute to the strength of the state without necessarily demanding the compensatory rights of citizens. Yet many remained uncomfortable with this logical inconsistency, with the notion of nonuniversal citizenship based on universal rights. Many blacks and whites alike looked forward to a time of final progress when citizenship would become as universal for national residents as subjecthood was for royal ones. Believing that the borders of population and the boundaries of citizenship should be coterminous, they argued that the presence of unfree people fatally destabilized the wider American family. Yet they often disagreed sharply on the right remedy for this moral and legal discrepancy.[41]

As Russell Parrott surveyed the situation, it seemed clear to him that all who served the nation earned the right to full membership in the nation. Just as black family love survived even the terrible reaping of slavery, so African American love of country yet grew from the rich loam of family. Recounting the contributions of U.S. blacks to the war effort, from noncombat work in Philadelphia to active-duty service by black seamen in celebrated naval battles of the war, he argued that "the black bore his part, stimulated by the pure love of country, which neither contempt nor persecution can eradicate from his generous heart." For Parrott, the case was clear. Black people had lent their strength to the country from the moment of colonization right through the worst days of the current crisis. They loved their families, from spouses to children to fellow countrymen, without reservation. In return, they should be admitted as full members of the American family, as citizens with political rights and emotional privileges that each reinforced the other.[42]

Figure 15. This antislavery tract makes family rupture the symbolic heart of critiques of the slave trade. Again, the inclusion of the child cowering behind the mother serves to emphasize that this is a family being torn apart. "The husband and wife, after being sold to different purchasers, violently separated: probably never to see each other more," illustration from *The Mirror of Misery* (New York: Samuel Wood, 1814), Collections of the Library Company of Philadelphia.

Free blacks across the Northeast sounded this refrain again and again. When George Lawrence stepped up to the pulpit of the African Methodist Episcopal Zion Church in New York City on January 1, 1813, to deliver a speech in commemoration of the fifth anniversary of the abolition of the slave trade, he had family love and public life on his mind. He told an audience of free blacks that the Atlantic slave trade had "pierce[d] the hearts of our ancestors, separated and dashed asunder the most sacred ties of nature." When slave traders seized people for sale, they "separated them from their dearest relatives; the aged parent from the tender child; the loving husband from the affectionate wife." Such crimes cast individual Africans into lives of misery (Figure 15).[43]

Dashing the "sacred ties" of love also had serious public consequences for the contemporary United States. When loving husbands and wives, tender parents and children, were torn apart, the emotional basis of community allegiance was destroyed as well. "The glory of a people is union; united in bonds of social love, they become strong and vigorous," Lawrence argued, "wise and discerning; they press undauntedly forward and are sure of conquest." Without family affection there could be no social love, without social love, no political unity or public progress.[44]

Lawrence left vague just what he meant by "conquest," but it seems likely he had several interrelated victories in mind: an African American triumph over slavery *and* a United States win against the British. He drew on Paul's Letter to the Ephesians to describe the importance of love in personal and public life alike. Expanding the claim that "union" was the highest glory of a people, he declared, "union is the foundation of liberty and its perfection is social love." For the United States to be fully united in its war efforts, and uncompromised in its promotion of liberty, its people must be joined by a love that started in family affection and grew outward to embrace the whole nation.[45]

Lawrence broached the topic of patriotism directly in his speech, making it difficult not to see his comments on family love, social love, and American liberty as closely connected. He had nothing but "gratitude towards that veteran band of patriots" who had achieved American independence and he asked his hearers to "rejoice for a nation rising" as the United States again confronted Great Britain. It would seem that Lawrence supported the war effort on principle. Yet he pointedly reminded the audience of free blacks in the church hall, "we make a part of this nation." If whites frequently forgot this fact, it was blacks' job to remind them. Putting it bluntly, he said, "this government founded on the principles of liberty and equality, and declaring them to be the free gift of God, if not ignorant of their declaration, must enforce it." Too often, Lawrence complained, the United States fell far short of its own founding commitments. To realize the revolutionary promise of liberty, all the nation's people must be bound not by chains but by love.[46]

Yet other free blacks in the North doubted that whites would ever recognize their positive contributions to the population, much less regard them as equals. Many began to search for a solution involving separation instead of union. In the very same month that Russell Parrott published his demand for citizenship rights, another free black leader, a Massachusetts merchant by the name of Paul Cuffee, presented a petition to Congress in which he asked for a special exemption from the Atlantic blockade then in effect in order to transport a shipload of free blacks from the United States to Sierra Leone. While he planned to take some trade goods along on the voyage, Cuffee's primary aim would be to help establish a colony of black freemen beyond the bounds of the United States.[47]

The white members of Congress debated whether the good of ridding the country of many free blacks would be outweighed by the bad in allowing a black man to engage in Atlantic trading at a time when whites were not authorized to do so. After "a debate of considerable length," Congress denied Cuffee permission to make the trip—but not before many had publicly shared their view that Cuffee's plan offered many "benefits to the United States particularly, from the establishment of an institution which would invite the emigration of free blacks, a part of our population which we could well spare." Faced with the awkward fact that blacks occupied a degraded status that placed them in the nation without making them of the nation, many whites regarded black removal as the best solution.[48]

When white men accused black ones of using wartime chaos in the capital as an opportunity for domestic attacks on white families, including sexual attacks on white women, they blamed them for twofold treachery. Not only would such acts signify a clear betrayal of national loyalties, but they would also represent the worst violation of the standards of civilized war. Charging black men with harboring so much as the desire to commit this dual crime provided a convenient excuse to deny them eligibility to join the full ranks of free U.S. citizens. Such rationalizations fed equally well into support for maintaining slavery and for movements to exile free blacks to new colonies.

Yet every time a white man—from a Connecticut minister like the Reverend Nathan Perkins to a Maryland military man like General Tobias Stansbury—dwelled on the possibility of black attacks on white women and children, he only reopened the question of how U.S. citizens could countenance those same acts being aimed at black families. As George Lawrence thundered in New York City in 1813, in Africa "the ravages of merciless power, extend like the besom of destruction, sweeping off [its] inhabitants without regard to age or sex." What did it say about the nation's true commitment to liberty, much less civility, that it could continue to profit for generations from violations of its own first principles of just warfare?[49]

An air of hypocrisy hung in the smoke over Washington. While blaming the British for forcing men to labor for the Royal Navy, U.S. politicians conducted the work of the republic in the shadow of the slave mart. While claiming to fight for liberty and family love, U.S. generals faulted their troops for daring to detour to defend their homes, even after every pretense of organized action had ended. And while the Madison administration brought General Winder to court for his failure to stand and defend the capital city, President James Madison himself was widely blamed for fleeing town along with everyone else.

For New England Federalists who had deplored the war from the start, the fall of Washington seemed to be the Republicans' final moment of truth. What effort of public relations could possibly recoup the loss of the capital? How could the people be rallied behind a flag of folly? Satirists seized on the image of the president galloping out of the capital as fast as his horse would carry him. In actuality, on the day of the invasion, Madison had taken an active if wholly ineffectual part in strategizing for defense. He had left town along the Bladensburg Road to reconnoiter with General Winder in Bladensburg, Maryland; unfortunately, it was the loss of Bladensburg that opened a clear path to the capital. Nevertheless, as soon as October 1814, the *Federal Republican*, a Federalist paper published in Georgetown, memorialized the president's rapid retreat from the capital as "the Bladensburg Races."[50]

Standing just five feet, four inches, in his stocking feet, Madison had the right physical build for a racing jockey and the ripostes began with this fact. "No jockey," claimed the *Federal Republican*, ever showed "greater dexterity in the management of his steed." Madison supposedly rode so hard, he was "overcome with fear" and "fairly out of wind." "When I took a survey of this jockey," said the anonymous newspaper columnist, "thinks I to myself, what a most admirable acquisition to a company of Comedians!" Variously comparing Madison to the hapless Don Quixote and calling him Napoleon "Bonaparte's Vice Roy," this Federalist brought out every critique he could to ridicule the president's performance, linking him to imbecility and to French-style imperialism all at the same time.[51]

The ultimate insult came with the suggestion that even the city's black inhabitants were ashamed and amused by Madison's actions. The fact that human bondage was practiced in the capital worked to the advantage of

Federalist war critics. Asserting that even enslaved people had observed how ridiculous the president looked in retreat, the writer added a flourish of black dialect saying, "while Pompey laughing thus did bawl / See Massa Jemmy beats 'em all!" Portrayed as a slaveholder and as a coward, James Madison (further belittled by the nickname "Jemmy") made an easy target for Federalist contempt. "Poor Madison, *'the greatest statesman in the world,'"* laughed the *Federal Republican,* "came in full tilt under the whip and spur." The president was an incompetent manager of an unwise conflict, a slave-owning statesman with no claim to the liberty he so blatantly failed to defend and uphold.[52]

Free black Federalists were the most scathing critics of all when it came to systematically dismantling the teetering structures of prowar rhetoric that equated impressment with slavery and claimed that the tragedy of ruptured family love among seamen could only be redressed through the remedy of war. In Brandon, Vermont, in February 1813, a free black minister by the name of Lemuel Haynes preached a sermon in honor of George Washington's birthday that took genuine love versus personal and political hypocrisy as its organizing theme.[53]

Lemuel Haynes had been born in West Hartford, Connecticut, in 1753 and raised as an indentured servant in the household of white New Englanders before being freed as an adult. He served in multiple military campaigns during the American Revolution and considered himself a true patriot. While little record remains of how and where he received his schooling, it is clear that he was a Puritan-influenced minister in the enlightened tradition of Jonathan Edwards. As such, he was well versed in the Edwardsian view of Christian love, which held that love, in its perfect form, should extend to all of heaven and earth, to "being in general," as Edwards put it. Pure love should not be put in the service of individual people or even of particular countries. As he surveyed the political landscape around him in 1813, Haynes concluded that people in the United States had all but forgotten the ideal character of love. He took as his text for the Washington's Birthday sermon a line from Romans 12:9, "Let love be without dissimulation," and he titled his sermon "Dissimulation Illustrated." For Haynes, nothing illustrated "dissimulation" like the sorry picture painted by prowar rhetoric equating slavery and impressment.[54]

Nearly deafened by the swell of voices calling for "love of country" in the era of 1812, Haynes shouted into the wind, *"Let love be without dissimulation.*

The word *dissimulation* is the same as hypocrisy." Haynes had a very specific contemporary example of hypocrisy in mind: "Our President . . . can talk feelingly on the subject of the impressment of our seamen. I am glad to have him feel for them. Yet in his own state, Virginia, there were, in the year 1800, no less than three hundred forty-three thousand, seven hundred ninety-six human beings holden in bondage for life!" Here again, the census came into political play. The problem, Haynes maintained, was that Madison, like so many of his followers, had failed to develop universal love, settling instead for a restricted brand of love that smacked of sinful self-interest. Haynes condemned the president, saying, "partial affection, or distress for some of our fellow creatures, while others, even under our notice, are wholly disregarded, betrays dissimulation." U.S. patriots could not claim that their love of country demonstrated *virtuous* love if their national feelings grew out of selfish attachments to only those people to whom they felt especially partial. Only when patriots extended their affections as freely to enslaved blacks as to impressed white seamen could they possibly claim that they went to war stirred by a virtuous love of liberty.[55]

Haynes, who as noted was a veteran of the Revolutionary War and claimed the right to offer critiques of patriotism on that basis, also rejected outright the widely current idea that virtuous patriotic love grew from romantic love. Romantic love was personal and partial by definition. Complaining that "the words *love to our country* . . . go cheap at the present day," Haynes dismissed such moral errors as just one more example of the dire French influence blinding American Republicans. His case in point was the rise of divorce in the United States and France. Divorces, he complained, were being "granted to almost every applicant, upon no other pretence than only they conceive that a new companion would be more agreeable to their lust, and render their lives more comfortable. In 1793, one thousand eight hundred divorces took place in Paris, in consequence of the French decree to abolish the ordinance of marriage." So-called love of country that grew mainly from sexual lust and passion could hardly be credited as either virtuous feeling or effective patriotism. Nevertheless, Haynes observed, "'tis not an uncommon thing to see men bellowing out their passions, with a kind of enthusiastic delirium, making the highest pretences to patriotism." If delirium was a strong word, Haynes did not use it lightly. Prowar commentators who claimed that war was some kind of romp, an enactment of sexual potency channeled into national militancy, entirely ignored the fact that battles were the source of mass suffering and death.[56]

Only pure and virtuous love of liberty could justify the costs of combat, never the tawdry "love of country" tainted by private passion that he saw flaunted all around him. Of those who enlisted willingly in this misbegotten war, Haynes said, "people may swagger and pretend great love to their country . . . pipe abroad that they have . . . acted their part well in the field of battle, and murdered a thousand men." But, he insisted, "this has nothing of that love recommended in my text." For all their claims to act on love, Haynes pointed out, "the poor disconsolate bereaved widow, and the hapless orphans have no place in their affections." Pure Christian love required extending affection to everyone, including the enslaved, and considering the full effects of wars on families. Politicians who claimed to have voted for war out of emotional sympathy with the suffering of sailors separated from their loved ones not only failed to feel for the enslaved but also seemed unconcerned that the war itself would destroy more families than had ever been harmed through the practice of impressment.[57]

Haynes opposed the War of 1812 as a Federalist, as an African American, and as a Christian man of God. For him, the real tragedy was "to see people intoxicated with zeal for their country, foaming out their rage and spite, offering the last drop of their heart's blood . . . sacrificing their profession of religion to political phrenzy, we pity their delusion." Haynes pleaded with his audience to cultivate "a rational affection" that began and ended with God and avoided the adulterating influence of personal passions.[58]

Haynes dismantled the puzzle box of prowar rhetoric, with its false floors and trick mirrors, piece by piece. He called hypocrisy by its name. He pointed out that liberty and slavery could never coexist, that tears shed for the lost love of seamen but not for that of slaves were nothing but empty show, that a war spurred by romantic love and lust could hardly be called rational or virtuous. His sermon of 1813 offered perhaps the most unsparing contemporary critique of the case for war made by anyone, black or white.

Perhaps most perceptively of all, Haynes broached the question of black membership in the American family head on. He daringly suggested that, by enslaving blacks, whites succeeded only in cutting *themselves* out of the national family. Reminding his largely white audience at the end of his sermon that the occasion of their gathering was the anniversary of the first president's birth, he informed them that Washington "was an enemy to slaveholding, and gave his dying testimony against it, by emancipating and providing for those under his care." Haynes then offered a prayer and a challenge: "O that his jealous surviving neighbors would prove themselves to be his legitimate children, and go do likewise!" According to Haynes, no one who failed to support the emancipation of slaves could claim to be a true child of Washington, a legitimate heir to the legacy of revolutionary liberty, or a full member of the American family. In this ingenious inversion, hypocritical whites, not enslaved blacks, were the ones in greatest danger of being cast forth from the nation.[59]

Still, Haynes left one key piece out of place in his summation. For all his clear-sighted vision on moral matters of black and white, Haynes did not seek a place for Indians in the American family. Telling his audience that even war opponents "may pray for our army, and ought to do," Haynes encouraged them to pray for peace and justice, that "swords may be beat into ploughshares, and spears into pruning hooks," then suggested that they should also pray that "the savages may be kept back from devastation and slaughter." This significant addition marked out Indians alone as a people beyond the civilized line that defined the U.S. population. Haynes's expedient choice to cast Indians as "savages" undercut his opposition to the conflict.[60]

When he demonized Indians as the agents of "devastation and slaughter," rather than arguing for their incorporation into the United States or, more radically still, advocating for full recognition of their territorial rights, Haynes proved how compelling the case for war actually was. The acquisition of Indian lands could potentially advance the material interests of all members of the U.S. population, both those already recognized as citizens and those who still aspired to that status. Despite the fact that western expansion and the increase in the internal slave trade went together, by the absolute measure of population increase, even enslaved blacks stood to gain from U.S. territorial aggression. Certainly property-owning free blacks stood to benefit from an increased availability of land. The war fully harmed only those native peoples who were *not* counted as any part of the nation.[61]

In the event, the words of the Reverend Lemuel Haynes, like those of so many other war opponents, gained very little currency. While his sermon was printed privately by the Washington Benevolent Society, which had sponsored his presentation, it was never reprinted. Haynes's ideas were neither quoted in newspapers from town to town nor picked up and reproduced in the many compendiums pouring from presses around the country. Federalist scolding about base lusts and sinful passions held far less appeal than did invitations to promote and protect family love of all kinds, including romantic love between husbands and wives. "Federal" Republicans of the kind critiquing the Madison

administration demanded a degree of emotional privation and personal discipline entirely out of step with the nation's eager turn toward a culture of ardor
and acquisitive politics of territorial expansion.

The satirical conceit of the Bladensburg Races, by contrast, caught the
imagination of war opponents and soon appeared in the press in many variations. By early January 1815, just before news of the war's end arrived on the
East Coast, the *Federal Republican* was advertising to its readers that a stand-
alone pamphlet containing "A New Poem, Called Bladensburg Races . . . in
Four Cantos," would soon be published and offered for sale. While copies of
that imprint do not seem to have survived, the poem was certainly written
and circulated widely. A full edition of the poem was reprinted in a Hartford
newspaper (in the very city that harbored the strongest Federalist opposition
to the war) by March 1815. And a pamphlet reprint of the poem from 1816
survives.[62]

The poem "in Four Cantos" lampooned claims that martial courage
stemmed from marital ardor, by featuring scenes in which the president "kiss'd
his loving wife" before charging off in fear. And it used the strong cultural
prohibition against involving women in warfare to make Dolly Madison the
target of ribald insinuations. Toying carefully and indirectly with the possibility that even the first lady could have been vulnerable to sexual advances in the
chaos of war, the poem said of Madison: "o'erjoy'd was he to find, Though bent
on running off, she'd still / His *honour* in her mind." By playing to the popular
taste for bawdy fun, while striving to embarrass Madison as much as possible,
this satire made the deeper point that romantic and sexual motivations for
war action were as indefensible as they were ineffective.[63]

⌒∞⌒

Jesse Torrey, who as the author of *A Portraiture of Domestic Slavery* offered
stinging commentary on the irony of seeing slavery in the capital of liberty,
also provided readers with a gruesome twist on the Bladensburg Races. Once
he saw enslaved people being paraded in front of the ruined seat of government, he forgot his original plan of touring Congress and instead began to
dig around for information on the prevalence of slavery in Washington, D.C.
As Torrey explained himself, "the tragedy of a company of men, women, and
children, pinioned and bound together with chains and ropes . . . and driven
as beasts of the harness, through the metropolis of that country of which I

had hitherto indulged both pleasure and pride . . . prevented my visit to the congressional hall that day." In the course of his subsequent sleuthing for cases of African American family separations through sale, he came across the story of a recently sold woman being transported south, who came to grief on the Bladensburg Road itself.[64]

Torrey recounted that, sometime around December 1815, "a female slave who had been sold in Maryland, with her child, on the way from Bladensburg to Washington, heroically cut the throats of both her child and herself with mortal effect." In relating this tale, Torrey aimed principally to dramatically underscore the desperation that enslaved people felt in being severed from their families and communities.[65]

Yet the tale of the woman who met death on the Bladensburg Road also gained political resonance because it inverted the satiric story of Madison's journey in every respect. She traveled in the opposite physical direction, from Maryland to D.C., and she sought not to save her life but to end it. While critics cast Madison's flight as proof of his cowardice, Torrey portrayed the enslaved woman's act as "heroic," an extreme gesture of despair and defiance against the dehumanization of the slave trade. Of course, Torrey made no direct comment on the president in presenting his tale. Still, given that Torrey published these anecdotes in 1817, by which time "Bladensburg Races" jokes had circulated widely, and given that he wrote with the destruction of the capital directly in mind, it is more than possible that he invited comparison between Madison and the slave woman deliberately.[66]

There is an apparent timelessness to claims that family pain provides a good measure of the moral depravity of those who inflict it. To this day, we are often asked after any tragic death to imagine the emotional turmoil of surviving family members. But the rhetoric of family love and family grief also enjoyed a special *timeliness* in 1812. Throughout early modern Europe and colonial British America, the family had functioned as a sort of ministate, providing everything that today comes under the rubric of various social-service agencies: church, school, hospital, poor house, house of correction, and old-age home all rolled into one. But in the nineteenth century, as many of these quasi-public functions were fading out, the family was growing in importance as a cultural symbol and emotional center as never before.[67]

In the early United States, family came to stand as a key emblem of American liberty. By 1812, British theorists like Thomas Malthus had argued against unfettered freedoms to marry and reproduce. At the same time, Indian families could be constituted through practices that Euro-Americans found deeply alien, including divorce, remarriage, and widespread captive adoptions. People had only to look around to see that African and African American families could be routinely broken through slavery, informal slave marriages easily violated by white masters, and enslaved parents and children parted. In this special context, white Americans came to view the love of family—of freely chosen love between husbands and wives and unbreakable attachments between parents and children—as a special privilege.

Yet Americans in the era of 1812 also came to argue that family ties should enjoy the status of something like natural rights. Beginning with the eighteenth-century Quaker activists who were the first British-American leaders in the antislavery movement, abolitionists had fought to show that enslaved people could feel all the same emotions as free ones. They documented that black people experienced deep suffering as the result of the terrible family splintering brought on by slavery. By the time of the War of 1812, a wide array of activists had begun to sound such themes. Still, Quaker voices remained prominent. Elias Hicks, better known as the eccentric religious reformer who inspired the so-called Hicksite Schism within Quakerism in the 1820s, devoted serious effort to the antislavery movement in this period. In New York, in 1814, he argued in a pamphlet called *Observations on the Slavery of Africans and Their Descendents*: "all nature is forced to yield when the husband is separated from a beloved wife and a wife from a beloved husband." Slavery, quite simply, owed nothing to nature, whereas nothing could be more natural than the mutual love of husband and wife. Once they made the conceptual leap from defining family love as a distinct privilege to regarding it as a universal right, white inhabitants of the United States had no easy way to keep black ones on the far side of the chasm.[68]

During the War of 1812, the idea that family love was a natural right that enjoyed greater respect in the United States than in any other nation took on added urgency because many regarded familial affection as the source of American patriotism itself. While whites remained strongly divided about whether a loyal black population deserved the reward of citizenship, few doubted that a disloyal black population spelled disaster. If whites undermined the family ties of blacks, did they not inadvertently lay the emotional ground for political subversion? If familial and national ties were linked, then any family fractures posed threats to national fealty.

In Philadelphia, where Russell Parrott spoke eloquently on black love of country, another free black leader, his friend and mentor James Forten, launched his own forceful objections to slave sales on just these terms in 1813. He said: "many of our fathers, many of ourselves have fought for the Independence of this country. Do not then expose us to sale. Let not the spirit of the father behold the son robbed of that Liberty which he died to establish." Forten spoke out at a particular moment of crisis, when the Pennsylvania legislature was considering a bill requiring even free black parents to enter their children in a special state registry, and to see their children sold off as slaves if they did not comply. Yet his comments had wide applicability.[69]

Warming to his theme, Forten insisted that blacks and whites were "born to the same hopes, created with the same feeling, destined for the same goal" of freedom. He then demanded of his white readers, "you who are perusing this effusion of feeling, are you a parent? Have you children around whom your affections are bound? . . . To you we submit our cause. The parent's feeling cannot err. By your verdict we will stand or fall—by your verdict live slaves or freemen." According to Forten, unfettered family affection was the defining characteristic of Americans, black and white, the most important dividend of independence, and a priceless national inheritance. Whites who ignored these precepts—by selling black sons away from their fathers—forfeited one of the most precious legacies of freedom.[70]

As these many varied comments on family love make clear, nineteenth-century commentators focused as much on parental love as on spousal love when speaking of liberty. While far from identical, these different varieties of affection were deeply interconnected. And each was especially fraught for blacks denied both the right to marry legally and the right to maintain child custody. While free blacks had somewhat greater assurance of family autonomy than did enslaved ones, Forten refused to let anyone forget how fragile even the rights of free people of color remained. While Euro-Americans enjoyed a growing sense of entitlement to family love and family independence, blacks remained obliged to accept an increasingly archaic definition of family.

In colonial British America, "family" in the modern nuclear sense of husband, wife, and children had actually mattered far less than the household. Everyone who lived under one roof under the direction of the adult male head, whether servant or slave, wife or child, counted as part of the "family." Indeed, in the colonial period, Euro-American children of every rank commonly passed many years of their childhoods as indentured servants in households other than those of their parents, learning needed skills and contributing a valuable and fairly flexible supply of labor. Only by the early nineteenth century did the expectation grow that white children should ideally reside from birth to maturity in the household of their natal family. At that point, parent-child separations became a mark of social dislocation and subordination, an experience to be endured by blacks and perhaps by Indians but less and less by whites, especially those of higher rank. For upper- and middle-class white Americans, parent-child ties rapidly became as sacrosanct as marital bonds had been for generations.[71]

Abolitionists writing during the war years bemoaned the family ruination brought on by slavery every bit as loudly as any war booster complaining about savage Indians attacking white women and children at home. In New York, in 1814, Samuel Wood, the same printer who produced a tract for Quaker Elias Hicks, published a large collection of case studies under the title *The Mirror of Misery; or, Tyranny Exposed* (see Figure 16). The book featured varied excerpts from British abolitionist tracts and focused especially on interviews with ship captains and other participants in the slave trade. The goal was to document that, under slavery, "husbands and wives, parents and children, are parted with as little concern as sheep and lambs by the butcher."[72]

Samuel Wood's 1814 compendium focused particularly on how slavery disrupted reproduction. If American apologists for the slave system like Virginia's John Taylor sometimes went so far as to claim that enslaved American blacks enjoyed fuller reproductive rights than did supposedly free British whites, Wood's examples effectively shattered such claims. He charged that, under slavery, "women were, in general, considered to miscarry from the cruel treatment they met with." One captain whose testimony was included in the book said that he personally had witnessed "a woman seated to give suck to her child, roused from that situation by a severe blow from the cart whip" while another said that he had "known pregnant women so severely whipped as to have miscarried in consequence." Beyond the emotional provocation created by such accounts, Wood and his fellow antislavery activists were offering evidence that slavery itself was highly unnatural; it interrupted that most celebrated of natural female functions, the bearing and rearing of children.[73]

To these anecdotal accounts, the Wood volume added sensationalist narrative poems. One pair of couplets, for example, described the plight of a pregnant woman who died in premature childbirth at the hands of a violent master:

While the lash tore her tir'd and tortur'd frame
The pangs of labour prematurely came.
She clasped her murdered infant to her breast!
Stretch'd her sore limbs, and sunk in endless rest!

Gruesome as this depiction of maternal-fetal murder was, other poems made clear that an infant's birth augured no better fate for mother or child. A second set of verses claimed:

I know a foetus, in mere wanton play
Sold from its mother in whose womb it lay.
Unhappy mother! Doom'd for months to bear
The luckless burden thou wert not to rear!

Selling a newborn into slavery amounted to both emotional and economic theft; this woman's labor in carrying her child to term went utterly uncompensated. Poems like this showed slave masters as monstrous, portraying their wanton greed as reaching so deep as to breech a mother's womb.[74]

Personal as the pain depicted in such poems was, Samuel Wood clearly intended such tales to have political reverberations. Wood was not merely an antislavery activist, someone who critiqued the conditions of slavery while accepting the necessity of the institution's existence, but a full abolitionist, someone who worked for the total abolishment of slavery. Had he been merely an antislavery activist, Wood might easily have subtitled his "mirror of misery": *cruelty* exposed, using the emotional charge of his material solely to make a sentimentalist case against slavery. However, rather than emphasize only whites' failure of sympathy, their lack of mercy, he attributed the actions of slave owners to "tyranny." As an abolitionist, Wood stressed that slavery was the work of political and domestic despots, of people unequal to the standards of liberty.[75]

By the time of the War of 1812, the renewed confrontation with Britain made it difficult to treat slavery as anything other than a fundamental challenge to America's founding political philosophy. Ironically, then, slavery's apologists began to see real utility in painting slavery primarily as a private tragedy, and one that harmed slavers as much as the enslaved. If focusing on slave feeling had been radical back in the mid-eighteenth century—at a time when many whites seriously entertained the idea that enslaved people were naturally devoid of emotional sensitivity—by the early nineteenth century attention to the emotional experiences of the enslaved had come to serve far more conservative functions. If emotional costs were the real problem with slavery, then compassion provided a cheap solution. By this logic, slaveholders could ameliorate the emotional suffering of the enslaved by improving certain conditions of their lives without facing any practical or moral necessity to fully emancipate them.[76]

Jesse Torrey's life and work perfectly illustrate how shows of emotion could allow slavery's supporters to avoid effecting more concrete changes. Torrey, trained as a physician, devoted many years of his adult life to trying to establish a system of free public libraries across the states. In fact, the initial impetus behind his 1815 trip to Washington seems to have been a desire to promote his library scheme to officials in the capital. Torrey's self-image as a man of letters and a literary sentimentalist proved fundamental to his anti-slavery position.[77]

Among the many dramatic episodes Torrey uncovered, the case of another enslaved woman on the Bladensburg Road, this one of a mother who tried but failed to commit suicide, gained special attention. Taken to a Bladensburg way station on her journey south, the woman took the opportunity of what was supposed to be a brief stopover to jump out an open window. The woman survived with a broken spine but an unbroken spirit and Torrey went to interview her. He recounted that he "asked her what was the cause of her doing such a frantic act." She replied, "they brought me away with two of my children, and wouldn't let me see my husband—they didn't sell my husband and I didn't want to go." She added that she was "sorry now that I did it—they have carried my children off with them." The unnamed woman, meanwhile, remained at Bladensburg, further cementing that town's status as a site of national disgrace.[78]

At first glance, this story of a wife and mother's anguished separation from her family seems very much in step with the emerging conventions of anti-slavery literature. When Torrey's book appeared in 1817, this story earned its own illustration, a graphic representation of slavery's utter desolation. Yet even more telling than the story itself was Torrey's reaction to it. Torrey declared in his characteristically ornate way that meeting the woman moved him to tears: "he that can behold this *'poor woman'* . . . without a *humid eye*, I will confess possesses a *stouter heart* than I do." For Torrey, his tears, not the enslaved woman's, were the whole point.[79]

Figure 16. This engraving, like many antislavery images, again pictures a mother and child, here in an especially tender pose. Yet Jesse Torrey has placed himself front and center in the picture, bathed in a wash of light, visually highlighting how his sentimental displays of concern for trafficked people allowed him to position himself as a heroic literary protagonist. "The Author noting down the narratives of several freeborn people of color who had been kidnapped," illustration from *A Portraiture of Domestic Slavery* (Philadelphia: J. Biorden, 1817), Library Company of Philadelphia.

For Torrey, every "confession" of tears was delicious. As he said of another "heart-rending scene" from which he had felt "compelled to avert [his] eyes"—the sight of a procession of slaves in front of the destroyed Capitol—if the sentimental author Lawrence "Sterne had been present . . . he would again have '*burst into tears*.'" Torrey's main interest was in the evidence of his own good heart. He made these shifts in his own emotions into the central arc of his story, figuring himself as both eminent author and literary protagonist, a quintessential man of sensibility.[80]

Suffering like Torrey's could be alleviated simply by redirection of the gaze, without any other ameliorative action at all. Torrey came close to making this argument openly when he declared, "Blessed, infatuated Columbia! The eyes and the hopes of weeping admiring nations are upon thee! Suffer not the lamp of public liberty to be smothered and extinguished by the gloomy shroud of private slavery!" All Torrey wanted was for slave sales to be outlawed in the capital so that they could cease to create public embarrassment (Figure 16).

Slavery not only could continue but should continue in private, so long as evidence of the practice was not allowed to tarnish American liberty in the eyes of the world.[81]

Torrey conveyed the attitude that the observer's emotional suffering mattered more than that of the observed. If, as Torrey evidently believed, emotional acuity varied with the degree of personal refinement, a viewer could feel distress at the sight of suffering without the humanity of the observed being in any way confirmed thereby. Torrey said outright that only a person of "morbid or mistaken humanity" would take the step of actually freeing enslaved people, or, as he put it, "turning [them] out of doors." He maintained that enslaved people were "morally and physically disqualified for securing an honest maintenance" and would be entirely unable to support themselves if emancipated. When a person of proven sensibility (such as a man who cried like Lawrence Sterne) did *not* feel stirred by a suffering object, the suffering could be said not to exist at all, regardless of the feelings of the object. If suffering had existed, it would have invariably excited sensibility in the observer! So Torrey could inveigh against the internal slave trade, then lapse contentedly into recommendations for maintaining the slave system.[82]

In fact, Torrey wholly betrayed the hollowness of his sympathy for the enslaved by adding the argument that the nation could not afford to allow abolition because *"our numerous white population* in several of the more southerly states" could not physically survive in the hot climate there without the benefit of black labor. He asserted that his "conviction" was that "the existence of Europeans (or white men) under the blaze of a torrid sun is dependent on African industry." For all that Torrey struck a pose of concern for the window jumper who had lost her husband and children, his true preoccupation was the ease and comfort of the *"numerous white population"*—a point he himself emphasized by putting the phrase in italics.[83]

Torrey kept population theory front and center in offering his analysis. He did take pains to promise that he was not "assent[ing] to the perpetual duration of involuntary servitude." But he insisted that slavery must endure as long as necessary to ensure the continuation of the nation's marvelous population progress. He demanded, "let the magnificent work of progressive and ultimate emancipation . . . be kept steadily in view . . . but let not the total depopulation of an immense tract of valuable *improved* country, be held forth as essential to its accomplishment." Here Torrey neatly encapsulated every argument of expansionist slaveholding Republican war hawks. The United States had earned the right to title over the lands of North America by "improving them," where Indians had not. Settlement was crucial to the process of improvement and here the black population played a twofold role. Enslaved blacks not only filled out the numbers of the nation's people but also provided the labor that allowed the numerous white population to flourish.[84]

When Torrey claimed blacks as his "brethren" and included them as members of the American family, he did so in the older sense of family as household. In effect, Torrey took a household view of the nation itself. He considered it proper for black members of the household to work in support of and under the direction of the white citizens who served as national household heads. In a tiered system of national membership rights, everyone in the populace contributed to population strength, but only the white population enjoyed the elevated status of citizens.

⚬∞⚬

When the British burned the White House, they torched the president's home, a place that was at once a national symbol and a domestic space. U.S. commentators charged that Admiral Alexander Cochrane and General Robert Ross, "the British naval and military commanders, immediately issued orders for and personally superintended the conflagration of the public buildings, with all the testimonials of taste and literature which they contained." These leaders, who should have known better, were directly responsible for the fact that "the capitol and the president's house . . . were, on the memorable night of the 24th of August, consigned to the flames." Depending on your perspective, this was either the worst possible humiliation for the United States or the ultimate disgrace for the British, who demonstrated by their attack on the national family home that they had no regard whatsoever for the principles of just and civilized war.[85]

American leaders from President James Madison to Secretary of State James Monroe pressed hard to ensure that the latter interpretation would take hold among people in the United States. Madison reacted within a week of the attack with a proclamation to the nation claiming that by setting the capital to flames the British had "exhibit[ed] a disregard of the principles of humanity and the rules of civilized warfare . . . which must give to the existing war a character of . . . barbarism." These charges were so explosive that the president's proclamation was reprinted nearly one hundred times in newspapers across in the country in the first two weeks after it appeared in the

Daily National Intelligencer on September 3, 1814. When Monroe followed up with a formal letter to Cochrane, on September 6, he sounded almost exactly the same note, protesting that the British had pursued a "system of desolation . . . contrary to the views and practice of the United States . . . revolting to humanity, and repugnant to the sentiment and usages of the civilized world." Such American critiques of British barbarism and lack of civility implied that the United States alone maintained the traditions of decency that respected family sanctity and protected liberty (Figure 17).[86]

Yet Cochrane had anticipated these types of objections and had actually sent a threatening letter to the secretary of state on August 18, six days before the attack, warning that while he had committed to "resort[ing] to severities which are contrary to the usage of civilized warfare . . . with extreme reluctance and concern," he had been "compelled to adopt this system of devastation" by the U.S. provocation in sacking York, the capital of Upper Canada. In essence, Cochrane offered insult before injury, asserting that the blameworthy conduct of some American soldiers (which had never had official approval from the U.S. command) would set the course of formal British policy.[87]

Cochrane's letter too was reprinted dozens of times in the weeks after the attack, no doubt with very different receptions depending on the politics of the reader. Some saw the British success against Washington as evidence of God's displeasure with slavery. But many more saw the torching of the capital as evidence that U.S. violations of slave families shrank in significance when compared to British efforts to lay siege to the homes and hearths of all American families, from the humblest hovel to the president's house.

The touchiness of the situation was captured by a British sympathizer named James Ewell. Ewell was a U.S. physician who stayed in occupied Washington to tend the British troops and wrote a highly revealing postwar memoir of his experiences. Ewell allowed General Ross to establish a headquarters in his house. In his memoir, Ewell reported an exchange in which he questioned Ross about burning the city, saying that he did not suppose the general "would have burnt the president's house, had Mrs. Madison remained at home." Ewell noted with satisfaction that the general replied, "no, sir, I make war against neither Letters nor Ladies; and I have heard so much praise of Mrs. Madison that I would rather protect than burn a house that sheltered such an excellent lady." Ross did not deny that civilized warfare required the protection of women. However, the larger implication of this conversation was

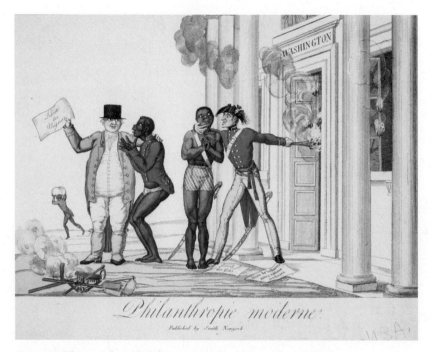

Figure 17. This complex political cartoon speaks volumes. The portly white man is a caricature of "John Bull," the satiric embodiment of Great Britain. He waves in his hand a paper reading "Liberté des Négres" [Liberty for Negroes]. A British redcoat sets fire to a federal-style building labeled "Washington," while treading on two more signs, one reading "Droits des Gens" [Rights of Man], the other reading "Droit de la Guerre entre nations civilisées" [Rights of War between civilized nations]. Meanwhile, both white men are embracing scantily clad and grotesquely caricatured black men, who have thrown down the rakes, hoes, and scythes of plantation labor and are instead donning British uniforms and taking up swords against the United States. The soldier-slave couple on the right side of the picture are exchanging an explicit and lascivious glance. In the background, a bare-bottomed black man in a British red coat appears to be stealing a bale of cotton. Altogether then, this print clearly conveyed the idea that American blacks were a total menace: murderous, thieving, and sexually deviant. The British, meanwhile, were fat greedy tyrants who applied the ideal of liberty to blacks but not to whites. Their profound disrespect for the rights of man and the conventions of civilized warfare was matched only by the depths of their sexual depravity. "Philanthropie Modern" [Modern Philanthropy], broadside, New York, c. 1814, Collections of the American Antiquarian Society.

that when the Madisons fled the capital and vacated the White House, they both betrayed personal cowardice and negated any claim that the space was a private residence rather than a public building.[88]

Ewell played with more than one kind of fire in recounting this episode. His verbal minuet with the general tacitly acknowledged that when the British sacked private homes, their attacks could extend as far as the marital bed. Rape was widely regarded as the most reprehensible military tactic, the last stop on the road to barbarity. Ewell reported that, in taking over his house for a headquarters, the general had promised him "he could never think of trespassing on the repose of a private family" since, as a husband and father himself, he was bound to *venerate the sanctities of the conjugal and domestic relations.*" Yet both Ewell and Ross well knew that Hampton and Havre de Grace, two towns along the Chesapeake, were widely reported in the American press to have been the site of mass rapes during British bombardments the previous spring.[89]

An official report of inquiry by the U.S. Congress published in July 1813 (which upon being reprinted became popularly known by the title *Barbarities of the Enemy*) asserted directly that "innocent victims of infernal lust at Hampton" had been left to suffer by "British officers whose duty, as men, required them to protect every female whom the fortune of war had thrown into their power." Even more inflammatory, first-person testimony reprinted in the report asserted that "the unfortunate females of Hampton who could not leave the town were suffered to be abused in the most shameful manner not only by the venal savage foe but by the unfortunate and infatuated blacks who were encouraged by them." Again, the specter of status inversions in which black men could attack white women neatly symbolized all that was at stake in the U.S. fight for liberty against the British.[90]

If they would tolerate such enormities, would the British really have protected the president's wife and respected his role as national household head if she had remained at home without him? Ewell rushed to assure his readers that the British did regard some moral codes as inviolate, but many remained unconvinced. Ewell's version of events rankled one reader so much that it sparked the publication of a satiric rebuttal. The satirist, calling himself Julius Scaliger (after a physician of the Italian Renaissance), excerpted Ewell's account with his own acid commentary added. To Ewell's quotation of Ross's claim that "he could never think of trespassing on the repose of a private family," Scaliger added parenthetically: "see the history of Hampton and Havre de Grace." Scaliger then reprinted Ewell's query, "I suppose General . . . you would not have burnt the President's house . . . had Mrs. Madison remained at home" but did not deign to include the general's witty bit of repartee claiming that he did not make war on letters or ladies. Instead, Scaliger interjected sarcastically, "What a pity that Mrs. Madison had not known that by 'remaining at home' she would not have been roasted." With the capital a wreck and the army in ruins, sarcastic critiques of British civility were the last balm left for U.S. wounds.[91]

As the pseudonymous physician "Julius Scaliger" well understood, claims that the British, in tandem with blacks and Indians, violated the principles of just war were powerful medicine indeed. Household attacks and wartime rapes defied the most important republican tenets, from property rights to the right of consent. Each time a U.S. inhabitant ridiculed such behavior, the murky moral ills of a nation both entrenched in slavery and bent on expanding its territory seemed less troubling. Doubts about the comparative worth and depth of American liberty seemed less urgent if the British-sponsored alternative was mass rape and civilian death.

One popular Republican diatribe (an essay datelined, "From the *Liberty Hall*") that made the rounds of print in the summer and fall of 1814, insisted Britain had "made a league with the Hell Hounds of America to butcher our fair ones, and helpless infants, and is endeavouring to excite insurrection among the slaves." As this article explained the situation of the nation:

> It is not possible that a free man in America, with common rationality, can be so blinded as not to see, nor so case-hardened as not to sympathise with his fellow citizens, who are toiling in British bottoms, while their families are left to struggle with the ills of fortune, without a guide. If this is not sufficient to rouse you to action, turn your attention to Hampton and other places, where the British have landed. Their barbarities have not been confined to those able to resist: but has burst forth on decrepit, old and sick men, on delicate females! Too horrid to particularize! Of the same kind is the conduct of their savage allies.

As the wartime crisis reached a fever pitch, American complaints began to run together, with British impressment, slave insurrections, Indian attacks, and sexual aggression all listed as symptoms of the same British disease.[92]

The summer and fall of 1814 brought the war to a critical pivot point. The British controlled the Eastern Seaboard and, by October that year, Federalist legislators in Massachusetts were calling a convention to demand constitutional reforms. Delegates soon gathered in Hartford, the home base of many of the war's most vocal dissenters, in December 1814. Yet the gathering ultimately amounted to little; the tepid demands that emerged from the conference were soon swept away in the ongoing course of events. In the interim, nearly lost amid the eddies of bad news swirling around Washington was a significant development that promised well for the continuing growth and expansion of the nation.[93]

In August, the very same month in which the capital fell to the British, General Andrew Jackson wrested an enormous land cession from Creek Indians in Georgia and Alabama: 22 million acres relinquished to the United States at the Treaty of Fort Jackson. At the time of its occurrence, the treaty garnered barely a mention in even the most nationalistic of papers, *The Daily National Intelligencer*. Yet in the event, this land cession would prove to be one of the most lasting legacies of the war years and among the most powerful precedents for the future. Meanwhile, the image of white American citizens as the most devoted defenders of civilized behavior and civil democracy survived stronger than ever.[94]

According to Doctor James Ewell, he and his wife had initially shared the alarm of their fellow Washingtonians, who feared that British attacks would mainly target women. He related that "the fearful apprehension, that the horrid scenes exhibited by the enemy in Hampton and Havre de Grace were about to be acted in Washington" had left him "palsied with horror," while his wife "wild with terror . . . fell into convulsions." And he asserted that he personally had watched as members of the Madison administration fled town, saying he had "beheld the unfortunate secretary of war and SUITE, in full flight, followed by crowds of gentlemen on horseback, some of them loudly bawled out as they came on, '*fly, fly: the ruffians are at hand!* . . . for God's sake send off your *wives* and *daughters*, for the ruffians are at hand!'" Yet if Ewell hoped to heap ridicule on Monroe and his fellow Republican leaders by relaying this gossip, he inadvertently revealed the power and prevalence of this line of rhetorical attack.[95]

Ewell said that he and Admiral George Cockburn had shared a good laugh about the British reputation for sexual tyranny, with the general teasing Mrs. Ewell, "Pray, madam, what could have alarmed you so? Did you take us for savages?" The Royal Navy man was ready with his own explanation, saying, "Ay madam, I can easily account for your terror. I see, from the files in your house, that you are fond of reading those papers which delight to make devils of us." As Cockburn rightly observed, newspapers played a key part in popularizing a sexually charged war culture—along with print media of all kinds, from novels and poems to posters and plays.[96]

Cockburn may have diagnosed the problem, but he could not offer any cure. British claims of their own decency held little appeal against white American readers' delight in tales of British, black, and Indian sexual savagery versus American gallantry. Ultimately, the culture of patriotic ribaldry had far more sway with the public at large than did legalistic arguments about liberty or moralistic lectures about sinful passions. American men who pictured themselves as the successful suitors and sturdy defenders of the nation's women felt few qualms about positioning themselves as virile and virtuous proponents of liberty. Concerted complaints about the aberrant sexual behavior of Britain and its allied peoples helped inoculate the United States against charges that Americans were the ones engaged in the worst abuses of liberty, from their reliance on slavery to their defiance of Indian territorial rights.[97]

Rather than confront the true facts of the family devastations white slaveholders and slave traders inflicted on the nation's black inhabitants, much less attempt to resolve the paradox of the land of liberty's reliance on slavery, war boosters in Washington tried to shift the conversation. Talk now centered on the threat that the British, along with their black and Indian supporters, imposed to all white American families, up to and including the first family of James and Dolley Madison. Amid such chatter, the faint cries of hypocrisy voiced by the likes of Lemuel Haynes were easy enough to drown out. As the war dragged on and the practical and rhetorical options left open to the United States declined, the issue of British affronts to white American domesticity claimed an ever greater share of public attention. Instead of advancing from debates about the definition of the American family to real discussions of expanding the rolls of the American citizenry, U.S. men could simply focus on British depravity. Instead of facing charges of neglect of duty in surrendering Washington, the troops who deserted to defend their own firesides could congratulate themselves on their romantic chivalry.

Indeed, if the republic seemed gravely endangered in the fall of 1814, patriotic demands for sexual decency signaled that the country's Republicans were poised for a rapid resurgence. Even as the dust settled over D.C., Andrew Jackson was marching off for New Orleans, where a massive last-minute victory against the British was about to bring him lasting fame as the best defender of the nation's "delicate females." In the meantime, printers at their presses and ordinary folks on streets and in sitting rooms were tuning up the ballads that would herald Jackson's success.

Conclusion

❦

Ardor and Triumph

NEW ORLEANS, JANUARY 1815

After the many disasters, surrenders, defeats, desertions, and general embarrassments that the United States endured in the War of 1812, the tide of history finally reversed itself on the Mississippi River, a few miles south of New Orleans, on January 8, 1815. On that great day, General Andrew Jackson led a patched-together force of regular soldiers, militiamen from Tennessee and Kentucky, Baratarian pirates, and French, Spanish, Anglo-American, and African American residents of New Orleans to a stunning victory against the British. Hunkered down behind earthworks along the east side of the river line, Jackson's troops first waited patiently for the invading British regulars to exit their boats and begin the tough scramble up the banks, then picked them off by the dozens. At the end of the fight, the British had suffered some twenty-six hundred casualties, while Jackson had racked up just thirteen. Reporting the results back to Washington three days later, he declared: "Louisiana is now clear of its enemy." The whole country was tremendously relieved—with the possible exception of one man.[1]

If George Poindexter had only known how spectacularly well the battle would end, he might not have spent the day indoors, cradling a slightly bruised arm in a sling and claiming to be too injured to join in the action. Yet if he had not been trying to distract everyone from gossiping about his trumped-up injury, he might not have spread around another story, the one that would decisively shape the way Americans of the era came to understand not just the battle of New Orleans but also the very nature of Britain and the United States.[2]

George Poindexter was a judge and sometime congressional delegate from the Mississippi Territory when he joined up with Major General George

Carroll as a volunteer aide in late December 1814. Poindexter later claimed that he had done so in order to "excite among the citizens of the Territory in which I reside a spirit of vigorous and manly resistance to the invaders of our soil." Apparently, Poindexter was not planning to provide an *active* example.[3]

The morning of January 8 found Poindexter not out on the ramparts, where the rest of Carroll's troops performed brilliantly, but rather safely ensconced inside Carroll's headquarters. It apparently came as a "severe shock," then, when "an eighteen pound shot . . . passed through the quarters . . . which threw a number of bricks from the wall against [his] left side and arm." Although, by Poindexter's own admission, it was "true that bruises, or contusions only were produced by the blows . . . received, and that the skin was very little, if any, broken," he bandaged up his arm and exempted himself from active duty for the rest of the day. That evening, the battle over, he retreated to the safety of the city of New Orleans to seek medical treatment and to try to stay ahead of the tattle.[4]

What Poindexter claimed to have heard on his travels was almost incendiary enough to obliterate interest in his own conduct. As he wrote in a letter to the editors of the *Mississippi Republican* that was rapidly reprinted in Washington, and then repeated countless more times after that: "the watch-word and countersign of the enemy on the morning of the 8th was BEAUTY & BOOTY." With these words, Poindexter trumpeted a motto that would sound far and wide—not on the lips of British soldiers and officers, who unequivocally denied ever having uttered them at all, but from the mouths of triumphant American Republicans.[5]

Poindexter wrote in his letter, "Comment is unnecessary on these significant allusions held out to a licentious soldiery," but quickly went on to offer a few. "Had victory declared on their side," he explained, "the scenes of Havre de Grace, of Hampton, of Alexandria . . . would without doubt have been reacted at New Orleans, with all the unfeeling and brutal inhumanity of the savage foe with whom we are contending." Poindexter's story was perfectly poised to sum up every rhetorical claim the Americans wanted to make against the British. He repackaged the most provocative charges to come out of the siege of Washington with a hugely satisfying new twist: this time British readiness to defy the most basic standards of decency had only resulted in their total defeat.[6]

Commentators in the capital could not resist the Poindexter story, quickly making it central to any account of Jackson's victory. Hezekiah Niles, ever ready to warm up his press and heat up his rhetoric, declared from the pages of his *Weekly Register:* "'BEAUTY AND BOOTY'—These words. Or, in other terms, RAPE AND ROBBERY, were the British watch-word and countersign on their attack of the defenses of *Orleans* on the ever-to-be-remembered 8th of January . . . '*Beauty and booty'*—rejoice, virgins of *Orleans*, that the ravishers . . . your intended spoilers have perished." For anyone uncertain about just what "beauty and booty" referred to, men like Niles eagerly supplied the definition. For contemporaries, such descriptions also helped to fix the meaning of the war itself. In a contest to claim the mantle of liberty, American soldiers fought for love of country while British forces sought only sexual debauchery.[7]

New England Federalists dismissed Poindexter's claims out of hand. Newspapers across the region quickly jumped to assure readers that "the story about the British counter-sign and watchword, *Beauty and Booty* turns out to be sheer fabrication." Investigative journalists tried to set the record straight with papers like the *Salem* (Massachusetts) *Gazette* and the *Concord* (New Hampshire) *Gazette* reporting: "'*Beauty and Booty'*—The democrats are endeavouring to give currency to the falsehood that these were the watch-words of the British in their attack on N. Orleans." These papers managed to trace the rumor to its source, explaining, "this story was forged by George Poindexter, formerly a member of Congress, and notorious for his ferocity and want of honest principle."[8]

Back in Poindexter's home territory of Mississippi, numerous antagonists, including the editor of the *Mississippi Republican*, challenged the truth of the watchword story. Hoping to discredit Poindexter entirely, they revealed the story of Poindexter's dereliction of duty on the day of the climactic battle. Poindexter responded to the charges by word and deed. He published a written rebuttal called *A Villain's Censure Is Extorted Praise* in which he offered the feeble excuse of his "bruises" and "contusions" as an explanation for his conduct. While this sheepish personal account of skin that was "very little broken, if any" did not go far to exonerate him, Poindexter did find satisfaction through other means.[9]

By March 1815 his arm had apparently recovered sufficiently to allow him to storm the offices of the *Mississippi Republican* and attack the editor there. As the *Burlington* (Vermont) *Gazette* reported, "Poindexter* was arrested . . . for an assault on the Editor of the Republican." The *Burlington Gazette* added an incredulous note: "*The story of '*Beauty and Booty*,' since contradicted, rests

solely on the word of this man." Federalists regarded stories of British depravity as unlikely to the point of absurdity.[10]

Poindexter, however, did have the last word and the last laugh. The story
of "Beauty and Booty" soon swept across the country, inspiring pointed commentary wherever it spread. It seemed the tale was simply too good to let go.
People could not resist repeating it in part because it helped to cement the
importance of the New Orleans victory in the public mind. In reality, Jackson's tremendous feat had no impact whatsoever on the formal outcome of the
war. As politicians in the capital soon learned, the celebrated action of January 8 took place some two weeks *after* negotiators had signed a formal peace
treaty with Britain in Ghent on December 24, 1814. But because of the delay
in the transmission of transatlantic news, information about New Orleans
had arrived in Washington before an announcement of the treaty. In the war's
final irony, the United States at last achieved a significant triumph only after it
no longer mattered from a negotiating perspective.[11]

Yet if timing prevented the Battle of New Orleans from being a true
"signal victory," the story of "Beauty and Booty" still sent a strong signal. And
it was exactly the message that American Republicans wanted to give. As
General Andrew Jackson's friend and biographer John Eaton explained in an
account of the battle he published in 1817, "*Booty and Beauty* was the watchword of Sir Edward Pakenham's army, in the battle of the 8th. Its criminality
is increased, from being the act of a people, who hold themselves up to surrounding nations, as examples of everything that is correct and proper." From
the beginning, the War of 1812 had been fought as a contest over the meaning
and validity of American claims to champion liberty in an expansionist age.
Whereas British commentators like Thomas Malthus had tried to seize the
moral high ground by critiquing American imperialism, the story of "Beauty
and Booty" helped mire the British in the muck of their own hypocrisy. As
Eaton observed, they could no longer "hold themselves up" as the standard to
which Americans should aspire.[12]

Besides making great gossip, the watchword scandal polished the U.S.
image as a uniquely virtuous nation bent on preserving the most fundamental form of liberty—sexual consent—from British perfidy. Each person who
passed on the story of "Beauty and Booty" helped validate assertions that
American men fought for country because of the romantic ardor they felt for
their wives and sweethearts. In doing so, U.S. soldiers enacted a love of liberty
entirely different from British tyranny.[13]

∞

On February 16, 1815, when the House of Representatives met to debate an official congressional resolution of thanks to Jackson, the image of the general as the defender of the women of New Orleans loomed large. On that day, Charles Jared Ingersoll, a lawyer and member of the Democratic-Republican Party from Philadelphia, took the floor to declare, "I have found it impossible to think—I have been only able to feel these last three days." For Ingersoll and his fellow members of the House of Representatives, it was not so much the preceding *ten* days that stirred them—the ten days since word had arrived of the victory at New Orleans—but only the preceding *three*. What had happened so very recently to transport Ingersoll?[14]

The diplomatic communiqué announcing the peace accord at Ghent had arrived in the capital on February 13. Ingersoll rejoiced: "with the tidings of this triumph from the south, to have peace from the east, is such a fullness of gratification as must overflow all hearts with gratitude." Yet, Ingersoll who no doubt had been emotionally transfixed by the news from Ghent, knew this was not the only sensational report circulating in the city. In fact, Poindexter's letter became known in Washington on the very same day that the Treaty of Ghent did; his letter was reprinted there in the *Daily National Intelligencer* on February 13.[15]

For Representative Ingersoll, all these events cascaded together in one rush of glory. Even as he celebrated the peace treaty, he also reminded his fellow members of Congress that British officers had "offered beauty and booty—in other words rape and rapine, as the reward of victory." He chortled, "thus led and thus invited the British army made its storm. Their discomfiture is without example. Never was there such disparity of loss." The supposed decision of the British to authorize extreme measures had only produced an extraordinary defeat.[16]

Jackson's success in New Orleans had been news for well over a week, but it was Poindexter's sensational claims that really electrified the country. As one newspaper editorialist explained the scale of the triumph, "our raw militia are . . . [too] great an overmatch for veteran troops even when excited on by the promise of 'Beauty and Booty.'" The virtues of American ardor had won the day over vile British lusts.[17]

Time and again, from Detroit to Buffalo to Washington to Alexandria, amateur militias had failed to stand up to the professional forces of the British

Army, putting defense of their own households far ahead of service to the country. Even at New Orleans, this pattern had persisted. If George Poindexter was almost alone in shirking the fight on the left bank of the Mississippi, the situation on the opposite bank had looked much different. There the troops had deserted with the same regularity displayed by so many previous service members. Yet at the end of the day, the performance of the main body of troops told a welcome new narrative. Ingersoll boasted that when "the gallant and generous inhabitants of the West flew to arms . . . it was in many cases more than a thousand, in all cases more than five hundred miles from home." At the climactic moment, Jackson's troops transformed the story, proving that the nation's men could perform perfectly in battle. And they could do so out of concern for more than their own private homes; their love for wives and sweethearts had at last blossomed into patriotic love of country.[18]

Ingersoll predicted that all divisions between northerners and southerners, Republicans and Federalists would be swept aside by the news. He exclaimed, "for the first time during this long, arduous, and trying session, we can all feel alike—we are all of one mind—all hearts leap up to the embraces of each other." Ingersoll's remarks were quickly published in Washington and did in fact reach the eyes of New England readers from Vermont to Massachusetts. After years of division, the whole nation could experience the emotional catharsis brought about by the notion that American men had protected their women.[19]

Ingersoll proved both right and wrong in his assessment of how the news coming out of New Orleans would affect the nation as a whole. New England Federalists were dismayed to hear the British portrayed as monstrous rapists and hardly delighted to have westerners from Tennessee and Kentucky rise to national prominence as the truehearted defenders of the nation. Some even went so far as to declare, as did a writer in the Salem, Massachusetts, *Gazette*: "fictions respecting 'British Barbarities' are the garbage on which democracy fattens." Yet the Federalist Party would never again gain success at the federal level, whereas Andrew Jackson would soon become the face of a new kind of democratic politics. Even if the claims against the British *were* nothing but rubbish, it was also true that the forces of popular democracy were gaining political weight.[20]

One of the first effects of the story of "Beauty and Booty" was to seal the fate of the Federalist Party. Every time Federalists tried to discount the reliability of George Poindexter (and no other individual person ever appeared to corroborate the watchword claim), Republicans stepped forward to accuse them of aiding and abetting the British. A New York paper published under the title the *National Advocate* complained, for example, "it is, indeed, singular, to observe how ignorant some of our federal newspapers appear to be concerning the little peccadilloes of the magnanimous cidevant enemy." Sarcasm aside, the point was that the Federalists hurt only themselves when they denied the reality of recent British cruelty.[21]

Laughing about the fact that Poindexter had accosted the Mississippi editor who had tried to expose him, the *National Advocate* continued by claiming that Federalist-allied editors had "dexterously caught at the story of the exceedingly well-cudgeled editor of the *Mississippi Republican* . . . because Mr. Poindexter . . . let out that terrible secret of 'Beauty and Booty,' which is so little to the honor of its munificent patrons." In this telling, the British invocation of rape was reprehensible, but Poindexter's good old-fashioned fisticuffs were only as much as the doubters of "Beauty and Booty" deserved.[22]

As such critiques mounted, even traditional centers of Federalist strength became the staging ground for sallies against them. A newspaper calling itself the *Boston Patriot* charged in April 1815 that the residents of that city who tried to "deny that 'Beauty and Booty' were the 'countersign' and 'watch-word' of the enemy at New Orleans on the night preceding the action of the 8th Jan" only proved themselves to be the "advocates and friends" of "monsters" notorious for "barbarous and infernal conduct." Failure to believe the story of "Beauty and Booty" came close to treason. "Ladies of Hartford," warned the *Hartford Mercury*, addressing the women of the city that had so recently been the center of Federalist war resistance, "do you not know that during the late war many of your fair countrywomen have been dishonored, polluted, and ravished by British officers?" The article warned all U.S. women to "take not to your bosoms . . . men who are yet warm from the conflagration of your villages and your Capitol; and whose ears are not yet free from the cries of ravished females." American men and women alike could prove their patriotism by cleaving only to each other.[23]

In the America of 1812, patriotism was supposed to grow from the romantic love of men and women. The story of "Beauty and Booty" provided the perfect ending for this popular tale. Throughout 1815, cities and towns across the country threw festive dinners and dances at which men and women alike gathered to celebrate the coming of peace and to repeat the patriotic myth of how

General Jackson had saved the women of the country from certain rape. In Wilmington, Delaware, in March 1815, for example, celebrants offered toasts urging, "May the defenders of Beauty and Booty live forever in the breasts of their grateful countrywomen." Women could show their own love of country by offering their affections to the men who gave them protection.[24]

Women might have no political rights, but they did have patriotic duties. Another guest at the Delaware event praised "Columbia's fair—whose love and patriotism has stimulated the youths of our country with a sense of justice and love for her laws." This toaster continued by urging the nation's women to "grow with her rising prosperity and cement by a just and faithful union those bands which neither foreign nor domestic foes can assail." In the aftermath of the war, as at its outset, romantic love and marriage "bands" featured as both the first obligation and the finest privilege of American patriots.[25]

Similar sentiments dominated at a gala held in South Carolina later the same month. That affair also concluded with round after round of toasts. To "'Beauty and Booty'—The British countersign at New Orleans" went the sarcastic tribute of one drinker, while another reveler raised a glass to "Admiral Cockburn, so celebrated for burning, may he eternally have the heart-burn." Spelling out exactly how patriotic love was supposed to function, another guest toasted "the Fair of America—Their smiles will ever nerve the arm of the patriot soldier and stimulate him to deeds of immortal glory—*Haste to the wedding—9 cheers*." Despite the real and growing reservations of some U.S. women about the economic inequities of marriage as well as the burdens of reproduction, war boosters cast women's continued willingness to love and marry as matters of crucial importance to the country.[26]

If one impact of the "Beauty and Booty" claim was the discrediting of Federalists, another was the reengagement of the nation's women. While many white women of the era gladly staked their membership in the population by entering marriages and bearing children, others had begun to express reservations and attach qualifications to their consent (Figure 18). Part of the beauty of "Beauty and Booty" was the way it allowed men to gloss over the public question of women's citizenship and the personal issue of inequality in marriage to focus instead on the protection men provided women against the most degrading forms of violence. Framing Jackson's victory at New Orleans as a strike against sexual assault helped men maintain the proposition that, even in the absence of any other economic or political rights, wives owed unquestioned allegiance to their husbands and their nation in return for simple protection from rape.

Figure 18. This needlepoint (embroidered during the run-up to the war) by 16-year-old Lucy Huntington of Norwich, Connecticut, suggests women's and New England Federalists' reservations about the war. Hector, a Trojan, leaves his wife and son to fight to his death against the Greeks. Adromache, his wife, clings to his shoulder, while a nursemaid holds their baby in the background. Here the useless sacrifice of war is poignantly foreshadowed. Hector leaves just one son, where he might have had many, and leaves his grieving wife a widow. "Hector Taking Leave of His Family," Lucy Coit Huntington (1794–1818), Norwich, Conn., 1810, Collections of the Metropolitan Museum of Art.

In reality, the Treaty of Ghent imposed no legal changes on either the United States or Great Britain in terms of territory or policy. The United States gained not one inch of Canadian ground nor did it succeed in forcing the British to renounce the practice of impressment. All that the two countries agreed to was a return to the status quo antebellum. Yet Republicans such as Charles Jared Ingersoll insisted nevertheless that something important had been accomplished by the war.[27]

Ingersoll closed his remarks to Congress by repeating his belief that the people of the United States had at last been drawn together by the common emotional experience of victory over a rapacious foe. "Who does not rejoice that he is not an European! Who is not proud to feel himself an American?" he demanded of those assembled in the chamber. Brushing aside the point that the Treaty of Ghent had simply returned relations between the United States and Britain to their prewar condition, he insisted "no matter what the terms of the treaty may be, the effects of this war must be permanently prosperous and honorable. The catastrophe at Orleans has fixed an impress, has sealed, has consecrated the compact beyond the powers of parchment." Though New Orleans had no legal effect that could be recorded in documents, it had a strong emotional one written in Ingersoll's heart.[28]

Ingersoll enthused, "for the richest kingdom in Europe, I would not exchange my American citizenship—for the most opulent endowment I would not surrender the delight which I derive from the feelings of this moment." Ingersoll proclaimed that emotion alone was enough reward for him and for the nation. Just as he demanded no greater concession from the British than his right to experience the "feelings of the moment," he seems to have assumed that no one in the United States, be they full legal citizens like him or simple inhabitants, could desire more than to share in the general delight.[29]

⁐∞⁐

Even in the midst of the conflict, many war supporters had argued that emotional arousal was not only the most important impetus for marshaling patriotism but also the central achievement sought by American belligerents. In such a situation, it mattered less who took up arms to fight than who opened their hearts to feel. Sharing in the emotional experience of patriotism created real and recognized contributions to the strength of the nation even in the absence of any concerted action. So long as all inhabitants of the United States, motivated by love for their families and love for their country, supported the continued right of U.S. settlers to people new ground, particular military encounters factored less than the promotion of general feeling.

This was just the view of the prowar minister Alexander McLeod (the New Yorker who had argued explicitly that love of spouse and love of nation were two sides of the same coin and that true liberty could not flourish unless a man was as free to choose "his country as his wife, his ruler as his servant"). By the close of the war, McLeod could celebrate that as an "effect of the contest, the American name, respected abroad, will communicate at home the impulse of patriotism." He went on to explain just exactly how the "impulse" of patriotism could be "communicated." He predicted that "the love of country ... will be revived by *this second war of independence* ... as well as [by] the growing influence of domestic literature." Though his own preferred genre was the sermon, McLeod recognized the crucial role that all kinds of literature— poems, stories, songs, and plays—played in transmitting love of country from one person to another.[30]

McLeod stated explicitly what many writers simply assumed: when it came to the War of 1812, the pen was mightier than the sword. He proclaimed that the "arts will cherish that passion," that is to say love of country, "in the breasts of the rising generation." Steeped in the persuasive words of home-brewed literature, "hereafter, they will take honorable pride in the deeds of their statesmen and warriors; and it will be felt by themselves and known to others, that on the question of foreign opposition, they are all Americans." American soldiers did not need to win battles; American statesmen did not need to win treaty concessions. All that the nation needed was for all inhabitants to agree that the essence of being American lay in the freedom to pursue romantic love and the opportunity to maximize reproduction. And nothing could better make that case than a popular culture centered on links between love and war.[31]

No sooner did peace break out than an anonymous Baltimore playwright produced a new work that defied traditional divisions between history plays and romances in a way that deftly illustrated the interworking of martial and marital concerns. Since military ardor and romantic passion each reinforced the other, the author decided that comedy and drama were better combined as one. The playwright offered audiences a nice little production he called *The*

Battle of New Orleans; or, Glory, Love and Loyalty; An Historical and National Drama in Five Acts. Nothing promoted the feelings of nationalism like an emotionally compelling narrative.[32]

The Baltimore play retold the story of General Andrew Jackson's triumph while following the trials and tribulations of two pairs of star-crossed lovers: Edward and Charlotte, Theodore and Louisa. Edward, a single young man, seeks the hand of Charlotte but is refused permission from her father, who judges him to be too lowly and poor to wed his daughter. Undeterred, Edward tells him, "I hold a commission in the service of my country, and that I deem a grade of honor, higher than mere money." Edward then fights beside Jackson and in reward wins the hand of Charlotte, who has always given him her heart. The American soldier and his lovely lady thus exemplify the ideal that patriotic women should reserve their affections for men of national merit. At the same time, they enact the idea that when young American men and women were allowed to make their own courtship decisions free of parental interference, their choices embodied the national commitment to free democratic consent.[33]

Theodore and Louisa, meanwhile, are a married couple who become separated when the British force Theodore into a press gang. When the British general Edward Pakenham tries to compel Theodore to fight against his country, he refuses and eventually makes his escape. He briefly reunites with Louisa—who has taken refuge in an Ursuline convent in New Orleans in order to protect her virtue in her husband's absence—then joins up to fight for Jackson. The twin plots of the two couples cleverly sum up both major threads of American war rhetoric, with one pair exemplifying how a man's love of country could win him the love of a woman even in the absence of riches, the other showing how British depravity separated husbands and wives while putting women's virtue at risk. Here, as ever, as the play's title reminded people, "glory, love and loyalty" were all of one piece.

The playwright never forgot that the romance plot mattered little unless it also brought to life the principles of patriotic participation that had framed General Andrew Jackson's efforts at New Orleans from beginning to end. He studded the fictional dialogue of his dramatis personae with transcriptions from authentic military correspondence and speeches that came out of New Orleans. One key strategic selection came with an actual speech made by Jackson on the eve of the battle with the British. Jackson, as quoted by the Baltimore playwright, had assembled his forces and demanded: "what man but feels this cause . . . who hears me now and would not bleed for freedom; have you a wife or daughter, think of Hampton!" Men who could not be roused by the idea that their women could be raped would be motivated by nothing.[34]

The fact that Jackson supposedly made this speech *before* the battle—and his friend and biographer John Eaton reported his speech in a similar way when he published his *Life of Andrew Jackson* two years later—shows why the story of "Beauty and Booty" gained such traction *after* the war. It fit neatly into the very narrative that Jackson and the Republicans had always wished to tell. The Baltimore playwright made the watchword scandal the capstone of his play when he closed the last line of the last scene with an ironic twist on the British motto. In his version of events, Jackson's men celebrated the connections between "glory, love, and loyalty" by shouting loudly "Duty and beauty are Columbia's shield."[35]

Like the Baltimore play, novels of the period could also combine genres in unconventional ways to emphasize the influence of romantic love on public events. In 1816, a New York author by the name of Samuel Woodworth produced a work that artfully blended a romance novel with a complete military history of the war. He created, in the process, a sustained dramatization of the contributions of romantic passion to patriotism. Woodworth gave his book the unwieldy but highly suggestive title *The Champions of Freedom; or, The Mysterious Chief, a Romance of the Nineteenth Century, Founded in the Events of the War Between the United States and Great Britain, Which Terminated in March 1815.* The book neatly defied genre divisions by combining seduction plots worthy of sentimental literature with realistic accounts of all the major battles of the war. Now little noticed, the title was popular enough in its day to go through two printings, one in 1816 and a second in 1818.[36]

Champions of Freedom follows the travels and trials of "our hero" George Washington Willoughby through many unintentionally comic episodes. He tries to follow the courageous example of the mysterious ghost of an Indian chief who floats about dispensing advice about valor even as Willoughby slaughters live "savages." He seeks to earn the heart of his chosen love—the chaste and virtuous Catharine—even as he engages to "flesh his maiden sword" (as Woodworth put it) both on the field of battle and in the bed of a fallen seductress named Sophia. Through it all, Willoughby struggles to achieve balance between his own needs and desires and the obligations he owes his country.[37]

The prowar faction had long struggled with the conundrum that the very emotions they attempted to manipulate in order to motivate men for war could also be the feelings that fatally undermined military effectiveness. If romantic ardor was supposed to propel men to defend their wives and sweethearts, too often it only resulted in mutinous refusals to stir far from their own firesides. The country required a kind of love that built on the personal to uplift the national. This was just the breakthrough that Representative Ingersoll celebrated after New Orleans and it proved crucial to the plot resolution of Woodworth's novel.

As the novel unfolds, George finds himself repeatedly torn between virtuous love of his country—and of the country lass named Catharine—on the one hand, and the sinful passions he feels for a Boston acquaintance, the temptress Sophia, on the other. The Mysterious Chief intervenes regularly to try to keep George on the path of righteousness as he enlists in the U.S. Army, even as he continues his dalliance with Sophia. At the close of volume 1, the Mysterious Chief intones, "While your country claims your services, she alone must possess your heart—to her your undivided affections must be devoted." Knowing that George chafes under this advice, the Chief concludes by promising, "when the Champions of Freedom have secured her temple . . . then, and not until then, you may with honor yield to the sway of virtuous love." The Chief casts love both as dangerous distraction and as sweet reward.[38]

The fulcrum of Woodworth's plot becomes the tension between George's desires for Catharine and for Sophia, between virtuous love and wanton lust. Yet George cannot be united even with Catharine unless and until the United States reaches accord with Britain. The Mysterious Chief lectures him on the lure of self-love and casts the indulgence of private romance over love of country as just that. He counsels George to defer the pleasure of romantic gratification until after the war concludes. Only in this way can George safely agree with his dear friend (and the husband of his sister), who declares: "WOMAN ever has been, still is, and always will be the main spring, the *primum mobile* of every masculine achievement." Here again, love and lust serve as prime movers, the motivating force behind military action. The friend demands, "We may talk of Patriotism—we may prate of Fame; but who could feel the one or seek the other but for the sake of woman?" Americans claimed a clear military advantage in their freedom to love and marry.[39]

The trick was not to put the cart before the horse and place love of a woman before love of country. George, having learned his lesson, does not wed until the war is won. Woodworth confided to readers: "George led his Catharine to the Altar of Hymen, on the very day that the ratification of the treaty of PEACE was celebrated." The reward of women's love was to come only after service to country had been rendered.[40]

Yet for all that Woodworth seemed to bring his convoluted story to a tidy conclusion, something still haunts the novel like a Mysterious Chief: the knowledge of the underside of American nationalism in the era of 1812. When George and Catharine retire to enduring happiness in Ohio, in what Woodworth had described earlier in the novel as "the verdant landscapes of his native country," they settle down to raise a family on what had only recently been Indian ground. Territorial ambitions and the rising white population receive little direct notice in the novel. Still, the fundamental fact that happy endings for Americans required the displacement of Indians was one of the ghosts disturbing the national rest in the postwar period. The "Champions of Freedom" had fought for something that looked a lot like imperialism when viewed through the eyes of an Indian chief.[41]

⟨∞⟩

The Reverend John Lathrop had opposed the War of 1812 from the outset. A Princeton graduate back when it was still the colonial-era College of New Jersey, Lathrop had spent some time as an Indian missionary in the 1760s, supported Massachusetts patriots in resisting the British during the Revolution of 1776, and then settled down to a long career in a Boston pulpit. Lathrop loved his country, a point he had amply proven in his youth, yet he could not countenance the rise of the Democratic-Republican Party nor the nation's turn toward war. He understood exactly the links between family love and liberty that the prowar faction was trying to forge and saw clearly the way such definitions of freedom spelled disaster for Native Americans.[42]

As he laid out his views in a pair of sermons published under the title *The Present War Unexpected, Unnecessary, and Ruinous*, in July 1812, Lathrop rebuked war supporters for both their immediate incentives and their ultimate aspirations in going to war. On the use of sensual passion to spur military action, Lathrop said, "we pray that 'God . . . would humble the pride and subdue the lusts and passions of men, from whence wars proceed.'" On the probable impact of the war on Indians, he added that he and his congregation prayed that God "would dispose the people of these States to do justice to the Indian tribes, to enlighten, and not exterminate them." Yet by the end of the war, it would be all too clear to Lathrop that his prayers had gone unanswered.[43]

In the first days of the peace, Lathrop rushed to bring to press one of the earliest histories of the war to be written. The pamphlet he produced was a brief thirty-two-page production, yet it bore the weighty title: *A Compendious History of the Late War; Containing an Account of All the Important Battles, and Many of the Smaller Actions, Between the American, and the British Forces, and Indians in the Years 1811, 1812, 1813, 1814, 1815*. Lathrop's lengthy title offered readers no romantic diversions or titillating promises of love. Instead, it offered the straight-up thesis that the War of 1812 could only be correctly understood when considered as a fight against Indians. Tellingly, he refused to date the beginning of the conflict from the formal congressional declaration of war against the British in 1812. Instead, he insisted that it had truly begun the year before with the first concerted efforts by General William Henry Harrison and others to defeat the Shawnee Confederacy led by Tecumseh.[44]

Lathrop did try to entertain readers with a sort of fable, but it was not the kind of thing designed to spark anyone's sensual passions. Explaining that he was "possessed of several anecdotes, which express the fears and apprehensions, which the Indians on the western borders have long entertained," Lathrop regaled his audience with one about an Indian chief and an American general who sat together on a log near the edge of a river. The Indian, who was seated on the far side of the log away from the stream, kept asking the general to slide over and make more space for him. As Lathrop told the tale, "the General replied, you will push me into the water. The native of the wilderness answered—So you white people, intend to make us poor Indians, remove, little by little, and then push us into the water where the sun goes down." The moral of the story could have been written by Thomas Malthus—who had complained years before that "if America continue increasing, which she certainly will do . . . the Indians will be driven further and further back into the country, till the whole race is ultimately exterminated." By the close of the War of 1812, with the surging popularity of Andrew Jackson the Indian fighter, it was clear to anyone with eyes to see that continuing continental expansion would be the chief legacy of the war.[45]

While the Treaty of Ghent was most remarkable for all the things it did not do—it did not end impressment much less result in the British surrender of Canada—one of its omissions came to have far-reaching consequences. The British had convinced their Indian allies to fight beside them by promising that when war ended they would demand permanent recognition of Indian land rights between the Ohio River and the Great Lakes. These were just the areas where the United States had recently begun rapid settlement. Yet at the negotiating table in Ghent, the British dropped the demand for an Indian buffer zone against American expansion. The result was that, once the war ended, the British would no longer arm Indians nor would they raise a hand to protect Indian land. The decision to do nothing at Ghent meant everything to the Indians who faced certain dispossession from that day forward.[46]

By 1815, John Lathrop was a rapidly aging man of seventy-five, destined, as it turned out, to die the very next year in 1816. Born in 1740, he had witnessed a world transformed by the lure of liberty more than once. Perhaps he was weary as he compiled his brief history of the war, one that he had once hoped would be more "compendious." In the final lines of that work, Lathrop offered a prayer that was in one sense a last lamentation, in another sense a surprising parting benediction. He pled: "From past sufferings, the American people will be warned against future evils. Should heaven see fit to diminish the population of the older, and more crowded parts of the world, we hope and pray, the desolating judgment may not be sent to this young country." Lathrop was a patriot to the end. Though he, perhaps more than any other U.S. citizen of his generation, saw and deeply opposed the aggression against Indians that drove the War of 1812, he could not bring himself to wish that the United States population would suffer. On the contrary, he, like more prominent founding fathers from Benjamin Franklin to Thomas Jefferson, relished the idea that America was a young country with a growing population on a spacious land. And he believed that, as such, the United States might yet prove a haven for the liberty fast being lost in the old world.[47]

◦◦◦

The full triumph of the prowar position came not only because of the sheer mass appeal of a model of patriotism based in romantic love but still more because of the fundamental fact that every inhabitant of the United States did have a stake in seeing the advance of the U.S. population. Small wonder then that when James Madison came to reflect on the significance of the war in a presidential message he offered at the end of 1815, he declared his pleasure in the fact that "the United States are in the tranquil enjoyment of a[n] . . . honorable peace. . . . The strongest features of its flourishing condition are seen, in a population rapidly increasing, on a territory as productive as it is extensive."

Madison's summation of the war emphasized once again the significance of population expansion and territorial extension as the best measure of national progress.[48]

When the members of Congress came to vote on a resolution of thanks to Jackson, they avoided being as explicit in invoking the phrase "Beauty and Booty" as Ingersoll had been during debate. They made no direct reference to Jackson's popular stature as the savior of the sexual purity of New Orleans women. But they did comment that the magnitude and magnificence of the war's final rout could best be calculated by using population as the scorecard. The formal declaration in praise of Jackson, as ultimately published by the Senate, thanked him and his troops for "obtaining a most signal and complete victory over the enemy, with a disparity of loss on his part unexampled in military annals." If population expansion measured the might of empires, then British casualties added up to American triumph. The Senate also complimented Jackson and his troops "for their uniform gallantry and good conduct." In contrast to General Hull, whose disastrous defeat had begun the war, General Jackson rose to fame as a "gallant" soldier, a man equally remarkable for his amorous attentions to ladies and his daring opposition to foes.[49]

꩜

In writing his biography of General Andrew Jackson, John Eaton set out deliberately to elevate him in ways that invited direct comparison to the fallen General William Hull. Whereas Hull had given up more than two thousand prisoners, Jackson had inflicted over two thousand casualties. Whereas Hull, a hero of the American Revolution, had preferred to be in command of a disciplined professional army, Jackson proved himself capable of winning with a ragtag militia. Most of all, while Hull faced a capital trial for the way he had allowed the ardor of his men to be "insensibly abated," Eaton stressed repeatedly that Jackson had risen to greatness through the "natural ardor of his temper" and that in every campaign he was everywhere among his troops "inspiring them with the ardor that animated his own bosom."[50]

When it came time to describe the events at New Orleans, Eaton provided an account of Jackson's speech to his men that made absolutely clear the link between passionate arousal and patriotic action. Eaton claimed that Jackson faced special difficulties in encouraging love of country because, "composed as our army was, of heterogeneous materials, Frenchmen, Spaniards, and natives, it required constant efforts to keep alive excitement." Yet nothing could awaken "excitement" like the potential of sexual threat.[51]

Asserting that Jackson had made his address with the definite goal of inspiring the men "to preserve their ardour and devotion to their country," he provided a florid and detailed recounting of the speech featured in the Baltimore play, "Glory, Love, and Loyalty." Eaton's Jackson exhorted: "look to your liberty, your property, the chastity of your wives and daughters. Take a retrospect of the conduct of the British army at Hampton . . . and every bosom, which glows with patriotism and virtue, will be inspired with indignation." By directly invoking Hampton and the rapes that had occurred there in his effort to prod his men to action, Jackson relied explicitly on the idea that the War of 1812 was as much a fight *against* sexual tyranny as a struggle *for* any more positive definition of liberty.[52]

The British took little notice of such rhetoric in 1815. For every story of the British at Hampton, they could counter with one about the United States at York. While not denying the occurrence of isolated atrocities, the British felt confident that leaders on both sides understood and respected the conventions of civilized war. Had Andrew Jackson allowed New Orleans to be the climax of his career and slid from there into an obscure retirement, the British would probably never have either known or cared about the "Beauty and Booty" scandal.

As things turned out, however, Andrew Jackson had ambitions to overtake the White House. To kick off what turned out to be an unsuccessful bid in 1824, his good friend John Eaton rereleased his hagiographic biography, *The Life of Andrew Jackson*. When Jackson again ran for president in 1828, this time successfully, Eaton published a third edition of the biography. Once Jackson occupied the executive office, his popularity spurred yet another release of the book, this one in time for his second inauguration in 1833. With Jackson's increased prominence, Eaton's version of the story of "Beauty and Booty" finally reached the notice of the British. They could hardly ignore the charge as presented in the quasi-official biography of a standing president.[53]

By 1833, of course, the British general Edward Pakenham, the man who had supposedly supplied the watchword, had been dead for eighteen years, having met his death on January 8, 1815. He could hardly rise from the grave to contradict the allegation. Yet six of his surviving subordinate officers swore oaths that no such countersign had ever been used. Under the leadership of Lieutenant-General Sir John Lambert, who had been Pakenham's second in command at New Orleans, they signed a statement saying that they could each "unequivocally deny that any such promise was ever held out to the army, or that the watchword asserted to have been given out was ever issued." They explained that "the refutation of the above calumnies not having before appeared [was] solely to be attributed to their not having come to the knowledge of the undersigned" until the publicity surrounding the 1833 reissue of Eaton's *Life of Andrew Jackson* brought them to light.[54]

Lambert's testimony was widely published in the American press at that point and preserved for posterity in 1834 in a book published in London called *Refutation of Aspersions*. The book concluded that "certainly the refutation of the charge as stated in Major Eaton's Book is, though tardy, complete." However, if the refutation was complete, so was the making of Jackson's reputation. He was president; John Eaton was his secretary of war. Whatever the true facts at New Orleans, those two men had nothing left to prove.[55]

In the aftermath of the victory at New Orleans, the story of "Beauty and Booty" proved an equally useful rhetorical tool in the hands of any ordinary white man who chose to wield it. If U.S. men could not claim that they invariably or exclusively upheld equal marriage rights—since they so obviously denied them to both free and enslaved blacks, so often refused to recognize them for Indians, and so routinely demanded that white women enter marriage contracts as unequal economic partners—they *could* trumpet the fact that they systematically avoided mass rapes. The real beauty of the story of "Beauty and Booty," as it came to be elaborated, was that it showed white men and black men fighting side by side to protect white women and black women alike from gang-style sexual attacks by British forces. Contemporaries celebrated black contributions to Jackson's victory and made explicit claims that the British had planned to target black and white women alike for assault. Poindexter's inspired piece of gossip helped men, from leading politicians to family patriarchs, pivot away from marriage as the measure of liberty and toward a less demanding symbolic standard.[56]

Simply forgoing mass rape as a military tactic set a rather low bar for liberty. As a foundation for freedom, sexual consent provided an even easier model than the marriage contract itself, one that could even be compatible with slavery. No matter the ambiguities of any individual sexual encounter, no matter the fact of widespread sexual aggression against enslaved women, white men could congratulate themselves for upholding freedom so long as they avoided using gang-style assaults as a weapon of war. Proslavery apologists argued that any inhabitant of the United States who could sire or bear children actually enjoyed a key form of liberty. Even enslaved people denied the ability to rear their own children to adulthood could at least claim the basic right to create progeny. Ultimately, sexual consent was a form of acquiescence difficult to distinguish from coercion—and one that neither required nor imparted deeper political rights.[57]

Populating the nation, adding to the country's strength in numbers, became at once the basic requirement and the main reward for national belonging. While black men and all women were denied full status as citizens, and thus most forms of democratic participation in the nation, members of these groups nevertheless made tangible contributions to the country as components of the population. With reproduction made the essence of freedom, even married women and enslaved blacks could be said to enjoy the most fundamental form of rights.

Stirring calls for love of country and patriotic participation in the population helped postpone difficult debates about the possibility of universal citizenship for all the nation's inhabitants. Not for decades would white women or people of color be able to claim full citizenship, yet white men of all classes would continue to expand and enjoy their roles as American family founders. In fact, the final advantage of regarding mass rape as the true mark of tyranny was that it made any other kind of sexual congress sufficient to establish the fiction of voluntary compliance.

Only the people of Indian nations were cut off from population membership as the most fundamental form of democratic participation. And U.S. boosters could claim this resulted directly from Indians' own tragic choices. If only Indians would abandon their own political and familial allegiances (not to mention their traditional communal land-holding practices) and consent to become supporting members of the U.S. population, they too could become unequal citizens and quasi-willing contributors to the country.

When Eaton and men of his ilk insisted that the top British commander, General Pakenham, had made mass rape official policy at New Orleans, they did more than just advance a general moral critique. They compiled evidence for a very specific argument; the British had no right to condemn U.S. territorial expansion as a threat to liberty if their own imperial wars from America to India rested on sexual tyranny. In fact, the "Beauty and Booty" smear worked directly to remind people on both sides of the Atlantic that British forces in India had already earned widespread notoriety for rapacious behavior.[58]

In a closely watched 1795 trial to unseat Warren Hastings (then the British governor-general of India) from his post, the British philosopher Edmund Burke had publicly described Hastings's crimes against Indian women by saying: "Virgins . . . publically were violated by the lowest and wickedest of the human race," while "wives were torn from the arms of husbands and suffered the same flagitious wrongs." Not only did U.S. newspapers report on the trial at the time it occurred, but they also kept its memory vivid in the public mind by referring to it throughout the 1810s.[59]

In April 1815, in the immediate aftermath of the war, columnists writing for Washington, D.C., area newspapers made easy reference to "the trial of Hastings" to convince Americans that "with all the boasted freedom of their government and liberty of their press, the English nation is . . . little acquainted with the true history of English possessions in Asia." As a direct reminder of British domination in India, rape made a great issue to cudgel the British with. American printers stood ever ready to burnish the image of the United States and tarnish that of the British by publishing tales of British rapacity. After all, every argument that tarred the British Empire with tyranny made it easier to believe in that earnest American oxymoron, the "Empire for Liberty."[60]

∽∞∾

Today, Americans no longer devote much time or attention to thinking about the War of 1812. If the conflict was, as many in the prowar faction claimed at the outset, simply a "second war of independence," it hardly seems worth pausing over. Why linger on a confrontation that did no more than confirm the results of the first?

Yet on closer study, the war emerges less as historically insignificant than as morally inconvenient. We tend to consider the era between 1812 and 1865 as a relatively slow period in American military history. It's called the "antebellum era" as if the only war that mattered were the Civil War. Yet these are the decades in which the nation would spread over the continent. From the moment the War of 1812 ended, the United States added a new state to the union each year for six years straight, a process halted temporarily only by the crisis over slave representation that resulted in the Missouri Compromise. In 1816 Indiana joined the United States, followed by Mississippi in 1817, Illinois in 1818, Alabama in 1819, Maine in 1820, and Missouri in 1821. Each of these border states had been under at least the partial control of Indians before the War of 1812; the U.S. ability to legally annex these new states resulted directly from its victory. Before the Civil War began, vast new territories would be won in the Mexican War and the nation's land claims would reach the Pacific. Once the Civil War ended, the legal process of formally incorporating these lands as official states would continue unabated. The shadow of the War of 1812 is longer and deeper than we often care to recognize.[61]

The nation never did wholly disavow the desire for aggregate increases in land and people that had driven the war from the start. The anti-Malthusian vision of 1812 would persist through civil war and world wars for almost two centuries as territorial annexation and population augmentation remained key national projects. In the aftermath of the War of 1812, U.S. commentators did their best to convince themselves and the world that the incorporation of new lands was a matter of natural right, of divine (and manifest) destiny. Yet taking time to absorb the popular atmosphere during the War of 1812 reveals that these developments resulted from the concerted political decisions and deliberate cultural commitments of wide swaths of the American populace.

If we think of the War of 1812 today at all, we are apt to remember it most as the occasion for the composition of our national anthem. Francis Scott Key, who bore witness to the failed British offensive on Baltimore just weeks after the fall of Washington, kept the flame of patriotism alive by penning a poem proclaiming that, at the end of that battle, "our flag was still there." This was then and remains today a vivid vision. Yet the fact is that Key's poem did not gain official status as the most important song in the country until a bill making it the official national anthem finally passed Congress in 1931—more than a century after it was written.[62]

At the time the war ended, another song held as much, if not more, sway with the public. This was a little ditty called "The Hunters of Kentucky," written by none other than Samuel Woodworth, the novelist behind the *Champions of Freedom* (Figure 19). Relaying Poindexter's claims about the British watchword in verse form, Woodworth rhymed:

You've heard, I s'pose, how New-Orleans
Is famed for wealth and beauty—

There's girls of every hue it seems.
From snowy white to sooty.
So Pakenham he made his brags,
If he in fight was lucky,
He'd have their girls and cotton bags,
In spite of old Kentucky.

Woodworth closed the song by boasting that the British "took to flight / And left us all the beauty," and scorned effete antiwar New Englanders by saying, "send for us Kentucky boys and we'll protect ye ladies." Woodworth's song was printed and reprinted in broadside form all across the country with different illustrations and rhyming variations in each new edition. In other words, one of the most popular national songs in the postwar period invoked just the kind of ardent desire sure to stir action—to hasten the Federalist Party's extinction; to cement national devotion; to augment population; and to motivate continuing territorial expansion—the desire to claim American Beauty.[63]

For months after his victory at New Orleans, Andrew Jackson made the rounds of celebratory parties and dinners, stopping in to be admired by adoring throngs. Jackson was already readying himself for his coming role as both champion of democracy and advocate of permanent Indian removal. Attended by local dignitaries as well as members of Madison's cabinet, these quasi-public appearances helped further build up his stature with the governing class in the capital. As a newspaper reported in December 1815, "Public dinners have been given in honor of Gen. Jackson in Georgetown and Alexandria. The citizens of Washington are preparing an elegant Ball and Supper." The article went on to describe the toasts that Jackson and the other guests offered at the Georgetown dinner.[64]

On that gala occasion, Jackson could already envision himself as a leader on the national level and he took the chance to get in a good dig at the fading New England Federalists. With an eye toward those whose war resistance had perhaps come close to calls for secession, he offered a toast to "Union, the sure basis of our political existence." The secretary of the navy turned his thoughts to Francis Scott Key and raised his glass to "the star spangled banner, in peace may it always wave, in war victoriously." Commodore David Porter, another officer of the navy, gave the final toast of the evening. With

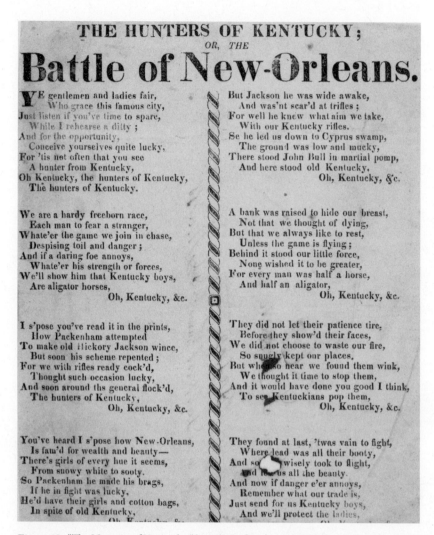

THE HUNTERS OF KENTUCKY;
OR, THE
Battle of New-Orleans.

YE gentlemen and ladies fair,
　Who grace this famous city,
Just listen if you've time to spare,
　While I rehearse a ditty ;
And for the opportunity,
　Conceive yourselves quite lucky,
For 'tis not often that you see
　A hunter from Kentucky,
Oh Kentucky, the hunters of Kentucky,
　The hunters of Kentucky.

We are a hardy freeborn race,
　Each man to fear a stranger,
Whate'er the game we join in chase,
　Despising toil and danger ;
And if a daring foe annoys,
　Whate'er his strength or forces,
We'll show him that Kentucky boys,
　Are aligator horses,
　　　　Oh, Kentucky, &c.

I s'pose you've read it in the prints,
　How Packenham attempted
To make old Hickory Jackson wince,
　But soon his scheme repented ;
For we with rifles ready cock'd,
　Thought such occasion lucky,
And soon around ths general flock'd,
　The hunters of Kentucky,
　　　　Oh, Kentucky, &c.

You've heard I s'pose how New-Orleans,
　Is fam'd for wealth and beauty,
There's girls of every hue it seems,
　From snowy white to sooty.
So Packenham he made his brags,
　If he in fight was lucky,
He'd have their girls and cotton bags,
　In spite of old Kentucky,
　　　　Oh, Kentucky, &c.

But Jackson he was wide awake,
　And was'nt scar'd at trifles ;
For well he knew what aim we take,
　With our Kentucky rifles.
Se he led us down to Cyprus swamp,
　The ground was low and mucky,
There stood John Bull in martial pomp,
　And here stood old Kentucky,
　　　　Oh, Kentucky, &c.

A bank was raised to hide our breast,
　Not that we thought of dying,
But that we always like to rest,
　Unless the game is flying ;
Behind it stood our little force,
　None wished it to be greater,
For every man was half a horse,
　And half an aligator,
　　　　Oh, Kentucky, &c.

They did not let their patience tire,
　Before they show'd their faces,
We did not choose to waste our fire,
　So snugly kept our places.
But when so near we found them wink,
　We thought it time to stop them,
And it would have done you good I think,
　To see Kentuckians pop them,
　　　　Oh, Kentucky, &c.

They found at last, 'twas vain to fight,
　Where lead was all their booty,
And so wisely took to flight,
　And left us all the beauty.
And now if danger e'er annoys,
　Remember what our trade is,
Just send for us Kentucky boys,
　And we'll protect the ladies,
　　　　Oh, Kentucky, &c.

Figure 19. "The Hunters of Kentucky," broadside, [n.p.], c. 1815, Collections of the American Antiquarian Society.

it, he summed up just how love of country was supposed to work in America in the era of 1812. He hailed "the feelings of patriotism and duty opposed to the watchword of 'beauty and booty.'" It is all too easy to imagine the assembled merry makers tilting back their heads and quaffing down the last of their drinks.[65]

Notes

Preface

1. Paul R. Weidner, ed., "The Journal of John Blake White (Continued)," *South Carolina Historical and Genealogical Magazine* 43, no. 2 (April 1942): 103–117, quotation on 113, and Paul R. Weidner, ed., "The Journal of John Blake White (Continued)," *South Carolina Historical and Genealogical Magazine* 43, no. 3 (July 1942): 161–174, quotation on 162.

2. Weidner, "Journal of John Blake White" (April 1942), 113, 117. For an example of White's work as a playwright, see White, *Modern Honor, a Tragedy in Five Acts* (Charleston [S.C.]: J. Hoff, 1812). The play, written and performed in 1812 just before war was declared, was a sentimental seduction tale with the moral that dueling was a tragic mistake. It stands out now for its vivid description of family life as the very definition of happiness, a theme that anticipated much prowar rhetoric. One set of main characters, a married pair, celebrates the "celestial love" of rearing children in their own likeness and are told how lucky they are that "your children bear the badges of you both." See White, *Modern Honor*, 11.

3. For statistics, see Donald R. Hickey, *The War of 1812: A Forgotten Conflict* (Urbana: University of Illinois Press, 1989), 302, Bruce Catton, *The Civil War* (New York: Houghton Mifflin Harcourt, 2004), 152–154.

4. The classic work on print culture in early America is Michael Warner, *Letters of the Republic*, and the best exploration of the role of print, especially newspapers, in the creation of American nationalism is David Waldstreicher, *In the Midst of Perpetual Fetes*. Trish Loughran, by contrast, has recently sought to challenge the idea that the institutions of the public sphere, including print culture, produced anything like a "national public." The most recent work on print culture urges us to accept these contradictions, understanding, as Robert Gross puts it, that "print could exercise its influence in opposing ways. . . . It contained the multitudes and contradictions of the sprawling nation it served." See Warner, *Letters of the Republic: Publication and the Public Sphere in Eighteenth-Century America* (Cambridge, Mass.: Harvard University Press, 1990); Waldstreicher, *In the Midst of Perpetual Fetes* (Chapel Hill: University of North Carolina Press, 1997); Loughran, *The Republic in Print: Print Culture in the Age of U.S. Nation Building, 1770–1870* (New York: Columbia University Press, 2009), 92; and Gross, introduction to Mary Kelley and Robert A. Gross, eds., *A History of the Book in America*, vol. 2: *An Extensive Republic:*

Print, Culture, and Society in the New Nation, 1790–1840 (Chapel Hill: University of North Carolina Press, 2010), 4.

5. In some contexts, it is useful to see the War of 1812 as part of a long continuum of Anglo-American wars for empire in North America, a proposition advanced persuasively in Fred Anderson and Andrew Cayton, *The Dominion of War: Empire and Liberty in North America, 1500–2000* (New York: Viking, 2004). Yet in other ways, the war marks an important historic departure as the first to be fought in a stable modern democracy with volunteer troops in the midst of a political election cycle.

Few historians have considered the War of 1812 in this light. For the origins of modern "democratic wars," historians and political scientists are more likely to begin by examining the American Revolution or the French Revolution, then skip forward to the twentieth century. Yet eighteenth-century revolutions of national formation were significantly different, from a cultural and political standpoint, than wars fought *after* the settled establishment of constitutional democracy, conflicts in which formal recorded votes for war were taken by officials accountable to a wide electorate. If we overlook this distinction, we miss the chance to examine the process by which public opinion forms and public support builds for conflicts in which democratic participation is in itself a key form of war mobilization. On warfare and democracy, see Dan Reiter and Allan C. Stam, *Democracies at War* (Princeton: Princeton University Press, 2002); Edward D. Mansfield and Jack L. Snyder, *Electing to Fight: Why Emerging Democracies Go to War* (Cambridge: MIT Press, 2005); and Samuel Issacharoff, "Political Safeguards in Democracies at War," *Oxford Journal of Legal Studies* 29, no. 2 (2009): 189–214.

The war provides a crucial opportunity to understand the role of cultures of persuasion in the making of modern democratic wars. As Michael D. Pearlman remarks, in 1812, there was little preexisting mechanism in place for the molding of public opinion. The idea of party politics and the concept of "loyal opposition" enjoyed no acceptance in the United States. Yet while Pearlman notes that "Republican ideologues still believed that 'patriotic ardor'" could carry the war effort, he focuses his own analysis much less on "ideologues" than on military planners, on the practical limitations faced by a nation fighting a war with inadequate infrastructure. He argues that the war's most significant challenges came not in the definition of goals but in the area of means. In fact, there is much to be gained from investigating the channels through which the nation debated its goals and the extent to which the populace became unified behind them. See Pearlman, *Warmaking and American Democracy* (Lawrence: University Press of Kansas, 2002), esp. 1–4, 72–78, quotation on 78. For more on the politics of declaring war in 1812, see J. C. A. Stagg, *Mr. Madison's War: Politics, Diplomacy and Warfare in the Early American Republic, 1783–1830* (Princeton, N.J.: Princeton University Press, 1983), 110–119 and see Hickey, *War of 1812*, 44–46.

6. Hickey, *War of 1812*, 1–3, figures on 303.

7. "Era of Good Feelings," Boston *Columbian Centinel*, 12 July 1817, 2. The phrase proved popular immediately and was reprinted at least twenty times in newspapers from Maine to Virginia within the first month after appearing in the *Centinel*. Here and throughout, estimates of newspaper publication frequency are based on searches in the digitized collections of America's Historical Newspapers by Readex, a division of NewsBank http://www.newsbank.com/readex/?content=96.

To date, most analysis of the early American public sphere has relied on the model, put forth by Jürgen Habermas, of print as a rational realm of critical inquiry. Habermas believed that reason was absolutely central to the proper functioning of the public sphere, that a free press would allow the development of well-considered democratic debates. Likewise, Benedict Anderson, writing on the rise of nationalism, argued that print played a special part in allowing people to form new connections with each other. Yet whereas Habermas stressed rationality, Anderson made clear in his discussion of how people create "imagined communities" that the emotional element of public life is fundamental and cannot be denied.

If we are to understand the role of print culture in the formation of early American nationalism, then, it would seem that we must incorporate Anderson's insights about emotion into Habermas's model of the public sphere. Anderson's ideas alone are not enough, however, to explain the role of emotion in the formation of patriotic public culture in the early United States. For Anderson argued that, "regardless of the actual inequality and exploitation that may prevail in each, the nation is always conceived as a deep, horizontal comradeship." Yet in reality, in the United States in 1812, the highest ranking white male citizens quite deliberately enforced a multilayered hierarchical society with marked status differentials between white and black, man and woman, citizen and alien, as well as between Federalist and Democratic-Republican, North and South, city and country, and merchant and farmer. And while Anderson considered that the most important emotion of nationalism was always "brotherly love," in the fractured social and political atmosphere of 1812, invocations of heterosexual love and reproductive desires proved to be much more prevalent.

What we need is a model of print culture that blends Habermas's emphasis on popular discord and debate, rather than consensus, with Anderson's recognition of the centrality of emotion in the rise of national aggression. The emotional content of public prints in the era of 1812 worked to rouse the people of the United States to enact sexual and territorial desires, to seek to produce children and populate the land, without creating a sense of "horizontal comradeship." American patriotic print culture in 1812 promoted coordinated actions and common purposes without in any sense conferring on them a common or unified identity devoid of status divisions. As Trish Loughran has recently pointed out, this fundamental lack of unity, of common identity, would become all too obvious with the coming of the Civil War. I add a crucial corollary: there *was* sufficient common purpose to allow for uninterrupted imperial expansion across North America during these decades. This point can only be explained by recognizing that parallel emotions could help disparate people to merge their pursuit of interests without requiring them to meld their identities. Every U.S. resident, regardless of legal or social status, had some basic stake in increasing reproduction and expanding land occupation. The anomalous place of Indians in this scheme is one of the central issues of this book.

See Habermas, *The Structural Transformation of the Public Sphere*, trans. Thomas Burger (Cambridge, Mass.: MIT Press, 1991); Anderson, *Imagined Communities: Reflections on the Origin and Spread of Nationalism*, revised edition (London: Verso, 1991), 7; and Loughran, *Republic in Print*.

On the relationship of Anderson to Habermas, see Robert A. Gross, "Print and the Public Sphere in Early America," in Melvyn Stokes, ed., *The State of U.S. History* (New York: Oxford University Press, 2002), 245–246. On the importance of reason to

Habermas, see Martin Jay, *Marxism and Totality: The Adventures of a Concept from Lukács to Habermas* (Berkeley: University of California Press, 1984), 467.

8. James Madison, "Proclamation of the President, June 19, 1812," as quoted in *War Declared Against Great Britain, with an Exposition of Its Motives* (Washington, D.C.: s.n., 1812), 27.

9. Daniel Webster, *An Address Delivered Before the Washington Benevolent Society at Portsmouth, July 4, 1812* (Portsmouth, N.H.: Oracle Press, [1812]), 5. On Webster's place in Federalist war dissent, see Lawrence Delbert Cress, "'Cool and Serious Reflection': Federalist Attitudes Toward War in 1812," *Journal of the Early Republic* 7 (Summer 1987): 123–145, quotation on 140–141.

10. Webster, *Address Before the Washington Benevolent Society*, 26.

11. "Communication," Charleston *City Gazette*, 6 August 1813, 3, and Weidner, "Journal of John Blake White" (April 1942), 113. Federalist use of emotions like fear and horror to try to discredit the war is extensively documented and discussed in Rachel Hope Cleves, *The Reign of Terror in America: Visions of Violence from Anti-Jacobinism to Antislavery* (Cambridge: Cambridge University Press, 2009), 153–193.

12. Some scholars, such as Christopher Looby, have recently challenged the significance of print culture in early America, both because limited distribution networks meant there really was no such thing as "mass culture" and because so much of people's lives were still dominated by face-to-face interactions and vocal language. While in no way denying the importance of face-to-face exchanges (which I analyzed at length in *Passion Is the Gale*), I would resist the idea of limiting our analysis of print culture simply because it does not meet the modern definition of "mass." As James W. Cook has recently pointed out, every generation since Gutenberg has seen stunning increases in the possibilities for the simultaneous distribution of and widespread access to cultural content. For example, the arrival of forms of instantaneous "mass" communication, like television, which seemed to mark the mid-twentieth century as the definitive moment in the development of mass culture, now seem quaint compared to the speed and worldwide distribution of culture via the Internet. Rather than trying to define just how wide and how fast the distribution of cultural content must be before it can qualify as "mass," Cook proposes that we take contemporaries' own perceptions seriously and analyze "historically specific sense[s] of ubiquity" (and efforts to achieve the same) on their own terms. While the current analysis of cultural productions during the War of 1812 cannot establish in detail the tenor of reception, it remains significant that a wide swath of the American public, from elected politicians to professional newspapermen to casual authors, took to print to try to shape collective public opinion. See Christopher Looby, *Voicing America: Language, Literary Form, and the Origins of the United States* (Chicago: University of Chicago Press, 1996); Nicole Eustace, *Passion Is the Gale: Emotion, Power, and the Coming of the American Revolution* (Chapel Hill: University of North Carolina Press, 2008); and Cook, "The Return of the Culture Industry," in James W. Cook, Lawrence B. Glickman, and Michael O'Malley, eds., *The Cultural Turn in U.S. History* (Chicago: University of Chicago Press, 2009), 294–296.

13. Samuel Woodworth, *The Champions of Freedom* . . . (New York: Baldwin, 1816), 226. Taken from Dryden's play *Love Triumphant or Nature Will Prevail*, these lines were first uttered by a besotted sister to justify her incestuous feelings for her brother on the grounds that her love motivated him to achieve glory for the nation. In seventeenth-century Britain, harnessing sexual love to national valor came freighted with moral complications.

Yet Woodworth's out-of-context quotation gave no indication of the problematic origins of the lines he quoted. Woodworth presented the quotation straight, giving his readers no hint that these lines by a British playwright had offered more warning than encouragement on the subject of love and war.

14. James W. Cook has recently advocated a return to the theories of Theodor Adorno on the "culture industry," a shift that would take us back beyond the work of his student Jürgen Habermas. What I find useful in Adorno (distinct from Cook's summation) is his critique of irrationality in mass culture, his contention that with its speed and uniformity the cultural industry "positively debars the spectator from thinking." Because there is no room for emotion in the Habermasian public sphere, it is very tempting to reengage with Adorno and his focus on the power of the irrational. However, Adorno's mid-twentieth-century concerns with fascism and advanced capitalism clearly don't apply neatly to the early national period. There is no full-blown totalizing "industry" in the sense that Adorno outlines. Rather, as Michael Denning explains it, in early America, the "products of the culture industry . . . can be understood neither as forms of deception, manipulation and social control, nor as expressions of a genuine people's culture, opposing and resisting the dominant culture." In a nascent and growing democracy that nevertheless requires entrenched social stratification, ordinary members of the population and political elites produce culture together in a sometimes combative but often symbiotic process. In the context of Andersonian nationalism rather than Adornian totalitarianism, the emotional work of mass culture is a simultaneously high/low phenomenon. See Adorno, "The Culture Industry: Enlightenment as Mass Deception," in Max Horkheimer and Theodor W. Adorno, Gunzelin Schmid Noerr, eds., and Edmund Jephcott, trans., *Dialectic of Enlightenment: Philosophical Fragments* (Stanford, Calif.: Stanford University Press, 2007), 100, and Denning, *Mechanic Accents: Dime Novels and Working Class Culture* (London: Verso, 1987), quoted in Cook, "The Return of the Culture Industry," 293.

15. On how the amygdala and frontal insula can "tilt the pinball machine," see Jonathan Haidt, "The New Synthesis in Moral Psychology," *Science*, 18 May 2007: 998–1002. Piercarlo Valdesolo and David DeStono argue that "environment-induced feelings of positivity at the time of judgement might reduce the perceived negativity, or aversion 'signal,' of any potential moral violation and, thereby, increase utilitarian responding." See Valdesolo and DeStono, "Short Report: Manipulations of Emotional Context Shape Moral Judgment," *Psychological Science* 17, no. 6 (2006): 476–477, quotation on 476.

For the sake of analytic simplicity, not to mention clarity of results, experimental psychologists tend to study one kind of affective priming in isolation, investigating the impact of either positive or negative stimuli alone. In real life, however, unlike in the lab, both kinds of affective priming can occur in tandem, pushing people's emotional responses from different angles but in the same direction. In rousing people for war, for example, stimulating feelings of avoidance toward the enemy while simultaneously provoking positive desires to approach allies has obvious advantages. In revealing the interplay of such emotional effects and their roles as causal agents of broad political change, historical case studies have something unique to offer emotions scholars in other disciplines.

16. Burke's treatise on *The Sublime and Beautiful* went through two different Philadelphia imprints in 1806 and were then followed a year later by the release in Boston of a collected edition of his work. See Edmund Burke, *A Philosophical Inquiry into the Origin of our Ideas of the Sublime and Beautiful* (Philadelphia: D. Johnson, 1806) and (Philadelphia: Samuel F. Bradford, 1806). All citations are to the latter edition. See also Edmund Burke,

The Works of the Right Honourable Edmund Burke . . . First American, from the Last London Edition (Boston: West and Greenleaf, 1807).

17. Burke, *Philosophical Inquiry*, 268.

18. Burke, *Philosophical Inquiry*, 268.

19. Taylor uses the conceit of a "civil war" primarily to explore borderland tensions between Canadian loyalists and American republicans, who took very different views of the British Empire, but he touches repeatedly on Federalist vs. Democratic-Republican divides and U.S. sectional strife as well. See Alan Taylor, *The Civil War of 1812: American Citizens, British Subjects, Irish Rebels, and Indian Allies* (New York: Knopf, 2010). On "picnic hampers" at Bull Run, see William C. Davies, *Bull Run: A History of the First Major Campaign of the Civil War* (Baton Rouge: Louisiana State University Press, 1977), 239.

20. Burke, *Philosophical Inquiry*, 271.

21. Burke, *Philosophical Inquiry*, 271–272.

Chapter 1: Celebrating Love, Liberty, and Progeny

1. Hezekiah Niles, "Treason, Rebellion, Revolution," *Niles Weekly Register*, 28 March 1812, 58, and Hezekiah Niles to James Madison, Baltimore, 17 July 1817, James Madison Papers, Library of Congress (hereafter cited as Madison Papers). On Niles's biography, see John Smith Futhy and Gilbert Cope, *History of Chester County, Pennsylvania* (Philadelphia: L. H. Everts, 1881), 669, and Philip R. Schmidt, *Hezekiah Niles and American Economic Nationalism: A Political Biography* (New York: Ayer Publishing, 1982), 6, 308, nn. 13, 14. Niles was so supportive of the war hawk faction that in 1828 he named a son Henry Clay Niles!

2. See Hezekiah Niles, "Malthus on Population," *Niles Weekly Register*, 28 March 1812, 66. The first number in this article series was Niles, "Malthus on Population, an Analytical Review of the 'Essay on the Principle of Population, by T. R. Malthus, A.M.' with Some Remarks More Particularly Applicable to the Present and Probable Future State of the United States," *Niles Weekly Register*, 28 September 1811, 52.

3. On the causes of the war, and the political controversy it caused within the United States, see J. C. A. Skaggs, *Mr. Madison's War: Politics, Diplomacy, and Warfare in the Early American Republic, 1783–1830* (Princeton, N.J.: Princeton University Press, 1983).

Historian Henry Adams, descendant of the Adams presidents, insisted that the War of 1812 had been the project of southerners and westerners. Summing up Adams's perspective, Marie-Jeanne Rossignol remarks, "the War of 1812 distinguished the United States as perhaps the first country to throw itself into a war that it dreaded in the hope that war itself would create the spirit of war." The fact of such ambivalence hints at the reasons why emotional rhetoric would assume such importance in Republican prowar efforts. See Adams, *History of the United States During the Administrations of James Madison*, vol. 2 (New York: Library of America, 1986), 210, and Rossignol, *The Nationalist Ferment: The Origins of U.S. Foreign Policy, 1792–1812* (Columbus: Ohio University Press, 2004), 189.

4. While historian Susan Klepp has recently documented in masterful detail the rise in women's desires for family limitation over the course of the eighteenth and nineteenth centuries, she also notes that "there is some evidence that women in underpopulated regions embraced the image of the heroic mother who sacrificed herself for the good of the whole through her abundant childbearing." My findings corroborate Klepp's suggestion that patriotic rhetoric demanded that women bear children for the nation. Of course, just as the war

itself was highly controversial, so too was the pronatalist stance espoused by many of the war's advocates. Still, the most recent research by demographers like J. David Hacker indicates that marital fertility remained high across the country through 1860 and was especially elevated in "frontier" areas. My evidence from the 1812 era indicates that this was no accident. Population expansion was explicitly understood as the surest means of laying territorial claim to new "underpopulated regions." See Klepp, *Revolutionary Conceptions: Women, Fertility, and Family Limitation in America, 1760–1820* (Chapel Hill: University of North Carolina Press, 2009), 274, and Hacker, "Rethinking the 'Early' Decline of Marital Fertility in the United States," *Demography* 40 (November 2003): 605–620, quotation on 605.

A focus on the interworking of population and patriotism in the early republic presents an opportunity to respond to the call of scholars such as Ann Laura Stoler for an "intimate history of empire." True, important recent work prods us to consider women's roles in imperialism. Amy Kaplan's evocative phrase "manifest domesticity" has highlighted the "spatial and political interdependence of home and empire." Yet the trope of midcentury domesticity, with its emphasis on the civic importance of women's moral virtue and sexual passivity, falls short of explaining the dynamics of an earlier period. In the era of 1812, fertile women figured as the natural companions of virile male warriors. See Stoler, "Tense and Tender Ties: The Politics of Comparison in North American History and (Post) Colonial Studies," *Journal of American History* 88 (December 2001): 829–865, quotation on 831; Stoler, ed., *Haunted by Empire: Geographies of Intimacy in North American History* (Durham, N.C.: Duke University Press, 2006); and Kaplan, *The Anarchy of Empire in the Making of U.S. Culture* (Cambridge, Mass.: Harvard University Press, 2005), 25.

5. On overpopulation as a perceived problem in sixteenth- and seventeenth-century Britain, and on Richard Hakluyt's prescription of overseas colonization as the solution, see Edmund S. Morgan, *American Slavery, American Freedom* (New York: Norton, 2003), 30–31. See also the discussion and accompanying footnotes in Kathleen M. Brown, *Good Wives, Nasty Wenches, and Anxious Patriarchs: Gender, Race, and Power in Colonial Virginia* (Chapel Hill: University of North Carolina Press, 1996), 22–23, 381, n. 30. Recent research suggests that by the eighteenth century, British opinion had begun to swing the other way, with Enlightenment-era analysts such as Adam Smith as well as Stephen Addington and Richard Price arguing that population should be regarded as an important national resource. Malthus's *Essay on Population* thus represented a significant and lasting intervention in this debate, returning Britain to a stance in favor of limiting population. On Benjamin Franklin's and Adam Smith's converging ideas on population, see David Waldstreicher, "Benjamin Franklin, Capitalism, and Slavery," in Waldstreicher, ed., *A Companion to Benjamin Franklin* (Oxford: Wiley-Blackwell, 2011), 212. And see also S. J. Thompson, "Parliamentary Enclosure, Property, Population, and the Decline of Classical Republicanism in Eighteenth-Century Britain," *Historical Journal* 51 (2008): 621–642, and E. A. Wrigley and R. S. Schofield, *The Population History of England, 1541–1871* (Cambridge: Cambridge University Press, 1989), 404–406.

6. On the multifaceted tensions leading to open conflict between Britain and the United States, with an emphasis on the desire of U.S. slaveholders to conquer Canada in order to neutralize Indians and expand slavery, see Jon Latimer, *1812: War with America* (Cambridge: Belknap/Harvard University Press, 2010), esp. 25–32.

7. For a review of British hypocrisy regarding American sovereignty rights that emphasizes the significance of America's defense of the citizenship of its natural-born

subjects, see Alan Taylor, *The Civil War of 1812: American Citizens, British Subjects, Irish Rebels, and Indian Allies* (New York: Knopf, 2010), esp. chap. 4.

8. Debate on the role of print in the development of nationalism and political factionalism continues to be vigorous. Most recently, Jeffrey L. Pasley has argued for the recognition of what he calls, "newspaper politics," claiming that partisan printers played crucial roles in the democratization of American life from the 1760s to the 1830s. Taking a contrarian stance is Trish Loughran, who argues that print simply could not bind together a nation that did not have the necessary physical infrastructure to support integration and that in any case desired no such outcome, given the localized loyalties and outlooks of most Americans in the first century of U.S. history. I find merit in both arguments. What I call the "popularization" of political economy fits well with Pasley's ideas on democratization. Meanwhile, I find Loughran's insistence that we err in looking for nationalism in a country rent by factionalism to be very useful. I would add, analogously, that seamless unity was not sought in a country that was quite willing to incorporate varied kinds people into the nation on vastly different terms and conditions. (See the extensive discussion on "population" below.) Still, for all the limitations on nationalism, the fact remains that the War of 1812 presented a critical moment in which nationalism became a goal and a problem, at least for those who supported the war. Loughran does not consider the War of 1812 in her analysis (nor the Mexican War, which created similar tensions). The key here is to realize that in these "antebellum" wartime emergencies, nationalism developed not in the service of sectional or socioeconomic unity, but rather in support of imperialism. The very idea that the entire first half of the nineteenth century can be usefully described as the period before *the* war, the Civil War, needs to be rethought. See Pasley, *"The Tyranny of Printers": Newspaper Politics in the Early American Republic* (Richmond: University of Virginia Press, 2003), esp. 17–22, and Loughran, *The Republic in Print: Print Culture in the Age of U.S. Nation Building, 1770–1870* (New York: Columbia University Press, 2009), esp. 3–14. On the Mexican War and U.S. imperialism, see Amy S. Greenberg, *Manifest Manhood and the Antebellum American Empire* (Cambridge: Cambridge University Press, 2005).

9. Matthew Mason notes, "Both Britons and Americans claimed to be the standard bearers of human liberation in the Age of Revolution." See Mason, "The Battle of the Slaveholding Liberators: Great Britain, the United States, and Slavery in the Early Nineteenth Century," *William and Mary Quarterly*, 3rd ser., 59, no. 3, *Slaveries in the Atlantic World* (2002): 665–696. See also Mason, *Slavery and Politics in the Early American Republic* (Chapel Hill: University of North Carolina Press, 2006), and Christopher Leslie Brown, *Moral Capital: Foundations of British Abolitionism* (Chapel Hill: University of North Carolina Press, 2006). The Samuel Johnson quotation appears in Brown, *Moral Capital*, 122.

10. Donald Winch notes that the *Essay on Population* was viewed in its day as a "sign of that skepticism or hostility towards the [French] revolution in Britain that set in during the final years of the century and was to continue throughout the Napoleonic wars. By association, at least, Malthus's work acquired a conservative or counter-revolutionary complexion that tempts comparison with Edmund Burke's *Reflections on the Revolution in France* (1790)." Winch adds that although Malthus saw himself as occupying a philosophical middle ground *between* Godwin (who celebrated the French Revolution) and Burke, "the conservative reputation of Mathus's *Essay* needs to be mentioned in any account of why 'Malthusian' acquired a negative connotation in some circles in his lifetime." See Winch, ed., *Malthus: An Essay on the Principle of Population (Cambridge Texts in the History of Political Thought* (Cambridge: Cambridge University Press, 1992), ix.

11. On the new subtitle for the second edition of the essay published in 1803, see also Samuel Hollander, ed., *Malthus' Essay on Population: The Six Editions (History of British Economic Thought)* (Taylor and Francis, 1996), and on the changes Malthus made to his essay between editions, see Hollander, *The Literature of Political Economy* (New York: Routledge, 1995), 247.

12. The third London edition of Malthus corresponds to the first American one. See T. R. Malthus, *An Essay on the Principle of Population; or, A View of Its Past and Present Effects on Human Happiness with an Inquiry into Our Prospects Respecting the Future Removal or Mitigation of the Evils which It Occasions . . . First American from the Third London Edition* (Washington, D.C.: Weightman, 1809). Subsequent citations of Malthus are from this first American edition. The official 1810 census (the third, following those of 1790 and 1800) was published as United States Census Office, *Aggregate Amount of Each Description of Persons within the United States of America and the Territories thereof, Agreeably to Actual Enumeration Made . . . 1810* (Washington, 1811).

13. Malthus, *Essay on Population*, 9–10.

14. Census numbers were reported in almanacs all across the country. These statistics might be national numbers, local numbers, or both. Especially suggestive were wartime almanacs that featured military news and highlights amid the census numbers. An example of this form is a twenty-page almanac from 1813, which featured daily weather predictions, narratives of five naval battles, a brief census report, and little else. See Thomas De Silver, *Desilver's Naval Almanac, for the Year of Our Lord 1814 . . . Containing . . . Some Interesting Particulars Relative to the Navy of the United States . . . Embellished with Five Prints of the American Naval Victories* (Philadelphia: Thomas De Silver, [1813]), [18]. For a geographically varied selection of examples of almanacs that includes census information, chosen from among many dozen, see George Hough and Daniel Cooledge, *Concord Pocket Almanac for the Year of Our Lord 1811* (Concord, N.H.: Geo. Hough & D. Cooledge, 1810), 96–100; Timothy Alden, *Alden's New Jersey Register and United States Calendar for the Year of Our Lord, 1811* (Newark: William Tuttle, 1811), 135; *Browne & Co.'s Cincinnati Almanac for the Year of Our Lord 1813* (Cincinnati: J.W. Browne, 1812), 8; and Thomas H. Whitney, *Whiteney's New Orleans Directory and Louisiana & Mississippi Almanac for the Year 1811* (New Orleans: author, 1810), ii.

Scholars such as Martin Bruckner have recently made us aware of the degree to which territorial ambitions infiltrated every element of American popular culture down to the creation of the new academic subject of geography featured in elementary school classrooms. He asserts, "The rhetoric of empire was the result of the programmatic diffusion of geographical knowledge in American schools and the widespread implementation of territorializing habits into the canon of national education. . . . During the early decades of the nineteenth century, the literary function of geography was undergoing a critical metamorphosis from stabilizing the union to mobilizing the desire for empire." The corollary to this is that the public was also engrossed by the progress of the country's population, eagerly keeping up with census reports and using population levels as comparative index of national strength and imperial potential. See Bruckner, *The Geographic Revolution in Early America: Maps, Literacy, and National Identity* (Chapel Hill: University of North Carolina Press, 2006), 240, 243.

15. Franklin advertised his pamphlet for sale in the *Pennsylvania Gazette* on 4 December 1755, saying it was "lately published in Boston, and to be sold at the NEW PRINTING OFFICE, in Market street, Philadelphia." The text quoted here is Benjamin

Franklin, "On Population: Observations on the Increase of Mankind, Peopling of Countries, &c.," in *Memoirs of the Life and Writings of Benjamin Franklin . . . together with the Whole of His Political, Philosophical, and Miscellaneous Works*, vol. 4 (Philadelphia: William Duane, 1809), 184–191, quotation on 190.

On the political and scientific context of Franklin's pamphlet, see Joyce Chaplin, *The First Scientific American: Benjamin Franklin and the Pursuit of Genius* (New York: Basic Books, 2006), 141–144.

16. Malthus, *Essay on Population*, 2–3.

17. Franklin, "On Population," 184, and Malthus, *Essay on Population*, 5.

18. Franklin, "On Population," 185, and Malthus, *Essay on Population*, 6.

19. Franklin, "On Population," 185–186.

20. See, for example, Franklin, "On Population," as cited above.

21. The composition date of this letter is uncertain. Albert Henry Smyth notes that the original rough draft of the letter, in the collections of the American Philosophical Society, is undated and that the conventionally accepted date of 1768 may be inaccurate. See "Benjamin Franklin to John Alleyne, Craven Street, August 9, 1768," in Smyth, ed., *The Writings of Benjamin Franklin*. vol. 5 (New York: Macmillan, 1907), 156.

For early American reprints, see, for example: "Early Marriages: Original Letter from Dr. Franklin, to John Alleyne, Esquire," *Freeman's Oracle or New-Hampshire Advertiser*, 3 February 1789; "Letter from Dr. Franklin to John Alleyne Esquire," Fredericktown, Md., *Republican Advocate*, 4 March 1803; "From the Republican Advocate Letter from Dr. Franklin, to John Alleyne, Esquire," New York *American Citizen*, 12 March 1803; "Letter from Doctor Franklin, to John Alleyne, Esquire," Easton, Md., *Republican Star*, 15 March 1803; "On Early Marriage. An Original Letter from Dr. Franklin to John Alleyne," Randolph, Vt., *Weekly Wanderer*, 15 December 1806; "On Early Marriages," *New York Weekly Museum*, 16 July 1814.

22. Franklin, "On Early Marriages," *New York Weekly Museum*. On eighteenth-century emphasis on the civic role of nursing mothers, see Londa Schiebinger, "Why Mammals Are Called Mammals: Gender Politics in Eighteenth-Century Natural History," *American Historical Review* 98 (April 1993): 382–411.

23. Franklin, "On Early Marriages," *New York Weekly Museum*. This was not Franklin's only humorous effort in this vein. Susan E. Klepp recounts how Franklin popularized a fraudulent account of one Polly Baker, the colonial woman who supposedly bore twenty children (the first five out of wedlock), the better to add strength to the number of the king's subjects. See Klepp, *Revolutionary Conceptions*, discussion on 215.

24. Mason Locke Weems, *Hymen's Recruiting-Serjeant; or, The New Matrimonial Tattoo, For the Old Bachelors* (Philadelphia: H. Maxwell, 1800). On Weems as an author and entrepreneur, see Christopher Harris, "Mason Locke Weems's Life of Washington: The Making of a Bestseller," *Southern Literary Journal* 19 (Spring 1987): 92–101. Steven Watts highlights the moral components of the *Hymen* pamphlet in Watts, "Masks, Morals, and the Market: American Literature and Early Capitalist Culture, 1790–1820," *Journal of the Early Republic* 2 (Summer 1986): 127–150, quotation on 142.

25. Weems, *Hymen's Recruiting-Serjeant*, [i] & 16. See also Weems, *Hymen's Recruiting Serjeant; or, The New Matrimonial Tat-too, For the Old Bachelors . . .* , 5th ed. (Philadelphia: John Bioren, 1806). A sixth edition with the same title was printed "for the author" in Philadelphia in 1816 and an unnumbered edition under the title also appeared from an unknown publisher in Greenfield, Mass., in 1817.

26. "Miscellany: From the Port Folio," Brattleboro, Vt., *The Reporter*, 28 November 1803; "From the Port Folio: Two Are Better than One," Middlebury, Vt, , *Middlebury Mercury*, 17 July 1805; "Miscellaneous Selections: The Lay Preacher," *Portland Gazette and Maine Advertiser*, 26 October 1807; "Miscellany: The Lay Precher," Danville, Vt., *North Star*, 7 November 1807; "Miscellany: The Lay Preacher," Chester, Vt., *Green Mountain Palladium*, 23 November 1807; "Two Are Better than One," *Boston Mirror*, 13 January 1810; "Miscellany from the Port Folio: The Lay Preacher," Dover N.H., *Dover Sun*, 27 August 1814; "From the Port Folio: The Lay Preacher," Middletown, Conn., *Connecticut Spectator*, 21 September 1814.

Demographic data on age of marriage are imprecise, but it appears that early marriage remained the norm throughout the early nineteenth century (though average age at marriage would increase by mid- to late century). Hacker observes, "nuptiality declined between the colonial period and 1890, when the Census office first published data on marital status. . . . The trend in marriage before 1850 was also likely upward, although the magnitude of the increase remains unclear." The mean age at marriage for white women was 23 in 1850, while inexact estimates place it between 22.7 and 21 in 1780, either "implying that there was little change between 1780 and 1850" or at most implying "a 2-year increase in white women's age at marriage between 1800 and 1850." See Hacker, "Rethinking the 'Early' Decline," 609.

Documenting the political debate swirling around these demographic trends makes clear how much personal marriage decisions were made with an awareness of public consequences. Many people did defy the war. Many did resist geographic expansion. And many did oppose the strains of unlimited family size. But these were tough trends to reverse. The shift in momentum, in both politics and demographics, came extremely slowly. In the era of 1812, domestic life and military policy remained very much intertwined.

27. The *Port Folio* essay omitted any mention of the national implications of maximized reproduction. It could be that over time the political content of Franklin's advice leached out of popular memory. Perhaps more likely, it was sometimes bleached out by partisan editors. The *Port Folio* was an avowedly Federalist paper published by a man named Joseph Dennie who made his life's work the preservation of the fading Federalist legacy. On the politics of the *Port Folio*, see William C. Dowling, *Literary Federalism in the Age of Jefferson: Joseph Dennie and the Port Folio, 1801–1812* (Columbia: University of South Carolina Press, 1999), and Catherine O'Donnell Kaplan, *Men of Letters in the Early Republic: Cultivating Forums of Citizenship* (Chapel Hill: University of North Carolina Press, 2008), esp. chap. 5.

28. Thomas Jefferson to Jean Baptiste Say, 1 February 1804, Thomas Jefferson Papers, series 1, general correspondence. 1651–1827, Library of Congress (hereafter cited as Jefferson Papers).

29. Jefferson to Say, 1 February 1804, Jefferson Papers.

30. Remarking on this Jefferson letter, Drew McCoy makes the important point that the president rejected Malthusian analysis as incompatible with his vision for a virtuous agrarian republic. However, McCoy does not note that Malthus explicitly singled out U.S. takeovers of Indian lands in his *Essay on Population* and that, in rejecting Malthus, Jefferson did as much to file a brief for imperialism as for republicanism. See McCoy, *The Elusive Republic: Political Economy in Jeffersonian America* (Chapel Hill: University of North Carolina Press, 1996), 190–195.

On the importance of marriage as a means to achieving republican manhood, see Mark Kann, *A Republic of Men: The American Founders, Gendered Language, and Patriarchal*

Politics (New York: New York University Press, 1998), esp. chap. 4, "The Family Man and Citizenship."

31. Donald Winch notes that "Malthus reluctantly came to the conclusion at the end of the war in 1814–15 that a measure of protection from foreign competition should be retained. In the eyes of many of his contemporaries . . . adherents of Adam Smith's 'system of natural liberty' almost to a man this constituted an act of apostasy, a departure from the general principle of free trade between nations . . . evidence of a corrupt allegiance or bias in favour of the interests of the land-owning aristocracy." See Winch, *Malthus*, x.

See also Roger Whatmore, *Republicanism and the French Revolution: An Intellectual History of Jean-Baptiste Say's Political Economy* (Oxford: Oxford University Press, 2001), 143, 206, and Samuel Hollander, "On Malthus's Physiocratic References," *History of Political Economy* 24, no. 2 (1992): 369–380.

32. Referencing research on the U.S. reception of Malthus that dated from the 1930s, Drew McCoy assumed that "few Americans read [Malthus's] work" and that few "commentators paid any attention to Malthus in the early years of the nineteenth century." I argue, to the contrary, that informal opposition to the basic ideas of Malthusianism was popular, widespread, and politically significant. See McCoy, *The Elusive Republic*, 192.

33. [William Wirt], "For the Enquirer," Richmond *Enquirer*, 11 August 1804.

34. [Wirt], "For the Enquirer." William Wirt is the exception that proves the rule when it comes to using Malthusian attitudes as a political indicator. As a putative Republican, Wirt should logically have opposed Malthus and supported population growth. After all, he was a protégé of Jefferson and Madison who became U.S. attorney general in the Monroe administration. Yet Wirt was never comfortable with republicanism and ultimately rejected the party and its politics outright. Reviewing Wirt's career as a whole, Michael Oberg argues that over time he adopted markedly antidemocratic ideas, became "a strong proponent of regulatory measures" at the national level (anathema to the physiocratic basis of Jeffersonian approaches to population), and ultimately ran in opposition to Andrew Jackson in order to challenge the emergence of the new Democratic Party in the presidential election of 1828. For anyone aware of his anonymous promotion of Malthus in 1804, what Oberg describes as Wirt's eventual "drift from Jeffersonian ideals" may have come as little surprise. See Oberg, "William Wirt and the Trials of Republicanism," *Virginia Magazine of History and Biography* 99, no. 3: 305–326, quotation on 307.

35. "For the Enquirer: The Rainbow-Series 2d," Richmond *Enquirer*, 17 November 1804.

36. [William Wirt], *The Rainbow: First Series Originally Published in the Richmond Enquirer* (Richmond: Ritchie & Worsley, 1804).

37. See Allen C. Clark, "Roger Chew Weightman, a Mayor of the City of Washington," *Records of the Columbia Historical Society, Washington, D.C.* 22 (1919): 62–104, quotation on 62. In describing Weightman as a publisher, I follow Rosalind Remer. Remer notes that while printers had to *sell* political treatises of many varieties, they often published only those that aided their own views: "publishing could be an act of political self-definition." See Remer, *Printers and Men of Capital: Philadelphia Book Publishers in the New Republic* (Philadelphia: University of Pennsylvania Press, 2000), 29, 75.

38. "*Malthus on Population*, Proposal for Publishing by Subscription," *United States Gazette*, 30 November 1807, 3. Weightman published along with J. Milligan, who placed the first advertisement in the Philadelphia paper *United States Gazette*, indicating that Samuel F. Bradford would take subscription orders from Philadelphia patrons. This set

off an "ad blitz" of ten separate subscription notices in Washington, Philadelphia, and New York newspapers in November and December 1807, including one in the *New York Commercial Advertiser* on 3 December 1807, 3, and one in the *National Intelligencer and Washington Advertiser* on 4 December 1807, 4. Weightman took care to include the essay excerpt in each advertisement, always crediting "The Rainbow" or the *Enquirer.*

39. "The American Press . . . Malthus's Treatise" [no headline], *American Citizen*, 17 May 1809. This commentary was reprinted exactly (without attribution) in "The American Press . . . Malthus's Treatise" [no headline], New York *Republican Watch-Tower*, 19 May 1809.

40. Donald Hickey, *The War of 1812: A Forgotten Conflict* (Urbana: University of Illinois Press, 1989), 17, 21–22.

41. John Bristed, *Hints on the Bankruptcy of Britain and Her Resources to Maintain the Present Contest with France* (New York: Sargeant, 1809), 64; "To the Editors of the Public Advertiser," New York *Public Advertiser*, 19 June 1809; "To the Editors of the Public Advertiser," *New York Journal*, 21 June 1809, 4; and "To the Editors of the Public Advertiser," Sag Harbor, N.Y., *Suffolk Gazette*, 1 July 1809, 2.

42. Loammi Baldwin, *Thoughts on the Study of Political Economy* (Cambridge: Hilliard & Metcalf, 1809), 12

43. Baldwin, *Thoughts on the Study of Political Economy*, 5–6.

44. Baldwin, *Thoughts on the Study of Political Economy*, 5–6.

45. Niles, "Malthus," 28 September 1811.

46. On Hezekiah Niles's political attitudes and wartime service in the era of 1812, see Phillip R. Schmidt, *Hezekiah Niles and American Economic Nationalism: A Political Biography* (New York: Arno, 1982), esp. 46–51.

47. Niles, "Malthus," 28 September 1811. Compare Malthus, *Essay on Population*, 43–47.

48. Niles, "Malthus," 28 September 1811. Compare Malthus, *Essay on Population*, 47, 77.

49. "The Floridas," *Niles Weekly Register*, 26 September 1812. In an editorial introduction, Niles noted that the article was a reprint and offered his personal approval of the contents: "For the following sketch, containing much interesting matter, we are indebted to the Nashville (Ten.) 'Clarion.'"

50. Niles, "Malthus," 12 October 1811. Compare: Malthus, "Chapter VI, Of the Checks to Population among the Ancient Inhabitants of the North of Europe," *Essay on Population*, 132–133. The work referred to was "Tacitus's *Germania*, which was the most broadly recognized source for ancient northern Europe." See Kristoffer Neville, "Gothicism and Early Modern Historical Ethnography," *Journal of the History of Ideas* 70, no. 2 (2009): 213–234, quotation on 216.

51. Niles, "Malthus," 12 October 1811.

52. Niles, "Malthus," 12 October 1811, emphasis in original, and Malthus, *Essay on Population*, 143.

53. Niles, "Malthus," 12 October 1811. Niles referred to the French naturalist Georges-Louis Leclerc, Comte de Buffon, author of the multivolume *Histoire Naturel* (completed in the 1780s). Ironically, Buffon's work was already in wide disrepute in the United States, not least because of his theory that all plants and animals degenerated on the continent of North America, a stance that Thomas Jefferson, among others, took great pains to refute. See Howard C. Rice, Jr., "Jefferson's Gift of Fossils to the Museum of

Natural History in Paris," *Proceedings of the American Philosophical Society* 95 (December 1951): 597–627.

Malthus would continue to be invoked by both proponents and opponents of U.S. slavery for decades to come, leading Dennis Hodgson to conclude that "there was no general 'American' appraisal of Malthus, but there was a 'Northern' and a 'Southern' appraisal." See Hodgson, "Malthus's *Essay on Population* and the American Debate over Slavery," *Comparative Studies in Society and History* 51, no. 4 (2009): 742–770, quotation on 744.

The notion that the fertility of Africans was adversely affected by a supposed lack of sexual morality was endemic to British America. Katherine Paugh has shown in detail how such attitudes served important political and economic interests of Caribbean slaveholders who claimed the right to exercise sexual surveillance over enslaved women the better to improve the plantation labor supply. See Paugh, "Rationalizing Reproduction: Race, Disease, and Fertility in the British Caribbean and the Atlantic World during the Age of Abolition, 1763—1833," Ph.D. diss, University of Pennsylvania, 2008.

54. For a summary of the battle, see John Sugden, *Tecumseh, a Life* (New York: Holt, 1999), 231–239. On contemporary suspicions of British involvement, see Solomon Aiken, *An Address to Federal Clergymen* (Boston: author, 1813), 27.

55. Niles, "Malthus," 28 March 1812,

56. Niles, "Malthus," 22 August 1812.

57. Niles, "Malthus," 22 August 1812. This was, of course, the formal position of the Republican Party. But where scholars have repeatedly noted the connection between land and equality in the American imagination, they have not taken note of the integrally related issue of reproduction.

58. Niles, "Malthus," 22 August 1812.

59. Niles, "Treason, Rebellion, Revolution," 28 March 1812.

60. For a discussion of sectional tensions, particularly as they related to the issue of slavery in the War of 1812, see Elizabeth R. Varon, *Disunion! The Coming of the American Civil War, 1789–1859* (Chapel Hill: University of North Carolina Press, 2008), 37. For a summary of Federalist war opposition, with emphasis on fears of the French, see Rachel Hope Cleves, "Fighting the War of 1812," in Cleves, *The Reign of Terror in America: Visions of Violence from Anti-Jacobinism to Antislavery* (Cambridge: Cambridge University Press, 2009), 153–193, esp. 161–162. On the related British view of U.S. motives for war, which dismissed the issues of neutrality and impressment, and emphasized the attempted conquest of Canada, see Jon Latimer, *1812: War with America* (Cambridge, Mass.: Harvard University Press, 2007), 1–59.

61. "National Politics," Philadelphia *Weekly Aurora,* 19 June 1810, 1, and "Economical Almanac," *New Hampshire Patriot,* 5 May 1812, 4. For reprints from the *New Hampshire Patriot,* see "Miscellany from the Yankee Economical Almanack," Hudson, N.Y., *Bee,* 19 May 1812, 1; "Economical Almanack," *Alexandria [Va.] Gazette,* 23 May 1812, 4; "Miscellaneous. Economical Almanac," Amherst, N.H., *Farmer's Cabinet,* 25 May 1812, 4; "Economical Almanac May," Kennebunk, Maine, *Weekly Visitor,* 6 June 1812, 4; "Matrimony," Middletown *Connecticut Spectator,* 14 December 1814, 4. All but one of these five reprints was in New England or upstate New York. The *Alexandria Gazette,* for its part, was an opposition Federalist paper in Virginia that took a strong stand against the war. On the paper's politics, see Myron F. Wehtje, "Opposition in Virginia to the War of 1812," *Virginia Magazine of History and Biography* (January 1970): 65–86, especially page 67.

62. George Bourne, *Marriage Indissoluble and Divorce Unscriptural* (Harrisonburg, [Va.]: Davidson and Bourne, 1813), 20–21. On Bourne's biography, see John W. Christie and Dwight L. Dumond, *George Bourne and "The Book and Slavery Irreconcilable"* (Dover, Del.: Historical Society of Delaware, 1969).

63. Bourne, *Marriage Indissoluble and Divorce Unscriptural*, 20–21.

64. John Taylor, *An Inquiry into the Principles and Policy of the Government* (Fredericksburg, [Va.]: Green and Cady, 1814), 543. Taylor's politics resist easy categorization in that he was both profoundly anti-British and radically antiwar. On the far fringe of the Republican Party, he displayed deep distrust of aristocratic social and political forms and of the centralization of executive power, believing that the country had drifted too far toward the political philosophy propounded by John Adams and his allies, authors of the *Federalist Papers* "signed Publius" (Taylor, *An Inquiry*, [v]). He argued that "the measures arising from the spirit early infused into executive power by its American form were armies, war, penal laws, and an increase of executive power. . . . These are English effects, and evil effects" (Taylor, *An Inquiry*, 174). Still, he remained enough of a party loyalist and wartime patriot that he made no direct critique of Madison anywhere in his 656-page *Inquiry*.

65. Taylor, *An Inquiry*, 545. William Appleman Williams has argued that Taylor's work in the *Inquiry* "provided the basis for all non-imperial philosophy" as it later developed in the United States and that, paradoxical as it may seem, "a southern slave owner made the best case against empire as a way of life." I argue that Taylor's belief that liberty could be compatible with slavery so long as it allowed for the supposedly more fundamental freedom of unrestricted fertility compromised his antiwar stance in a fatal way. However genuine his stated aversion to war and empire, in rejecting Malthusian analysis of the role of excessive population growth in necessitating and motivating imperial aggression, he irreparably undermined his own position. That southern and western slaveholders remained the chief proponents of U.S. imperial actions throughout the nineteenth century only deepens the historical importance of this analytical point. See Williams, *Empire as a Way of Life: An Essay on the Causes and Character of America's Present Predicament Along with a Few Thoughts About an Alternative* (Oxford: Oxford University Press, 1982), 49.

66. Tacitus's work seems to have been broadly familiar to early Americans. A cursory search of the Readex's digitized "Early American Newspaper Series" for "Tacitus" in the years 1810–1815 reveals 678 newspaper citations for Tacitus, including many booksellers' advertisements offering for sale an imported translation of his work by Arthur Murphy: "Murphy's Tacitus."

67. Niles, "Malthus," 12 October 1811. Compare Malthus, *Essay on Population*, 132–133. I have been unable to find any similar passage from Tacitus in Malthus.

68. Niles, "Malthus," 12 October 1811. Without knowing exactly from which edition of Tacitus Niles drew (and whether he read Tacitus in Latin or in translation), one cannot determine how much Niles embroidered Tacitus's observations himself. However, an early twentieth-century translation of Tacitus by Princeton University classics professor Duane Reed Stuart suggests that Niles made as free with Tacitus as he did with Malthus. Stuart renders the relevant passages from Tacitus as "the women and children usually accompanied a barbarian army in the field" and "death at the hands of their own compatriots was to be preferred to falling into the power of the enemy. The behavior of the German women . . . was actuated by the same motives." Niles omitted the reference to children in battle while adding an emphasis on emotional ardor. In combination, these

apparent changes would have magnified the association between battlefield performance and romantic love. See Stuart, *Tacitus, The Germania with Introduction and Notes* (New York: Macmillan, 1916), 44–45.

69. Hezekiah Niles to James Madison, Baltimore, 17 July 1817, Madison Papers.

70. On the ethnic variety of Euro-Americans in the U.S. population in 1810, see Campbell Gibson, "The Contribution of Immigration to the Growth and Ethnic Diversity of the American Population," *Proceedings of the American Philosophical Society* 136 (June 1992): 157–175.

Jay Fliegelman famously focused attention on the concomitant decline of fathers and the rise of democracy in the United States. Julie Ellison is one of the first scholars to have noted that writers eager to "shape republican narratives to the geopolitics of North America" produced works "justifying the mixture of patriotism and romance." See Fliegelman, *Prodigals and Pilgrims: The American Revolution Against Patriarchal Authority* (Cambridge: Cambridge University Press, 1982), and Ellison, *Cato's Tears and the Making of Anglo-American Emotion* (Chicago: University of Chicago Press, 1999), 77–78.

71. Michel Foucault's lectures, *Security, Territory, Population*, first published in English in 2007, provide a useful starting point for understanding the Enlightenment context of early American ideas. Foucault asserts that in the eighteenth century, "the population as a political subject, as a new collective subject absolutely foreign to the juridical and political thought of earlier centuries [was] appearing." He argues that "the population as a collective subject is very different from the collective subject constituted and created by the social contract." Members of the population do not consent to government so much as they submit to management. All those who interact with state institutions (through tax collection, public health, or the penal system, to cite several of Foucault's examples) are members of the population regardless of whether or not they can also claim status as members of the political citizenry.

Foucault's notion of "population" describes well how white male citizens imagined that many noncitizens would be incorporated into the nation in the United States in 1812. Members of "the population" were neither royal subjects nor democratic citizens, but a new category entirely. Foucault offered "population" as a capacious term to be applied to *all* the inhabitants of varying social and political status that together make up the "collective subjects" of the nation. He wrote using grain scarcity as a case study and, in his analysis, the "population" refers to all those whose access to grain must be regulated by the apparatus of the state. In other words, in Foucault's conceptualization, *everyone* is a member of the "population" because *everyone* is a consumer of grain. Linked neither to lineal descent nor to legal consent, population afforded a universal category in which affiliation could be achieved through joint participation. Anyone who contributed productive or reproductive labor, anyone whose life was subject to state regulation, contributed to the population of the nation. When considered as a category of analysis, "population" has an explanatory power that exceeds that of citizenship. There was no necessary correlation between population membership and political rights.

In the United States in 1812, almost anyone who could bear arms or bear children counted as a member of the "population." Some members of the population (in Foucault's schema, the privileged few who are suppliers as well as consumers of grain) held the additional distinction of being "citizens," persons with recognized political and civil rights. But everyone, male or female, young or old, black or white, native born or new immigrant, who inhabited the nation constituted its population—everyone that is except the one class of people that remained in but not of the nation—Native Americans. While Native Americans were denizens of North America, they were not residents of the United States in any meaningful sense.

Foucault's theory of "population" accounts for this anomalous category with the term the "people." In this special sense, "the people . . . are those who resist regulation of the population, who try to elude the apparatus by which the population exists." In nineteenth-century America, Native Americans (who shared space within the territorial claims of the nation without constituting part of the U.S. population, without accepting government regulation) constituted "the people." See Foucault, Michel Senellart, ed., Graham Burchell, trans., *Michel Foucault: Security, Territory, Population: Lectures at the College de France, 1977–1978* (New York: Picador, 2007), 42–44.

72. My reading of Foucault's use of the terms "population" and "people" is distinct from that provided in Nancy Armstrong and Leonard Tennenhouse, "The Problem of Population and the Form of the American Novel," *American Literary History* 20 (Winter 2008): 667–685, discussion on 682 and n. 12, 684.

73. Baldwin, *Thoughts on the Study of Political Economy*, 8–9.

74. Benedict Anderson (and those like Joyce Appleby and coauthors who have followed him) often refers to the unifying potential of emotion to create national "identity." Yet the notion of "identity" itself is problematic. It may be more useful to ask how emotion can spur joint exploits. See Joyce Oldham Appleby, Lynn Avery Hunt, and Margaret C. Jacob, *Telling the Truth About History* (New York: Norton, 1995), 93–94, and Rogers Brubaker and Frederick Cooper, "Beyond 'Identity,'" *Theory and Society* 29 (2000): 1–47, discussion on 4.

75. Fred Anderson and Andrew Cayton say in summation that "the War of 1812 climaxed a long series of border wars provoked by competition for control of the territory whose waters drain into the Great Lakes and the Gulf of Mexico east of the Mississippi River, a final struggle to gain the power to control the cultural and political landscape of eastern North America." Anderson and Cayton, *Dominion of War*, 229.

Political philosophers like Susan James remind us that there is an inherent connection between passion and action. In fact, James shows that Cicero, classical inspiration to many self-styled republicans of the 1812 era, claimed that implicit in the notion of "libido" is a disposition to action, a will to acquire a desired good. For white Americans of the early republic, the object of political desire was Indian lands. See James, *Passion and Action: the Emotions in Seventeenth-Century Philosophy* (Oxford: Oxford University Press, 1997), 5. There were no fewer than a dozen American reprints of Cicero in Latin translation published in the United States between 1802 and 1816 in which the concept of "libido" was discussed. See, for example, *Narrationes excerptæ ex Latinis scriptoribus servato temporum ordine dispositæ; or, Select Narrations taken from the Best Latin Authors Justin, Quintus Curtius, Cæsar, Cicero, Titus Livius, Sallust, Suetonius, and Tacitus* (Philadelphia: John F. Watson and Joseph Delaplaine, 1813).

76. James Madison, "President's Message Washington City, Dec. 5. This day at 12 o'clock . . ." [Boston, 1815], broadside in the collections of the American Antiquarian Society (AAS), Worcester, Mass.

77. Thomas Jefferson to William Short, 28 November 1814, Jefferson Papers.

78. Thomas Jefferson to Pierre Samuel du Pont de Nemours, 31 December 1815, Jefferson Papers. Although wartime letters from Madison to de Nemours do not survive, a number of letters from de Nemours to Madison indicating their close affinity remain

in the latter's correspondence. For example, in a letter dated 30 April 1813, de Nemours wrote to congratulate Madison on the news of his recent reelection to a second term in office: "the continuation of your virtuous and courageous administration appears to me extremely necessary for my second homeland" (translation mine from the French). See Pierre Samuel du Pont de Nemours to James Madison, 30 April 1813, Madison Papers.

79. "Petition to Congress by Citizens of the Eastern States," March 1816, Clarence Edwin Carter, ed., *The Territorial Papers of the United States*, vol. 17, *The Territory of Illinois, 1814–1818* (Washington, D.C.: U.S. Government Printing Office, 1950), 321–322. Where demographers once treated the availability of land as a simple environmental factor that encouraged greater reproduction as if through some constant law of nature, scholars now emphasize that the very idea of a "frontier" is a cultural and political construct. As Lee L. Bean et al. analyze the idea, "Opportunities arise on the frontier not simply because available land provides new opportunities. The institutional structures that govern access to and distribution of land must be considered. . . . 'No family system can be understood apart from the political economic context in which it is found.' . . . The concept of the frontier essentially presents a region . . . within which the political-economic system supports relatively open access to resource exploitation." See Bean, Geraldine P. Mineau, and Douglas L. Anderton, *Fertility Change on the American Frontier: Adaptation and Innovation* (Berkeley: University of California Press, 1990), 242.

80. Governor Ninian Edwards to Secretary of War William Crawford, Kaskaskia, Illinois Territory, 26 September 1816 in Carter, *The Territorial Papers of the United States*, vol. 17, 399.

81. "Early Marriage, an Extract," *Carlisle* [Pa.] *Gazette*, 1 November 1815, 4.

82. Again, exercise of these personal freedoms and obligations was in no objective sense an adequate equivalent of full civil rights. However, the substitution of private for public liberties did play an often overlooked, yet historically significant, part in helping white political leaders rationalize the highly circumscribed nature of American freedom. As I will argue at length in later chapters, African Americans and white women resisted this unequal bargain. To the extent that any performed the supportive, subordinate patriotic roles demanded of them (and many explicitly resisted), they did so only as a strategic first step toward the ultimate aim of claiming full citizenship.

Chapter 2: Failures of Feeling as National Disasters

1. Robert Lucas, "The Robert Lucas Journal," ed. John C. Parish, *Iowa Journal of History and Politics* 4, no. 3 (1906): 343–437, quotations on 410, 363, 413 (hereafter cited as Lucas Journal).

2. Lucas Journal, 413–415.

3. Colonel Lewis Cass to Secretary of War William Eustis, 10 September 1812 as quoted in *Sketches of the War Between the United States and the British Isles* (Rutland, Vt.: Fay and Davison, 1815), 34.

4. Charge 3, 4th specification, "Charges Exhibited by Order of the Secretary of War Against General Hull," as recorded in *Sketches of the War*, 42. (Slightly different wording of this charge appeared in *Report of the Trial of Brig. General William Hull: Commanding the Northwestern Army of the United States by a Court Martial Held at Albany on Monday 3d January, 1814* [New York: Eastburn, Kirk, and Co., 1814], 14: "the general ardor of the troops in the prosecution of the war insensibly abated.")

5. Charge 3, 4th specification, "Charges Exhibited," 42.

6. Cass to Eustis, 31–35.

7. Cass to Eustis, 35.

8. *Report of the Trial*, 40.

9. As Steven Novak has noted, "American thought was in transit from an Age of Reason to an Age of Feeling" in precisely this period, with youth culture playing a key part in the new emphasis on emotion as a mark of morality. See Novak, *The Rights of Youth: American Colleges and Student Revolt, 1798–1815* (Cambridge: Harvard University Press, 1977), 88. On the themes of "generational conflict" and "generational rivalry" in the early republic, see Daniel A. Cohen, "Arthur Mervyn and His Elders: The Ambivalence of Youth in the Early Republic," *William and Mary Quarterly* 43 (July 1986): 362–380, and Rodney Hessinger, *Seduced, Abandoned, and Reborn: Visions of Youth in Middle-Class America* (Philadelphia: University of Pennsylvania Press, 2005).

10. On Hull's commission, see William Hull, *Memoirs of the Campaign of the Northwestern Army of the United States, a.d. 1812* (Boston: True and Greene, 1824), 34.

11. *Report of the Trial*, 56; Hull, *Memoirs*, 35.

12. *Report of the Trial*, 56, 57.

13. *Report of the Trial*, 44, 65.

14. *Report of the Trial*, 66.

15. "Extract of a Letter from a Gentleman of Respectability at Pittsburg, Dated July 20, 1812," New York *War*, 1 August 1812; "Extract of a Letter from an Officer in General Hull's Army, to a Gentleman in Baltimore, Dated Sandwich, (U. Canada), July 15," Hartford *Connecticut Mirror*, 10 August 1812; "Copy of a Lettter from Colonel Cass to General Hull. Sandwich, Upper Canada, July 17, 1812," Easton, Md., *Republican Star or Eastern Shore General Advertiser*, 18 August 1812; "Upper Canada," New York *Western Star and Harp of Erin*, 8 August 1812.

16. "[Report from] Frankford, Kentucky, August 5, 1812," Philadelphia *Poulson's American Daily Advertiser*, 19 August 1812, and Boston *Repertory and General Advertiser*, 21 August 1812. Both articles note the loss of Michilmackinac. The *Rhode Island American* first reported the ceasefire on August 21. See "The Armistice," Providence *Rhode Island American*, 21 August 1812.

Distrust between Hull and Dearborn preceded the war. As the *Rhode Island American* noted in its next issue, it was common knowledge that Hull had "refused the office of Brigadier-General, unless he could hold his command independent of Dearborn, and receive his orders directly from the Secretary of War." "The Armistice," Providence *Rhode Island American*, 25 August 1812.

For Hull's correspondence, see William Hull to William Eustis, 21 July 1812, 29 July 1812, and 4 August 1812, Clark Historical Library, Central Michigan University.

17. See, for example, "Copy of a Letter from Colonel Cass to General Hull," in the following: Easton, Md., *Republican Star or Eastern Shore General Advertiser* 18 August 1812; Boston *Repertory and General Advertiser*, 18 August 1812; Charleston, S.C., *Times*, 19 August 1812; *The Saratoga* [N.Y.] *Patriot*, 19 August 1812; and Hallowell, Maine, *American Advocate*, 20 August 1812.

18. On European theories and colonial anxieties about the possible physical alteration and moral degeneration of Europeans in North America, see Susan Scott Parrish, *American Curiosity: Cultures of Natural History in the Colonial British Atlantic World* (Chapel Hill: University of North Carolina Press, 2006), esp. 82–102.

19. Hugh Williamson, *Observations on the Climate in Different Parts of America . . . To Which Are Added, Remarks on the Different Complexions of the Human Race: With Some Account of the Aborigines of America* (New York: Swords, 1811), 171.

20. Alexander von Humboldt, *Researches Concerning the Institutions & Monuments of the Ancient Inhabitants of America . . . Translated into English by Helen Maria Williams* (London: Longman, 1814), 32. Because Humboldt was a member of the American Philosophical Society, which added his book to its collections once the 1814 English translation appeared, American intellectuals would have had ample opportunity to be apprised of the continuing strength of such views.

21. On connections between cold and melancholy in humoral theory, see Joyce Chaplin, *Subject Matter: Technology, the Body, and Science on the Anglo-American Frontier, 1500– 1670* (Cambridge, Mass.: Harvard University Press, 2001), esp. 121.

22. Samuel Stanhope Smith, *An Essay on the Causes of the Variety of Complexion and Figure in the Human Species* (New Brunswick, N.J.: J. Simpson, 1810), 209.

23. For Smith's critique of England, see, "Of Laws Relative to a State of War and of Neutrality," in Samuel Stanhope Smith, *The Lectures Collected and Improved which Have Been Delivered for a Series of Years in the College of New Jersey on the Subjects of Moral and Political Philosophy* (Trenton, N.J.: Fenton, 1812), 369–386.

At about the same time that Smith contradicted Kames, Parrish notes that Benjamin Smith Barton, writing on *The Generation of the Opossum of North America* (Philadelphia: S. Merritt, 1813), took time to critique Buffon. I would point out that the timing of the publication of this piece may well be significant; Barton's need to counter Buffon may evidence generalized wartime anxieties. See Parrish, *American Curiosity*, 134.

24. Williamson, *Observations on the Climate*, 3, 17, 67. Here Williamson sets out to prove that no "frigidity" in the American climate inhibited courage, whereas he states elsewhere that those in warm climates were often suspected of want of courage. Which endangered courage, heat or cold? Williamson, in fact, sought to establish that a temperate climate prevailed in the United States. His rhetorical weaving arose in large part from the fact that by the time he wrote in the early nineteenth century, he had to reply to centuries of prior theorists, writers united only by their critical views of the American hemisphere, but not by any consensus about its actual climate!

25. Robert Lucas to Major William Kendall, 12 August 1812, Lucas Journal, 407. Common modern assumptions about the antithetical relationship between romantic ardor and martial ardor, summed up in the Vietnam era protest slogan "make love not war," often take as their starting point Sigmund Freud's hopeful claim, in the 1933 essay "Why War?," that "if the propensity for war be due to the destructive instinct, we have always its counter-agent, Eros, to our hand." Political psychologist David G. Winter, for example, in recent comments on "Power, Sex, and Violence," cites these lines from Freud in an effort to describe how we might "tame or temper power so that we can live with it as well and peaceably as we can." Freud invited such views by declaring in the same essay, "we assume that human instincts are of two kinds: those that conserve and unify, which we call 'erotic' . . . or else 'sexual' . . . and secondly the instincts to destroy and kill, which we assimilate as the aggressive or destructive instincts." See Freud, "Why War?" in James Strachey, ed. and trans., *The Standard Edition of the Complete Psychological Works of Sigmund Freud*, vol. 22 (London: Hogarth, 1964), 197–215, and Winter, "Power, Sex, and Violence: A Psychological Reconstruction of the 20th Century and an Intellectual Agenda for Political Psychology," *Political Psychology* (June 2000): 383–404, quotation on 395.

However, Freud's full views on the connections between sex and violence were more complex than these comments initially seem to suggest. Discussing what he called "the lust for aggression and destruction," Freud argued that "the stimulation of these destructive impulses by appeals to idealism and the erotic instinct naturally facilitate their release." In other words, far from believing that sex necessarily counteracted violence, Freud theorized that the "lust for aggression and destruction" could be "release[d]" by the "erotic instinct." To the extent that Freud did believe that love or "Eros" could act as a "counter-agent" to war, what he seems to have had in mind was a generalized love of humankind. Immediately after making the positive claim for "eros" as counteragent, Freud asserted, "all that produces ties of sentiment between man and man must serve as war's antidote." Allying himself with traditional Judeo-Christian precepts, he continued, "religion uses the same language: Love thy neighbor as thyself. . . . All that brings out significant resemblances between men calls into play this feeling of community, identity, wherein is founded, in large measure, the whole edifice of human society."

And in fact, when writing on the subject of sexual love, as opposed to disinterested love of humankind, modern psychologists, including David Winter, most often conclude by stressing that "violence acquire[s] properties of sexual arousal and satisfaction and vice versa," not least because "power, violence, and sexuality all share a dimension of sympathetic nervous system arousal." Precisely because all kinds of ardor share the same neural circuits, each can be used in the excitation of the other. See Winter, "Power, Sex, and Violence," 393.

26. "By This Morning's Mail," *Carlisle* [Pa.] *Gazette*, 28 August 1812; "Important!," New York *Statesman*, 31 August 1812; and "General Hull," *Alexandria* [Va.] *Gazette*, 12 September 1812.

27. "Evacuation of Canada! And Surrender of Detroit!" *Cooperstown* [N.Y.] *Federalist*, 12 September 1812.

28. Cass to Eustis, 35.

29. "Washington, September 11," Washington, D.C., *Courier*, 16 September 1812; "The Statement of Col. Cass," Philadelphia *Poulson's American Daily Advertiser*, 22 September 1812; "Letter of Col. Cass," Charleston, [W.]Va., *Farmer's Repository*, 25 September 1812.

30. William Hull, "To the Inhabitants of Canada!," in *Sketches of the War*, 20.

31. Hull, "To the Inhabitants of Canada!," 18; *Report of the Trial*, 38.

32. *Report of the Trial*, 40.

33. *Report of the Trial*, 49.

34. Lucas Journal, 375; *Report of the Trial*, 43.

35. *Report of the Trial*, 56.

36. "The Soldier's Drill and Fare," in "A Song Composed on the Cause and Progress of the Present American War," BDSDS 1814 (General Broadside Collection, AAS).

37. See the signed cover page of the Isaiah Thomas Collection of Broadside Ballads at the AAS. Clare Lyons describes a key shift in early national culture toward the masculinization of middle-class sexuality and the concomitant restriction of women's sexuality to the bodies of the lower classes. My research suggests that the masculinization of sexuality accompanied the militarization of American society in the era of 1812. See Lyons, *Sex Among the Rabble: An Intimate History of Gender and Power in the Age of Revolution*, *Philadelphia, 1730–1830* (Chapel Hill: University of North Carolina Press, 2006).

Sharon Block offers a brief discussion of the ways in which British "assaults on women's bodies became publicly noteworthy as assaults on the body politic" of the United States during the War of 1812, but discusses sexuality only in the negative without analyzing the passionate metaphors invoked to rouse Americans themselves to war. See Block, *Rape and Sexual Power in Early America* (Chapel Hill: University of North Carolina Press, 2006), 230–233, quotation on 233.

38. "On Hobbies," *A National Song-Book Being a Collection of Patriotic, Martial, and Naval Songs and Odes, Principally of American Composition* (Trenton, N.J.: James Wilson, 1813), 50.

39. "How to Nail 'Em," *The American Muse: or, Songster's Companion* (New York: Smith & Forman, 1814), 18.

40. "The Soldier's Return," in BDSDS 1810, AAS.

41. "The Soldier and His Fair Maid Together with Hard Times," AAS Broadside Ballads from the Collection of Isaiah Thomas, vol. 1 (hereafter cited as Thomas Collection Broadsides).

42. On the reproductive work of enslaved women, see Jennifer L. Morgan, *Laboring Women: Reproduction and Gender in New World Slavery* (Philadelphia: University of Pennsylvania Press, 2004). Historian Linda Kerber's enduring evocation of "republican motherhood" has fixed in our minds the notion that women of the republic could only secure virtue by sublimating their sexuality. However, in highlighting the determination of nineteenth-century Americans to restrict ideals of female sexuality to "moderate desire, inherent sexual reserve, and a natural inclination to chastity" (in the words of Clare Lyons), scholars have underplayed an important corollary. Women were expected to render sexual service to the nation both by inspiring fighting men and by bearing children. When contained within the confines of marital love, white women's sexuality could be validated, even valorized. See Kerber, *Women of the Republic: Intellect and Ideology in Revolutionary America* (Chapel Hill: University of North Carolina, 1980), 285, and Lyons, *Sex Among the Rabble*, 394.

43. "Love of Country," in *A National Song-Book*, 112.

44. *The Battle of Plattsburg* ([Boston]: Nathaniel Coverly, [1814?]).

45. Leonard Withington, "Rustic Love: A Dialog in Two Acts," New Haven, 1814. Mss. Dept., Octavo vols., "W," 10, AAS.

46. Withington, *Rustic Love*, 23, 37.

47. Withington, *Rustic Love*, 26.

48. On the importance of love in Aristotle's model of politics, see Russell Bentley, "Loving Freedom: Aristotle on Slavery and the Good Life," *Political Studies* 47 (1999): 100–113.

As noted, one striking aspect of U.S. militaristic rhetoric in the era of 1812 is that it appears to have appealed less to homosociality than to heterosexuality. Anderson writes of *amor patriae* as something akin to a universal and timeless emotion, saying, "It may appear paradoxical that the objects of all these [national] attachments are 'imagined.' . . . But *amor patriae* does not differ in this respect from the other affections, in which there is always an element of fond imagining." Yet we must interrupt assumptions of the timeless characteristics of "love of country" if we are to truly understand the particular ways in which Americans of the early republic drew on love in projects of death.

Scholars have only just begun to take stock of this fact. Julie Ellison, for example, notes in passing in a discussion of John Dennis's 1704 play *Liberty Asserted* that, although traditionally "Roman drama . . . pits reproductive against homo-social relations, and sets both against abstract law," by the eighteenth century, English playwrights eager to "shape republican narratives to the geopolitics of North America," produced works "justifying the mixture of patriotism and romance." My aim in this project is to begin to understand just why such a "mixture of patriotism and romance" proved so peculiarly potent in American republicanism and attendant militarism. See Anderson, *Imagined Communities: Reflections on the Origin and Spread of Nationalism*, rev. ed. (London: Verso, 1991), 7, 154, and Ellison, *Cato's Tears and the Making of Anglo-American Emotion* (Chicago: University of Chicago Press, 1999), 77–78.

49. Matthew Carey, "The Crisis No. 2," [Philadelphia, 1814], BDSDS 1814, AAS.

50. "Brigadier General William Hull to Secretary of War William Eustis, Sandwich, Upper Canada, 29 July 1812," *Michigan Pioneer and Historical Collections* 40 (1929): 424–426, quotation on 426. Hull referred to this and earlier letters at the trial. See *Report of the Trial*, 37. Few military historians have cared to defend Hull. Among his detractors are Walter Borneman, *1812: The War that Forged a Nation* (New York: HarperCollins, 2004), 69, and J. C. A. Stagg, *Mr. Madison's War: Politics, Diplomacy, and Warfare in the Early American Republic, 1783–1830* (Princeton, N.J.: Princeton University Press, 1983), 205. An exception is Robert S. Quimby, *The U.S. Army in the War of 1812: An Operational and Command Study*, 2 vols. (East Lansing: Michigan State University Press, 1997), 1: 46–48. However, Donald R. Hickey has recently asserted that Quimby offers the defense "unaccountably," a view I do not share for the reasons outlined below. See Hickey, "The War of 1812: Still a Forgotten Conflict?" *Journal of Military History* 65, no. 3. (2001): 741–769, quotation on 744, n. 17. Still, while I am obviously skeptical of the charges against Hull, my primary aim is less to argue his guilt or innocence as a "coward" than to examine the political import of emotional accusations, to understand how and why issues of ardor and cowardice could become fit subjects for a court-martial and central preoccupations for a society.

51. *Report of the Trial*, 58.

52. *Report of the Trial*, 57.

53. *Report of the Trial*, 40.

54. John Lathrop, *The Present War Unexpected, Unnecessary, and Ruinous, Two Discourses Delivered in Boston* (Boston: J.W. Burditt, 1812), 11.

55. Kiah Bayley, *War a Calamity Greatly to Be Dreaded* (Hallowell [Maine]: Cheever, 1812), 5–6.

56. "Lust, *n.*," "Lustful, *a.*," "Lustfully, *ad.*," "Lusting, *n.*," and "Lustily, *adv.*," in Noah Webster, *A Compendious Dictionary of the English Language in Which Five Thousand Words Are Added to the Number Found in the Best English Compends* (New Haven, [Conn.]: Hudson and Goodwin, 1806), 181.

57. William Allen, "Columbia's Prayer," [Newport, R.I., 1812], BDSDS 1812, AAS.

58. John Smith, *An Apology for the Friends of Peace* (Haverhill, Mass.: W.B. & H.G. Allen, 1812), 13.

59. Jacob Catlin, *The Horrors of War* (Stockbridge, [Mass.]: H. Willard, 1813), 8.

60. Smith, *An Apology for the Friends of Peace*, 18.

61. David Osgood, *A Solemn Protest Against the Late Declaration of War* (Cambridge, [Mass.]: Hilliard and Metcalf, 1812), 9, 14–15.

62. Benjamin Bell, *A Sermon Preached at Steuben April 1813: In Which Are Shewn the Evil Effects of War* (Sangerfield, [N.Y.]: J. Tenny [1814]), 76–77.

63. *Resolves of the General Court of the Commonwealth of Massachusetts* (Boston: Russell, Cutler, 1814), [351].

64. Lucas Journal, 411.

65. Lucas Journal, 410; *Sketches of the War*, 48.

66. Appendix, *Report of the Trial*, 1–6.

67. *Report of the Trial*, 110.

68. Appendix, *Report of the Trial*, 99. For biographical information on Snelling, see Helen Dunlap Dick, "A Newly Discovered Diary of Colonel Josiah Snelling," *Minnesota History* 18, no. 4 (1937): 399–406.

69. *Report of the Trial*, 110.

70. *Report of the Trial*, 108.

71. *Report of the Trial*, 108.

72. *Report of the Trial*, 106.

73. Benjamin Rush, *Medical Inquiries and Observations, upon the Diseases of the Mind* (Philadelphia: Kimber and Richardson, 1812), 259–261.

74. Webster, *A Compendious Dictionary of the English Language*, 224.

75. Richard Brown, *An Essay on the Truth of Physiognomy, and Its Application to Medicine* (Philadelphia: Thomas Stiles, 1807), 10–11.

76. *The Columbian Reader . . . Designed for the Use of Schools* (Otsego, N.Y.: H. & E. Phinney, 1810), 82; George Brewer, *The Juvenile Lavater . . . Calculated for the Instruction and Entertainment of Young Persons* (New York: R. M'Dermut & D.D. Arden, 1815).

77. Of Branagan's many published editions of this work, three are now extant: Thomas Branagan, *The Charms of Benevolence and Patriotic Mentor, Being an Essay on the Utility and Propriety of Organizing Benevolent Associations*, 2nd ed. (Philadelphia: author, 1812); Branagan, *The Charms of Benevolence and Patriotic Mentor; or, The Rights and Privileges of Republicanism, Contrasted with the Wrongs and Usurpations of Monarchy* (Philadelphia: Johnson and Patterson, 1813); Branagan, *The Charms of Benevolence and Patriotic Mentor; or, The Rights and Privileges of Republicanism, Contrasted with the Wrongs and Usurpations of Monarchy*, 5th ed. (Philadelphia: W. Spence and E. Jones, 1814).

78. *Report of the Trial*, 106.

79. *Report of the Trial*, 107.

80. *Report of the Trial*, 107.

81. *Report of the Trial*, 107.

82. Bell, *A Sermon Preached at Steuben*, 8.

83. Samuel Whelpley, *The Fall of Wicked Nations, A Sermon, Delivered in the First Presbyterian Church, Newark, September 9th, 1813, a Day of Fasting and Humiliation* (New York: Pelsue and Gould, 1813), [3].

84. Whelpley, *The Fall of Wicked Nations*, 15–16.

85. "Washington City, Wednesday, Nov. 4 The President . . . This Day Communicated . . . the Following Message to Congress," [New York?, 1812], BDSDS 1812, AAS.

86. Jacob Bigelow, *The Wars of the Gulls: An Historical Romance* (New York: Dramatic Repository, 1812), 33.

87. Frederick Augustus Fidfaddy, *The Adventures of Uncle Sam in Search After His Lost Honor* (Middletown, [Conn.]: Richards, 1816), 66, 78. As quoted, these verses are reversed from their order in the original.

88. *Report of the Trial*, 107.

89. On Lucas, see Parish's introduction to Lucas Journal, 344. On Cass, see Willard Carl Klunder, *Lewis Cass and the Politics of Moderation* (Kent, Ohio: Kent State University Press, 1996). On Dearborn, see Hull, *Memoirs*.

90. "Lewis Cass, Ohio Militia Third Division, to James Madison," 30 September 1809, Madison Papers.

91. *Report of the Trial*, 107, 114.

92. Thomas Clark, *American Chronology, from the Discovery of the Western World, Till May 3, 1814: By Thomas Clark, Author of the Naval History of the United States* (Philadelphia: Carey, 1814), 1, 52.

93. *Report of the Trial*, 21.

94. *Report of the Trial*, 21; *Sketches of the War*, 49.

95. Steven Watts claimed that D. H. Lawrence was only "half-right" when he observed of "American consciousness" in the early nineteenth century: "Destroy! Destroy! Destroy! hums the under-consciousness. Love and produce! Love and produce! cackles the upper consciousness. And the world hears only the Love-and-produce cackle. Refuses to hear the hum of destruction underneath." My aim here, in accord with Lawrence, is to understand more fully how refusals to hear "the hum of destruction" grew out of fantasies of love. Watts was right to insist that the war seemed to promise "inner peace and psychic coherence," yet he goes too far in arguing that the war "provided an opportunity for enterprising, willful, self-controlled individuals to prove their mettle." My contention, arising out of William Hull's observations at trial, is that far from testing white American mens' mettle, the vicarious emotional "experience" of violence as pleasure allowed armchair commanders to imaginatively avoid the true consequences of war. See Watts, *The Republic Reborn: War and the Making of Liberal America, 1790–1820* (Baltimore: Johns Hopkins University Press, 1987), 216, 289.

Tony Ballantyne and Antoinette Burton have recently urged historians to pay fuller attention to the body's "capacity as an archive for the pleasures of human experience and the violences of history." Analysis of emotional fantasies in which violence and pleasure are conflated provides a key opportunity to do just this. See Ballantyne and Burton, eds., *Bodies in Contact: Rethinking Colonial Encounters in World History* (Durham, N.C.: Duke University Press, 2005), 406.

Chapter 3: Romantic Stories of Republican Conquest on the Great Lakes

1. "Oliver Perry to William Jones, Secretary of the Navy, Lake Erie, 10 September 1813, 4 PM," in United States Congress, Senate Committee on National Affairs, *Letter from the Secretary of the Navy, of the Twenty-seventh Instant, to the Chairman of the Naval Committee, Together with Sundry Documents* (Washington, D.C.: Weightman, 1813), 9.

2. *Commodore Perry, or, The Battle of Erie, Containing a Full and Accurate Report of the Proceedings of Congress in Relation to the Gallant Officer and His Signal Victory on Lake Erie* (Philadelphia: Thomas Desilver, 1815), 8, 9 (hereafter cited as *Full and Accurate Report*). The debate was reported contemporaneously in a capital newspaper. See "Navy Department, Dec. 27, 1813," Washington, D.C., *The Senator*, 6 January 1814, 1–2.

On Fromentin's career, see Peter J. Kastor, *The Nation's Crucible: The Louisiana Purchase and the Creation of America* (New Haven, Conn.: Yale University Press, 2004) 183–184, 276, n. 3.

3. *Full and Accurate Report*, 10. On this moment in Charles Tait's senate career, see Charles H. Moffat, "Charles Tait, Planter, Politician, and Scientist of the Old South," *Journal of Southern History* 14, no. 2 (May 1948): 206–233, esp. 214–215.

4. *Full and Accurate Report*, 11. This chapter, like this book as a whole, aims to advance a new cultural history of politics in the early republic. Specifically, this chapter seeks to explore the "cultural work" performed by marriage—in story, in metaphor, and in practice— in diverse cultural genres—from national political speeches to popular broadside ballads— during the War of 1812. As Jane Tompkins explained the concept of "cultural work" in plain terms a quarter century ago: "literary texts . . . should be studied because they offer powerful examples of the way a culture thinks about itself, articulating and proposing solutions for the problems that shape a particular historical moment." Tompkins also noted that "forms of non-fictional discourse, when set side by side with contemporary fiction, can be seen to construct the real world in the image of a set of ideals and beliefs in exactly the same way that novels and stories do." My research shows the permeability of boundaries in early American life that allowed marriage to do cultural work across many barriers scholars once regarded as inviolate, not only divisions of genre but also of high and low culture, personal life and politics, domestic household conduct and international affairs. During the War of 1812, discussions of marital love helped address complex questions about the meaning of American liberty. In the face of military disappointments, marital imagery helped score rhetorical triumphs. See Tompkins, *Sensational Designs: The Cultural Work of American Fiction, 1790– 1860* (Oxford: Oxford University Press, 1985), xv, xi.

5. British commentators repeatedly described their nation as the last citadel of liberty in Europe. See, for example, Jon Latimer, *1812: War with America* (Cambridge, Mass.: Harvard University Press, 2010), 19, 35. On Britain's India problem, see Christopher Leslie Brown, *Moral Capital: Foundations of British Abolitionism* (Chapel Hill: University of North Carolina Press, 2006), 203–205.

6. Historians such as Nancy F. Cott posit connections between marriage and the nation, arguing that federal and state governments intervene in marriage regulations because the structuring of marriage is one key to ordering the state. While starting from the premise that nations have an interest in marriage, scholars have most often placed the emphasis of their research on the law, seeking to show how legal statutes shape social experience (and conversely, how social actions can influence legal theory). The related goal of this chapter is to interrogate more explicitly the *cultural meanings* of love and marriage for geopolitics and war. Rather than reporting on abstract analogies between love, marriage, and law, I seek here to document the frequency with which marital imagery played a tangible and immediate part in the representation and interpretation of particular political and military events. In the era of 1812, private feelings and actions could be loaded with the burden of expressing political commitments. See Cott, *Public Vows: A History of Marriage and the Nation* (Cambridge, Mass.: Harvard University Press, 2000), 10–11.

Despite a growing body of work by feminist scholars, the intricate intertwining of family history and political history still sometimes seems invisible. In their 2005 essay volume *Wither the Early Republic* John Larson and Michael Morrison concede that "legal and political historians are in fact noticing the ways conflicts within . . . [the] . . . private realms gradually enlarged the purview of government," yet they still claim that "relations between husbands and wives . . . did not rise to the level of public consideration." Without arguing that all the practical daily challenges of married life received due political attention (there is much evidence, in fact, that issues like rape within marriage were considered largely outside the sphere of government action), I do wish to make clear how central the *symbolism* of love and marriage was to the very language of politics and how important stories about marriage were to the popular evaluation of the events of high politics. See Larson and Morrison, *Wither the Early Republic: A Forum on the Future of the Field* (Philadelphia: University of Pennsylvania Press, 2005), 196.

7. *Full and Accurate Report*, 9.

8. Donald R. Hickey details these events in *The War of 1812: A Forgotten Conflict* (Urbana: University of Illinois Press, 1989), 141–143, including the quotation on militia failures at Buffalo from General George McClure, 142. He sums up the setbacks by saying that "by the end of the year, the Niagara Valley was in flames" (143).

9. Jon Latimer notes that "for the United States in 1812 the goal was to conquer Canada. . . . The United States achieved none of its war aims, and in these terms, the War of 1812 must be seen as a British victory." See Latimer, *1812*, 3–4.

10. *Full and Accurate Report*, 13, 17. Military historian Donald R. Hickey concludes that "the Battle of Lake Erie lacked any broader significance." See Hickey, *Don't Give Up the Ship! Myths of the War of 1812* (Urbana: University of Illinois Press, 2006), 128.

11. Samuel R. Brown, *Views on Lake Erie, Comprising a Minute and Interesting Account of the Conflict on Lake Erie . . .* (Troy, N.Y.: Francis Adancourt, 1814), 9, 10, 11. The complete text of this account of *Erie* was also included in a longer work by Brown that went through three editions: Samuel R. Brown, *Views of the Campaigns of the Northwestern Army &c.* (Troy, N.Y.: Francis Adancourt, 1814), (Burlington, Vt.: Samuel Mills, 1814), and (Philadelphia William G. Murphey, 1815). Samuel R. Brown (1775–1817) is identified in the "Condensed Biographical Dictionary," William Harrison De Puy, *Encyclopaedia Britannica*, vol. 25 (1893), 1698.

12. Brown, *Views on Lake Erie*, 11. Brian Connolly notes in passing that "the problem of liberty was central to the marriage question" in the early republic, citing an intriguing case from 1811 in which a minister lost his pulpit for refusing to recognize a man's chosen marriage. See Connolly, "'Every Family Become a School of Abominable Impurity': Incest and Theology in the Early Republic," *Journal of the Early Republic* 30 (Fall 2010): 413–442, 442, quotation on n. 40.

13. Solomon Aiken, *An Address to Federal clergymen, on the Subject of the War Proclaimed by the Congress of the United States, June 18, 1812* (Boston: author, 1813), 23, and William Pinkney, *Letters of Publius to the People of Maryland* [Baltimore: Whig Office, 1812], 19.

14. "The Orphan Boy; The Galley Slave, and the Sailor's Return," c. 1812, American Antiquarian Society (AAS) Broadside Ballads from the Collection of Isaiah Thomas, vol. 1 (hereafter cited as Thomas Collection Broadsides). This song also appeared in a second poster: "The Dying Soldier together with the Galley Slave," c. 1812, Thomas Collection Broadsides, vol. 2.

15. "The Bloody Miller and Oh Cruel," BDSDS 1810, AAS.

16. Henry Clay, *Mr. Clay's Speech on the New Army Bill Delivered in the House of Representatives of the U. S. on the 8th and 9th January, 1813 in Reply to Mr. Quincy* (Alexandria, Va.: Corse & Rounsavell, [1813]), 15.

17. Pamphlet-length reprints included *Speech Delivered by the Hon. Henry Clay . . .* (Washington, D.C.: *Daily National Intelligencer*, 1813) and *Speech of the Hon. Henry Clay . . .* (Baltimore: Patriot Press, [1813?]). The passage quoted here was also excerpted in ten editions between 1814 and 1818 of the book-length work *The Olive Branch*, beginning with Mathew Carey, *The Olive Branch; or, Faults on Both Sides, Federal and Democratic* (Philadelphia: M. Carey, 1814), 154.

18. "Impressed Seamen from Salem!," *Salem* [Mass.] *Gazette,* 30 March 1813, BDSDS, 1813, AAS. Latimer argues that the British intended impressment only as a tool to prevent desertions by British subjects and that "the Royal Navy took great pains to investigate and repatriate genuine cases." See Latimer, *1812,* 17.

19. "The Poor Little Child of a Tar Together with Sweet Poll of Plymouth," Thomas Collection Broadsides, vol. 3, c. 1812.

20. "The American Patriot's War Song; or, An Appeal to Free Men," Thomas Collection Broadsides, vol. 1, c. 1812.

21. In his study of *The Female Marine,* a novel set during the war and published in 1816, Daniel Cohen argues in a similar vein that, in the parlance of war culture, "sexual virtue and sexual vice . . . represent the polar opposites of patriotism and disloyalty." Cohen makes the useful point that in the postwar period, marital metaphors could work to address the problem of national disunity, the difficult relationship between New England Federalists and southern and western Republicans. See Daniel A. Cohen, ed., *The Female Marine: Narratives of Cross-Dressing and Urban Vice in America's Early Republic* (Amherst: University of Massachusetts Press, 1997), 30–31.

22. Brown, *Views of the Campaigns,* 86.

23. Brown, *Views of the Campaigns,* 86.

24. Oliver Perry to William Jones, 13 September 1813, as quoted in *Letter from the Secretary of the Navy,* 10.

25. John Lewis Thomson, *Historical Sketches of the Late War Between the United States and Great Britain* (Philadelphia: Thomas Desilver, 1816), 160, preface. Desilver published two more editions in 1816, a fourth in 1817, and a fifth in 1818. If Thomson ever wrote anything else, the book has not turned up in the Shaw Shoemaker bibliography.

26. "Gallant," 5b, 7, *Oxford English Dictionary;* Noah Webster, "Gallant," in Webster, *A Compendious Dictionary of the English Language* (New Haven, [Conn.]: Hudson & Goodwin, 1806), 127.

27. This discussion of citizens vs. subjects hues closely to the terms and concepts discussed in James H. Kettner, "Subjects, Aliens, and Citizens," in Kettner, *The Development of American Citizenship, 1608–1870* (Chapel Hill: University of North Carolina Press, 1978), 3–13. The comparison of subject status to that of parent and child appears in Kettner. Many subsequent scholars have noted marital analogies for citizenship. A classic statement is in Jan Lewis, "The Republican Wife: Virtue and Seduction in the Early Republic," *William and Mary Quarterly* 44 (October 1987): 689–721, and see also Nancy Isenberg's more recent discussion of how the "marriage covenant . . . bore certain similarities to republican political theory" in *Sex and Citizenship in Early America* (Chapel Hill: University of North Carolina Press, 1998), 11.

28. Alexander McLeod, *A Scriptural View of the Character, Causes, and Ends of the Present War* (New York: Eastburn, Kirk, 1815), 212. On the life of Alexander McLeod, see Samuel Brown Wylie, *Memoir of Alexander McLeod, D.D.* (New York: Scribner, 1855), esp. 72.

29. McLeod, *A Scriptural View of the Present War,* 219.

30. Wendover's presentation of McLeod's sermons to Jefferson is discussed in Wylie, *Memoir of Alexander McLeod,* 226.

31. On U.S. citizenship policies in the Jeffersonian era, see Rogers M. Smith, *Civic Ideals: Conflicting Visions of Citizenship in U.S. History* (New Haven, Conn.: Yale University Press, 1997), 168. And see Isenberg, *Sex and Citzenship,* 147. Discussion of the indirect role of marriage in establishing a man's legal residency is mine, based on 1812 commentary; see below.

32. Alan Taylor summarizes contemporary debates about impressment, largely giving validity to the idea of "informal" naturalization, in which men simply declared their American citizenship without benefit of either British or American legal process. Taylor describes men's tattoos and purchase of forged citizenship papers as methods for self-made citizenship. Men's marriages could be added to the list. See Taylor, *The Civil War of 1812: American Citizens, British Subjects, Irish Rebels, and Indian Allies* (New York: Knopf, 2010), 102–106, and Smith, *Civic Ideals*, 156.

33. John Quincy Adams, *A Letter to the Hon. Harrison Grey Otis . . . on the Present State of Our National Affairs* (New Haven, Conn.: Sydney's Press, 1808), 18.

34. William Coleman, *Remarks and Criticisms on the Hon. John Quincy Adams's Letter to the Hon. Harrison Grey Otis* (Boston: Joshua Cushing, 1808), 15, and Aiken, *Address to Federal Clergymen*, 23. In addition to the reprint in Aiken, these same lines were also featured in multiple reprints of Matthew Carey's *The Olive Branch*, beginning with the first imprint of 1814 (196).

35. Massachusetts House of Representatives, *Report of the Committee of the House of Representatives of Massachusetts on the Subject of Impressed Seamen with the Evidence and Documents Accompanying It* (Boston: Russell and Cutler, 1813).

36. Massachusetts House, *Report of the Committee*, 24.

37. Massachusetts House, *Report of the Committee*, 35.

38. Joshua Penny, *The Life and Adventures of Joshua Penny a Native of Southold, Long-Island, Suffolk County, New-York, Who Was Impressed into the British Service* (New York: author, 1815).

39. Penny, *Life and Adventures of Joshua Penny*, 9.

40. Penny, *Life and Adventures of Joshua Penny*, 4 7–48.

41. Penny, *Life and Adventures of Joshua Penny*, 57. On self-divorce in England, see John R. Gillis, *For Better, for Worse: British Marriages, 1600 to the Present* (Oxford: Oxford University Press, 1985), 209–219.

42. Penny, *Life and Adventures of Joshua Penny*, 57.

43. Penny, *Life and Adventures of Joshua Penny*, 57. Studying anxieties about incestuous marriages, Brian Connolly has recently emphasized that we need "to reconsider the force of marriage and sentiment as agents of virtue in the early republic." Evidence from the 1812 era lends weight to this observation. While the *right* marriages could be a source of national virtue, the wrong marriage had the potential for treason. See Connolly, "Every Family Become a School of Abominable Impurity," 442.

44. "Eighth Naval Victory: LINES, *Composed on the Capture of His Britannic Majesty's Squadron on Lake Erie, by Commodore Perry*," c. 1812, Thomas Collection Broadsides, vol. 2. Punning allusions to the names of ships were a commonplace element of wartime commentary. For example, when the USS *Boxer* won an engagement, a political cartoon showed an American giving a British figure a bloody nose. See for example the broadside cartoon by William Charles, "A Boxing Match, or Another Bloody Nose for John Bull," c. 1812, Collections of the AAS.

Consent as a basic feature of American marriage grew out of Christian practice. See Cott, *Public Vows*, 10–11.

45. Scholars sometimes still treat early American sexual activity, especially extramarital "sporting culture," as a nebulous and difficult to trace "underworld," surviving only in fragments of letters, in scattered records of occasional legal proceedings, or in only recently discovered pornographic "flash" newspapers. Yet war propaganda of the 1812 era

shows that sexual imagery and metaphors were very much an "above ground" phenomenon that featured even in matters of high politics. See Patricia Cline Cohen, "Sex and Sexuality: The Public, the Private, and the Spirit Worlds," *Journal of the Early Republic* 24 (Summer 2004): 310–318.

46. Nancy F. Cott originated the idea of female "passionlessness" as normative in the nineteenth century, while Clare Lyons has recently spoken of an ideal of "inert female sexual desire" for middle- and upper-class women. Still, the evidence is much stronger for condemnation of nonmarital sexuality than of the marital kind. In the 1812 era, in the context of war culture, women's sexuality could still be valorized within the bonds of marriage. This is just the point Jan Lewis makes in arguing that in the early republic, "Attraction between the sexes . . . could be transformed into the bedrock of the nation!" Here I extend that concept beyond abstract models of nationalism to the specific development of patriotic militarism during the war. See Cott, "Passionlessness: An Interpretation of Victorian Sexual Ideology, 1790–1850," *Signs* 4 (Winter 1978): 219–236; Lyons, *Sex Among the Rabble: An Intimate History of Gender and Power in the Age of Revolution, Philadelphia, 1730–1830* (Chapel Hill: University of North Carolina Press, 2006), 311; and Lewis, "The Republican Wife," 702.

47. "Bainbridge's Victory; or, Huzza for the Constitution Once More!," c. 1812, Collections of the AAS. Scholarship on widespread participation in urban pleasure culture by middle- and upper-class men, including rural and suburban men on sightseeing trips as well as city dwellers, is now extensive. See Timothy Gilfoyle, *City of Eros: New York City, Prostitution, and the Commercialization of Sex, 1790–1820* (New York: Norton, 1992); Patricia Cline Cohen, *The Murder of Helen Jewett: The Life and Death of a Prostitute in Nineteenth-Century New York* (New York: Knopf, 1998); C. Dallett Hemphill, "Isaac and 'Isabella': Courtship and Conflict in an Antebellum Circle of Youth," *Early American Studies* (2004): 398–434; and Rodney Hessinger, *Seduced, Abandoned, and Reborn: Visions of Youth in Middle-Class America, 1780–1850* (Philadelphia: University of Pennsylvania Press, 2005).

48. Details on these naval encounters can be found in Hickey, *The War of 1812*, 96.

49. "The Uncourteous Knight or Flying Gallant," in "Black-Ey'd Susan" (Hartford, Conn.: B. & J. Russell, Jr., n.d.), in BDSDS 1813, AAS.

50. "The Yankee Sailor," c. 1812, Thomas Collection Broadsides, vol. 2.

51. "Black-Ey'd Susan"; see also the stand-alone copy in Thomas Collection Broadsides, vol. 1, c. 1812.

52. "Tom Starboard," c. 1812, Thomas Collection Broadsides, vol. 1.

53. "The American Constitution Frigate's Engagement with the British Frigate Guerrière," c. 1812, Thomas Collection Broadsides, vol. 2. On the *Guerrière*, see Hickey, *The War of 1812*, 93.

54. James Campbell, "Glorious Naval Victory Obtained by Commodore Bainbridge, of the United States Frigate Constitution, over His Britannic Majesty's Frigate Java" (Boston: Nathaniel Coverly, Jr.), Thomas Collection Broadsides (no vol. no. given).

55. "The Question," in "Perry's Victory," BDSDS 1813, AAS.

56. Scholars have traditionally emphasized either the ways in which women were excluded from formal politics or the ways in which they managed to pry access to some political privileges despite their restricted rights. My argument, by contrast, is that women's performance of domestic roles generally, and marriage specifically, constituted a critical kind of uncompensated political and cultural work. Nancy Isenberg notes that "antebellum

politicians and constitutional theorists argued that at marriage women agreed to give up their property . . . and . . . . . . to retreat from politics." See Isenberg, *Sex and Citizenship,* 127. Carol Smith-Rosenberg reaffirms that representative democracy in the early republic "banished women and the feminine from the political arena and the role of virtuous citizen." See Smith-Rosenberg, *This Violent Empire: The Birth of an American National Identity* (Chapel Hill: University of North Carolina Press, 2010), 126. Mary Ryan stresses that women never entirely disappeared from public, but "battered at the walls of the public sphere," while Rosemary Zagarri has shown that a period of revolutionary possibility occurred for women despite later political retrenchment. See Ryan, *Women in Public: Between Banners and Ballots, 1825–1880* (Baltimore: Johns Hopkins University Press, 1990), 17, and Zagarri, *Revolutionary Backlash: Women and Politics in the Early American Republic* (Philadelphia: University of Pennsylvania Press, 2007). Meanwhile, important work on "parlor politics" has shown how elite women's work as hostesses and salonières allowed them real political influence. See Catharine Algor, *Parlor Poltics: In Which the Ladies of Washington Help to Build a City and a Government* (Charlottesville: University of Virginia Press, 2000), and Susan Branson, *These Fiery Frenchified Dames: Women and Political Culture in Early National Philadelphia* (Philadelphia: University of Pennsylvania Press, 2001).

Ordinary women's personal actions were evaluated in implicitly political terms. The new point here is that, in discussing restrictions on women's *rights*—and their efforts to push back against those constraints—we should not lose sight of the fact that women of every period continued to perform political *duties* in the midst of their daily lives. While women did not enjoy the *privileges* of *citizens,* they did suffer the *obligations* of the *population* (to invoke again this useful new sense of the term from Foucault).

57. "Death of General Wolfe, Together with Susan's Lamentation," c. 1812, Thomas Collection Broadsides, vol. 3.

58. Susannah Rowson, *Sarah; or, The Exemplary Wife* (Boston: Charles Williams, 1813). Quotations from Rowson's correspondence appear in Marion Rust, *Prodigal Daughters: Susannah Rowson's Early America* (Chapel Hill: University of North Carolina Press, 2008), 3. Rust argues compellingly that Rowson's private writings make it impossible to ignore the political import of early American sentimental discourse or the intersections of commerce and geopolitics in the putatively feminine domestic realm. In tandem with Rust, I am arguing here for what Kathryn Kish Sklar has recently called "women's political history," that is, stories that "advance our understanding of women and gender at the same time that they advance our understanding of American political history." See Sklar, "The New Political History and Women's History: Comments on 'The Democratic Experiment,'" *History Teacher* (August 2006): 509–514, quotation on 514.

59. Rowson, *Sarah,* 4.

60. Rowson, *Sarah,* 5. The claim Amy Kaplan advances for the 1850s can be usefully applied to novels of the 1812 era: we must interpret "narratives of domesticity and female subjectivity as inseparable from narratives of empire and nation building." See Kaplan, "Manifest Domesticity," in Donald E. Pease and Robyn Weigman, eds., *The Futures of American Studies* (Durham, N.C.: Duke University Press, 2002), 113.

61. Rowson, *Sarah,* 13, 242.

62. McLeod, *A Scriptural View of the Present War,* 92.

63. McLeod, *A Scriptural View of the Present War,* 92, 98.

64. *Address of the Conferees of the Washington Republicans of Philadelphia, to the People of Pennsylvania* [Philadelphia: s.n., 1812], 7.

65. Charles G. Haines, *An Oration Delivered Before the Republican Citizens of Gilmanton and the Adjacent Towns on the Fourth of July, 1812* (Concord, N.H.: J. and W. R. Hill, 1812), [5], 19. On Haines's biography, see Edgar J. Wiley, "Charles Glidden Haines," in Wiley, *Catalogue of Officers and Students of Middlebury College, 1800–1915* (Middlebury, Vt.: Middlebury College, 1917), 41. Haines subsequently authored *Considerations on the Great Western Canal from the Hudson to Lake Erie* (Brooklyn: Spooner & Worthington, 1818).

66. Rowson, *Sarah*, 244. Sadly, Rowson apparently knew firsthand the limitations of American marriages; her own union appears to have subjected her to "emotional neglect and physical abuse." On Rowson's marriage, see Rust, *Prodigal Daughters*, 147–148.

67. Rowson, *Sarah*, 253. Writing before the "Atlantic turn," Jan Lewis interpreted this novel as an indictment of republicanism's weakness, its reliance on perfect virtue. Yet a comparison of Rowson's treatment of love in the United States vs. Britain suggests a more explicitly feminist and nationalist reading, one in which Rowson was not so much exposing the Achilles heel of republicanism as challenging American republicans to live up to their own ideals. See Lewis, "The Republican Wife," 714–715.

68. Rowson, *Sarah*, 24, 250–251.

69. Judith Shklar identified "earning" as well as "voting" as key "attributes of the American citizen." See Shklar, *American Citizenship: The Search for Inclusion* (Cambridge, Mass.: Harvard University Press, 1995), 3. The issue of married women's property rights would not receive legal redress for decades. See Isenberg, *Sex and Citizenship*, 168–185.

70. [Sarah Savage], *The Factory Girl* (Boston: Munroe, Francis, & Parker, 1814). Sarah Savage was a very distant cousin of the famous writer Nathaniel Hawthorne. Her life and work are discussed briefly in Margaret B. Moore, *The Salem World of Nathaniel Hawthorne* (Columbia: University of Missouri Press, 1998), 111.

71. Savage, *The Factory Girl*, 62. For the historiography on republican wives and mothers, the articulation of the concept, and the limits of its efficacy, see Linda Kerber, "The Republican Mother: Women and the Enlightenment—An American Perspective," *American Quarterly* 28 (1976): 187–205; Lewis, "The Republican Wife"; and Ruth H. Bloch, "The Gendered Meanings of Virtue in Early America," *Signs* 13, no. 1 (1987): 37–58.

72. Savage, *The Factory Girl*, 69, 85, 107. In this way, the book is far more subversive than earlier critics have taken it to be. Cathy Davidson, for example voiced "disappointment with the assimilationism" of the book. See Cathy N. Davidson, *Revolution and the Word: The Rise of the Novel in America*, exp. ed. (New York: Oxford University Press, 2004), 12.

73. Savage, *The Factory Girl*, 102. See Marylynn Salmon, *Women and the Law of Property in Early America* (Chapel Hill: University of North Carolina Press, 1989).

74. "Oliver Perry to William Jones, Secretary of the Navy, Put-in-Bay, 13 September 1813," quoted in U.S. Congress, *Letter from the Secretary of the Navy*, 1 0–11.

75. "Oliver Perry to William Jones, Secretary of the Navy, Put-in-Bay, 13 September 1813," quoted in U.S. Congress, *Letter from the Secretary of the Navy*, 11. This letter is in marked contrast to what one newspaper praised as the "Spartan brevity" of Perry's 10 September 1813 letter to General William Henry Harrison: "we have met the enemy and they are ours." See "We Have Met the Enemy," *Baltimore Patriot*, 23 September 1813, 2. Today this is Perry's best remembered line. But in his own day, his longer description was much valued. For examples of newspaper reprints of the extended Perry-to-Jones letter of

13 September, from Maine to North Carolina, see "Seventh Naval Victory," Wilmington, Del., *American Watchman*, 25 September 1813, 2; "Seventh Naval Victory," Richmond *Enquirer*, 28 September 1813, 2; "Further Particulars: Copy of a Letter from Commodore Perry to the Secretary of the Navy," Portsmouth, N.H., *Intelligencer*, 30 September 1813, 2; "North-Western News: Commodore Perry," Morristown, N.J., *Palladium of Liberty*, 30 September 1813, 2; "Seventh Naval Victory," New Bern, N.C., *Carolina Federal Republican*, 2 October 1813, 2; "Copy of a Letter from Com. Perry to the Secretary of the Navy," Cooperstown, N.Y., *Otsego Herald*, 2 October 1813, 2; "Further from Lake Erie," Kennebunk, Maine, *Weekly Visitor*, 2 October 1813, 2; "Copy of a Letter from Commodore Perry to the Secretary of the Navy," *Portland Gazette and Maine Advertiser*, 4 October 1813, 2.

76. Samuel Woodworth, *The Heroes of the Lake* (New York: S. Woodworth, 1814), 11. On Woodworth's career, see Joseph J. Letter, "Reincarnating Samuel Woodworth: Native American Prophets, the Nation, and the War of 1812," *Early American Literature* 43, no. 3 (2008): 687–713.

77. Woodworth, *Heroes of the Lake*, 12.

78. Woodworth, *Heroes of the Lake*, 13.

79. Woodworth, *Heroes of the Lake*, 37.

80. Benjamin Allen, *Columbia's Naval Triumphs* (New York: Inskeep and Bradford, 1813), 51–52, 53.

81. Ann Marie Plane argues that "marriage and family practices actually aided the formation and maintenance of colonial domination." See Plane, *Colonial Intimacies: Indian Marriage in Early New England* (Ithaca, N.Y.: Cornell University Press, 2000), xii.

82. "Trial for Murder!" (Boston, [1813]) BDSDS 1813, AAS.

83. Middlebury College, "Commencement. Middlebury College, August 18, 1813," BDSDS, 1813, AAS. For biographical details, see the entries "Samuel Nelson" and "Horatio Conant" in Wiley, *Catalogue of Officers and Students of Middlebury College*, 15, 28. Commenting on the Crevay case, Daniel R. Mandell argues both that there was "growing elite sympathy for Indians" and that "Anglo-Americans, regardless of class shared many perceptions of remnant Indians in southern New England." See Mandell, *Tribe Race, History: Native Americans in Southern New England, 1780–1880* (Baltimore: Johns Hopkins University Press, 2008), 175–176.

84. "Trial for Murder!" Richard D. Brown argues that the outcome of this case confirms that during the War of 1812 Indians could still receive equal justice under U.S. law. My emphasis is on the cultural origins of the crime and the political importance of propaganda publicizing the punishment. Brown, "'No Harm to Kill Indians': Equal Rights in a Time of War," *New England Quarterly* 81 (March 2008): 34–62.

85. Alexander McLeod, *Negro Slavery Unjustifiable* (New York: T. & J. Swords, 1802). Nancy F. Cott argues that "the denial of legal marriage to slaves quintessentially expressed their lack of civil rights. To marry meant to consent, and slaves could not exercise the fundamental capacity to consent." See Cott, *Public Vows*, 33.

86. McLeod, *Negro Slavery*, 18, 17, 6. Amy Drew Stanley notes that "by the late 1830's antislavery literature focused on violation of the marriage contract, as abolitionists made a mission of revealing slavery's unspeakably private dimensions." Evidence from the 1812 era demonstrates the early emergence of marriage as an antislavery theme and illustrates that beyond the private dimension, slave marriages posed public problems for American political theory. This point is elaborated at length in chap. 5, below. See Stanley,

From Bondage to Contract: Wage Labor, Marriage, and the Market in the Age of Emancipation (Cambridge: Cambridge University Press, 1998), 24.

87. Noting that "marriage policy underlies national belonging," Nancy F. Cott argues that denying enslaved people the right to formal marriage provided an important means of excluding them from citizenship, while the invalidation of Indian plural marriages served a similar function. See Cott, *Public Vows*, 5.

88. *An Address to the Fair Daughters of the United States Calling on Them for Their Advice and Interest in the Present Important Crisis* (New York: Southwick & Pelsue, 1811). On the racial underpinnings of "fair sex" ideology, see Pauline Scholesser, *The Fair Sex: White Women and Racial Patriarchy in the Early American Republic* (New York: New York University Press, 2002).

Chapter 4: Demographic Strategies and the Defeat of Tecumseh

1. On the military and political significance of the Battle of the Thames, see R. Douglas Hurt, *The Indian Frontier, 1763–1846* (Albuquerque: University of New Mexico Press, 2002), 135, and Walter R. Borneman, *1812: The War that Forged a Nation* (New York: HarperCollins, 2004), 161. For statements on war captives, see below.

2. "From Gen. Harrison to Gen. Vincent. Head-Quarters, Fort George. 3d Nov. 1813," New York *National Advocate*, 7 January 1814, 2.

3. "From Gen. Harrison to Gen. Vincent," 2.

4. "From Gen. Harrison to Gen. Vincent," 2. On traditional practices of captive taking among the Iroquois, see Daniel K. Richter, *The Ordeal of the Longhouse: The Peoples of the Iroquois League in the Era of European Colonization* (Chapel Hill: University of North Carolina Press, 1992), 35.

5. Scholarship makes clear that Indians were keenly aware of the impact of rising Euro-American populations on Indian land rights. See, for example, James H. Merrell, *Into the American Woods: Negotiations on the Pennsylvania Frontier* (New York: W.W. Norton, 2000), 277–278.

6. "From Gen. Harrison to Gen. Vincent," 2. Roy Harvey Pearce noted long ago that "tales of barbarity and bloodshed, however true at base and however 'serious' in intent, were everywhere the thing." See Pearce, "The Significances of the Captivity Narrative," *American Literature* 19 (March 1947): 1–20, quotation on 10.

"Unborn children being cut from wombs" was a common feature of atrocity stories throughout the colonial and early national periods. Peter Silver has noted their "unmatchably tight cluster of associations with vulnerability." Here I underscore that feticide had symbolic meanings for Indians as well as for whites and that these meanings stemmed not only from a desire to provoke feelings of horror but also from practical calculations about the importance of population in determining the outcome of imperial rivalries. See Silver, *Our Savage Neighbors: How Indian War Transformed Early America* (New York: W.W. Norton 2007), 84–86, quotation on 85.

June Namias, in her comprehensive survey of two centuries of captivity narratives from 1675 to 1870, emphasizes that "placing women and children at the center of so many cultural works . . . exposed a basic vulnerability of white women and children, and by extension the entire enterprise of Euro-American settlement." I agree and would stress an important corollary. Centering accounts on competition for women and children made clear the strategic importance of population resources. Reproduction and migration shaped colonial contests at every stage and took on increased prominence in the crisis of war and in the context of Malthusian-era theory. See Namias, *White Captives: Gender and Ethnicity on the American Frontier* (Chapel Hill: University of North Carolina Press, 1993), 272.

7. Here I follow Linda Colley in quoting Michel Foucault: "Perhaps we should see this literature of [captivity] ... neither as a spontaneous form of popular expression, nor as a concerted programme of propaganda and [moralization] from above; it was a locus in which [different] investments of [empire] met—a sort of battleground around the crime, its punishment and its memory." Colley's excellent article and apposite quotation from Foucault deserve citation, although readers should note that Colley mistakenly transcribes "moraliza-tion" as "mobilisation." I point out her transcription error because I, in fact, argue that the combination of popular expression and concerted propaganda that found its locus in captivity narratives *did* serve key functions in emotional provocation and war mobilization even as this literary form also betrayed profound moral ambivalence. See Foucault, *Discipline and Punish: The Birth of the Prison*, trans. Alan Sheridan (London, 1977), 67, quoted in Colley, "Going Native, Telling Tales: Captivity, Collaborations and Empire," *Past and Present* 168 (August 2000): 170–193, quotation on 192–193.

The Harrison letter was reprinted (under various headlines) at least two dozen times in the following newspapers: *New York Spectator*, 8 January 1814; Harrisburg, Pa., *Chronicle*, 10 January 1813; Easton, Md., *Republican Star*, 11 January 1814; *New York War*, 11 January 1814; *Philadelphia Weekly Aurora*, 11 January 1814; Salem, Mass., *Eseex Register*, 12 January 1814; Brooklyn, N.Y., *Long Island Star*, 11 January 1814; Bridgeport, Conn., *Republican Farmer*, 12 January 1814; *Boston Independent Chronicle*, 13 January 1814; Utica, N.Y., *Columbian Gazette*, 18 January 1814; Newark, N.J., *Centinel of Freedom*, 18 January 1814; *New Haven Columbian Register*, 18 January 1814; Portsmouth *New Hampshire Gazette*, 18 January 1814; Elizabethtown *New Jersey Journal*, 18 January 1814; Hudson, N.Y., *Northern Whig*, 18 January 1814; Portland, Maine, *Eastern Argus*, 18 January 1814; Charleston, [W.]Va., *Farmer's Repository*, 20 January 1814; Newport *Rhode Island Republican*, 20 January 1814; Brattleboro, Vt., *Reporter*, 22 January 1814; Windsor *Vermont Republican*, 24 January 1814; Washington, Pa., *Washington Reporter*, 24 January 1814; Middlebury, Vt., *Columbian Patriot*, 26 January 1814; Cooperstown, N.Y., *Otsego Herald*, 29 January 1814; and Burlington *Vermont Centinel*, 4 February 1814.

8. The classic statement on the characteristically American genre of captivity narratives is Richard Slotkin's *Regeneration Through Violence: The Mythology of the American Frontier, 1600–1860* (Middletown, Conn.: Wesleyan University Press, 1973). Noting that captivity narratives are "generally regarded by scholars as one of the few distinctively American literary genres," Annette Kolodny argues that "for both their authors and their readers, Indian captivity narratives have mirrored the aspirations and anxieties of successive generations." To date, however, these narratives have not been examined in the context of the first-ever war declared in a modern constitutional democracy, the chief aim of this chapter. See Kolodny, "Among the Indians: The Uses of Captivity," *Women's Studies Quarterly* 21 (Fall–Winter 1993): 184–195, quotations on 186, 187.

I allude here to "the incantatory lines of the prologue" to Longfellow's *Evangeline*, a work in the nationalist tradition formalized by James Fenimore Cooper that stretched back to the 1812 years and would still "play well to a nation becoming infatuated with its Manifest Destiny" by the time Longfellow published in 1847. See Ron McFarland, *The Long Life of Evangeline: A History of the Longfellow Poem in Print, in Adaptation, and in Popular Culture* (Jefferson, N.C.: McFarland, 2009), 38, 37.

Pauline Turner Strong notes that for decades both before and after the 1826 publication of James Fenimore Cooper's *The Last of the Mohicans*, "the captivity theme . . . persisted in Anglo-American literature and popular culture as a pervasive mode of representing a distinctively Euro-American identity." See Strong, *Captive Selves, Captivating Other: The Politics and Poetics of Colonial American Captivity Narratives* (Boulder, Colo.: Westview Press, 2000), 2.

As is the case with Strong, scholars of captivity narratives have most often examined them for the insights they allow into issues of identity, for the avenues they open to understanding how early Americans located the self in social and cultural space. The "politics" of the narratives are taken to be purely discursive. Yet during the War of 1812, captivity narratives took on direct, active political meaning and served explicitly imperial geopolitical purposes.

9. Building on the insights of Julie Ellison, Michelle Burnham has argued that sentimental captivity narratives helped forge "associations between emotion and historical events . . . [and] offered an ideal entry point into the discourse of history and into the project of nation building." Burnham argues that "moving between the realm of feeling and that of history . . . captivity histories serve . . . as an affective model of what [she] call[s] the imperialist audience." Curiously, however, Burnham, like so many other scholars, does not interrogate how such imperialist audiences were built during the War of 1812, skipping directly from the 1790s to the Jacksonian era. See Burnham, *Captivity and Sentiment, Cultural Exchange in American Literature, 1682–1861* (Hanover, N.H.: University Press of New England, 1997), 94.

10. Theda Perdue documents the importance of adoption in Indian population strategies in the Southeast, noting that "clan ties organized native societies and only birth or adoption into a clan conveyed tribal citizenship. . . . Marriage did not provide clan ties as only birth or adoption did that." Indian adoption thus implied a sort of total absorption into a previously alien culture that would have been especially threatening to U.S. whites. See Perdue, *Mixed Blood Indians: Racial Construction in the Early South* (Athens: University of Georgia Press, 2005), 20–21.

11. Although the British themselves deplored Indian murders of women and children, they denied that they could possibly defend their forts without Indian assistance or that they could control the way Indians waged war. On these points, see Alan Taylor, *The Civil War of 1812: American Citizens, British Subjects, Irish Rebels, and Indian Allies* (New York: Knopf, 2010), 167.

12. Samuel R. Brown, *Views of the Campaigns of the North-Western Army, &c. Comprising, Sketches of the Campaigns of Generals Hull and Harrison* (Troy, N.Y.: Adancourt, 1814), 61.

13. Brown, *Views of the Campaigns*, 77, and "A Brilliant Victory: Extract of a Letter from Gen. Harrison to the Department of War," Washington, D.C., *Universal Gazette*, 22 October 1813, 1.

14. Brown, *Views of the Campaigns*, 77.

15. Brown, *Views of the Campaigns*, 61, 77. The other editions were published by Samuel Mills in Burlington, Vt., in 1814 and by Griggs & Dickinsons in Philadelphia in 1815. The briefer excerpt focused on Erie contained the anecdote about the "ladies" of Malden only: Samuel R. Brown, *Views on Lake Erie, Comprising . . . the Conflict on Lake Erie, Military Anecdotes* (New York: Adancourt, 1814), 51.

16. As Richard Drinnon notes in a survey of American expansionism from the Pequot War to the Philippines, "racism defined natives as nonpersons within the

settlement culture and was in a real sense the enabling experience of the rising American empire." Yet whereas Drinnon relies informally on the concept of sexual repression (and its sublimation into violence), I argue, instead, that in the era of 1812 cultural productions evoked both disgust and desire directly but differentially, the better to harness limbic drives for war. See Drinnon, *Facing West: The Metaphysics of Indian-Hating and Empire-Building* (Norman: University of Oklahoma Press, 1997), xxv–xxviii, quotation on xxvii.

17. Elias Darnell, *A Journal Containing an Accurate and Interesting Account of the Hardships, Suffferings, Battles, Defeat, and Captivity of Those Heroic Kentucky Volunteers and Regulars Commanded by General Winchester, in the Year 1812, 1813, also Two Narratives, by Men, That Were Wounded in the Battles of the River Raisin, and Taken Captive by the Indians* (Paris, Ky.: Joel R. Lyle, 1813). As Gary L. Ebersole notes, "the white male fantasy involving the exotic native female has shown remarkable staying power" and is shown in "the unmistakable presence of this complex in many captivity narratives." This general fact makes the demonization of Indian women in war-era narratives all the more remarkable and analytically significant. See Ebersole, *Captured by Texts: Puritan to Postmodern Images of Indian Captivity* (Charlottesville: University Press of Virginia, 1995), 209.

My analysis here consequently refines that of June Namias, who, in analyzing the period from 1764 to 1820 collectively, concludes that "erotic motifs occur within the captivity literature, extending the possibilities of sexual encounters across racial, ethnic, and cultural lines." While this is useful as a generalization, it obscures the propagandizing particulars of writing published during the War of 1812, which took care to paint Indians as sexually repulsive. For example, when Namias cites a bathing scene from the James Smith *Treatise on the Mode and Manner of Indian War* (for a fuller discussion of Smith's *Treatise*, see below), her evidence for the work's eroticism comes not from the text itself, but from an illustration included in the 1849 edition of the work. In the 1812 edition, the bathing scene is not presented as a sensual one but rather as a terrifying one in which Smith "apprehended that [he] was to be drowned" and expressed no attraction or arousal when he subsequently found that he was only to be "washed and rubbed . . . severely." See Namias, *White Captives*, 92–93, quotation on 97, and Smith, *A Treatise on the Mode and Manner of Indian War . . . Ways and Means Proposed to Prevent the Indians from Obtaining the Advantage* (Paris, Ky.: Joel R. Lyle, 1812), 30.

18. Darnell, *A Journal* (1813), 45–46.

19. Darnell, *A Journal* (1813), appendix, 2.

20. Darnell, *A Journal* (1813), appendix, 5, 6.

21. Mary Smith, *An Affecting Narrative of the Captivity and Sufferings of Mrs. Mary Smith* (Providence, R.I.: L. Scott [1815]). Christopher Castiglia discusses the Mary Smith narrative and notes that the description of her daughters' torture was lifted directly from a 1799 narrative by Frederic Manheim. See Castiglia, *Bound and Determined: Captivity, Cross-Dressing, and White Womanhood from Mary Rowlandson to Patty Hearst* (Chicago: University of Chicago Press, 1996), 107.

For an account of a "heroine [who] took off the scalps of her vanquished enemies," see Jonathan Carver, *Travels Through the Interior Parts of North America in the Years 1766, 1767, and 1768* (Walpole, N.H.: Isaiah Thomas, 1813), 185. The heroine also murders her captor in: Abraham Panther, *A Very Surprising Narrative, of a Young Woman, Discovered in a Rocky-Cave; After Having Been Taken by the Savage Indians, of the Wilderness; in the Year 1777* (Jaffrey, N.H.: [Salmon Wilder?], [1814]). The highly popular Panther narrative was first published in 1788 and went through fifteen editions through 1824. It was little altered in the wartime edition. In the context of the war, one of the more interesting aspects of the tale is that the heroine ran away from home after her father refused her marriage choice. Although her captor (referred to as an Indian in the title and text of most editions, but called a "giant" within the text of the 1814 edition) asked her to marry him, he agreed to sleep the night without molesting her. While some scholars have interpreted the story as one of near rape, the encounter actually seems to suggest that "civilized" fathers refused to grant the right of free marriage choice acknowledged even by "savage Indians" at their own risk.

22. Smith, *An Affecting Narrative*, 13.

23. Smith, *An Affecting Narrative*, 13. Annette Kolodny noted how the Mary Smith narrative helped bolster support for Andrew Jackson's anti-Indian campaigns, but not how it formed part of a comprehensive war culture in the era of 1812. See Kolodny, "Among the Indians," 188–189.

24. [John Finch], *The Soldier's Orphan* (New York: Van Winkle, 1812), 74. The book was published May 2, just over a month before the declaration of war, at which point the imminent possibility of conflict was obvious to all observers.

25. Carver, *Travels*, 141. Many of the particulars of Carver's published account, including his many silent quotations from previous works, were described and debunked in Edward Gaylord Bourne, "The Travels of Jonathan Carver," *American Historical Review* 11 (January 1906), 287–302. However, the authenticity of the underlying manuscript journal on which the published version was partially based has recently been established in John Parker, ed., *The Journals of Jonathan Carver and Related Documents, 1766–1770* (St. Paul: Minnesota Historical Society, 1976), 54–55.

26. Carver, *Travels*, 190, 203. Carver discusses at-will divorces on page 205. Sharon Block skillfully unpicks the complex of Euro-American attitudes toward Indian sexuality, noting that whites believed Indian men were not sexually aggressive toward Euro-American women both because Indian women were sexually loose and easily available and because effeminate Indian men did not have the wherewithal to perform patriarchal sexual roles. See Block, *Rape and Sexual Power in Early America* (Chapel Hill: University of North Carolina Press, 2006), 228–229.

27. "The Adventures of Henry Bird," *Analectic Magazine* 6 (January–June 1815): 295–301. The story was reprinted as *The Narrative of Henry Bird, Who Was Carried Away by the Indians, After the Murder of His Whole Family in 1811* (Bridgeport, Conn.: s.n., 1815). The *Analectic Magazine* enjoyed considerable prominence during the war years, having been published under the editorship of literary light and U.S. Army volunteer Washington Irving between 1813 and 1814. On Washington Irving's editorship, nationalist activities, and military service during the War of 1812, see Andrew Burstein, *The Original Knickerbocker* (New York: Basic Books, 2007), 95–97.

28. *The Narrative of Henry Bird*, 5.

29. *The Narrative of Henry Bird*, 5.

30. *The Narrative of Henry Bird*, 7, 8.

31. Peter Williamson, *The Authentic Narrative of the Life and Surprising Adventures of Peter Williamson* (New York: James Oram, 1807). This is the first American edition to include the Long-Crawford tale as a story-within-the-story of the Williamson narrative. In an 1809 edition and in two 1813 editions, the Williamson narrative (including the Long-Crawford story) was presented as a double feature with another entirely separate narrative, also often published independently, regarding the exploits of a U.S. Navy man,

John Paul Jones. The wartime reprints, both titled *The Life, Travels, Voyages, and Daring Engagements of Paul Jones . . . to which Is Prefixed, The Life and Adventures of Peter Williamson*, were published by H. C. Southwick in Albany, N.Y., in 1813, and by John Russell, Jr., in Hartford, Conn., in 1813. I have chosen to quote from the wartime edition, but note that it is essentially identical to that of 1807.

32. Williamson, *Life and Adventures* (1813), 51.

33. Williamson, *Life and Adventures* (1813), 55, 57. Precisely because Euro-American popular culture portrayed unmarried Indian women as sexually promiscuous, white women faced additional pressures to confine their own sexuality within Christian marriages. See Tiffany Potter, "Circular Taxonomies: Regulating European and American Women Through Representations of North American Indian Women," *Early American Literature* 41, no. 2 (2006): 183–211.

34. For comparison with earlier editions, see, for example, Peter Williamson, *French and Indian Cruelty: Exemplified in the Life, and Various Vicissitudes of Fortune, of Peter Williamson* (York: Nickson, 1757), in which the Long-Crawford wedding story appears on 42–49. The basic Williamson story of Indian captivity appeared in pirated editions in America throughout the eighteenth century, with many variations in wording and content, sometimes published on its own and other times as part of compilations with other tales. These editions contained so many discrepancies that Peter Williamson was sometimes called Peter Wilkinson. (And the full Williamson story began and ended in Britain, the story of his Indian captivity being but part of the tale.) However, careful examination of the Indian captivity section of each American edition of the Williamson narrative reveals that the story-within-the-story of the Long-Crawford wedding was omitted from all of them until 1807. Editions published under the title *Affecting History of the Dreadful Distresses of Frederick Manheim's Family to which Are Added the . . . Sufferings of Peter Wilkinson* (with the relevant section pages) included H. Ranlet, [Exeter, N.H.]: 1793, 25–42; D. Humphreys (Philadelphia: 1794), 19–31; James Oram (New York: 1798), 17–29; Henry Sweitzer (Philadelphia: 1800), 19–31; and Adams and Wilder ([Leominster, Mass.]: [1800]), 12–23. In addition, there was Peter Williamson, *Sufferings of Peter Williamson, One of the Settlers in the Back Parts of Pennsylvania* (Stockbridge, [Mass.]: [Loring Andrews], 1796).

35. Williamson, *Life and Adventures* (1813), 70–71.

36. Williamson, *Life and Adventures* (1813), 72 & 75.

37. Williamson, *French and Indian Cruelty* (1757), 49.

38. In actuality, as many contemporaries insisted and modern scholars generally agree, Indians did not rape women as a tool of war. On this point, see Block, *Rape and Sexual Power*, 223.

39. "From Gen. Harrison to Gen. Vincent," 2.

40. For reprints of the Prevost speech (all published without headline), see the Boston *Repertory*, 29 January 1814, 1; Windsor, Vt., *Washingtonian*, 31 January 1814, 2: Boston *Gazette* 31 January 1814, 1; and Lexington, Ky., *Reporter*, 19 February 1814, 3.

41. *Boston Gazette*, 31 January 1814, 1.

42. Susannah Willard Johnson, *A Narrative of the Captivity of Mrs. Johnson Containing an Account of Her Sufferings, During Four Years, with the Indians and French* (Walpole, N.H.: David Carlisle, Jr., 1796). The second edition, under the same title but "corrected and enlarged," was published by Alden Spooner in Windsor, Vt., in 1807.

43. Susannah Willard Johnson, *A Narrative of the Captivity of Mrs. Johnson Containing an Account of Her Sufferings, During Four Years, with the Indians and French Together*

with an Appendix, Containing the Sermons, Preached at Her Funeral and That of Her Mother with Sundry other Interesting Articles, 3rd ed., corr. and considerably enl. (Windsor, Vt.: Thomas M. Pomroy, 1814). Until very recently, many scholars have written of Johnson as if she were the sole author of her text. However, Lorrayne Carroll has convincingly affirmed long-standing suspicions that from the first edition of 1796, the authentic facts of Johnson's captivity were shaped and narrated by a group of men in Walpole, New Hampshire, including the credited publisher of the first edition, David Carlisle, and a local lawyer named John C. Chamberlain. Although Carroll confines her analysis to "the production and representation of authorship in the first edition," she makes the useful general point that "the Johnson *Narrative* enacts the historiographical goal of interpreting the past so that its readers will be directed to a politicized reading of their present."

Carroll associates the 1796 edition with Federalist politics, but there is no reason to think that the 1814 edition, published in Vermont rather than New Hampshire, hewed to this tradition. My own research strongly suggests that revisions to the 1814 edition were also the handiwork of someone other than Johnson; see below. See Carroll, "'Affecting History': Impersonating Women in the Early Republic," *Early American Literature* 39, no. 3 (2004): 511–552, quotations on 521, 546, n. 27, 527.

44. Johnson, *A Narrative*, 3rd ed., 3–5. As Rebecca Blevins Faery has argued in a related context, "white women, their bodies and their sexuality, [were] positioned as guardians of the boundaries of race to serve the territorial and political purposes of white men and their claim to dominance." See Faery, *Cartographies of Desire: Captivity, Race, and Sex in the Shaping of the American Nation* (Norman: University of Oklahoma Press, 1999), 9.

45. Johnson, *A Narrative*, 3rd ed., 6–7.

46. "Psalm and Odes: For the Fourth of July 1812" [New London, Conn.?: 1812], broadside in the collections of AAS.

47. George Fowler, *A Flight to the Moon; or, The Vision of Randalthus* (Baltimore: Millenberger, 1813).

48. Fowler, *A Flight to the Moon,*1 3–14.

49. Fowler, *A Flight to the Moon,* 144.

50. Kathryn Zabelle Derounian-Stodola, in her survey of several centuries of captivity narratives by and about women, notes that "almost all the women's accounts emphasize that captivity sundered families." It is all the more striking, then, that in the era of 1812, narratives like that of Susannah Johnson broke this pattern to emphasize instead white women's continued maternal powers even in captivity. See Derounian-Stodola, *Women's Indian Captivity Narratives* (New York: Penguin, 1998), xxi.

51. Johnson, *A Narrative*, 3rd ed., 32, 33, 33, 34. The entire story in which Johnson revisits the scene of her daughter's birth and a monument is erected in her honor is an invention of the wartime 1814 edition. The material quoted here is from a footnote inserted only in the 1814 edition.

Scholarly confusion on this issue has been rampant. In 1999, for example, Ian Kenneth Steele and Nancy Lee Rhoden asserted unequivocally that the account of the stone monuments was included in the 1807 version of the *Narrative*. This simply is not the case. In both the 1807 edition and the 1814 edition of the *Narrative*, the story of Captive's birth appears in chap. 2, "History of Our Journey Through the Wilderness, Till We Came to the Waters That Enter Lake Champlain," which corresponds to pages 38–44 of the 1807 edition and pages 31–38 of the 1814 edition. The body of the text in these two editions is virtually identical. However, the 1814 edition adds an extended footnote in compressed type on pages 32–35 that recounts the existence of the monuments for the first time. This long recitation, written in the first person in the voice of Susannah Johnson, appears nowhere at all in the 1807 edition. See Steele and Rhoden, *The Human Tradition in Colonial America* (New York: Rowman & Littlefield, 1999), 269.

52. Johnson, *A Narrative*, 3rd ed., 34.

53. Finch, *The Soldier's Orphan*, 180.

54. Finch, *The Soldier's Orphan*, 183–184.

55. Finch, *The Soldier's Orphan*, 74–75.

56. Finch, *The Soldier's Orphan*, 75. Though he offers no specific analysis of the War of 1812, Richard Drinnon notes that "Indian-hating identified the dark others that white settlers were not and must not under any circumstances become, and it helped them wrest a continent and more from the hands of these native caretakers of the lands." See Drinnon, *Facing West*, xxvii–xxviii.

57. Johnson, *A Narrative*, 3rd ed., 34.

58. Johnson, *A Narrative*, 3rd ed., 35. The trope of verdant farms replacing dark woods was perennial in Euro-American colonizing culture. See Merrell, *Into the American Woods*, 27.

59. Johnson, *A Narrative*, 3rd ed., 35. In this respect, it seems telling that the genealogical records added to the 1814 edition of the *Narrative* documented generations of the Willard family, that is of Susannah's family of origin, rather than of her husband's family, the Johnsons. Despite European traditions of tracing descent through fathers, in the 1812 era it was *women's* reproductive work that gained special attention.

60. Johnson, *A Narrative*, 3rd ed., 34, 35. To be clear, the 1814 *Narrative* contains two poems supposedly featured on the memorial stones, the actual verses on the stone ("When trouble's near the Lord is kind / He hears the captive's cry; / He can subdue the savage mind / And learn it sympathy") and the four additional lines addressed to mothers that I discuss here. The lines on the Lord teaching the savage sympathy were entirely conventional by this time. See, for example, the discussion of "Christian emotion" among Indians in Nicole Eustace, *Passion Is the Gale: Emotion, Power, and the Coming of the American Revolution* (Chapel Hill: University of North Carolina Press, 2008), 347–348.

61. Johnson, *A Narrative*, 3rd ed., 32–33. A 1907 reprint of the 1814 edition of the *Narrative*, still referenced by scholars, quotes a local New Hampshire history as saying "in substance that Mrs. Johnson negotiated for these monuments, prepared their inscriptions, and directed that the smaller stone should be placed upon the spot where her child was born, while the larger should mark the place where the Indians encamped." See Horace W. Bailey, ed., *A Narrative of the Captivity of Mrs. Johnson, Reprinted from the Third Edition* (Springfield, Mass.: H.R. Hunting, 1907), xii–xiii.

Christopher Castiglia has cited this 1907 edition recently. See Castiglia, *Bound and Determined*, 224.

Even Carroll, in her otherwise excellent interrogation of the circumstances and authorship of the Johnson *Narrative*, seems to accept the monument story at face value, directly citing the 1876 local New Hampshire history relied on by Horace Bailey in 1907. See Carroll, "Affecting History," 546, n. 27.

62. There was some precedent for the erection of stone markers in memory of women who lived both as historical people and as literary characters. When the deceased Elizabeth Whitman was fictionalized as Eliza Wharton in the 1797 novel *The Coquette* (the

very same year in which Johnson supposedly began looking for the site of her labor and delivery), avid fans of the book made so many tourist trips to Whitman's grave that her tombstone was worn to a nub. See Bryan Waterman, "Elizabeth Whitman's Disappearance and Her 'Disappointment,'" *William and Mary Quarterly* 66 (April 2009): 325–364, esp. 350–357.

63. Christopher Castiglia makes the useful point that, as a genre, female-narrated captivity tales throughout history have "offered American women a female picaresque, an adventure story set, unlike most early American women's literature, outside the home." Yet this argument needs refining for the specific era of 1812. The most striking feature of many wartime accounts is the way in which women were positioned as heroic for managing to continue to meet traditionally *female* obligations even when cut off from civilization. Furthermore, for the war years, Castiglia's contention that female-narrated captivity tales evidence women's "ambivalent relationships to the rhetoric of westward expansion" (in comparison to the confident assertions of men) does not hold up. See Castiglia, *Bound and Determined*, 4, 6.

On the other hand, if we accept and extend Lorrayne Carroll's analysis of the phenomenon of "rhetorical drag" by applying it to these overlooked verses, we must incorporate the fact that this female heroine's supposed words were actually written by men and that the pronatalist attitudes "Johnson" evinced may have better reflected men's ideas about women's proper place within an imperial settler republic than women's own views. See Carroll, "Affecting History," 512, and Carroll, *Rhetorical Drag: Gender Impersonation, Captivity, and the Writing of History* (Kent, Ohio: Kent State University Press, 2006).

64. Much current scholarship downplays the idea that early U.S. nationalism was purely antagonistic to Britain, noting an enduring conflicted strain of Anglophilia in American culture. See, for example, Leonard Tennenhouse, *The Importance of Feeling English: American Literature and the British Diaspora, 1750–1850* (Princeton, N.J.: Princeton University Press, 2007), and Elisa Tamarkin, *Anglophilia: Deference, Devotion, and Antebellum America* (Chicago: University of Chicago Press, 2008). Most recently, Sam W. Hayes has effectively emphasized the enduring ambivalent pull of the British counterexample. See Hayes, *Unfinished Revolution: The Early American Republic in a British World* (Charlottesville: University of Virginia Press, 2010).

65. "From Gen. Harrison to Gen. Vincent," 2.

66. "From Gen. Harrison to Gen. Vincent," 2.

67. M[ichael] Smith, *A Geographical View of the British Possessions in North America* (Baltimore: P. Mauro, 1814), 248. The District of Virginia copyright was filed on 1 January 1814, in the immediate weeks after news of Harrison's victory spread.

One of the many reasons for this rhetorical power is supplied by June Namias, who observes that, for men, "placing women and children at the center [of captivity tales] may have been a way of recognizing their worst anxieties of being unable to provide adequate protection without admitting to weakness" (Namias, *White Captives*, 264).

68. Darnell, *A Journal* (1813), 52.

69. Darnell, *A Journal* (1813), 52–53. In fact, the British did *not* pay Indians for taking scalps, but, as Alan Taylor observes, claims that they did make for great American propaganda. See Taylor, *The Civil War of 1812*, 208–210.

70. Darnell, *A Journal* (1813), 53.

71. Elias Darnell, *A Journal Containing an Accurate and Interesting Account of the Hardships, Suffferings, Battles, Defeat, and Captivity of Those Heroic Kentucky Volunteers*

and Regulars Commanded by General Winchester, in the Year 1812, 1813, also Two Nar-
ratives, by Men, That Were Wounded in the Battles of the River Raisin, and Taken Captive
by the Indians . . . To Which Is Added a Geographical Description of the North-Western Sec-
tion of the State of Ohio, or That Part to which the Indian Title Has Not Been Extinguished
(Frankfort, Ky.: Robert Johnson, 1814), 56.

72. Darnell, *A Journal . . . To Which Is Added a Geographical Description* (1814), 56.

73. Darnell, *A Journal . . . To Which Is Added a Geographical Description* (1814), 64.

74. Caleb Bingham, *The Hunters; or, The Sufferings of Hugh and Francis, in the Wilder-*
ness a True Story (Boston: Samuel T. Armstrong, 1814).

75. Bingham, *The Hunters*, 33–34.

76. Carver, *Travels*, 191.

77. Fowler, *A Flight to the Moon*, 55.

78. See James F. Brooks, *Captives and Cousins: Slavery, Kinship and Community in the*
Southwest Borderlands (Chapel Hill: University of North Carolina Press, 2001).

79. On adoption and slave labor among Indian captives, see Richter, *Ordeal of the Long-*
house, 69. And see Jon Parmenter, "After the Mourning Wars: The Iroquois as Allies in
Colonial North American Campaigns, 1676–1760," *William and Mary Quarterly* 64 (January
2007): 39–76. William Cronon comments on northeastern Indians' low fertility in the same
discussion in which he compares men's vs. women's relative caloric contributions to Indian
societies, arguing that they each made important offerings through their respective activites
of hunting and farming. It seems to me useful to link these observations and to regard Indian
men's and women's respective reproductive contributions (of capturing and bearing children)
through a similar lens of complementarities. See Cronon, *Changes in the Land: Indians, Colo-*
nists, and Ecology in New England, rev. ed. (New York: Hill and Wang, 2003), 41–44.

80. On the burgeoning Indian slave trade, see Allan Gallay, *The Indian Slave Trade:*
The Rise of the English Empire in the American South (New Haven, Conn.: Yale University
Press, 2003), and Christina Snyder, *Slavery in Indian Country: The Changing Face of Cap-*
tivity in Early America (Cambridge, Mass.: Harvard University Press, 2011).

81. The definitive account of the Eunice Williams captivity, and the cultural anxieties provoked by her subsequent refusal of repatriation, is John Demos, *The Unredeemed*
Captive: A Family Story from Early America (New York: Knopf, 1994).

Castiglia notes that as a genre, one appeal of captivity narratives for female audiences
was "the potential value for women of reading captivity stories as a way . . . to express other
forms of constraint." See Castiglia, *Bound and Determined*, 4.

82. Bingham, *The Hunters*, 8. John Williams's account first appeared as Williams,
The Redeemed Captive Returning to Zion (Boston: B. Green, 1707) and went through a
dozen American editions until the final one of 1811 cited here. This time, the Williams
account was combined with another famous narrative: Williams, *The Captivity and Deliv-*
erance of Mr. John Williams, Pastor of the Church at Deerfield, and Mrs. Mary Rowland-
son . . . Written by Themselves (Brookfield, Mass.: Hori Brown, 1811). As Rowlandson had
famously returned from captivity, her tale was no doubt included in this double feature as
a counter to the bitterness of the Eunice Williams story.

83. Bingham, *The Hunters*, 33.

84. "Speech of Tecumseh," Lexington, Ky., *Reporter*, 6 November 1813, 3.

85. "Speech of Tecumseh," 3. Reprints appeared in the following newspapers, all
except one under the headline "Speech of Tecumseh": Washington, Pa., *Reporter*, 8,
November 1813, 4; Charlestown, [W.]Va., *Farmer's Repository*, 11 November 1813, 2;

Wilmington, Del., *American Watchman*, 13 November 1813, 2; New York *Commercial Advertiser*, 13 November 1813, 2; Harrisburg, Pa., *Chronicle*, 15 November 1813, 2; Boston *Independent Chronicle*, 15 November 1813, 1; *Alexandria* [Va.] *Gazette*, 16 November 1813, 3; Utica, N.Y., *Columbian Gazette*, 16 November 1813, 2; Worcester, Mass., *National Aegis*, 17 November 1813, 2; Bridgeport, Conn., *Republican Farmer*, 17 November 1813, 3; Baltimore *Evening Patriot*, 18 November 1813, 2; Carlisle, Pa., *Kline's Weekly Carlisle Gazette*, 19 November 1813, 1; Portsmouth, N.H., *War Journal*, 19 November 1813, 1; New Haven, Conn., *Columbian Register*, 23 November 1813, 4; Morristown, N.J., *Palladium of Liberty*, 25 November 1813, 1; Newport *Rhode Island Republican*, 25 November 1813, 2; Brattleboro, Vt., *Reporter*, 27 November 1813, 2; *Pendelton* [S.C.] *Messenger*, 4 December 1813, 3; and it appeared as "Indian Eloquence," Windsor *Vermont Republican*, 29 November 1813, 4.

86. J. F. H. Claiborne, *Life and Times of Gen. Sam. Dale, the Mississippi Partisan* (New York: Harper and Bro., 1860), 60. On Claiborne as a southern planter, see Elmo Howell, *Mississippi Home Places: Notes on Literature and History* (Memphis: Roscoe Langford, 1988), 12–16. On Claiborne's writing career, see James B. Lloyd, *Lives of Mississippi Authors, 1817–1967* (Jackson: University Press of Mississippi, 1981), 88–91.

On the colonial origins of ventriloquism, see Joyce Chaplin, *Subject Matter: Technology, the Body, and Science on the Anglo-American Frontier, 1500–1676* (Cambridge, Mass.: Harvard University Press, 2003), 26–27.

87. On Claiborne's relation to Dale, who died in 1841, including the admission that Claiborne had taken down Dale's recollections "some years ago" by the time the biography was published in 1860 and that the first manuscript Claiborne had prepared from Dale's remarks had been "lost by the sinking of a steamer on the Mississippi," see Claiborne, *Life and* Times, vii–viii. What all this means is that Claiborne's account of Tecumseh's "very words" was based at best on his recollections of a conversation held some twenty years earlier with Dale, a man who was himself relying on the memory of a speech delivered another thirty years before that—a speech he almost certainly did not hear and could not have understood even if he somehow had witnessed it.

On the actual conditions of Tecumseh's meeting with the Creeks, including the fact that no white person heard or made record of it, see John Sugden, *Tecumseh, a Life* (New York: Holt, 1999), 243–246. Confirming Sugden's persuasive account, I find no contemporary descriptions of the speech in searching Readex newspaper databases and Early American Imprints collections. By contrast, upon publication in 1860, the Tecumseh speech portion of the Dale biography gained enough immediate notice that an excerpt was reprinted in an Ohio newspaper: "From Claiborne's Life of General Sam. Dale, Tecumseh Eloquence—His Speech in a War Council," *Daily Ohio Statesman*, June 1, 1860, 1.

88. J. F. H. Claiborne, *Mississippi as Province, Territory, and State*, vol. 1 (Jackson, Miss.: Power and Barksdale, 1880), 317. This version of the Claiborne fiction has survived to be treated as fact in Robert V. Hine and John Mack Faragher, *The American West: A New Interpretive History* (New Haven, Conn.: Yale University Press, 2000), 127. Hine and Faragher cite Robert Remini, *Andrew Jackson: The Course of American Empire, 1767–1821* (Baltimore: Johns Hopkins University Press, 1998), 188, and Remini in turn cites Claiborne as his sole source for Tecumseh's speech.

On the prevalence of racial projection in white American life, see Mechal Sobel, *Teach Me Dreams: The Search for Self in the Revolutionary Era* (Princeton, N.J.: Princeton University Press, 2002), 56.

89. On the history of Paris, Ky., see the entries "Bourbon County" and "Paris" in John E. Kleber, ed., *The Kentucky Encyclopedia* (Lexington: University Press of Kentucky, 1992), 104, 710, and on the Lyles' biographies, see William Henry Perrin et al., *Kentucky: A History of the State* (Louisville: F.A. Battey, 1888), 492.

Gregory Evans Dowd notes that Tecumseh experienced "powerful feelings of betrayal" as a result of British failures to strike the United States at this time and that in his final battle he was rumored to have removed his British uniform and donned his own buckskin in symbolic statement that he fought as an autonomous Shawnee and not as a British vassal. See Dowd, *War Under Heaven: Pontiac, the Indian Nations, and the British Empire* (Baltimore: Johns Hopkins University Press, 2002), 273.

90. James Smith, *An Account of the Remarkable Occurrences in the Life and Travels of Col. James Smith (Now a Citizen of Bourbon County, Kentucky) During His Captivity with the Indians in the Years 1755, '56, '57, '58, and '59* (Lexington, Ky.: John Bradford, 1799), and Smith, *Treatise*. The descriptive note is on the title page of Smith, *Treatise*.

91. Smith, *Treatise*, 30–31.

92. Smith, *Treatise*, 30, and Darnell, *A Journal* (1813), appendix, 2.

93. Jervis Cutler, *A Topographical Description of the State of Ohio, Indiana Territory, and Louisiana* (Boston: Charles Williams, 1812), iv, 115.

94. John Rodgers Jewitt, *A Journal, Kept at Nootka Sound* (Boston: author, 1807) and John Rodgers Jewitt, *A Narrative of the Adventures and Sufferings, of John R. Jewitt* (Middletown [Conn.]: Seth Richards, 1815).

95. Jewitt, *Journal*, 14, 30.

96. Additional printings of Jewitt's *Narrative* were by Loomis & Richards (Middletown [Conn.]: 1815) and Daniel Fanshaw (New York: 1816). The broadside song appeared as "The Poor Armourer Boy, a Song . . . Adapted to the Case of John R. Jewitt" ([Middletown, Conn.]: Loomis & Richards, [1815]).

97. Jewitt, *Journal*, 6. Jewitt had originally pitched his tale as a story of "slavery." In 1807, with the close of the Atlantic slave trade, this must have seemed an especially current issue. Yet Jewitt had offered no philosophical thoughts or political comments in his text. He had made no mention of American liberty, nor had he offered praise for republican democracy.

Alsop quickly redrew Jewitt's marriage from an arrangement in which the Nootka chief imposed a match with a fisherman's daughter to a scene in which Jewitt was allowed to select his bride himself at a leisurely feast in which multiple maidens were paraded before him, including the neighboring chief's seventeen-year-old daughter, whose hand he finally took and whose bridal gifts included "two young male slaves to assist . . . in fishing." However much Alsop departed from the facts by claiming, essentially, that Jewitt had married a rich princess, his version came closer to the "truth" as U.S. readers thought they knew it. Stories of common European men consorting with Indian princesses, their civilized superiority more than a match for savage nobility, had been popular from the time that John Smith wove yarns about Pocahontas. In this innovation, then, Alsop stuck to convention.

Yet, in so doing, Alsop provided a partial exception that proved a general rule: during the active years of the war, Indian women were most often portrayed as unappealing beasts. Even though he portrayed Jewitt's Indian wife as a princess, Alsop stopped short of claiming that Jewitt had sired a child with the woman, instead inventing the story of the adoption of the chief's son. Meanwhile, in the far more plausible 1807 *Journal*, published by Jewitt alone, he had taken a different stance. Jewitt had remarked on his reluctance to marry among the Indians by saying that it was "very much against my inclination to take one of these heathens for a partner." Moreover, it proved a short step from disinclination to disgust. In narratives written in the midst of the fighting, writers would go to extremes to depict Indians as revolting beyond measure. See Jewitt, *Narrative*, 138, vs. Jewitt, *Journal*, 30.

98. Jewitt, *Narrative*, 138, 160. Jewitt mentioned the chief's son six times in his *Journal*, each time to remark that he had danced after a feast. See 16, 24, 30, 31, 32, 42.

99. Jewitt, *Narrative*, 160, 161. While early European colonists had initially noted that Indians bathed more frequently and appeared to keep themselves far cleaner than Europeans did, by the mid-eighteenth century, Euro-American commentators were claiming superior cleanliness as a mark of enhanced civility. See Kathleen M. Brown, *Foul Bodies: Cleanliness in Early America* (New Haven, Conn.: Yale University Press, 2009), 157.

100. Jewitt, *Narrative*, 190.

101. Smith, *Treatise*, 18, 21–22, alternate spellings of Shawnee in original.

102. Brown, *Views of the Campaigns*, 73–74, quotations on 74.

103. Brown, *Views of the Campaigns*, 73.

104. Brown, *Views of the Campaigns*, 73–74.

105. Brown, *Views of the Campaigns*, 74.

106. Willie Blount to William Eustis, Knoxville, Tenn., 25 June 1812, as reprinted in *Message from the President of the United States, Transmitting a Report of the Secretary of War, Relative to Murders Committed by the Indians in the State of Tennessee* (Washington, D.C.: Roger C. Weightman, 1813), 15.

107. Willie Blount to William Eustis, 26 June 1812, in *Message from the President*, 17. The Crawley story circulated widely in Tennessee before making its way to Washington. Blount wrote to Eustis that the story had been "copied from a Nashville paper, and transmitted for your information" and that the newspaper item in turn quoted an "Extract of a Letter from Mr. William Henry to John I. Henry, Esq. of William County, Tennessee, Dated St. Stephens, Mobile, 26th June, 1812." See Blount to Eustis, 26 June 1812, 16, 17.

108. William Eustis to Willie Blount, War Department, 7 August 1812, and Willie Blount to William Eustis, Nashville, Tenn., 14 October 1812, in *Message from the President*, 18, 19.

109. J. C. A. Stagg attributes Eustis's departure to his failures at army recruitment, while Donald R. Hickey points to generalized Republican dissatisfaction with Madison's war cabinet. See Stagg, *Mr. Madison's War: Politics, Diplomacy, and Warfare in the Early American Republic, 1783–1830* (Princeton, N.J.: Princeton University Press, 1983), 277, and Hickey, *The War of 1812: A Forgotten Conflict* (Urbana: University of Illinois Press, 1989), 106.

110. Smith, *Treatise*, 47. The text of this 1812 edition of the Smith work contains a footnote indicating that the text was "taken from page 81" of the 1799 edition, which indeed it was. Given that over half the material from the 1799 edition was cut from that of 1812, it seems significant that these comments on marriage and "propagation" were deemed important enough to preserve.

111. Cutler, *Topographical Description*, 218. W. J. Rorabaugh concluded that between 1800 and 1830, U.S. alcohol consumption exceeded five gallons per capita, "a rate nearly triple today's consumption," while Mark Edward Lender and James Kirby Martin place the estimate even higher, at seven gallons. Regardless, all agree that the years 1810 to 1830 marked an historic high in U.S. alcohol consumption. See Rorabaugh, *The*

Alcoholic Republic: An American Tradition (New York: Oxford University Press, 1979), 8, and Lender and Martin, *Drinking in America: A History* (New York: Simon and Schuster, 1987), 46. Peter C. Mancall notes that "the stereotype of the drunken Indian . . . evolved from colonists' views of the unalterable inferiority of Indians." See Mancall, *Deadly Medicine: Indians and Alcohol in Early America* (New York: Cornell University Press, 1997), 26–27.

112. Fowler, *Flight to the Moon*, 154.

113. For the 1815 edition of the Swan narrative issued in tandem with the "Message from the President," see the facsimile edition: Eliza Swan, *An Affecting Account of the Tragical Death of Major Swan* (New York: Garland, 1978), in the collections of the Library of Congress. This edition is not mentioned in the Evans-Shaw-Shoemaker Early American imprints catalog, which includes only another 1815 imprint: Eliza Swan, *An Affecting Account of the Tragical Death of Major Swan, and of the Captivity of Mrs. Swan and Infant Child, by the Savages* (Boston: H. Trumbull, [1815]). This imprint, available in the collections of the AAS and digitized by Readex, is the one quoted here.

The existence of the 1978 Garland edition, with its mention of the "Message from the President," is flagged in a recent anthology featuring the Swan narratives, *Liberty's Captives*. However, the editors of the anthology do not appear to have identified the 1813 Weightman edition of *The Message from the President* as the one referred to in the Swan volume. See Daniel E. Williams et al., eds., *Liberty's Captives: Narratives of Confinement in the Print Culture of the Early Republic* (Athens: University of Georgia Press, 2006), 239–254, quotation on 240.

On the biographical basis of the Swan narrative, see, Williams et al., *Liberty's Captives*, 240.

114. Swan, *Affecting Account*, 2.

115. Swan, *Affecting Account*, 5.

116. Swan, *Affecting Account*, 5.

117. Swan, *Affecting Account*, 5.

118. Swan, *Affecting Account*, 6.

119. See Susan E. Klepp, *Revolutionary Conceptions: Women, Fertility, and Family Limitation in America, 1760–1820* (Chapel Hill: University of North Carolina Press, 2009), 274, and J. David Hacker, "Rethinking the 'Early' Decline of Marital Fertility in the United States," *Demography* 40 (November 2003): 605–620, discussion on 605.

120. Swan, *Affecting Account*, 8, and Thomas Jefferson to William Short, November 28, 1814, Jefferson Papers. Daniel E. Williams et al. note that Swan's reference here to what "history informs us" reveals that her narrative was deliberately constructed within the conventions of captivity narratives as literature. See Williams et al., *Liberty's Captives*, 241.

In contrast to my focus on Swan's maternal fortitude, June Namias casts Swan as an archetype of the "fragile flower" because she was helpless to avenge herself. See Namias, *White Captives*, 37–40.

121. Swan, *Affecting Account*, 18.

122. Swan, *Affecting Account*, 24. Susannah Willard Johnson likewise avoided claiming kinship with her Indian captors and attributed their show of humanity after the birth of her child to their mercenary desire to sell the child into slavery. She reported that, after she gave birth in a "booth" made of branches, "my master looked into the booth and clapped his hands with joy, crying, two monies for me, two monies

for me." Johnson, *A Narrative*, 3rd ed., 32. Both stories underscore the *productive* value of reproduction.

Yael Ben-Zvi uses the Johnson *Narrative* as a primary example of how captivity narratives "employ elaborate strategies of separation and resist potential erosions of cultural boundaries in order to construct the foreignness of Native Americans for an implied Anglo-American readership." Of this scene in Johnson, specifically, he notes perceptively that "the denial of Native American emotions within a sentimentalist text represents Native Americans as foreign both to Johnson and to her readers." See Ben-Zvi, "Ethnography and the Production of Foreignness in Indian Captivity Narratives," *American Indian Quarterly* 32 (Winter 2008): 9–32, quotations on 10, 16.

123. Swan, *Affecting Account*, 8, 3, 4, 7, 8, 21.

124. William Henry Harrison to Legislative Council and House of Representatives of Indiana Territory, "Annual Message," 12 November 1810, in Logan Esarey, ed., *Messages and Letters of William Henry Harrison*, in *Indiana Historical Collections* 7 (1922): 492–493.

125. "Extract of a Letter from Gen. M'Arthur to the Secretary of War: Detroit, Oct. 6, 1813," which appeared under the headline "A Brilliant Victory: Extract of a Letter from Gen. Harrison to the Department of War," Washington, D.C., *Universal Gazette*, 22 October 1813, 1.

126. Examples of reprints (which featured both letters in the text, regardless of headline) include "Extract of a Letter from Gen. M' Arther to the Secretary of War Detroit, Oct. 6," Plattsburgh, N.Y., *Northern Herald*, 26 October 1813, 3, and "Letter from Ge. Harrison to the Department of War H. Q. Sandwich U. C. Sept 30," *Dover* [N.H.] *Sun*, 30 October 1813, 1.

127. "From the Franklin Chronicle," New York *War*, 2 November 1813, 84. This report was reprinted as "Lexington, (Ky.) Oct. 23" in these newspapers: New York *Mercantile Advertiser*, 11 November 1813, 2; Albany, N.Y., *Albany Gazette*, 15 November 1813, 3; Hartford, Conn., *American Mercury*, 16 November 1813, 3; *New Haven Register*, 16 November 1813, 3; Brooklyn *Long Island Star*, 17 November 1813, 1; Bridgeport, Conn., *Republican Farmer*, 17 November 1813, 4; Morristown, N.J., *Palladium of Liberty*, 18 November 1813, 2; Goshen, N.Y., *Orange County Patriot*, 23 November 1813, 1; and as "Lexington, (Ky.) Oct. 22," Wilmington, Del., *American Watchman*, 20 November 1813, 2.

128. "Circus," Advertisement, Philadelphia *Poulson's American Daily Advertiser*, 1 November 1813, 3.

Chapter 5: Liberty, Slavery, and the Burning of the Capital

1. Jesse Torrey, *A Portraiture of Domestic Slavery in the United States: With Reflections on the Practicability of Restoring the Moral Rights of the Slave, Without Impairing the Legal Privileges of the Possessor* (Philadelphia: J. Biorden, 1817), 33. For the phrase "beautiful white freestone," see T. H. Palmer, ed., *The Historical Register of the United States, Part II for 1814*, vol. 4 (Philadelphia: Palmer, 1816), 41.

2. Torrey, *A Portraiture of Domestic Slavery*, 33. Torrey's deliberate juxtaposition of republican liberty and American slavery is well known, the connections he drew to the War of 1812 less so. See, for example, Mary Beth Corrigan, "Imaginary Cruelties? A History of the Slave Trade in Washington, D.C.," *Washington History* (Fall–Winter 2001–2002): 4–27.

3. The British wielded the facts of American slavery as a rhetorical weapon against the United States. William Stanhope Lovell, a commanding naval officer in the 1814 British assault on the Chesapeake, complained, for example, "'Republicans are certainly the most cruel masters and greatest tyrants towards their fellow men. . . . American liberty consists in oppressing the blacks beyond what other nations do.'" For the British perspective on the war, see Jon Latimer, *1812: War with America* (Cambridge, Mass.: Harvard University Press, 2007), 167. Matthew Mason calls the War of 1812 an "important milestone in the international politics of slavery." See Mason, "The Battle of the Slaveholding Liberators: Great Britain, the United States, and Slavery in the Early Nineteenth Century," *William and Mary Quarterly* 59 (July 2002): 665–696, quotation on 668. For a comprehensive overview of Atlantic slavery, see Ira Berlin, *Many Thousands Gone: The First Two Centuries of Slavery in North America* (Cambridge, Mass.: Harvard University Press, 2000).

4. The phenomenon of family separations was widespread. Walter Johnson estimates that "of the two thirds of a million interstate sales made by traders in the decades before the Civil War . . . fifty percent destroyed a nuclear family." Ira Berlin notes that "the internal slave trade proved to be a source of enormous profit, what one Maryland newspaper called 'an almost universal resource to raise money.'" Adam Rothman adds that the development of an internal slave trade "molded the slave system in the United States into the destructive form that it assumed in the decades leading up to the Civil War." See Johnson, *Soul by Soul: Life Inside the Antebellum Slave Market* (Cambridge, Mass.: Harvard University Press, 2001), 19; Berlin, *Many Thousands Gone*, 265; and Rothman, *Slave Country: American Expansion and the Origins of the Deep South* (Cambridge, Mass.: Harvard University Press, 2007), x.

5. On U.S. slaveholders' self-serving embrace of John Locke's claim that slavery was a legitimate outcome of just war, see Ari Helo and Peter Onuf, "Jefferson, Morality, and the Problem of Slavery," *William and Mary Quarterly* 60 (July 2003): 583–614, discussion on 589.

6. Torrey, *A Portraiture of Domestic Slavery*, 37.

7. In one of the first uses of the phrase, commentators in Ohio declared in June 1812 that, "the holy flame of patriotism burns with inextinguishable luster—all . . . are preparing for the second war of independence." The phrase was used throughout the war and remains current today. See "Western Patriotism," *Providence* [R.I.] *Patriot*, 6 June 1812, 2, and A. J. Langguth, *The Americans Who Fought the Second War of Independence* (New York: Simon and Schuster, 2006).

8. Palmer, *Historical Register*, vol. 4, 41.

9. Palmer, *Historical Register*, vol. 4, 56.

10. Palmer, *Historical Register*, vol. 4, 56.

11. On the absolute centrality of black women's labor, in the sense of both production and reproduction, to the development of the early U.S. economy and society, see Jennifer L. Morgan, *Laboring Women: Gender and Reproduction in New World Slavery* (Philadelphia: University of Pennsylvania Press, 2004).

12. "Mr. Russell to the Secretary of State, Dated London, Sept. 17, 1812," in "State Papers Laid before Congress 12th Congress—2d Session," 1–226 in Palmer, *The Historical Register*, vol. 1 (Philadelphia: Palmer, 1814), 86. Note: There is an idiosyncrasy in the pagination of vol. 1. That pagination runs from 2–164 and then reverts to page 1 on what would otherwise be page 165. The page numbers cited here are from the second run of pagination within vol. 1.

13. "Mr. Russell to the Secretary of State," 86. On the concept of commodification in Atlantic slavery, see Stephanie E. Smallwood, *Saltwater Slavery: A Middle Passage from Africa to American Diaspora* (Cambridge, Mass.: Harvard University Press, 2008).

14. "Mr. Russell to the Secretary of State," 86.

15. The letter was printed twice in 1812 as a stand-alone pamphlet by the congressional printer in: *Message from the President of the United States, Transmitting Copies of a Communication from Mr. Russell to the Secretary of State . . . November 12, 1812, Read and Ordered to Lie on the Table* (Washington, D.C.: Weightman, 1812), and *Message from the President of the United States, Transmitting Copies of a Communication from Mr. Russell to the Secretary of State . . . November 12, 1812, Printed by Order of the Senate of the United States* (Washington, D.C.: Weightman, 1812).

The letter was reprinted in the following newspapers: "Mr. Russell to Mr. Monroe, Dated London, September 17, 1812," Newport *Rhode-Island Republican*, 3 December 1812, 3; "Documents Accompanying the President's Message to Congress, on November 18, 1812," Morristown, N.J., *Palladium of Liberty*, 3 December 1812, 1; "Documents Accompanying the President's Message to Congress, on November 18, 1812," Windham [Conn.] *Herald*, 3 December 1812, 1; "Mr. Russell to the Secretary of State: London, Sept. 17, 1812," *Baltimore Patriot*, 4 January 1813, 1; and "Impressment: For the Patriot," Providence [R.I.] *Patriot Columbian Phoenix*, 20 August 1814, 2.

Finally, Russell's lettter was included in two editions of Palmer's contemporary compendium, both published in 1814, the first edition cited above as well as in a second edition by the same title, 86.

16. [John Lowell], *The Antigallican; or, The Lover of His Own Country . . . Wherein French Influence, and False Patriotism, Are Fully and Fairly Displayed: By a Citizen of New-England* (Philadelphia: Cobbett [1798]), 49, and [John Lowell], *Mr. Madison's War: A Dispassionate Inquiry into the Reasons Alleged by Mr. Madison for Declaring an Offensive and Ruinous War Against Great Britain* (Boston: Russell & Cutler, 1812). This pamphlet was a Boston blockbuster and went through four editions by the publishers Russell and Cutler in 1812 alone. On Lowell's biography, see Betty Farrell, *Elite Families: Class and Power in Nineteenth-Century Boston* (Albany: SUNY Press, 1993), 65. John Lowell was the half-brother of the early industrialist Francis Cabot Lowell, founder of the famous Lowell Mills.

This would not be the last time Russell could be accused of exhibiting a highly problematic brand of patriotism. A decade later, in 1822, Russell would try to offer political advantage to Henry Clay by forging documents purporting that John Quincy Adams had deliberately caved in to the British at the Treaty of Ghent, where the war eventually ended. Adams rebutted the charges and exposed Russell's fraud in a book-length pamphlet—with the result that Russell's dubious patriotic career ended once and for all. On Russell's ignomious end, see Lynn H. Parsons, *John Quincy Adams* (New York: Rowman & Littlefield, 1999), 168, and Walter R. Borneman, *1812: The War that Forged a Nation* (New York: HarperCollins, 2004), 299–300.

17. [John Lowell], *Perpetual War the Policy of Mr. Madison: Being a Candid Examination of His Late Message to Congress* (Boston: Stebbins, 1812), 59.

18. See Nathan Perkins, *The National Sins and National Punishment in the Recently Declared War* (Hartford, Conn.: Hudson and Goodwin, 1812).

19. Perkins, *National Sins*, 13, 16.

20. Perkins, *National Sins*, 23.

21. Perkins, *National Sins*, 23.

22. Perkins, *National Sins*, 18.

23. Perkins, *National Sins*, 17.

24. Perkins, *National Sins*, 18.

25. For a useful brief summation of the aims, efforts, and ultimate failure of the African colonization movement, see Allan E. Yarema, *American Colonization Society: An Avenue to Freedom?* (Lanham, Md.: University Press of America, 2006). And see Eric Burin, *Slavery and the Peculiar Solution: A History of the American Colonization Society* (Gainesville: University Press of Florida, 2008).

26. Torrey, *A Portraiture of Domestic Slavery*, 37.

27. Torrey, *A Portraiture of Domestic Slavery*, 33. In his coupling of racist attitudes with antislavery politics, Torrey was utterly typical of his time. Rachel Hope Cleves notes, "most antislavery Federalists embraced a racial 'middle ground,' advocating civil inclusion and political rights for African Americans while demanding social subordination. . . . Northeastern Federalists viewed African Americans as ignorant and degraded, yet they acknowledged the oppressive forces faced by black people." See Cleves, "Hurtful to the State: The Political Morality of Federalist Antislavery," in Matthew Mason and John Craig Hammond, eds., *The Politics of Slavery in Revolutionary America and the Early Republic* (Charlottesville: University of Virginia Press, 2011), 219.

28. Torrey, *A Portraiture of Domestic Slavery*, vi.

29. In fact, historian Robert H. Gudmestad has documented that the internal slave trade "grew in scale and became more open in the years following the War of 1812." See Gudmestad, *A Troublesome Commerce: The Transformation of the Interstate Slave Trade* (Baton Rouge: Louisiana State University Press, 2003), 3.

30. *Report of the Committee Appointed on the Twenty-Third of September Last to Inquire into the Causes and Particulars of the Invasion of the City of Washington by the British Forces in the Month of August, 1814* (Washington, [D.C.]: A. & G. Way, 1814), [i].

31. "Letter of General Armstrong, Late Secretary of War," as cited in *Report of the Committee*, 74–83, quotation on 83, and *Sketches of the War, Between the United States and the British Isles* (Rutland, Vt.: Fay and Davison, 1815), 422.

32. Winder's actions and fate are detailed in a biography of his son: see Arch Fredric Blakey, *General John H. Winder, C.S.A.* (Gainesville: University of Florida Press, 1990), 26. See also Walter R. Borneman, *1812: The War that Forged a Nation* (New York: Harper Collins, 2005), 234. On Armstrong, see Donald R. Hickey, *The War of 1812: A Forgotten Conflict* (Urbana: University of Illinois Press, 1989), 202.

33. Palmer, *Historical Register*, vol. 4, 43, and Frank A. Cassell, "Slaves of the Chesapeake Bay Area and the War of 1812," *Journal of Negro History* 57 (April 1972): 144–155, discussion on 150–152. On black service to the United States in defense of the capital, see Keith Melder, "Slaves and Freedmen," *Wilson Quarterly* 13 (1989): 76–83, discussion on 82.

34. "General [Tobias] Stansbury's Report, Baltimore, November 15, 1814," in *Report of the Committee*, 187. On the persistent American fixation on the possibility of rapes of white women by black men, see Martha Hodes, ed., *Sex, Love, Race: Crossing Boundaries in North American History* (New York: New York University Press, 1999), esp. 356.

35. On Parrott's religious and literary leanings, see *An African American Miscellany Selections from a Quarter Century of Collecting, 1970–1995* (Philadelphia: Library Company of Philadelphia, 1996), 44, and on his wartime organizing efforts, see Julie Winch, *A*

Gentleman of Color: The Life of James Forten (New York: Oxford University Press, 2003), 174–175.

36. Russell Parrott, *An Oration on the Abolition of the Slave Trade* (Philadelphia: Stiles, 1814), 6.

37. Parrott, *An Oration*, 6.

38. Parrott, *An Oration*, 8, 10.

39. Historian Alan Taylor argues that "the War of 1812 pivoted on the contentious boundary between the king's subject and the republic's citizen." See Taylor, *The Civil War of 1812: American Citizens, British Subjects, Irish Rebels, and Indian Allies* (New York: Knopf, 2010).

40. When considered as a category of analysis, "population" has an explanatory power that exceeds that of citizenship. Classic studies of U.S. citizenship, including work by James H. Kettner and Rogers M. Smith, often treat its marked limitations as a matter of flawed logic or unfulfilled promise. More recent scholarship informed by feminism and by critical race theory, from the work of Carol Smith-Rosenberg to that of Evelyn Nakano Glenn, insists that there was nothing accidental about restrictive definitions of citizenship, that rhetorically and materially, the privileges of white male citizenship gained significance only when counterposed to the status of the noncitizen. Yet even this more critical appraisal of citizenship still rests on the analysis of exclusion. Because it does, it cannot account for the ways in which wartime demands for the productive and reproductive labor of *all* the nation's inhabitants required, on the contrary, a new vocabulary of provisional inclusion. Nor can the concept of citizenship explain crucial distinctions in the noncitizen status of women, blacks, and Indians. I argue that "population" best describes how contemporaries imagined that many would be incorporated into the nation. Linked neither to lineal descent nor to legal consent, "population" afforded a universal category in which affiliation could be achieved through action. Significantly, population offered only a limited kind of social and cultural inclusion, one that demanded patriotic service without conferring political privileges. See Kettner, *The Development of American Citizenship, 1608–1870* (Chapel Hill: University of North Carolina Press, 2005); Smith, *Civic Ideals: Conflicting Visions of Citizenship in U.S. History* (New Haven, Conn.: Yale University Press, 1999); Smith-Rosenberg, *This Violent Empire: The Birth American National Identity* (Chapel Hill: University of North Carolina Press, 2010); and Glenn, *Unequal Freedom: How Race and Gender Shaped American Citizenship and Labor* (Cambridge, Mass.: Harvard University Press, 2004).

41. Here and throughout the following discussion, use of the term "population" follows that of Michel Foucault. A detailed explanation of these issues as they relate to Foucault (and to Indians) appears in chap. 1, n. 71. See Foucault, Michel Senellart, ed., Graham Burchell, trans., *Michel Foucault: Security, Territory, Population: Lectures at the College de France, 1977–1978* (New York: Picador, 2007), 42–44.

42. Parrott, *An Oration*, 13.

43. George Lawrence, *An Oration on the Abolition of the Slave Trade* (New York: Hardcastle and Van Pelt, 1813), 8.

44. Lawrence, *An Oration*, 9.

45. Lawrence, *An Oration*, 10.

46. Lawrence, *An Oration*, 11.

47. See Paul Cuffee, "Memoirs of the Life of Paul Cuffee, the Interesting Negro Navigator," *Belfast Monthly Magazine*, October 31, 1811: 284–292, and *A Bill to Authorise the President of the United States to Permit the Departure of Paul Cuffee from the United States, with*

a Vessel and Cargo for Sierra Leone, in Africa, and to Return with a Cargo [Washington, D.C.: s.n., 1814]. Although the majority of free blacks in the United States preferred to remain and continue the freedom struggle in the nation in which they had been born and raised, Alexander X. Byrd makes the important point that the very existence of Sierra Leone upended the traditional narrative Anglo-Americans preferred to tell—in which Africa stood for petty despotism and sin, Britain and America for freedom and enlightenment. By voyaging *to* Africa and *away* from America in the quest for freedom, U.S. blacks made a symbolically important strike against U.S. claims to be a citadel for liberty. Reversing the traditional Atlantic crossing in which Africans traveled west to bondage, migrants to Sierra Leone traveled east to freedom. See Byrd, *Captives and Voyagers: Black Migrants Across the Eighteenth-Century British Atlantic World* (Baton Rouge: Louisiana State University Press, 2009).

48. A historical account of Cuffee's congressional petition appears in Palmer, *Historical Register*, vol. 3, 100–103, quotation on 102. For a modern account, see, Frankie Hutton, "Economic Considerations in the American Colonization Society's Early Effort to Emigrate Free Blacks to Liberia, 1816–36," *Journal of Negro History* 68 (Autumn 1983): 376–389, discussion on 376 and 377.

49. Lawrence, *An Oration*, 8.

50. "Communication: The Bladensburg Races," Georgetown, D.C., *Federal Republican*, 7 October 1814, 1.

51. "Communication: The Bladensburg Races," 1.

52. "Communication: The Bladensburg Races," 1. On Madison, slavery, and the international public-relations problem of slave sales in the capital, see Don Edward Fehrenbacher and Ward M. McAfee, *The Slaveholding Republic: An Account of the United States Government's Relations to Slavery* (Oxford: Oxford University Press, 2002), esp. 67.

53. Lemuel Haynes, *Dissimulation Illustrated: A Sermon Delivered at Brandon, Vermont, February 22, 1813, Before the Washington Benevolent Society; It Being the Anniversary of Gen. Washington's Birth-day* (Rutland, [Vt.]: Fay & Davison, 1814).

54. Haynes, *Dissimulation Illustrated*, 3. For a wonderful biographical and spiritual portrait of Haynes, see John Saillant, *Black Puritan, Black Republican: The Life and Thought of Lemuel Haynes, 1753–1833* (Oxford: Oxford University Press, 2003), esp. the discussion of *Dissimulation Illustrated*, 68–71. For a discussion of Jonathan Edwards and the *Treatise on Religious Affections*, in which he developed the concept of general love, see George Marsden, *Jonathan Edwards: A Life* (New Haven, Conn.: Yale University Press, 2003), 284–290.

55. Haynes, *Dissimulation Illustrated*, 4, 10.

56. Haynes, *Dissimulation Illustrated*, 18, 13.

57. Haynes, *Dissimulation Illustrated*, 6, 8, 17

58. Haynes, *Dissimulation Illustrated*, 17.

59. Haynes, *Dissimulation Illustrated*, 22. As Henry Louis Gates, Jr., has written, from the Enlightenment onward, writers in the black literary tradition have been "demanded to write [them]selves into the human community." The inversion Haynes performs here in writing blacks into the American family is one more example of this work, of what Gates calls "Signifyin(g)," the process through which "a discrete black text interacts with and against its critical context," that context being the white "textual world that a black text echoes, mirrors, repeats, revises, or responds to in various formal ways." See Gates, *Figures in Black: Words, Signs, and the "Racial" Self* (Oxford: Oxford University Press, 1989), xxi, xxxi, xxxii.

60. Haynes, *Dissimulation Illustrated*, 21.

61. On the relationship between U.S. expansion across the North American continent and the increased dimensions of the internal slave trade in the years following the War of 1812, see Steven Deyle, "The Irony of Liberty: Origins of the Domestic Slave Trade," *Journal of the Early Republic* 12 (Spring 1992): 37–62, esp. 45.

62. See "A New Poem, Called Bladensburg Races or, the Devil Take the Foremost: In Four Cantoes," *Federal Republican*, 10 January 1815, 1, and "For the Connecticut Herald, A New Poem Called the Bladensburg Races," New Haven *Connecticut Herald*, 7 March 1815, 1. The full pamphlet was published (presumably not for the first time, though this seems to be the earliest surviving edition) as *The Bladensburg Races, Written Shortly After the Capture of Washington City, August 24, 1814* ([Washington]: Printed for the purchaser, 1816). The text of this 1816 edition is substantially the same as that which appeared in the *Connecticut Herald* in 1815, though interestingly, the 1816 edition contains Americanized spellings ("honour" corrected to "honor," for example). Brief colloquial references to the president's flight as "the Bladensburg Races" (containing neither the full original prose satire nor the subsequent comedic poem) indicate that this became a widely popular form of ridicule. See, for example, the reference to the "Captain-General of the democratick party who won the prize in the Bladensburg races," in the Providence *Rhode Island American*, 4 July 1815, 3.

63. "A New Poem Called the Bladensburg Races," *Connecticut Herald*, 7 March 1815, 1, emphasis in original.

64. Torrey, *A Portraiture of Domestic Slavery*, 40.

65. Torrey, *A Portraiture of Domestic Slavery*, 45.

66. Torrey, *A Portraiture of Domestic Slavery*, 45.

67. On the early modern conception of the family as a "little commonwealth" that provided all services and most discipline for its members, see John Demos, *A Little Commonwealth: Family Life in Purta New England*, 2nd ed. (New York: Oxford University Press, 1999). On the increasing importance of the domestic realm as a symbolic sphere of virtue, see Ruth Bloch, "The Gendered Meanings of Virtue in Revolutionary America," *Signs* 13, no. 1 (Autumn 1987): 37–58, and Marilyn Westercamp, *Women in Early American Religion, 1600–1850* (New York: Routledge, 1999).

68. Elias Hicks, *Observations on the Slavery of Africans and Their Descendents* (New York: Samuel Wood, 1814), 19. On the Hicksite Schism, see E. Brooks Holifield, *Theology in America: Christian Thought from the Age of the Puritans to the Civil War* (New Haven, Conn.: Yale University Press, 2005), 320–327.

On emotion in eighteenth-century Quaker antislavery activism, see Nicole Eustace, *Passion Is the Gale: Emotion and Power on the Eve of the American Revolution* (Chapel Hill: University of North Carolina Press, 2008), esp. 37–42, 264–265.

69. James Forten, *Letters from a Man of Colour on a Late Bill Before the Senate of Pennsylvania* [Pennsylvania: s.n., 1813], 2.

70. Forten, *Letters from a Man of Colour*, 6.

71. In his landmark study of the U.S. domestic slave trade, Walter Johnson suggests the special burden and stigma of the family ruptures routinely imposed on the enslaved, proposing that slaveholders should be called "family separators in a land of organic social relations." See Johnson, *Soul by Soul*, 22.

On household governance, see Mary Beth Norton, *Founding Mothers and Fathers: Gendered Power and the Forming of American Society* (New York: Vintage, 1997). On children as servants, see Demos, *A Little Commonwealth*, 120, and on broader historical and changes cultural views of childhood, see Stephanie Grauman Wolf, *As Various as Their Land: The Everyday Lives of Eighteenth-Century Americans*, reprint ed. (Fayetteville: University of Arkansas Press, 2000), esp. chap. 4, "The Invention of Childhood."

72. *The Mirror of Misery; or, Tyranny Exposed. Extracted from Authentic Documents, and Exemplified by Engravings* (New York: Samuel Wood, 1814), 4. Wood's volume was very successful in his day. He published it at least three times, in 1807, in 1811, and again in the wartime 1814 edition cited here. All editions appear to be substantially the same and are not numbered as separate editions. The 1807 and 1814 are readily available in digital form. The 1811 edition is now rare; a copy is in the collections of the Library Company of Philadelphia.

73. See John Taylor, *An Inquiry into the Principles and Policy of the Government* (Fredricksburg, [Va.]: Green and Cady, 1814), 543, and *The Mirror of Misery*, 5, 6.

74. *The Mirror of Misery*, 29, 35.

75. Christopher Leslie Brown draws a useful distinction between "anti-slavery" and "abolitionism" in the eighteenth century that I am here extending to the nineteenth. Anti-slavery activists could be critical of some but not all aspects of slavery, whereas nineteenth-century abolitionists, having achieved the legal end of the Atlantic slave trade, worked for the abolishment of slavery and emancipation of the enslaved. See Brown, *Moral Capital: Foundations of British Abolitionism* (Chapel Hill: University of North Carolina Press, 2006), 17–18, n. 14.

76. In pointing out the limits of sympathy as a vector for social change, I follow Julia Stern's brilliant critique of the limits of the culture of sympathy as a vehicle for antislavery activism. See Julia A. Stern, *The Plight of Feeling: Sympathy and Dissent in the Early American Novel* (Chicago: University of Chicago Press, 1997), 25. See also Karen Halttunen, "Humanitarianism and the Pornography of Pain in American Culture," *American Historical Review* 100 (April 1995): 303–334. For an alternative view, see Elizabeth B. Clark, "'The Sacred Rights of the Weak': Pain, Sympathy, and the Culture of Individual Rights in Antebellum America," *Journal of American History* 82 (September 1995): 463–493.

77. On Torrey's biography, especially his lifelong interest in promoting libraries, see, Edward Harmon Virgin, "Life of Jesse Torrey," in Virgin, ed., *The Intellectual Torch: Developing a Plan for the Universal Dissemination of Knowledge and Virtue by Means of Free Public Libraries* (Cambridge, Mass.: Harvard University Press, 1912), vii–xxii.

78. Torrey, *Portrait of Slavery*, 43. Robert H. Gudmestad traces the political fate of this sensational story in the House of Representatives, arguing that the tale was most often repeated as a tactical move by defenders of slavery who wished to prove that their moral sensibilities had not been deadened by the institution of slavery. See Gudmestad, *A Troublesome Commerce*, 35–39.

79. Torrey, *Portraiture of Slavery*, 44. Literary theorist Elizabeth Barnes offers a perceptive related critique of how "sympathy ultimately brings us back to ourselves." See Barnes, *States of Sympathy: Seduction and Democracy in the American Novel* (New York: Columbia University Press, 1997), 4–5, 7.

80. Torrey, *Portraiture of Slavery*, 34. Writing on sentimental novels, Barbara M. Benedict makes a similar point about the limits of sympathetic identification, saying, "The sympathetic spectator knows, as he or she watches, that he or she can only approximate knowledge of the other's feelings. Indeed, the very process by which one vicariously experiences another's feelings reminds one of the distance between one and another. . . . Even while sentiment was seen as universal, it was a mark of naturally high class." See Benedict,

Framing Feeling: Sentiment and Style in English Prose Fiction, 1745–1800 (New York: AMS Press, 1994), 11, 13.

81. Torrey, *Portraiture of Slavery*, 38.

82. Torrey, *Portraiture of Slavery*, 27.

83. Torrey, *Portraiture of Slavery*, 29.

84. Torrey, *Portraiture of Slavery*, 29.

85. Palmer, *Historical Register of the United States*, vol. 4, 42.

86. "By the President of the U. States of America. *A Proclamation*," Washington, D.C., *Daily National Intelligencer*, 3 September 1814, 2, and "Copy of a Letter from Mr. Monroe to Sir Alex. Cochrane, Vice Admiral, &c. &c. . . . September 6, 1814," Washington, D.C., *Daily National Intelligencer*, 9 September 1814, 2. The reprints of these letters are simply too numerous to cite.

87. "Copy of a Letter from Vice-Admiral Cochrane to Mr. Monroe . . . 18th August, 1814," Washington, D.C. *Daily National Intelligencer*, 9 September 1814, 2. On York as a justification for the burning of Washington, see Hickey, *The War of 1812*, 130.

88. James Ewell, *The Medical Companion . . . with . . . a Concise and Impartial History of the Capture of Washington* (Philadelphia: Anderson & Meehan, 1816), 642.

89. Ewell, *Medical Companion*, 639, emphasis in original. On Hampton and Havre de Grace, see Hickey, *The War of 1812*, 153–154. Rapes were only documented at Hampton, but attacks on the two towns tended to be lumped together.

90. *Barbarities of the Enemy Exposed in a Report of the Committee of the House of Representatives of the United States Appointed to Inquire into the Spirit and Manner in which the War Has Been Waged by the Enemy* (Worcester, Mass.: Isaac Sturtevant, 1814), 10, 111. The report with these quotations was also reprinted in Palmer, *Historical Register of the United States*, vol. 2, 263.

91. Julius Scaliger, *Eulogium on the Capture of Washington, or, Bilious Fever* (Baltimore: New Porcupine Press, 1816), 15, 16.

92. See "From the Liberty Hall," Washington, Ky., *Union*, 19 April 1814, 3. And see reprints of "From the Liberty Hall" in Clinton *Ohio Register*, 12 July 1814, 178; Bedford, Pa., *True American*, 13 July 1814, 1; and Bedford, Pa., *True American*, 7 September 1814, 1.

93. The classic study of the Hartford Convention remains James Banner, *To the Hartford Convention: The Federalists and the Origins of Party Politics in Massachusetts, 1789–1815* (New York: Knopf, 1970). For a contrarian view that Federalists at Hartford were a truly seditious threat to the nation, see Richard Buel, Jr., *America on the Brink: How the Political Struggle over the War of 1812 almost Destroyed the Young Republic* (New York: Macmillan, 2005).

94. See the very brief notice, "Extract of a Letter from Col. B. Hawkins to the Secretary at War, Dated 'Creek Agency, 16th Aug. 1814,'" Washington, D.C., *Daily National Intelligencer*, 4 September 1814, 1.

95. Ewell, *Medical Companion*, 634.

96. Ewell, *Medical Companion*, 641.

97. While black men may have had a sharply limited ability to share in this vision, those free black men who supported the war also advocated for according black males the same rights and duties as husbands and fathers allowed to white ones. Russell Parrott, for example, especially lamented the way the slave trade interrupted the manly activities of black husbands and fathers. His prototypical enslaved person was a family man making

useless entreaties to slave traders to allow him to fulfill his appointed patriarchal role: "in vain he tells them that numerous offspring depend upon him for sustenance; that an affectionate wife looks with anxious solicitude for his return." See Parrott, *An Oration*, 7.

Conclusion

1. "Copy of a Letter from Major General Jackson, to the Secretary of War, Dated Head-Quarters, 7th Military District, 13 January, 1815," Washington, D.C., *Daily National Intelligencer*, 6 February 1815, 2.

2. George Poindexter, *To the Public*, "*A Villain's Censure is Extorted Praise*" [Lexington, Ky.: s.n., 1815], 4.

3. Poindexter, *To the Public*, ii.

4. Poindexter, *To the Public*, 4. The centerpiece of Poindexter's self-defense was the claim that he did not leave camp to seek treatment until *after* the battle had ended. There seems no reason to doubt that claim, but also little reason to see it as doing much to rehabilitate his reputation; he freely admitted to sitting out active duty with a sham injury.

5. The letter "George Poindexter to Messrs. Isler and McCurdy," was published as "From the Mississippi Republican-Extra, New-Orleans, Jan 20., 1815," Washington, D.C., *Daily National Intelligencer*, 13 February 1815, 2. On Peter Isler, J. McCurdy, and the editorship of the *Mississippi Republican*, see Douglas Crawford McMurtrie, *A Bibliography of Mississippi Imprints, 1798–1830*, Heartman's Historical Series no. 69 (New York: Book Farm, 1945).

6. "From the Mississippi Republican-Extra."

7. Hezekiah Niles, "From a Late *Boston Centennial*," *Niles Weekly Register*, 25 February 1815, 410.

8. For the claim of "sheer fabrication," see "Beauty and Booty," *Boston Daily Advertiser*, 18 March 1815, 2; *Boston Repertory*, 18 March 1815, 2; *Connecticut Journal*, 20 March 1815, 2; *Hallowell* [Maine] *Gazette*, 29 March 1815, 4; and *Bennington* [Vt.] *Newsletter*, 10 April 1815, 2. For the link back to Poindexter, see "Beauty and Booty . . . from the *Salem Gazette*," *Concord* [N.H.] *Gazette*, 25 April 1815.

9. Poindexter named one "Samuel Brown and a few unprincipled confederates" for spreading the story of his dereliction of duty. The inference that the editors of the *Mississippi Republican* also questioned his veracity comes from published reports that he assaulted one of them: see below. Poindexter, *To the Public*, i.

10. "From the Mississippi Republican, March 8," *Burlington* [Vt.] *Gazette*, 14 April 1815, 3.

11. Here I share the position of Jon Latimer, who notes: "Some American writers have claimed that had it not been for the victory at New Orleans the British would have disavowed the Treaty of Ghent and attempted to retain the city, but this claim has no basis." See Latimer, *1812: War with America* (Cambridge, Mass.: Harvard University Press, 2007), 401.

12. John Henry Eaton, *The Life of Andrew Jackson, Major General in the Service of the United States Comprising a History of the War in the South, from the Commencement of the Creek Campaign, to the Termination of Hostilities Before New Orleans* (Philadelphia: M. Carey & Son, 1817), 352.

13. As historian Sharon Block alerts us, "rape by British soldiers became a propaganda tool of proportions unmatched in early American history." See Block, *Rape and*

Sexual Power in Early America (Chapel Hill: University of North Carolina Press, 2006), 236.

14. "House of Representatives, Thursday, 16th FEB. 1815: SUBSTANCE OF MR. INGERSOLE'S OBSERVATIONS ON THE PASSAGE *Of the Resolutions expressive of the thanks of Congress to Gen. Jackson, &c.*," Washington, D.C., *Daily National Intelligencer*, 20 February 1815, 2 (hereafter cited as "Ingersole's Observations").

15. "Ingersole's Observations," and "From the Mississippi Republican-Extra." On the date that news of Ghent arrived in Washington, D.C., see Donald R. Hickey, *The War of 1812: A Forgotten Conflict* (Chicago: University of Illinois Press, 1989), 298. Hickey dates the arrival of the news to February 13 on the basis of an article of 14 February 1815 in the *Daily National Intelligencer* reporting that "a rumor was afloat last evening, wearing stronger semblance of probability than any we have yet heard, importing the preliminaries of Peace had actually reached this country. The truth or falsity of the rumor must be determined in a few hours." See "Rumor of Peace!," *Daily National Intelligencer*, 14 February 1815, 2.

16. "Ingersole's Observations."

17. "Paragraphs from the Trenton T. American," Wilmington, Del., *American Watchman*, 4 March 1815, 3.

18. "Ingersole's Observations." For a contemporary account of the American desertions on the right bank of the river, see *History of the American War of Eighteen Hundred and Twelve from the Commencement until the Final Termination Thereof, on the Memorable Eighth of January, 1815, at New Orleans* (Philadelphia: M'Carty & Davis, 1816), 232.

19. "Ingersole's Observations." Ingersoll was quoted verbatim in *Essex* [Mass.] *Register*, 4 March 1815, 1; "Mr. Ingersoll's Speech," *Vermont Republican*, 13 March 1815; and *Pittsfield* [Mass.] *Sun*, 23 March 1815, 2.

20. "Beauty and Booty," *Concord* [N.H.] *Gazette*, 25 April 1815, 3. Federalists, of course, did not lose all cultural influence and did continue to enjoy local electoral success in many New England states. See Marshall Foletta, *Coming to Terms with Democracy: Federalist Intellectuals and the Shaping of American Culture* (Charlottesville: University Press of Virginia, 2001). Rachel Hope Cleves argues in particular that Federalist fear-based politics played a crucial part in the development of the antislavery movement. See Cleves, *The Reign of Terror in America: Visions of Violence from Anti-Jacobinism to Antislavery* (Cambridge: Cambridge University Press, 2009), esp. 230–275.

21. "For the National Advocate: A Democratic Judge," New York *National Advocate*, 7 April 1815, 2.

22. "For the National Advocate," 2. And see the reprint: "For the National Advocate: A Democratic Judge," Concord *New Hampshire Patriot*, 25 April 1815, 1.

23. "For the Boston Patriot: Beauty and Booty," *Boston Patriot*, 5 April 1815, 2. This article was reprinted as "From the Boston Patriot: Beauty and Booty," Hartford, Conn., *American Mercury*, 12 April 1815, 2.

"Enemies in War;—in Pece [*sic*] Friends," Hartford, Conn., *American Mercury*, 7 March 1815. And see the reprints: "Enemies in War;—In Peace Friens [*sic*]," Hudson, N.Y., *Bee*; 21 March 1815, 3, and "From the Hartford Mercury: Enemies in War, in Peace Friends," Washington, D.C., *Daily National Intelligencer*, 8 April 1815, 2.

24. "Wilmington, 8th March, 1815," Wilmington, Del., *American Watchman*, 8 March 1815, 3.

25. "Wilmington, 8th March, 1815," 3.

26. "For the City Gazette," Charleston, S.C., *City Gazette*, 6 April 1815, 2.

27. J. C. A. Stagg notes that Federalists "pointed out with sarcasm and bitterness that the administration had achieved none of its stated war objectives," a view shared even by some Republican critics. See Stagg, *Mr. Madison's War: Politics, Diplomacy, and Warfare in the Early American Republic, 1783–1830* (Princeton, N.J.: Princeton University Press, 1983), 500.

28. "Ingersole's Observations." As Jon Latimer observes, "for America the results of the war were largely psychological, and this was perhaps fitting, since attitudes of mind had generated it in the first place." See Latimer, *1812*, 400.

29. "Ingersole's Observations."

30. Alexander McLeod, *A Scriptural View of the Character, Causes, and Ends of the Present War* (New York: Eastburn, Kirk, 1815), 220.

31. McLeod, *A Scriptural View*, 220.

32. [C. E. Grice], *The Battle of New Orleans* (Baltimore: Commercial Press, 1815).

33. [Grice], *The Battle of New Orleans*, 17.

34. [Grice], *The Battle of New Orleans*, 30.

35. Eaton, *Life of Andrew Jackson*, 282, and [Grice], *The Battle of New Orleans*, 56.

36. Samuel Woodworth, *The Champions of Freedom . . .*, 2 vols. (New York: Baldwin, 1816), and Woodworth, *The Champions of Freedom . . .*, 2 vols. (New York: Baldwin, 1818).

37. Woodworth, *Champions*, vol. 2, 192.

38. Woodworth, *Champions*, vol. 1, 229.

39. Woodworth, *Champions*, vol. 2, 99.

40. Woodworth, *Champions*, vol. 2, 199.

41. Woodworth, *Champions*, vol. 1, 77. On this theme, see also Renée L. Bergland, *The National Uncanny: Indian Ghosts and American Subjects* (Hanover: University Press of New England, 2000). This fine book is one of few scholarly treatments on *Champions of Freedom* that I have found; it does not, however, take up the issues of love and patriotism I consider here.

42. On the details of Lathrop's earlier life and career, see Nicole Eustace, *Passion Is the Gale: Emotion, Power, and the Coming of the American Revolution* (Chapel Hill: University of North Carolina Press, 2008), 330–331, 443.

43. John Lathrop, *The Present War Unexpected, Unnecessary, and Ruinous, Two Discourses Delivered in Boston* (Boston: J. W. Burditt, 1812), 18–19.

44. Lathrop, *A Compendious History of the Late War; Containing an Account of all the Important Battles, and Many of the Smaller Actions, Between the American, and the British Forces, and Indians in the Years 1811, 1812, 1813, 1814, 1815* (Boston: J. W. Burditt, 1815).

45. Lathrop, *A Compendious History*, 8, and T. R. Malthus, *An Essay on the Principle of Population; or, A View of Its Past and Present Effects on Human Happiness with an Inquiry into Our Prospects Respecting the Future Removal or Mitigation of the Evils Which It Occasions . . . First American from the Third London Edition* (Washington, D.C.: Weightman, 1809), 9–10.

46. For an account of the British retreat from their original negotiating position that there should be an "Indian barrier" in the American West, see Hickey, *The War of 1812*, 289–293.

47. Lathrop, *A Compendious History*, 32.

48. James Madison, "President's Message Washington City, Dec. 5. This day at 12 o'clock . . ." [Boston, 1815], broadside in the Collections of the American Antiquarian Society (AAS), Worcester, Mass.

49. "Resolved by the Senate and the House of Representatives of the United States of America in Congress Assembled . . . ," in *Journal of the Senate of the United States of America . . . Begun and Held in the City of Washington, September 19, 1814* (Washington, [D.C.]: Weightman, [1815]), 382–384.

50. On Jackson's reliance on the militias of Kentucky and Tennessee, see *History of the American War of Eighteen Hundred and Twelve* (Philadelphia: McCarty and Davis, 1816), 231.

51. Eaton, *Life of Andrew Jackson* (1817), 281.

52. Eaton, *Life of Andrew Jackson* (1817), 282.

53. For later editions of Eaton's work, all containing the claim that "Beauty and Booty" was the British watchword, see John Henry Eaton, *The Life of Major General Andrew Jackson* (Philadelphia: S. F. Bradford, 1824), 380–381; Eaton, *The Life of Major General Andrew Jackson*, 3rd. ed. (Philadelphia: McCarty and Davis, 1828), 233; and [Eaton], *Memoirs of Andrew Jackson* (Philadelphia, 1833), 293.

54. James Stuart, *Refutation of Aspersions* (London: Gilbert and Rivington, 1834), 104. Stuart corresponded extensively with Lieutenant-General Sir John Lambert in preparing his documents. He provided copies of this correspondence as "Appendix No. II" in his book (102–105) and included extracts from U.S. newspapers proving that word of the denials had received wide American publicity as "Appendix No. III" (106–108). Donald R. Hickey concurs that "there is no credible evidence that the British planned to sack New Orleans" and notes that the Lambert declaration was published in the *Niles Weekly Register* on October 19, 1833. See Hickey, *Don't Give Up the Ship: Myths of the War of 1812* (Chicago: University of Illinois Press, 2006), 279–281, and 403, n. 13.

55. Stuart, *Refutation of Aspersions*, 108.

56. Contemporary accounts stress black participation at New Orleans, telling of how "requisition was made by general Jackson for negroes to work on the fortifications" while also noting that "the uniformed companies of the militia under the command of major Planche, [included] 200 men of colour, chiefly from St. Domingo." See *History of the American War*, 228, 229.

Jennifer M. Spear notes that free men of color in Louisiana in the early republic were valued for their militia service without being given any political rights. She also points out that from 1808 forward, law required that whites, free blacks, and enslaved people marry only within their own group, allowing the government to use "the regulation of sex to define the tripartite system's three racial castes." See Spear, *Race, Sex, and Social Order in Early New Orleans* (Baltimore: Johns Hopkins University Press, 2008), 185–186, quotation on 217.

57. It is also crucial to note that avoidance of military gang rapes did little to eliminate individual rapes. Indeed, as Jennifer M. Spear notes, rape was a capital crime "only when perpetrated 'on the body of any white woman or girl.'" In New Orleans, by legal definition, a woman of color could not be raped, a fact that allowed white men the "liberty" of sexual violation of nonwhite women without endangering their claims to uphold liberty. See Spear, *Race, Sex, and Social Order*, 188.

58. I thank Mary Maples Dunn for her suggestion that I investigate the connection between rape charges at New Orleans and the contemporary British reputation for sexual tyranny in India.

59. See Edmund Burke, *The Complete Works of the Right Honorable Edmund Burke*, 10 vols. (10: 88–89), cited in Nancy L. Paxton, "Mobilizing Chivalry: Rape in British Novels About the Indian Uprising of 1857," *Victorian Studies* 36 (Autumn 1992): 5–30, quotation on 5. For contemporary U.S. reports on the Hastings indictment and subsequent trial,

see, for example, "The Following Are the Titles of the Charges against Warren Hastings, Esq.," *Boston Gazette*, 21 April 1788, 2, and "Trial of Warren Hastings," Boston *Argus*, 12 August 1791, 1.

60. "From the Aurora: Political Views," Washington, D.C., *Daily National Intelligencer*, 12 April 1815. The *Weekly Aurora* was a Philadelphia newspaper that frequently published a column called "Political Views." The original of this particular column does not seem to have survived. Burke's testimony at the trial of Warren Hastings was referenced throughout the decade. See, for example, "Mr. Sheridan," Concord *New-Hampshire Patriot*, 2 October 1810, 4, and "Miscellany . . . Memoirs of the Late Honorable Richard Sheridan," Northampton, Mass., *Hampshire Gazette*, 31 December 1817, 4.

On Jefferson and the long legacy of his idea of "empire for liberty" (as well as Federalist critiques of the same), see Peter S. Onuf, *Jefferson's Empire: The Language of American Nationhood* (Charlottesville: University of Virginia Press, 2001), esp. 53–61.

61. Viewed in this light, the Civil War itself becomes only an interruption in a longer running continental project. By ending slavery, the Civil War put to rest a key part of the nation's population problem. It ended forever the embarrassment of slavery in the land of liberty. Yet that war did not end the question of whether all of the nation's denizens could claim to be equal citizens. Much remained unresolved regarding the status of women and Indians as well as that of newly freed blacks and later arriving immigrants.

62. On the adoption of the national anthem, see Lonn Taylor, *The Star-Spangled Banner: The Flag that Inspired the National Anthem* (Washington, D.C.: Smithsonian Institution, 2000).

63. The AAS has copies of at least three different versions of this broadside from 1815 as well as others from 1817, 1824, and beyond. See [Samuel Woodworth], "The Hunters of Kentucky; or, The Battle of New Orleans" ([New York: C. Brown, 1815?]); [Samuel Woodworth], "The Hunters of Kentucky; or, The Battle of New Orleans" ([United States: s.n., 1815?]); "The Hunters of Kentucky: As Sung by Mr. Ludlow, in the New Orleans and Western Country Theatres" ([New Orleans?: s.n., 1817?]); and [Samuel Woodworth], "The Hunters of Kentucky" ([Boston]: L. Deming, 1837).

64. "Public Dinners; Gen. Jackson; Georgetown; Alexandria; Washington," *Providence* [R.I.] *Patriot*, 16 December 1815, 1.

65. "Public Dinners," 1. A fascinating coda to the war and to Andrew Jackson's role in defining its meaning in terms of fertility and feeling emerged in 1828, the year Jackson was elected to the presidency. In rare instances, white Americans did actually adopt Indians, and Jackson, who sired no biological children of his own, was one of them. Following a victory against the Creek Indians in 1813, Jackson adopted an orphaned Indian infant boy named Lyncoya. While this act garnered little or no public attention at the time, obituaries published when the boy died of tuberculosis in 1828 make clear that the legend surrounding the circumstances of the event added nicely to the story line of maternal depravity among Indians. According to an article, "From the Nashville (Tenn.) Republican, June 17," the infant had been found in the aftermath of the fight "in the bloodiest part of the field, sucking at the breast of its dead mother, who had been killed, unfortunately, in the action." The account tried to establish immediately that U.S. soldiers regarded the mother's death as unfortunate, an occurrence due to her inappropriate appearance on the battlefield and not to any violation of the practices of just war by American troops. The paper reported that Jackson took immediate charge of the infant and that, "as many squaws had been taken, and some of them had children at the breast, he applied to these

298 Notes to Conclusion

to suckle it, offering a reward to any one who would preserve it. They all refused." By this account, Creek women failed utterly as mothers and proved unable to feel for the baby boy, whereas General Jackson was a man "whose heart was immediately interested in its preservation," and his wife Rachel, who cared for the boy, was "an amiable and benevolent lady." In actuality, it seems the "adoption" may have felt more like a kidnapping to the boy, who ran away repeatedly from the Jacksons to the Creek Indians during his short life. Nevertheless, for white Americans, the tale of the Jacksons' humanity vs. the Indians' depravity fit neatly with claims about the superiority and civility of American family feeling. [See "From the Nashville (Tenn.) Republican, June 17," Philadelphia, *National Gazette and Literary Register*, 3 July 1828, 3. The obituary was reprinted at least ten times in the month of July 1828 in newspapers across the Northeast. On Lyncoya's life and his frequent attempts to return to the Creek Nation, see Bertram Wyatt Brown, "Andrew Jackson's Honor," *Journal of the Early Republic*, 17 (Spring, 1997): 1–36, discussion on 32–33.]

Index

⟨◈⟩

Acknowledgments

⟨∞⟩

I am very grateful to the scholars and institutions that have helped advance this project. For fellowship support and for great encouragement, many thanks to the American Antiquarian Society, especially Paul J. Erickson and Caroline Sloat; the American Philosophical Society, especially Roy Goodman and Martin Levitt; and the Library Company of Philadelphia, especially James N. Green and Phil Lapsansky. Without their resources—in people as well as in print—this project would not have been possible. And thanks to my dear friends the Ginsberg-Peltz Family, whose hospitality greatly eased my stint at AAS.

Thanks to New York University for a year of sabbatical leave in 2010–2011, which allowed me time to complete the writing of this book. I am fortunate to have fascinating colleagues who have read and critiqued my work and, often more importantly, asked me to read theirs. In addition to the comments I received from members of the NYU Atlantic Workshop, directed by Karen Kupperman, and of the U.S. History Workshop, directed by Thomas Bender, I especially appreciate the many stimulating conversations with and crucial suggestions from: Lauren Benton, Jane Burbank, Frederick Cooper, Ada Ferrer, Richard Hull, Stefanos Geroulanos, Fiona Griffiths, Martha Hodes, Andrew Lee, Maria Montoya, T. Andrew Needham, Molly Nolan, Jeffrey Sammons, and Joanna Waley-Cohen. Great thanks to Linda Gordon and Jennifer L. Morgan, who each took time from hectic schedules to provide insightful written feedback on chapter drafts and project proposals.

I also benefitted greatly from the chance to workshop chapters in scholarly forums. Thanks to Andrew R. L. Cayton, Fred Anderson, Christopher Grasso, and Karin Wulf, conveners of the William and Mary Quarterly–Early

Modern Studies Institute Writing American History 2008 Authors' Workshop, for the chance to collaborate with a great group. It was a special pleasure to participate with John Demos, my undergraduate mentor and constant friend, who has done so much to promote attention to the stories in history. Drew Cayton, who started out as a reader for the press on my first book, has been a sustaining scholarly presence in my life for a decade now. Our ideas on emotion and empire jibed from the beginning and I truly appreciate the numerous ways, large and small, that he has encouraged and improved this project. Thanks to Daniel Richter, Director of the McNeil Center for Early American Studies, for the opportunity to appear at the Friday Seminar and to continue conversations and debates begun in my graduate school days. Special thanks to my old friends there, especially Amy Baxter-Bellamy, Dallett Hemphill, Susan Klepp, Michelle and Roderick McDonald, and Roz Remer. And great gratitude to Michael Zuckerman, convener, and Richard and Mary Dunn, hosts, for the chance to present work salon-style to a fantastic group; what a uniquely enriching and enlivening experience that was. And how fortunate I am to have had the three of them behind me on this book as on the first.

Conference participation is a great way to road-test ideas and I deeply appreciate comments and critiques received from Rachel Hope Cleves, Matthew Rainbow Hale, Kate Haulman, Lloyd Pratt, Barbara Rosenwein, Peter Stearns, Alan Taylor, and Serena Zabin. Extra thanks to Alan Taylor, who kindly took time to provide written comments on several chapter drafts.

Great thanks to three inspiring women who have contributed immeasurably to all of my work: Kathleen M. Brown, Jan Ellen Lewis, and Fredrika J. Teute. Kathy, dissertation director on my first project, encouraged this one from the very start. I am truly grateful for all the times she made herself available for consultation and all she continues to teach me. Jan devoted many hours to reading different drafts of various pieces of this project, always improving them immensely. I benefitted as much from her enthusiastic warmth as from her deep knowledge of women and gender, and culture and politics in the early Republic. Fredrika, editor of my first book, remained an important sounding board as I developed this one. I very much enjoyed the opportunity for lots of 1812 talk with her and Robert Parkman as we worked together to develop the conference, "Warring for America, 1803–1818," jointly sponsored by Omohundro Institute of Early American History and Culture, the Huntington

Library, the Department of History of New York University, and the John W. Kluge Center, Library of Congress.

The University of Pennsylvania Press has been a delight to work with. In the final stages of publication, Noreen O'Connor-Abel, Project Editor, and Tim Roberts, Project Manager, shepherded the book through production. The initial interest in the project shown by Early American Studies Series Editor, Daniel Richter, buoyed me from the beginning, while Dan's incisive comments on the full manuscript draft eased the final stages of writing. Series Editor David Waldstreicher's perceptive reading of the entire manuscript proved invaluable and I'm deeply indebted to him for his wholehearted support. Mike Zuckerman too contributed his inimitable brand of criticism on a late draft. He sets a high standard of scholarly generosity. Robert Lockhart's sympathetic vision as senior history editor helped me stay true to my own. Two anonymous readers for the press offered timely and detailed critiques. I am grateful also for the added efforts of the talented freelance editor Elizabeth Wolf.

Finally, my love to my family. Thanks, always, to my parents, Tom and Cely Eustace, who ever inspire me with their vitality, curiosity, and humanity. Hugs to Ned and Jeralyn Eustace for always being there, for carrying us up mountains and across states. Jaitrie Paul has become another pillar of our family and we are so grateful to have her in our lives. To my extended Klancnik family, Jim, Maggie, Gordon, Michelle, Amelia, Sara, Will, and Betty, thanks to you all for your steadfast friendship.

Jay, thank you for this life we share. With you, Jem, and Lex, I have learned to fly. All my life, I was only waiting for this moment to arise . . .